$\int 1.05$ ¢

Cardinal Giacomo Antonelli and
Papal Politics in European Affairs

Cardinal Antonelli.
Secretary of State to Pius IX.

Cardinal Giacomo Antonelli and Papal Politics in European Affairs

FRANK J. COPPA

State University of New York Press

Published by
State University of New York Press, Albany

©1990 State University of New York

Printed in the United States of America

For information, address State University of New York
Press, State University Plaza, Albany, N.Y., 12246

Library of Congress Cataloging-in-Publication Data

Coppa, Frank J.
    Cardinal Giacomo Antonelli and papal politics in European affairs
/ Frank J. Coppa.
        p.   cm.
    Bibliography : p.
    Includes index.
    ISBN 0-7914-0184-7. — ISBN 0-7914-0185-5 (pbk.)
    1. Antonelli, Giacomo, 1806-1876.   2. Cardinals—Italy—Biography.
3. Catholic Church—Relations (diplomatic)—Europe.   4. Europe-
-Foreign relations—Catholic Church.   5. Papal States-
-History—1815-1870.   I. Title.
BX4705.A625C67   1990
282'.092'4—dc19
[B]   89-4357
                                                                   CIP

10   9   8   7   6   5   4   3   2   1

Hist! here's the arch-knave in a
Cardinal's hat,

With the heart of a wolf, and the
stealth of a cat

(As if Judas and Herod together
were rolled),

Who keeps, all as one, the Pope's
conscience and gold,

Mounts guard on the altar, and
pilfers from thence,

And flatters St. Peter while stealing
his pence!

Who doubts Antonelli? Have
miracles ceased

When robbers say mass, and Barabbas
is priest?

From Perugia
John Greenleaf Whittier

Contents

Chapter One

Cardinal Giacomo Antonelli: The Myth and The Man

Giacomo Antonelli, the chief minister and advisor of Pope Pius IX (1846–1878), was one of the remarkable men of the nineteenth century. A figure of continental importance for almost three decades, he played a leading role as diplomatic agent in Europe and powerbroker in Rome. Contemporaries complained that the longest-reigning Pontiff confided only in Antonelli, refusing to discuss political affairs with any of the other cardinals.[1] Following the feverish succession of six ministers in the convulsive years from 1846 to 1848, Giacomo was to monopolize the Secretariate of State from the end of 1848 to his death in 1876—an extraordinarily long tenure in the history of Papal Rome.

Antonelli directed Vatican diplomacy during the tumultuous years when Russia, Austria, and France faced military defeat, the United States was divided by the Civil War, the Maximilian Affair troubled diplomats on two continents, Papal infallibility was proclaimed, Italy and Germany were unified, and the Roman Question, and the *Kulturkampf*, burdened the Papacy. He crossed swords with Cavour, Bismarck, and Napoleon III among others. He was disliked but respected by the Germans, baffled the English, and infuriated the politicians of the new Italy. No other Secretary of State, not even Ercole Consalvi under Pius VII, was seen to wield such influence. Small wonder that sovereigns and citizens courted his influence.[2]

The impact of this "Prime Minister" of the Pope transcended Europe and reached the new world.[3] "The life of this ambitious and indomitable statesman," read his obituary in the New York Times, "has embraced some of the most stirring moments in the history of the Church."[4] Since Antonelli supervised the ecclesiastical affairs of the Catholic Church, as well as the political interests

1

of the Papal States, his influence was far-reaching. Nonetheless, the man who sought to defend Rome from Italian nationalism, French opportunism, and an unfriendly *Zeitgeist,* has long been without an objective biography. A number of excellent articles have focused on the Cardinal, but to date no scholarly book has appeared in English on the alter ego of Pius IX (Pio Nono).[5]

Although neglected as a historical subject, the Cardinal was early a target of gossip and criticism.[6] Both his character and conduct were branded ignominious.[7] Regarded by the liberals as the incarnation of evil, his wealth, position, power, and the fact that he was a cardinal though not a priest, provoked scandal. Some doubted that he had any religious sentiment, charging that he was a mason.[8] In pride he was considered a match for Lucifer, in politics a disciple of Machiavelli. Described as Cesare Borgia and Machiavelli bound into one, he was transformed into an absolutely repellent figure. He was depicted as a monstrous fiend with "long, fang-like teeth," "thick lips" and the "grossest of appetites,"[9] and Gregorovius noted in his diary that while "the upper part of his face is clear cut and almost handsome, the lower ends in the animal."[10] Antonelli's face was described as "Egyptian" or "Asiatic" of "moorish hue" with "rolling, demonical" eyes and "eagle beak." His look was deemed glassy and penetrating and his smile cold, and at once immutable and eloquent. Characterized as ugly to the point of beastiality, his features supposedly betrayed him as the "perfect type of low, political adventurer. His soft hands were said to hide the hawk's talons, remorseless in their search and vise-like in their grip."[11]

Even those less hostile to Antonelli's policies were intrigued by the Cardinal's appearance.

> That sallow, intensely Italian face; those great black eyes, never at rest; those parted lips, that show the glittering teeth; the jet-black hair; the worn yet defiant look so full of intelligence, power, and pride, can belong to none but Antonelli. His very walk is a kind of stride, that speaks, as it were, of the super-abundant energy of one of the most remarkable men of the day—a man relied on by many as a minister of high courage, and eminent ability, but dreaded and detested by the revolutionary party.[12]

"His perfect manners were the shining armour of a complete control over anything which could reveal his thought," wrote another, adding, "and yet, while he sat silent, they suggested a charm which invited confidence."[13]

Descriptions of Antonelli's personality have been no less color-
ful than depictions of his appearance. He has been termed "vul-
gar," "coarse," "brutal," "avaricious," "venal," "ambitious," "sinister,"
"skeptical," and "sensuous," but alleged to be "slippery," "able" and
"artful" in his scheming. It was said that he fascinated like a si-
ren, which the family had as an emblem. Unfortunately, this
magic was misused as Antonelli was seen to be implacably driven
by greed for personal advancement. The plush carpeting and ex-
pensive furniture in his office in the secretariate of state was
deemed inappropriate for a minister of the Pope. Much was made
of the fact that he had his family ennobled, and supposedly nominated his brother Filippo governor of the Banca Romana, brother
Luigi, an administrator of the Pontifical Railroads, leaving his
brother Gregorio responsible for affairs in the countryside. All were
made counts including his youngest brother Angelo, who lived in
Paris.[14]

Filippo Antonelli's speculative maneuvers were held responsible for the financial plight of the Papal States, which was believed
to be aggravated by the Cardinal's massive fraud. A biographer of
Count Cavour claimed:

> During the quarter of a century between the return of Pius and
> Antonelli's death, the Cardinal Secretary amassed a fortune esti-
> mated at upwards of 60,000,000 lire. Wherever money passed,
> there he took his toll. He embezzled public funds, appropriated
> public estates, sold offices, honors and favors, blackmailed the
> rich, stript the poor. Whoever had an important suit must buy the
> Cardinal's good offices in order to receive a favorable verdict.[15]

Antonelli was believed to enrich himself by taking bribes and
exacting commissions from those he assigned public contracts, as
well as amassing vast sums by controlling the rise and fall of
prices. Even funds earmarked for the Pope or the religious orders
were allegedly directed into the pockets of his rapacious relatives.
Graft and corruption, claimed a spate of rumors, made Antonelli
the second richest man in Rome after Torlonia. The Cardinal was
condemned for substituting the nepotism of the Popes with that of
the Secretary of State.[16]

Reportedly, Antonelli enjoyed the company of attractive
women, provoking scandal which proliferated as lurid stories of
torrid affairs circulated. Adulterous relationships, it was whis-
pered, had been instrumental in advancing his career. His sexual

appetite, critics charged, was as insatiable as Casanova's and as perverted as De Sade's. This "debauched" lifestyle allegedly took an early toll. In 1847, when Antonelli received the Cardinal's hat from Pope Pius IX, he was supposedly so afflicted with venereal disease that he could barely walk. Apparently he did not mend his ways, for it was charged that at banquets and receptions, the Cardinal was exclusively preoccupied with women. Branding Antonelli one of the most "notorious libertines in Rome," Thayer wrote that it was not his free life style but the magnitude of his abuses that startled Papal society.[17] The "expose" of his alleged immorality increased with the years, and at the time of his death, many accepted the word of a young woman that she was his daughter.[18] This was only one of the many stories readily believed in Rome.

Maligned as a peasant from the mezzogiorno, he was described as callous to the point of having his carriage run over children in the streets of the capital and then transmitting a trifling sum of money to their parents. Reportedly, he responded to anguished pleas for assistance that those who had no bread should eat grass.[19] Little good, opponents observed, could be expected of the "insatiable vulture" whom they insisted was the nephew of the notorious assassin Gasperone, whose brigand's instincts he supposedly shared. The basis of the family fortune, they contended, was wealth derived from brigandage.[20] Edmond About wrote that criminal activity came naturally to the Antonelli family, due in part to the fact that they lived in Sonnino, a den of thieves more celebrated in the history of crime than all Arcadia in the annals of virtue. The author further asserted that hawks do not hatch doves, and had the young Antonelli followed a virtuous course, his village would have disowned him.

> The young man hesitated for some time on the choice of a profession. His vocation was that of all the inhabitants of Sonnino— to live in plenty, to indulge in every kind of pleasure, to be at home every where, to depend on no one, to domineer over others, to inspire fear in them if necessary, and especially to violate the laws with impunity. To attain an object so elevated, without exposing his life, which was always dear to him, he entered the theological seminary at Rome.[21]

The political policies of the man did not escape censure. He was condemned for working against the march of events and held responsible for the uncompromising attitude of Pius IX.[22] Many deemed him the implacable foe of reformism and the most decisive opponent of reconciliation with Italy. Thus, the Secretary of State rather than the Pope was held accountable for Rome's condemnation of Italian nationalism and unification. Pio Nono's decision to abandon his capital at the end of 1848, his opposition to the Roman Republic, and the intervention of France, Austria, Spain, and Naples against it in 1849, were all attributed to the "Machiavellian" Secretary of State. He was viewed as the opponent of a free press who believed that "newspapers should limit themselves to announcing functions in Papal chapels and giving interesting news of Chinese insurrections."[23] Small wonder he was considered responsible for the Syllabus of Errors which condemned both contemporary thought systems and political movements and shocked the liberal world.[24]

"The Pontiff, gracious in demeanor and endeared to the multitude of people by his misfortune and the vicissitudes which he has endured, has not been associated in the minds of most men with the wily, scheming, and haughty Cardinal who served his failing state so well."[25] Reports circulated that the Pope was sympathetic to the Italians, but Antonelli turned his head. It was also believed that the Pontiff would have remained liberal in his inclinations had it not been for the "unscrupulous" Secretary of State. "If I had Count Cavour as my Minister," Pius reportedly confessed in 1858, "I would grant my subjects a constitution."[26] Edmond About, writing in 1859, charged that it was Antonelli who prevented all intercourse between the Pope and his people and that he dominated a timid old man and a fettered population. For this and other reasons some viewed this "demon of the zelanti" as God's instrument to topple the temporal power.[27]

It was purported by his contemporaries that this "evil genius" dominated the Pope, although there was disagreement concerning the means he employed to achieve his total control. Some suggested that Antonelli became the arbiter of the Pontiff by nourishing him with adulation. Others argued that Antonelli pandered to the Pope's fear of his own subjects and the hesitations and doubts of his conscience to render him subordinate. It was even theorized that Antonelli mesmerized the Pope with his "evil eye" against which poor Pius was helpless, a process later revised and rendered more plausible for the modern public by terming it hypnotic suggestion.[28]

Whatever the technique for the alleged domination, it was repeatedly claimed that Pius was paralyzed by fear of the man who was supposed to serve him. The fact that he occupied the Vatican apartments directly above the Pope was interpreted as a reflection of his authority and arrogance. According to the rumors that circulated in Rome, more than once the link between the timid though generous Pope and his aggressive and ambitious minister was strained to the breaking point, but Pius did not dare to dismiss his "Satan."[29] Thus only the Cardinal's death could provide liberation for the Pope, and this explained why Pius did not grieve the loss of his Secretary of State. Supposedly, when Pius learned of Antonelli's death he said, "speak of him no more," as if finally a troublesome episode had been concluded.[30]

The stories of Antonelli's wiles and his reputation for duplicity were so pervasive, that even the United States' representative could not resist their allure. Thus, following his first interview with Antonelli, Alexander W. Randall wrote the American Secretary of State Seward, "I was careful in what I said to him, because I became satisfied, in a few minutes after the interview commenced, that he could understand and speak the English language."[31]

What do we know about the introspective and intensely loyal Cardinal Secretary of State who left no memoirs, and saw no need to provide an apologia for his life and service? For a long time, all too little: a few dates, some uncertain rumors, half-forgotten despatches and often insinuated slanders. These still remain the materials on which many of the generalizations and conclusions about Antonelli have been based. At the beginning of the twentieth century he remained an enigmatic figure, even in Rome.[32]

This study aims to separate fact from fiction, and the man from the myth, as it focuses upon both the person and policies of Antonelli. The Cardinal's personal life is not easily penetrated. It is encrusted by long-standing stories which the inner-directed, laconic Cardinal, little prone to reveal his private thoughts to those outside his family, did not choose to publicly challenge. Furthermore, the responsibilities of government which he eagerly assumed increasingly encroached upon and absorbed his private life. Nonetheless certain areas of his life can and should be scrutinized. For example, was the Cardinal as venal, lascivious, and unscrupulous as his detractors claim? Was his diplomacy as brilliant as still others insist? What motivated the Cardinal? It is hoped these questions will be answered in this biography of Giacomo Antonelli.

Other problems concerning the life and times of the Cardinal emerge. How can one account for his long tenure in office when most others found it difficult, if not impossible, to serve the temperamental Pius IX? What was the basis of the strict collaboration between the Cardinal, who was an aloof and calculating introvert, and his sovereign, who was an emotional, spontaneous extrovert? Of necessity, the work must therefore delve into the relationship between Pio Nono and his chief minister. What part, if any, did Antonelli play in provoking the counter-*Risorgimento*? Was he the architect or executor of the policy of Papal intransigence—or both? Was it at his insistence that the "liberal" Pope of 1846 was transformed into the "secondo Pio Nono" who abandoned both nationalism and constitutionalism? Did the Secretary of State help shape Pio Nono's ecclesiastical policies? These are some of the problems examined within the subsequent pages.

An objective examination of the Cardinal's personal and political life can be written now that the documents of the Secret Vatican Archive are available for the Pontificate of Pius IX. The Vatican papers, in conjunction with the neglected family papers in the State Archive of Rome, provide a good archival base for the long needed biography of the man who played a key role in shaping the events of the unification era. The papers of the family archive are particularly useful for an understanding of the early years and career of Giacomo Antonelli. Beginning in 1848, when the public figure increasingly consumed the private one and the Cardinal was entrusted with the herculean task of preserving the beleaguered state, the Vatican Archives prove indispensable. These archival sources are supplemented by an important and growing printed record, which includes part of the Cardinal's correspondence with the nuncios in Paris, Madrid and Vienna, as well as government documents and memoir material.

Chapter Two

First Years: The Antonelli Family

Giacomo Antonelli, the future cardinal and statesman, was born in Sonnino near Terracina in the southern tier of the Papal States on April 2, 1806, during the turmoil of the Napoleonic period. He was reared in a province in which the reforms of the enlightenment had not yet filtered, and a state still largely immune from many contemporary developments. Looking southward towards Naples, the area was controlled by large landowners, some ecclesiastic, others from the feudal aristocracy, who dominated the down-trodden peasantry and were served by a small middle class. The Antonelli's belonged to the latter.

Giacomo spent the first six years of his life in Sonnino, brushing the border of the Kingdom of the Two Sicilies. His birthplace was rustic but not poor, possessing a rich agriculture and profiting from the contraband trade with the Neapolitan Kingdom to the south. Nonetheless, it was not a rural paradise. Roads were poor where they existed, travel was difficult, and the administration was scandalously inefficient. Trade was hindered by the arrested condition of the infrastructure, the shortage of specie, the rapid turnover of officials (who were often venal), and brigandage, which threatened life and property. The atmosphere lent some credence to the later accusation that the family engaged in brigandage, and was related to the notorious Gasperone, who terrorized the region. In fact the Antonelli's shunned illegal activities; there were less dangerous, more productive means of amassing wealth by serving the official class which richly rewarded collaborators. This was the path pursued by the Antonelli's. Giacomo was the third son of a family which had long profited from official and private concessions.

In 1813, when Giacomo was seven, his family relocated to Terracina, which the extravagant Pope Pius VI had developed into a second Rome. The Pope frequently visited the area to supervise the construction of the Papal palace.

Pius VI, who was Pope since 1775, denounced the principles of the French Revolution of 1789. He rejected the notion that the Assembly had the right to unilaterally alter the status of the Church in France. In 1791, he condemned the Civil Constitution of the Clergy, which imposed a national and elective structure on the French Church. The outbreak of war in 1792 did not bode well for traditionalists such as Pius, who feared the export of the revolution. The Piedmontese had warned that should they succumb to the invasion, all of Italy would be in danger. Their prediction proved prophetic. Following the peace signed between Piedmont and Napoleon in May 1796, the French had access to the entire peninsula. Pius was troubled by Napoleon's proclamation that the population of the Papal States was to be liberated from their centuries of servitude. In May 1796, the Pope had no sooner arrived in Terracina than he was recalled to Rome by the deteriorating political situation. Papal efforts proved incapable of forestalling the French seizure of the Legations of Bologna, Ferrara, and the Romagna. Pius agreed to the Treaty of Tolentino (February, 1797) in the hope of preventing a French penetration south of the Legations. Skeptics doubted that the French had been satiated and the Pope shared their fear. In 1798, when the French threatened to invade what remained of the Papal States, Pius had some of the most valuable treasures of the Vatican spirited to Terracina, where he planned to seek refuge himself. His plans went awry and he found himself exiled to France where he died on February 20, 1799. His successor, Pius VII, never visited Terracina, which nonetheless remained important to the Papal court.

The French intrusion disrupted the torpor of Rome, exposing the provinces and its people to dangerous new currents. The nobility, both ecclesiastic and lay, proved most vulnerable. Although the Antonelli's were not noble, they served and were identified with a series of noble patrons. The family was related to the Terenzi of Sonnino, whose two brothers were priests. Don Giovanni served as the vicar general of Sonnino and Don Giacomo as a canon of the cathedral of Terracina. The latter had won the support of the Braschi Pope, Pius VI, who had a special interest in Terracina. Giacomo's early years were spent in the huge paternal house which had passed from one feudal family of the region to another and had been transferred to the Antonelli's by powerful patrons.

Connected to the directing class and the first families of the region by service, the Antonelli future looked promising.

Giacomo's grandfather had earned the friendship and gratitude of the influential Albani family, and served as country agent for the Colonna family. We do not know the original circumstances by which Domenico Antonelli senior entered the good graces of Gian Francesco Albani, one of the most noted cardinals of the period. The relationship proved fortunate for his son Domenico junior, who was born on March 14, 1769, five months after his father's death. His mother Rosalia was left with five daughters (Carminella, Rosaria, Fortunata, Grazia and Caterina) and one son, Casimiro Tommaso Maria Domenico Antonelli—Giacomo's father.

Rosalia, left alone to care for her children, was assisted by the Pellegrini, one of the first families of Sonnino, who helped sustain her during these difficult times. By dint of diligence, good connections, and hard work she managed to have her son Domenico educated outside of Sonnino. Thus, when he was ten or eleven years old, Domenico was enrolled in a college and most likely completed the seventh grade. Since he had a bent for agriculture, after graduation Domenico served as assistant land agent for the Pellegrini family, while Cardinal Albani bestowed an official appointment in the office of the Pontine Marshes, as well as a series of other contracts. Supported by powerful patrons, Domenico prospered and in a few years proved financially able to start a family.

In 1794, when Domenico was twenty-five years old, he married Loreta Mancini, the seventeen year old daughter of a substantial, propertied family, who brought him a considerable dowry. The marriage was personally as well as economically successful, with five sons and three daughters emerging from the union. In October 1795 the Antonelli's had their first child Rosalia, named in honor of Domenico's mother and sponsored at baptism by Benedetto Pellegrino and his wife Maria.[1]

Domenico Antonelli performed various tasks for Cardinal Albani in Terracina.[2] He also retained the protection and patronage of the wealthy Pellegrini. His problems arose from foreign developments and from the steady pressure of revolutionary France upon Papal Rome after Napoleon invaded the Legations and imposed the Peace of Tolentino upon the Pope. At the end of 1797, when the assassination of General Duphot led Napoleon to order General Berthier to march on Rome and encourage the formation of a Roman Republic, Domenico found himself in difficulty. Determined to remain faithful to the Pontifical regime which had been generous to him, his decision entailed risks. At the beginning of 1798, shortly after the French occupation of Rome, Sonnino was seized without a shot being fired and a tree of liberty was planted in the main square. However the following July, when almost all the centers of Southern Lazio rose against the foreigners, Sonnino likewise forced the French to withdraw. The success proved of brief duration, because the returning French exacted a heavy retribution. From September 23 to 29 the French military mission based in the parish church of Sant' Angelo ordered the execution of twenty-two Sonninese to terrorize the community into submission.

After Pius VI was dragged from the Eternal City in 1798, the Roman Republic which followed was staffed and supported by the middle classes which had unexpectedly gained the upper hand over the aristocracy and clergy. It thus proved advantageous to those lawyers, doctors, intellectuals and traders who collaborated with the new regime, but disastrous for the former directing class and its hangers-on such as the Antonellis. Many upper class Romans feared for their lives, leading some 15,000, lay and ecclesiastic members of this class to abandon the capital. Domenico assisted a number of Church dignitaries in their flight from Rome. Among the Roman prelates Domenico helped was his benefactor and protector, Gian Francesco Albani, who angered the French by his pro-Austrian attitude. Albani had abandoned the capital on the eve of the French entry, intending to cross into the Kingdom of Naples. However, he was refused admission because his passport had lapsed. Fearful for his life, the Cardinal called upon Domenico, who hid him in a small Neapolitan village before escorting him to Naples. Following this mission, Domenico returned to Sonnino, at which time Loreta again became pregnant. Their first son was born on October 13, 1799 and baptized Filippo Gregorio Luigi.[3] Domenico did not linger long at home, burdened by a series of responsibilities.

The French occupation of 1798–99 proved troublesome for Domenico Antonelli. Like other property owners, he was subject to forced requisitions and contributions as the French made outlandish demands. Perhaps worse, he was neither able to continue his activities in the Pontine Reclamation works nor fulfill his other contracts. Nonetheless, throughout the period of French control, Domenico rendered important services to the cause of his exiled sovereign and members of the curia. Small wonder that following the excesses of the Sanfedisti, the armed bands loyal to the Church and their traditional rulers, and the first restoration, Domenico was rewarded by another lucrative contract to take part in the reclamation work of the Pontine Marshes. This was but one of many favors that were to follow. The first year of the new century brought additional concessions. On February 22, he was made superintendent of the fief of Sonnino by Prince Colonna Goerni, once again a reward for his conduct during the Jacobin occupation. Thus, Domenico was at once involved in the baronial as well as the state administration, without being prevented from engaging in his own private enterprises. His income increased dramatically and he became a wealthy man.[4]

Domenico Antonelli emerged as one of the most influential, prudent, and enterprising country merchants of the Southern Lazio. He traded not only in the States of the Church but in the Kingdom of Naples, buying and selling agricultural products as well as wood, construction material, coal, and animals. During the second French occupation, he once more proved his loyalty by refusing to collaborate with the invaders, withdrawing exclusively to private affairs. International events thus conspired to prevent Domenico from fully exploiting the favorable disposition of the Pontifical regime. The Neapolitans entered Rome on September 30, 1799, preparing the way for the return of the future Pontiff. The French occupation and brief revolutionary experience had transformed neither the capital nor the countryside, and the revolutionary spirit disappeared with the Jacobins and the French.

Despite the fact that the new Pope, Barnaba Chiaramonti, Pius VII, sought to reconcile Rome and the Revolution and signed a concordat with the Emperor of the French in 1801, tensions ensued. Paris resented the fact that neither Pius nor the curia approved the political treaty which sought to make the Holy See a virtual French satellite.[5] This Papal independence and Rome's refusal to declare war against England led the French to seize most of the Pope's territory in 1808.[6] Pius VII, like his predecessor, was taken captive and subsequently held in Savona for more than three years, creating a dilemma for the faithful.[7] When Pius was deported, Domenico, who had remained loyal to the Papal government, was accused of brigandage and complicity in the guerrilla campaign against the French in the provinces of Velletri and Frosinone. A member of the family was condemned to death and executed by the French. Domenico barely escaped himself.

In 1811, when Giacomo was only five years old, his father was carted to Rome to be judged by the French military tribunal, on the charge of brigandage. Domenico was accused of being an accomplice by receiving stolen goods from one of his subordinates, Giovanni Giorgi, who had been captured by the police. If the charges had been proven, Domenico Antonelli would have been executed.

The entire clan fell under suspicion. The Antonelli family, including young Giacomo, was virtually housebound, fearful of the taunts and jeers of jealous neighbors delighted to see this powerful house humbled. The first campaign to discredit the Antonelli's commenced; it would not be the last. This influenced family behavior and especially the conduct of Loreta Antonelli, who abandoned her trusting and gregarious manner and became increasingly morose and suspicious. She transmitted her distrust of all outside the family to her offspring, as she waited to hear from her husband. Some four months elapsed without word from the imprisoned Domenico; the family agonized as it remained in the dark about the fate of its head and its future. On September 23, 1811 the French Military Tribunal determined that Domenico was innocent of the crimes attributed to him, and on September 30 granted him permission to return to Sonnino. Despite his acquittal, the charge of brigandage would continue to haunt Domenico and his sons. Early in October, Domenico found his way back to his frantic relatives.

Domenico Antonelli awaited better times, confident that Napoleon's enemies would eventually push the French out of the Peninsula and the Papal States. He preferred to wait in Terracina where he decided to transfer his family. The thought of settling in Terracina had long been in the mind of Domenico, who had planned to move in 1798 but was constrained by the French occupation. In 1808, another French occupation prevented the transfer. Following his acquittal, Domenico determined finally to go, and had a house readied for his arrival. At this juncture Loreta confided to her husband that she was expecting another child, and to spare her unnecessary strain, Domenico delayed the move to Terracina until 1813.

On February 2, 1813 Loreta Antonelli gave birth to Rosa Maria Purificata, and two months later the Antonelli's finally transferred to Terracina. Upon their entry, they found the Papal Palace occupied by the French and Pius VII, like Pius VI before him, a prisoner. The Antonelli's sought to avoid political matters, focusing upon their new home, which they found enchanting. Unlike their Sonnino residence, which was surrounded by other buildings, the home in Terracina was encircled by a vast garden, which delighted the children. By this time, Rosalia was eighteen years old and served as a surrogate mother. Filippo was fourteen, Gregorio eleven, Giacomo seven, Grazia six, Luigi three and the newborn Rosa only weeks old.[8]

While the Antonelli children basked in the comfort of their new home, their parents were encouraged by the news from abroad. Following the fall of Napoleon, Pius VII returned to Rome where he was enthusiastically welcomed. Furthermore, Cardinal Ercole Consalvi managed to regain most of the Papal territory at the Congress of Vienna. Those faithful to Rome, such as Domenico Antonelli, were thankful for this restoration, expecting that their loyalty would be repaid. Their expectations materialized. Antonelli was showered with concessions, including the contract for the construction of a new road, which reportedly netted him some 600,000 *scudi* (approximately 600,000 dollars). He was also accorded a contract to supervise the upkeep of some forty kilometers of the Via Appia, a profitable lease which the family kept for half a century. Following the restoration of King Ferdinand in Naples, Domenico was repaid for his earlier services by being granted the right to collect wood in certain royal forests, enabling him to engage in a lucrative timber trade.[9] By these and other government contracts, financial astuteness, entrepreneurial initiative, and a good dose of parsimony and perseverance, Domenico Antonelli amassed a considerable fortune.[10] This wealth assured the future of the Antonelli children, contributing to the success achieved by all of Domenico's sons.[11]

Domenico's enterprises, power, and prestige earned him the respect of the community in Terracina. His greatest priority was to make the position of his family secure, an ambition he transmitted to all of his sons and daughters. Intelligent and ambitious, Domenico determined that his children: daughters Rosalia, Grazia, Rosa Maria Purificata and his sons Filippo, Gregorio, Giacomo, Luigi and Angelo, should bring the family name and fortune to a new high. In pursuing this goal he astutely recognized the value of education and did not spare expense in providing it for his sons.[12]

The autumn of 1814, as traditionalism triumphed in the Papal States, Filippo and Gregorio, the two older Antonelli brothers, left for study in Rome. The choice of schools for the children was made by Domenico, to whom Loreta deferred in educational matters. Domenico sought not only instruction but contacts for his sons. In 1816, Domenico brought Giacomo to the capital to introduce him to the superiors of the Roman seminary. He also used the trip to seal his cordial relations with various prelates, and to visit Reginaldo

Angeli, who had supervised the activities of Filippo and Gregorio in Rome. Giacomo, like Filippo and Gregorio, was schooled by his father to manipulate the world with certainty and grace.

Domenico Antonelli was a devoted though severe and demanding father to his five sons. He taught them that success was a common enterprise which required cooperation and the subordination of private satisfaction for the common good. He did not hesitate to assign them roles and responsibilities. Filippo was required to settle in Rome to represent the family interests in the capital and to watch over his younger brothers studying there. Domenico knew Filippo to be tenacious in bringing projects to a successful conclusion, possessing a certain magnetism which enabled him to charm others. Domenico also realized that his oldest son could be short tempered and irritable, if not rude. Gregorio was trained by his father to assist him in the management of the family's extensive businesses and holdings at Terracina. Like Filippo, Gregorio was a tenacious worker possessing great common sense. In addition he was blessed with both amiability and calm, and enjoyed a stability that Filippo lacked. Giacomo, following in the footsteps of his two older brothers, was sent to study in Rome, where his father schemed to have him enter the administration of the state. Aware of Giacomo's quick mind and strong will, his father foresaw a brilliant career for his third son in government service, especially if he entered the priesthood.

It is true that Pius VII's Secretary of State, Consalvi, had sought to humanize and illuminate the temporal government and had proposed a series of administrative reforms that would have allowed laymen to enter judicial and administrative posts. Unfortunately, this program was frustrated by the zelanti who condemned innovation of any sort and tended to distrust the laity. This was underscored by the Motu proprio of July 6, 1816, which assured a predominantly clerical administration. This conservative course led Domenico Antonelli to conclude that those who wished to succeed in restoration Rome had to have an ecclesiastical background. Thus, even though Giacomo showed no inclination for the priestly life, he was entered in the Collegium Romanum.

In the Papal States the course of grammar and rhetoric lasted seven years, which Giacomo completed during the years 1816–1823. Domenico Silvagni, who attended classes with Giacomo at the Collegio Romano, later wrote that neither of them learned very much. Giacomo found the subjects boring and thought constantly about Terracina and his family. Like most others in Rome, he was little affected by news of the revolts in the Kingdom of Naples (1820) and Sardinia (1821). The tranquility of the Eternal City was not shattered; the clock of Europe seemed to have stopped in this city which did not follow the rhythm of contemporary society. However, Giacomo showed greater interest in the news that his father had acquired considerable property as a result of an agreement concluded with Prince Pontiatowski in 1821. The deal brought Domenico a number of estates and three great palaces: one in Rome in the Via Sant'Agata de Goti, a second in Ceccano, and a third in Terracina, as well as smaller palaces and houses. This transaction, which reinforced the family's wealth and standing in the community, created a sensation in the Papal States, arousing interest and jealousy.

Giacomo, although only fifteen, appreciated the importance of his father's acquisitions to his own lifestyle, but did not see how the revolutionary rumblings in the other states of the peninsula affected him. In response to his queries about the new properties, his father explained that the family responsibilities also had broadened and had to be borne by all. The following year Domenico signed another contract with the Apostolic Chamber increasing his power and profits as well as the family obligations.

As the Antonellis' stake in the Papal States increased so did Domenico's conviction that only an ecclesiastic in the family could safeguard their interests and position. At the same time he shied from imposing a religious life upon any of his sons, and waited for events to unfold. Privately he hoped that Giacomo would become the prelate the family required. In many ways Domenico considered his third son a combination of Filippo and Gregorio, possessing the intelligence, intuition, willpower, tenacity and fascination of the former and the calm and equilibrium of the latter.

The harassment Domenico experienced the summer of 1823 convinced him of the need for a ecclesiastic in the family to safeguard their interests. He was precipitously ordered to account for his administration of Papal affairs in Terracina and to refund the sum of 8,735 *scudi* to the treasury. Domenico attributed this "vendetta" to the factionalism and rivalry in the curia, making the need for protectors in the administration indispensable. Perhaps this is why in 1823 the seventeen year old Giacomo was enrolled in the University of the Sapienza. That very year Pius VII died and was replaced by Leo XII, elected by the zelanti. The climate in Rome was now decidedly conservative, as the new Pope imposed a strict censorship and encouraged the fanaticism of the *sanfedisti*.

In 1824 he issued the *Ubi primum* in which he denounced contemporary errors and the de-Christianization of society. Giacomo paid little attention to political developments and heard no criticism of the Papal regime in the Fausti household, where he resided. The Fausti's, like the Antonelli's, were intensely loyal to the Papal government and had profited from their devotion. Nonetheless, Domenico planned to bring Giacomo under closer family control.

While Domenico Antonelli had taken possession of the palace in Ceccano almost immediately, the family postponed occupying the palace in Rome. Plans were devised to have Loreta move to the capital with one of her daughters, and to have Giacomo live with them. This materialized at the end of 1825, when Domenico and his wife traveled to Rome for the jubilee and for the opening of their new residence. Some weeks before Giacomo was inscribed in the faculty of jurisprudence which he frequented with enthusiasm. Having finally found a subject that interested him, he applied himself diligently to his studies.[13]

At the Sapienza Antonelli remained jovial and fun loving. Following the conclusion of his courses in 1827 Giacomo lost contact with his friends for some time. He reappeared a changed figure, serious in manner, which was a marked contrast to his earlier behavior. Where and what Giacomo studied at this time is not certain; what is clear is that he planned to enter the prelatura, the higher civil and diplomatic service of the state. To prepare for his entry into this select circle Giacomo studied with Monsignor Nicola Manari of the Apostolic Chamber from November 1829 to March 5, 1830. The Monsignor was impressed by his open and alert mind, talent, and diligence.[14] Giacomo's energy and determination were matched by his ability and amiability, combining to assure his success.

Filippo Antonelli, the oldest brother, was no less talented or ambitious. While Giacomo's decision to enter the prelatura pleased his father, his brother Filippo delighted Domenico by establishing a relationship with the Countess Marianna, niece of Cardinal Ercole Dandini de Sylva. Filippo's fiancee provided an important link with a member of the Sacred College, an aristocrat from one of the oldest families in the state, and one of the most powerful prelates controlling the finances of the Holy See. The proposed marriage to the Cardinal's niece was perceived as useful to the entire family, which awaited the union with anticipation.

The marriage was ill-fated from the start. For one thing, a series of events conspired to postpone the nuptual. First was the death of Annibale Della Genga, Pope Leo XII, on February 10, 1829. Then Cardinal Dandini, the bride's uncle, had to enter the conclave to elect a successor. He emerged only after March 31 and the election of Francesco Saverio Castiglioni as Pius VIII. Pius would serve as Pope for a very short time. It was said in Rome:

> The eighth Pius was Pope,
> He lived and died, and no one took note.[15]

The Antonelli's, were perhaps the exception, for the conclave had led to the postponement of Filippo's long awaited marriage. It may have also contributed to another complication, for on June 29, 1829, the day after the wedding, the bride confessed to her husband that she was pregnant with another man's child. Although disappointed by Marianna's conduct, Filippo did not wish to lose the valuable association with the Cardinal. Dandini, determined to avoid scandal, settled matters by providing that the child would be the heir of the mother. The marriage would be preserved as a convenience with Filippo promising not to betray the secret. He had early sacrificed his personal happiness for his success and the well-being of the family, and now remained in a marriage which promised political and economic advantages at the expense of trust and love. Filippo's career, in fact, benefited from the Cardinal's financial contacts. Domenico and Gregorio profited from having the Cardinal as protector of Terracina, while plans were hatched to have Dandini support Giacomo's request to enter the prelatura. The Antonelli's determined to exploit the connection with Cardinal Dandini to the fullest.

Domenico exploited the good fortune of having the Cardinal in the family to direct his third son towards an ecclesiastical career, recognizing that the success attained by Filippo had whetted Giacomo's appetite. Since entry into the prelatura required celibacy, the desire to marry posed an obstacle, as had been the case with Gregorio. Domenico made it clear that the sacrifice of celibacy was more than compensated by the prospect of being eligible for almost any dignity in the state, including the cardinalate, which would enable the family to have a successor to Dandini. Giacomo welcomed the prospect, revealing that celibacy represented no problem for him.

Entry into the prelatura was difficult even for those having the support of an influential member of the curia. Competition was keen; candidates had to provide a handsome fee to the government and had to secure the approval of its membership. By tradition, aspirants to this office had to pay a number of visits to the seven voting prelates of the Tribunal of Justice in their residences or offices. The first visit they would make dressed as laymen. They then would be subject to the scrutiny and questioning of the judges. Only a few survived this first stage. A candidate who received the approval of at least two-thirds of the judges was permitted to make a second and crucial visit, this time dressed in clerical garb and subject to more intensive questioning. Others were now disqualified. If approved at this juncture, one was expected to provide the requiste fees before being assured admission and termed *Illustrissimo Monsignore.*[16]

In 1830, at the age of twenty-four, Giacomo passed the necessary examinations, and on June 22, 1830 his father supplied Giacomo with the sum of 1,500 scudi per year required to enter the prelatura.[17] The story that Pius VIII graciously lowered the fees for him is without foundation, as Domenico paid the full sum.[18] Giacomo's friends at the University, aware of his towering ambition, indomitable will, and critical mind, had expected him to succeed, but were surprised by the rapidity of his accession.[19] They did not appreciate the extent of his father's influence, reinforced by that of his brother Filippo, or the part played by Cardinal Dandini, who was indebted to the family. Domenico received a host of letters congratulating him on Giacomo's success, which was clearly perceived as the good fortune of the entire family.[20]

Domenico Antonelli, delighted to see Giacomo among the prelates trained in civil and canon law and earmarked for a career in the service of the state, basked in the fact that his third son found himself in a very privileged and powerful group. He expected that Giacomo, in turn, would show his filial appreciation for all that had been done for him by furthering the family's interests, as had Filippo. For the moment, Giacomo was not in a position to repay his debt, but he did express his gratitude by sending various small gifts to his father and brothers.[21] With those outside the immediate family circle, the Antonelli's showed themselves far less generous.[22]

Giacomo began his public career during a troubled period for Italy as a whole, and the Papal States in particular. In November 1830 Ferdinando II succeeded his father Francesco I as King of Naples. He resisted the pressure of Louis Philippe, who urged him to govern in a liberal manner, and did not listen to those like Luigi Settembrini, who urged him to seek the crown of Italy.[23] The attempted reforms of Pius VIII during his brief pontificate (1829–1830) had come to naught, except to raise the level of expectation and frustration of critics. It was Pius who had to respond to the July Revolution in Paris and he did so by immediately recognizing the new regime and urging the French clergy to swear allegiance to Louis Philippe. He thus refused to tie the fortune of the Church to the legitimate Bourbon branch in France, revealing that Rome could be flexible and preserve its independence vis-a-vis the secular regimes. In the eyes of some he had sown the wind and his successor would have to reap the whirlwind.

Early in 1831, the Camaldolese monk Bartolomeo Alberto-Mauro Cappellari was elected Pope and took the name Gregory XVI. This figure who was a champion of traditionalism and had written such works as "The Triumph of the Holy See and the Church against the Assaults of Innovators" was confirmed in his conservatism by the revolutionary events of 1830–1831.[24] Following his election the revolution long threatened in the Papal States erupted, overrunning the Marches and Emilia, and was suppressed only by Austrian intervention. The French, disturbed by this development, garrisoned Ancona to preserve the balance of power in Italy, insisting that a conference of the major powers (Austria, France, Great Britain, Prussia and Russia) be called in Rome to advise the Pope on reforms needed to avert future revolutionary outbursts.[25]

Pope Gregory resisted the call for a consultative assembly for the administration of the Papal States that was issued in the Memorandum of the Powers (1831), thus showing himself opposed to reform as well as revolution. In 1832 he issued *Mirari vos,* which condemned the entire liberal movement. By this and other measures he demonstrated his unwillingness to make any concessions at home.[26] Tommaso Bernetti, Gregory's Secretary of State until 1836 and a friend and role model for Giacomo[27], proved conservative, though not reactionary. "I think that the secularization of our government is inevitable," Bernetti wrote Giacomo, adding, "but such a development would bring about the total collapse of the ecclesiastical government."[28] All of this duly impressed Giacomo, who commenced his public career with a decidedly conservative outlook.

Following in the footsteps of his father Domenico and his older brother Filippo, Giacomo had learned what could be achieved and attained by serving the directing class. There was no positive role model available to him among those who sought to alter the course and policies of the existing regime. Thus, while the pragmatic Giacomo readily grasped the advantages of collaboration, he found none in confrontation. Small wonder that Giacomo, like Domenico and Filippo, thought of serving rather than directing, of preserving rather than restructuring. Like his father and brother before him, Giacomo's vision and ambition was limited.

Assigned in 1830 to the Superior Court of the Papal Government, which dealt with administrative matters, he was nominated secretary of the two tribunals by the next year and by 1832 was made a supplementary judge of the Civil Congregation of the Apostolic Chamber. By this time Giacomo enjoyed the support of the Cardinal Prefect of the Supreme Tribunal, Giovanni Francesco Falzacappa. The Tribunal of Justice was the epicenter of the judicial system of the Holy See and enjoyed maximum power and prestige. It was the superior court of the curia, above the diocesan and regional courts, and even above the Rota. Its functions focused upon procedural questions, and it could treat cases both of secular and ecclesiastical nature, thus functioning not only as a court of appeal but as a court of first instance.

In 1834 Giacomo received a new promotion, albeit not his first choice, when he was appointed assessor to the Criminal Tribunal in Rome. He soon assumed an important role in this body, both because of his recognized ability and because its President was preoccupied with his responsibilities as Governor of Rome.

Giacomo was most interested in diplomacy but realized that he could not immediately enter the diplomatic service since he lacked a title of nobility, a serious drawback in a service still dominated by the aristocracy. He had to prove himself by obtaining a fund of experience in the political administration, a move that did not appeal to Giacomo. He had reservations about the political administration for two reasons. First he feared the turn of events which might lead to a disaster out of the control of even the best administrator, who would nonetheless be burdened with the responsibility. Such a development could ruin even the most promising career. Secondly, he detested life in the periphery, far from the source of power in the capital. To realize his ultimate ambition, Giacomo was prepared to enter the political administration and endure exile in the provinces to prove himself to Rome.[29]

Chapter Three

Early Career: Giacomo Conquers Rome From the Provinces

In 1835 Giacomo, not yet thirty, transferred from the judicial to the provincial administration by being appointed Apostolic Delegate to the province of Orvieto. Those provinces of the Papal States beyond the Apennines were under the authority of Cardinal Legates, while those closer to the capital were administered by Apostolic Delegates. This was an extraordinary promotion for a young man and it convinced skeptics in Terracina that Giacomo's family had political as well as economic clout. It was marked by a celebration on April 9, 1835 in the church of San Giovanni of Terracina. That evening a band played before the Antonelli house, and that of the Sanguigini, in honor respectively of Gregorio and his sister Rosalia. The initiative for the festivities had been assumed by the canons of the collegial Church, who perceived that Giacomo's career had assumed a decisive turn. Adversaries of the family had questioned whether Giacomo could emerge from the labyrinth of the lower curia; his appointment to Orvieto removed all doubt.

Presently the term Apostolic Delegate has an exclusively ecclesiastical significance, but such was not the case in the first half of the nineteenth century when Giacomo was appointed to Orvieto. Introduced by Consalvi at the beginning of the century—until then the Papal States had been simply an aggregate of communes—they were inspired by the republican administration, much to the chagrin of conservatives. In the post Vienna Papal States the jurisdiction of an Apostolic Delegate was territorial and administrative, encompassing both civil and ecclesiastical functions. Thus, despite their clerical garb, the Apostolic Delegates were almost exclusively civil functionaries, similar in many respects to the prefects in the later Italian Kingdom. Residing in the capital city of the province, oftentimes directly opposite the Bishop, the Apostolic Delegate was his subordinate in religious matters but his equal, if not his superior, in terms of breadth of jurisdiction. In the mid 1830's there were only 14 Delegations in the Papal States against some 100 diocese. Only in Orvieto, in fact, the smallest of the Apostolic Delegations in size and importance, did the Apostolic Delegate and Bishop preside over the same territory, with the first exercising religious authority and the second civil power. Nonetheless, for a young man of twenty-nine, it was an important achievement.

Giacomo's appointment was promoted by a series of patrons. Since his first years as a member of the curia, Giacomo had won the goodwill of Cardinal Falzacappa, a friend of his father. He was designated to the position of Apostolic Delegate by Cardinal Domenico Gamberini, Secretary of State for Internal Affairs, upon the suggestion of the Secretary of State for Foreign Affairs, Cardinal Tommaso Bernetti. Concomitantly, his cause was advanced by Cardinal Luigi Lambruschini, long interested in Orvieto, which was almost a family fief. Finally, there was the wholehearted support of Pope Gregory XVI, who had very close relations with the Antonelli's, and with Filippo in particular.[1]

From the start of his career Giacomo's ability, self-confidence, tact, and pleasing personality won him the backing of some influential prelates, including Cardinals Zurla, Dandini, and Lambruschini. The first was Vicar of Rome, and a close companion of Pope Gregory, the second married his niece to Giacomo's brother, Filippo, while the last was soon to become Secretary of State. Lambruschini was absolutely enchanted with Giacomo, doing all within his means to advance the young man's career. Giacomo confided to his brother Filippo that the Cardinal constantly wanted him by his side.[2] These protectors were cultivated by the moral and financial support of his family, which Giacomo would never forget.[3] In the art of winning friends and influencing people, Giacomo had an incomparable teacher in his father and learned a lesson or two from his oldest brother Filippo, whom Giacomo idolized.[4]

In Orvieto, far removed from Terracina, Giacomo's world was filled by nostalgic family reminiscences and official responsibilities. He fought his loneliness by writing often to his brothers.[5] Although homesick, he sought to fulfill his functions and prove his competence. In his first letter from Orvieto, Giacomo revealed his determination to make a tour of the province to see firsthand whether the orders of the Secretary of State regarding preventive measures against the cholera were being enforced. Throughout the summer Giacomo did not complain about the climate, but found the winter in Orvieto considerably rawer than Terracina or even Rome. The winter of 1835–36 was particularly severe, with much snow and freezing rain, so that the Paglia River overflowed its banks. "It is deadly cold here," a depressed Giacomo wrote home on January 2, 1836, "we are everywhere surrounded by snow."[6] He longed for the sunshine of the Mezzogiorno.

Clearly unhappy in Orvieto, Giacomo strained to please the Papal government, including steps to improve the cultivation of hemp in the provinces. When an outbreak of cholera erupted, he proved courageous in confronting the crisis, preserving law and order through the imposition of restrictive measures. "The government is very pleased with me because I have done considerable under very difficult circumstances," Giacomo boasted in October 1835, adding that although he had been constrained to employ severe measures, there had been no disturbances as a consequence. Cardinal Luigi Lambruschini, who had been Archbishop of Genoa and was soon to be selected as Gregory XVI's Secretary of State (1836), assured Giacomo that the Pontiff appreciated the important services he had rendered.[7] Domenico, too, was proud of his prelate son confiding that the goodwill shown him by Gregory was gratifying to the entire family and should spur him to win new honors.[8]

Giacomo's success was attained at a price—the painful separation from his close-knit family. Alone in Orvieto his thoughts were homeward bound. In his correspondence with his father and brothers he rarely mentioned political issues, dwelling instead on domestic matters such as the food prepared for him, the dinner parties he gave and attended, and his struggles to remain within a limited budget. When circumstances restricted his correspondence, he subsequently notified one or another member of the family that only burdensome duties and lack of time had prevented him from keeping them posted on developments, reassuring his relatives that his health was excellent.[9]

When the young Apostolic Delegate sought to hold a festival in honor of the Assumption at Orvieto, and discovered that the condition of the treasury did not permit the expense, he called upon his brother, Filippo, to provide the funds. Likewise, when he learned that the anniversaries of the election and coronation of Pope Gregory XVI were to be celebrated respectively on February

2 and 3, 1836, he again appealed to Filippo. Giacomo explained that as Apostolic Delegate he was expected officially to sponsor some festivity for each of these occasions. To commemorate the election, he planned a meal, to which he intended to invite the chief public functionaries. To celebrate the coronation, he had decided to hold an evening reception inviting the nobility and other important personages of Orvieto as guests. Even these modest measures taxed his budget, so Giacomo asked Filippo to furnish both the funds and refreshments for the occasion. Among other things, he required at least fifteen pounds of the best pastries (he wanted to make a good impression), four bottles of rum, and glasses to serve the drinks.

During his first years as Apostolic Delegate, Giacomo was financially strapped, and relied upon his family to provide the means to fulfill his responsibilities and further his career. Filippo, charged with dispensing family funds, met Giacomo's needs, but cautioned restraint. In response to Filippo's advice to economize, Giacomo explained that he already cut his expenses in Orvieto to the bone. His monthly income was only 76 scudi and 33 baiocchi, and from this Giacomo had to pay the salaries of three servants and a coachman, which cost 30 scudi per month. Another 15 scudi were required for the maintenance of the horses, while four scudi were given to the priest who said mass for him, and served as his gentleman, and one scudo to the woman who carried water two miles to his residence. What remained was needed to pay for oil and coal (for light and heat), for the washing of clothes, as well as for food, bread, and wine. Luckily, he had only four extraordinary occasions he had to officially celebrate each year: the election and coronation of the Pope, the feast of the Assumption, and Christmas.[10]

Although Filippo, the oldest son, sometimes questioned Giacomo's requests, as much to assert his authority as to assure economy, they were always fulfilled. The Apostolic Delegate appreciated this, and remained devoted to his relatives and preoccupied with family matters, inquiring about the health and well-being of his parents, brothers and sisters, and even cousins. No matter how hectic his schedule, or how much he had to travel, Giacomo found the time to correspond with his relatives.[11] Moreover, he constantly strove to advance their interests, as they did his. Presumably Giacomo's hand was behind Filippo's appointment to the governing congregation of the province of Velletri. An advisory body appointed by the government, it included influential lay people such as Filippo Antonelli, who enjoyed the favor of high officials and whose talent was incontestable. At the beginning of January 1836, Giacomo succeeded in having the entire family inscribed among the nobility of Orvieto. This honor required fees amounting to 30 scudi, and once again Giacomo found it necessary to call upon Filippo.[12] This time there were neither questions nor calls for economy, for Giacomo was beginning to rival his older brother Filippo as chief champion of family interests. Domenico was proud of all of his sons, but increasingly delighted by the career and conduct of Giacomo.[13]

Giacomo, however, remained dissatisfied with his accomplishments, feared some new upheaval, and schemed to return to Rome. Governance of the provinces proved burdensome due to the widespread unemployment, massive poverty, shortage of food, outbreak of epidemics, brigandage in the countryside, and the plague of beggars in the cities. The broad economic and social malaise provided fertile ground for those who sought to sow the seeds of discontent, and generated innumerable difficulties for those like Antonelli responsible for the public tranquility. "It would be good," he wrote Filippo after only nine months at Orvieto, "if I could be made Auditor of the Tribunal of Justice," in Rome. He implored his older brother to see what he, or Cardinal Dandini, could do to realize this goal. Giacomo was disappointed when Filippo responded that the Pope was considering sending him to preside over another Apostolic Delegation. "I would consider such a transfer a disgrace," Giacomo wrote back, warning "I would be placed in a position of losing that small degree of credit that I have earned here."[14]

Nonetheless, the ambitious prelate had to resign himself to moving to Viterbo with only a brief visit to Rome.[15] Lambruschini confessed that he had initiated the transfer, convinced that no one but he was capable of keeping its difficult inhabitants under control. On July 4, 1836 Giacomo received a formal letter from the Secretary of State notifying him of the transfer from the delegation in Orvieto to that of Viterbo.[16] Thus after a fourteen month residence in Orvieto, he departed for Viterbo, going from the smallest of the historic cities of Lazio to the capital of the patrimony of St. Peter. Giacomo was not happy, he longed for the security and power found only in Rome.

Giacomo arrived in Viterbo during a difficult time, when poor harvests and the spread of cholera contributed to an outbreak of violence. The situation was so critical that Antonelli had to prohibit the holding of their fair—an unpopular decision which he forcefully upheld. Agitators took advantage of the situation to create fresh disturbances, which led the police and cavalry to fire upon angry demonstrators. The new Apostolic Delegate responded promptly to the disorders, effectively suppressing the explosion of violence. His actions were applauded in Rome by both the government and the Pope. However, such approval was not sufficient for Giacomo, who complained that he did not receive all the news from the capital.[17]

During his tenure at Viterbo, Giacomo thirsted for news of political developments and of family affairs. His Viterbo correspondence reveals the same family concerns earlier shown at Orvieto. Giacomo was relieved to hear that his father was in good health, and that all was well with the other Antonelli's.[18] He later learned that Gregorio had been stricken with a debilitating fever. Distressed by his brother's illness, he thanked God for the improvement in Gregorio's condition.[19] Meanwhile, he lost no time in endearing himself to the prosperous agrarian and mercantile interests of Viterbo, who expressed their appreciation by enrolling Giacomo and his entire family among the nobility. Thus he provided another honor for his relatives.

In mid-February 1837 an unexpected Papal directive ordered Giacomo to Civitacastellana to resolve the conflict between some of the outstanding citizens of the city and the Bishop. The balanced solution provided by the Apostolic Delegate was appreciated by both parties, earning him further praise in Rome, and adding to the reputation he had already earned by his handling of the disturbances in Viterbo. Giacomo hoped that appreciation for his performance would be translated into an assignment in Rome, but such was not the case. He was destined to remain away from the capital for another three years.

Anxious to return to the Eternal City, the Apostolic Delegate in Viterbo did not despair, knowing that Pope Gregory was well disposed toward him and his family. Indeed, Gregory paid a visit to Terracina, remaining there from April 23 to April 29, 1839. Unquestionably, the Antonelli's were the chief beneficiaries of the visit as Gregorio, mayor of Terracina, remained at the Pope's side throughout the visit, arranging most of the details of the trip. The family did more than offer Gregory XVI their hospitality, presenting him with a statue of Sophocles they had uncovered at San Felice Cicero. Pope Gregory, overwhelmed by their generosity, revealed his devotion to the family. Domenico, who constantly advanced Giacomo's interests, was promised that Giacomo would eventually be promoted to a major office.

Early in 1839 Giacomo heard that he had been appointed Apostolic Delegate to Macerata. A notable promotion which would serve as a stepping stone to the fulfilment of Gregory's pledge to Domenico. Macerata was the largest of the Provinces in extent and population. His appointment to this important position revealed Rome's confidence in him. Giacomo should have been content. However, he was not; he still aspired to return to Rome. Nonetheless, it was an honor he dared not refuse. While at Macerata the first stories of Giacomo's illicit relations with women began to circulate. In reality, in Macerata, as in Orvieto and Viterbo, Antonelli had very few contacts with women, even of the most public and legitimate sort. Very likely the rumors of his sexual license were spread by those who opposed his conservative policies, and they were legion in Macerata.[20]

Apparently Giacomo was sent to Macerata to uncover and eliminate the liberal underground organization which conspired against the conservative policies of Gregory XVI. He succeeded in large measure. The energy with which he fought the adversaries of the Pontifical regime earned him the enmity of part of the local population, while it increased his prestige in the capital, where a conservative atmosphere prevailed. Giacomo's determination to combat all enemies of Gregory's government won him high praise in Rome, which had earlier witnessed the publication of the Catechism on Revolution. "Does the Holy Law of God permit rebellion against the legitimate temporal sovereign?" it was rhetorically asked and the answer was, "No, never, because the temporal power comes from God." It was further argued that since one had to remain subject to God, one had also to remain subject to the prince who was his minister.[21] These were sentiments that Antonelli seemed to share.

Domenico Antonelli had taught his children, including Giacomo, not to seek false popularity, but to court the prince whose favors counted. This approach had served the family well in the past and played a major role in the plans charted for the future. Pleased by the many concessions granted by the Papal regime to his household, Domenico urged his children to show their appreciation, for that would make them all the more meritorious in the eyes of the government, and assure new favors.[22] Giacomo did not hesitate to express his gratitude, for at the end of 1840 the Pope fulfilled his dream, when he was recalled to the capital. In 1841 he was appointed Under-Secretary for Internal Affairs.[23] This was an important post, because, following the division of the Secretariate of State by Pope Gregory in 1833, the Secretariate for Internal Affairs had become the major central organ of the ordinary administration of the Papal States. Service in the Secretariate of the Interior provided Antonelli invaluable experience as well as a firsthand knowledge of the mechanism of the state.

Gregory also appointed Giacomo a canon of St. Peter's, which carried a pension of 30 scudi a month, providing him with the monthly sum of 50 scudi until such time as Giacomo was in a position to collect an income from the cathedral chapter.[24] Pending the arrival of his successor in the city and province of Macerata, Giacomo continued to govern with the title of pro-Delegate.[25]

Loreta and Domenico Antonelli were overjoyed that Gregory had made their Giacomo Under Secretary of State for the Interior. Loreta sought to have her son by her side, possibly in the same house. By this time Giacomo was becoming Domenico's favorite son; he viewed him as "an angel sent by heaven" to clean up the intrigues that plagued the capital.[26] Giacomo had emerged as standard bearer for the Antonelli's. Filippo, who had always been close to Giacomo, seems to have had mixed feelings about his younger brother's prominence. On the one hand, he realized that the appointment redounded to the honor and welfare of the entire family, and he welcomed it. On the other hand, he resented the fact that he, the eldest son, was in danger of losing his position as head of the family. These mixed feelings colored his conduct towards his prelate brother. Filippo's reaction to Giacomo was similar to that of Gustavo Di Cavour to his younger but more prominent brother, Camillo.

Filippo, noting the abundant room in the spacious family palace in Via Sant'Agata de' Goti, offered the first floor to the new Undersecretary of the Interior, convinced that this would spare Giacomo needless expense, while increasing the family prestige. He was surprised and angered by his brother's rejection of the offer, refusing to accept his explanation that he would have to be near the Vatican, where his office was located. The older brother listed the expenses entailed in establishing Giacomi in a private apartment suitable for his station and office, finding it incomprehensible that the Pope would not allow him to live at home. In the face of Giacomo's obstinate refusal, Filippo made it known that if he were prepared to pay for the apartment himself, he would pose no objections. However, if Giacomo thought of utilizing family funds for the enterprise, he, still keeper of the purse, would oppose the plan.

Giacomo might have appealed this decision and called for the intervention of his father. He chose not to do so, preferring to borrow from strangers rather than upset his parents by challenging his older brother's judgment. Thus he said nothing about Filippo's conduct, and only told his brother Gregorio, certain that he would not reveal his secret which both knew would upset their parents.[27]

Established in his own apartment in Rome, Giacomo remained near to Filippo and his mother, but missed the rest of the family, especially his father and his brother Gregorio, who were in Terracina. He wrote frequently there, anxious to be kept informed about everything happening.[28] While he sought to advance the interests of his brothers, he used discretion in fulfilling their requests. To the pleas of Angelo to find him an opening in Rome, Giacomo responded that his younger brother imagined he could create jobs at will. Giacomo recognized the need to avoid scandal or arouse the jealousy of others in the curia. Luckily, he was still relatively unknown, and had few enemies in the capital, for contrary to his plans, he had conquered Rome from the provinces. Nonetheless, as he climbed the political ladder in the capital, his prominence excited envy and provoked condemnation.

Following Antonelli's replacement of the indecisive and inactive Monsignor Roberti, who had served as Under Secretary to Cardinal Mario Mattei in the Interior, the Pope sought Giacomo out immediately, while Cardinal Mattei, a friend of the family, showered him with all sorts of courtesies. It is true that the Antonelli's still lacked entree to the aristocratic world of Rome, but they had ready access to Pope Gregory, Gustavo Moroni, the Pope's powerful chamberlain, accorded them preferential treatment, allowing and arranging Papal audiences at their pleasure.

During the course of 1841, Giacomo, still a lay prelate, decided to receive sacred orders up to the deaconate. Domenico and Loreta Antonelli, his parents, were elated to learn of his decision. Such a step, his father predicated, would at once provide Giacomo with divine assistance, while furthering his career. He was most anxious for his son to become a priest—a step which Giacomo scrupulously avoided, despite parental encouragement. Indeed, we do not know precisely when Antonelli became a deacon. The fact that the record indicates only his determination to become a deacon, without reference to the time and place of the solemnity, has led some to conclude that he never received even that order.[29] This is contradicted by his general acceptance as a deacon and his being accorded all of the privileges commensurate with that rank.

However, it is true that he never became a priest. There were limits to Giacomo's obsessive concern for career, and willingness to please his parents.

Antonelli's competence in economic matters, and knowledge of administration gained during the three and a half years of his tenure in the Ministry of the Interior, were important assets. Gregory's evident satisfaction with Giacomo's performance as Undersecretary of the Interior, and appreciation of his political conservatism, led to his appointment as Assistant to Cardinal Antonio Tosti, Minister of Finance, in 1844. Following Tosti's death in 1845, Giacomo became acting Treasurer-General and in April, 1845 was confirmed as Treasurer-General. Filippo applauded the promotion and abandoned his earlier diffidence towards his younger brother.[30] The prestige and power accruing from Giacomo's position overcame Filippo's personal pique. Meanwhile Giacomo quickly assumed the responsibilities of his new office, commissioning Angelo Galli to compile a balance sheet of the Papal financial system for the past decade.[31]

From the first, Antonelli expressed concerns about serving in the Ministry of Finance, noting that before he assumed office therein, he had pondered its problems from a theoretical point of view. Now he had to confront the hard reality.[32] His father foresaw that his son would perform well in the ministry he regarded as the most important and interesting in the state. To assure his success, no sooner had Giacomo entered the Treasury than Domenico wrote to the two men who presided over the Pope's government, Cardinal Lambruschini, Secretary of State, and Cardinal Mattei, Secretary of the Interior, imploring them to protect his son's interests as they had in the past.[33] The old and sickly Domenico still made every effort to conciliate the influential figures in the capital. He found them sympathetic towards Giacomo, and the entire family.[34]

Domenico, whose substantial estate had been accumulated through the years by serving and pleasing men of high station and important position, taught his sons that with a good manner one could obtain a great deal, and go far.[35] Conscious of Giacomo's extraordinary gifts, Domenico stressed that talent, though essential, was not sufficient to make one's mark. Charm and personality were also important, as was the need for protectors and patrons in high places. He therefore hoped that Giacomo, with his native intelligence, would know how to choose his friends, and above all have the good sense to retain the support of the Eminences of State, and the Holy Father.[36]

Giacomo learned the lesson well, for he employed his office to remain in almost continuous contact with the Pontiff, the Cardinals, and the Directors of the great establishments in Rome. With his self confidence, courteous ways, and conciliatory manner, Antonelli made friends easily and quickly won the esteem of all those who were in the good graces of the Pope and guided the ship of state. Although Giacomo was inner-directed and secure, not burdened by the psychological need for the approval of others, he recognized the political advantages of making himself liked. His self-confidence and amiability gave Giacomo an almost irresistible magnetism, to which his associates and superiors succumbed. Later some deemed Antonelli's extraordinary allure demonic. Whatever its basis, Gregory XVI seemed to succumb, nominating him in October 1842, to the commission to review civil and criminal regulations. In July 1844 he was named president of the commission.

Giacomo immediately revealed his competence in financial and economic matters; after only two months as Treasurer he solved the thorny problem of the Beauharnais appanage. The great powers had decided at the Congress of Vienna to provide compensation to the former Viceroy of Italy, and stepson of Napoleon, Eugene Beauharnais, by assuring him in appanage the property he held in the Marches. This enormous leasehold, which almost constituted a state within a state, had long troubled the Papal government, which could not produce the enormous sums needed to repurchase the concession. The new Treasurer proved equal to the task. He secured a loan of 3,750,000 scudi at the reasonable rate of six percent interest, and signed an agreement with a newly formed company, in which his brothers (and above all Filippo), played a prominent part, that divided the land into small plots and distributed it widely. This common-sense solution, which assisted the economy of the Marches, won the gratitude of Gregory, as well as that of the Curia.[37] It was accomplished by managerial competence rather than magic. The entire conservative establishment was pleased with the Treasurer, whose future seemed assured. This did not prevent, and indeed may have provoked, the rumor that the Antonelli's had illegally profited from the venture.

While Giacomo and Filippo were in the throes of tackling the problem of the appanage, word came from Terracina that Domenico was gravely ill. Their father, who had suffered from malaria since his youth and his work in the Pontine Marshes, in early March 1845, was stricken by an attack of pernicious fever. Giacomo, unable to leave Rome, prayed for him and secured the Pope's benediction. For a time Domenico seemed to recover, but on March 27 Giacomo received word of his death, which occurred two days earlier. He grieved at the loss, urging his brothers to assure that their father's wishes be respected and fulfilled. The first was to take adequate care of their mother, Loreta. The second was to further the prominence of the family, a goal which Domenico had steadfastly pursued.[38] He left a substantial estate, which assured the financial future of his children.

Filippo, Giacomo, and Gregorio all followed Domenico's advice to accommodate themselves to the thought and policies of the most influential figures of state. Allied to Lambruschini, who many considered a likely successor to Gregory, Giacomo was very much in the conservative camp, and one of those concerned by the threat of impending revolution in the Papal States, provoked by an increasing national and liberal sentiment and by Gregory's refusal to make any accommodation with reformism.[39] Giacomo's conservative stance accounts for the fact that he was among the few to attend Gregory on his death bed in June 1846. Antonelli, like Metternich, the Austrian Chancellor, regretted the Pope's death.[40] Confident of his ability and his family's influence, Giacomo awaited future events.

Chapter Four

Antonelli Accompanies Pio Nono on the Path of Reformism, 1846–1848

Giacomo Antonelli played a vital, if mundane, role during the course of the conclave which gathered the evening of June 14, 1846 to elect a successor to Gregory. He was charged with providing food and lodging for the foreign Cardinals, among the fifty, who met at the Quirinale Palace to elect the next Pope. Efficient, loyal, and taciturn, he was trusted by almost all in the curia. Gregorio hoped that his brother would use the opportunity to ingratiate himself with the most influential prelates, which Giacomo did, winning their esteem and admiration. The Antonelli's approved of all the main contenders for the Papal throne, having close ties to Luigi Lambruschini, leader of the conservative bloc, as well as Pasquale Gizzi, who had acquired a liberal reputation since praised in the pages of *Massimo D'Azeglio's Degli ultimi casi di Romagna*. (On the Recent Events in the Romagna). The family quickly adjusted to the election of Giovanni Maria Mastai-Ferretti on June 16. Filippo, the eldest brother, commented that the conclave could not have been more brief, nor its choice more worthy.[1] The Antonelli's campaign to ingratiate themselves with the new Pope had commenced.

There was anxiety among some members of the Antonelli family about the attitude and position of Mastai-Feretti, the Bishop of Imola, who became Pope Pius IX in June 1846. Rumor circulated that the new Pope was hostile to Giacomo because while Treasurer he had conceded too many favors to his brother, Filippo. As late as 1847 Filippo wondered whether his brother had the confidence of the new Pope.[2] Furthermore, Pius was perceived as a liberal in comparison to Gregory XVI, while Antonelli was associated with the zelanti, such as Lambruschini. Prior to assuming the chair of Peter, Mastai had indicated he did not understand conservative fears, preferring reform to reaction.[3] This did not bode well for the ultras and their circle. For these among other reasons, Giacomo worried about the treatment he would receive from Pius.

Following the Pope's coronation with the triple tiara on June 21, Giacomo wrote his brother Filippo, "We hope for the best from our new sovereign and that Terracina will not be forgotten."[4] Both Filippo and Gregorio, the two older brothers, knowing the importance of first impressions, expressed concern about Giacomo's meeting with the new Pontiff. "Giacomo almost immediately knelt before him," noted Filippo with relief, "and last night (the eve of the official announcement) had a long conference with him."[5] They were satisfied that all went well, for Giacomo received the same friendly treatment from Pius he had from his predecessor; the first link between the two men had been forged.

Giacomo, eminently practical, and a technocrat more than an ideologue or politician, sought to determine which way the wind was blowing before committing himself to any stance. Unlike those who were conservative by conviction, his views had been largely shaped by his desire to please the curia and advance his career. In light of the changed circumstances, he was prepared to alter his image, and commenced by quietly disassociating himself from the ultras in the capital. Meanwhile he sought to determine the intentions of the Pope. This was perhaps his most difficult task, for Pius seemed uncertain of his ultimate goal as well as the steps required to arrive at his destination.

The Pope, to the dismay of those about him, appeared to move in two directions. On the one hand he realized that the policies of Gregory, though motivated by the best of intentions, had failed to resolve the political and fiscal problems troubling the state. On the other, he hesitated alienating the conservatives, appointing a Commission of Cardinals that included such traditionalists as Mario Mattei, Tommaso Bernetti, and Luigi Lambruschini, to advise him on administrative and political issues. This encouraged Antonelli to continue to watch and wait, stressing the need to reorder state finances while shying away from all political judgments.[6]

Antonelli, the Minister of Finance, called for an equilibrium between income and expenses. Noting that it would be difficult, if not impossible, to increase entries, his report declared that only by cutting expenses could a balance be attained.[7] Antonelli, who knew firsthand from his provincial experience the close connection between high taxes and political discontent, consistently cautioned against an increase in taxes.[8] He did not know how Pius would receive his advice, and thus he continued to scrutinize the statements and actions of the new Pope, whose course was not easily charted. Meanwhile he prudently assumed a centrist position.

Convinced of the need for a strong Papacy for the well-being of the Church,[9] Pius had been critical of the slow and cumbersome Roman administration for some time, believing that the clerical government could be better atuned to the needs of its subjects. Mastai catalogued his criticism and suggestions in his "Thoughts on the Public Administration of the Papal States,"[10] which appeared in the fall of 1845. It was not the work of a liberal by conviction, but of a realist who recognized the need for change. Although far from a coherent plan, the proposal did favor the creation of some corporate body that would at once advise upon, and supervise, the administration of affairs.[11] The Pope also had recourse to the Memorandum of the Powers of 1831, and following his election had their suggestions brought forward for consideration.

There were limits to his reformism, however, as he indicated to Pietro Renzi, the leader of the insurrection in Rimini in September 1845, who visited to thank him for his amnesty. Conceding that Renzi's Reform Manifesto contained many useful suggestions, Pius refused to accept it in toto. "There is one article I do not consider just," he blurted out. "You recommend the secularization of the Government, as if it mattered what garments your rulers wear if they govern according to the laws of justice."[12] This opinion prevailed, as he consistently resisted the pressure of the French Ambassador, Pelligrino Rossi, who called for the secularization of the government. Pius believed secularization weakened and undermined religious authority, accounting for his reluctance to sanction it.[13]

The Pope, seeking improvements in his State, moved cautiously from the first, fearing radical change might prove detrimental to the interests of the Church. He openly acknowledged his lack of political expertise, having on one occasion confessed that his knowledge of politics ran from A to C.[14] For these reasons, as well as his desire to share responsibility, he relied upon the advice of the Commission of Cardinals, which in early July approved the political amnesty which was signed on July 16, exactly one month after his election, and made public the following day. Despite the restrictions imposed by the more conservative Cardinals,[15] the amnesty was the spark that transformed the Pope from a reformer to a revolutionary in the eyes of many. In Rome it provoked a collective delirium. To Pius' dismay, many who took advantage of this amnesty reverted to their revolutionary ways.[16] Their agitation flamed a broader upheaval, sweeping the Pope along a path he had not planned, as he found it difficult, if not impossible, to moderate the popular enthusiasm unleashed.

The unforeseen march of events worried Cardinal Pasquale Gizzi, the Pope's Secretary of State, who was closely associated with the Antonelli family. Called to the post by liberal opinion which knew the image rather than the man, Gizzi, far from being a liberal, was a centrist if not a conservative. Prepared to support the technical reforms that Giacomo advocated, Gizzi questioned the political changes sought by moderates and radicals alike, fearing that they would ultimately lead to the collapse of the temporal power. His cynicism stood in marked contrast to the optimism of the Pope.[17]

During these early, exciting months of the Pontificate, Pius relied upon Antonelli for a number of reasons. The Pope felt most comfortable with technical reforms, such as the development of a railway network in his State,[18] and in these matters Antonelli had proved his mettle, as had his brother Filippo, who was made a member of the National Society for Railroads in the Pontifical State.[19] The fiscal and technical talent of Filippo was widely acknowledged; only his and Giacomo's enemies condemned the appointment as a variant of nepotism. The Treasurer-General was called upon to ameliorate the public services, adjust the State's tariffs, reform the criminal and civil codes, and above all, put the financial house in order.

Antonelli, for his part, jettisoned his earlier conservative views, stressing the need for a moderate reformism, which more or less echoed the position of Pius. Thus Antonelli alluded to the unhappy position of the people, warning of the dangers of absolute power.[20] Antonelli analyzed and understood Pius better than the others around him, appreciating that his reformism was moderated by his obsessive concern that no measure be undertaken which might compromise his spiritual mission. Finally, he more than anyone else possessed the skills needed to cope with the pressing financial problem burdening the State. Perceptive, technically competent, and enjoying frequent access to the Pontiff, Antonelli transformed himself into a crucial force in Rome. Competence, rather than ideology, was his forte.

The problems of the Papal States called for strong leadership. Both inside and outside of the state, there were those who feared the outbreak of a revolution of discontent. Poverty was endemic in both the countryside and the cities as peasants, artisans, and workers all faced a deterioration in their already low living standard. The added poverty contributed to the increase in delinquency and to the unrest that seemed to prevail everywhere.[21] Restive and misgoverned, the lower classes in the state that divided the peninsula in half threatened to resort to violence. To restore calm, Pius proposed modernization, appreciating that the difficulties in his state were economic as well as political.[22] Unfortunately, he lacked the financial resources to fund an ambitious program. In fact, the financial situation of the State had reached crisis proportions. The task of the Commission of Cardinals, appointed to examine these problems, proved difficult.

During the course of the third session of the Commission, July 15, 1846, the need for immediate financial reform loomed large. The annual deficit of more than 60,000 scudi, their report stressed, could only be reduced by increasing entries or cutting expenses.[23] In its fourth session, August 26, 1846, Monsignor Giovanni Corboli-Bussi, assuming Antonelli's stance, insisted that an increase in entries was out of the question, so expenses would have to be curtailed. The Monsignor deemed this cut essential, for in 1846 the cost of the public debt amounted to 3,125,000 scudi—a sum which the State could not afford.[24] Pius, thus, found himself torn between the need to effect economies, and the desire to provide for the country's social ills. Confronted with this difficult choice, he sought assistance, calling upon Antonelli, who knew the finances of state inside and out.[25]

By this time Antonelli had abandoned the camp of the "Gregorians," who opposed reforms, and ranked among the "Pians," who favored them. He noted that the Pope was not discouraged by the conservative talk of a revolt, and supported his view that concessions would eliminate much of the discontent. "Why speak to me of revolutions," Pius retorted to the cautious, "abuses are the rebels which sap the foundations of empire."[26] Antonelli, who remained as Minister of the Treasury, seconded the progressive policy of his sovereign. He and Gizzi were perceived as the only liberals in the Council of Ministers, created by the Motu Proprio of June 12, 1847.

The new Council included heads of the principal administrative units of the State: the Cardinal Secretary of State, the Cardinal Camerlengo, the Cardinal Prefect of Waters and Roads, Monsignor Auditor of the Chamber, the Monsignor Governor of

Rome, the Monsignor Treasurer-General, and the Monsignor President of Arms. The Council was rendered necessary, read the communique of June 12, both for practical reasons and the need for order.[27] Antonelli, the painstaking administrator who had restored some sort of stability to the Treasury, was considered the most important figure in the "cabinet."

Giacomo was rewarded for his efforts by a grateful Pope. "I want to make you a Cardinal," Pius confided, during the course of his usual Saturday audience on May 23, 1847. Antonelli, just forty one years old, and Treasurer-General for less than three years, was surprised but pleased by the unexpected honor.[28] Pius fulfilled his promise on June 12, 1847, when Giacomo was made a Cardinal with the deaconal title of S. Agata alla Suburra, later exchanged for that of S. Maria in Via Lata. In addition to Antonelli and Monsignor Guiseppe Bofondi, deacon of the sacred Roman Rota, Pierre Giraud and Jacques Dupont were elevated to the Purple.

In his address to the assembled Princes of the Church, Pius said of Giacomo:

> We feel sure that you will all give a warm reception to another member, whom we have resolved to add to your order. It is our beloved son, Giacomo Antonelli, a man distinguished by his character, his integrity, his virtue, and his zeal for religion, and who, after having displayed alike courage and ability in the discharge of many and grave functions, has filled the office of Prefect of our Pontifical Treasury. In the exercise of the office we have recognized his incorruptible fidelity, his indefatigable labours, his great talent, his skill and prudence in the management of affairs, so that in decorating him with the purple, we have in view not only the importance of the office that he has filled, but the merits by which he has won our confidence and our special goodwill.[29]

The elevation of Antonelli to Cardinal pleased the French, as Louis Philippe sent his personal congratulations to Antonelli.[30] Various Princes of Germany did likewise.[31] The nomination was in part inspired by the Pope's desire to reinforce the party which favored reformism, and greater independence from Austria.[32] Equally important, was the Pope's determination to send Antonelli as Legate to Ravenna, a hot spot both because of the temperament of its inhabitants, and its proximity to the Austrian border. Pius believed that only the former Apostolic Delegate from Viterbo and Macerata could cope with the difficulties there. The appointment would remove Giacomo from Rome, but made him a Cardinal, and thus, was a considerable coup. The Antonelli's believed that the Secretary of State, Cardinal Gizzi, had promoted Giacomo for this high honor, and Filippo Antonelli personally thanked Gizzi for his efforts. The Secretary of State, however, would take no credit, indicating that "the idea was entirely that of the Pope," adding that "his pleasure was only that of being the first to hear of the decision."[33]

Filippo wrote Gregorio the good news, adding that the honor would require Giacomo to go to Ravenna as Legate. He prayed that divine providence would continue to guide Giacomo. Although not given to emotional outbursts or sentimentality, Filippo immediately made provision for his brother's new wardrobe, planned the festivities to celebrate the occasion, and sought to provide him with a residence in Ravenna. Filippo negotiated to rent the second floor of the house of Cardinal Bartolomeo Pacca in Ravenna for Giacomo. This plan was interrupted by the outbreak of disorders in the provinces and Rome.

In June 1847, in commemoration of the Pope's election one year earlier, over 20,000 demonstrators flocked to the capital. On June 17, the Pope blessed the flags of the fourteen districts of Rome. Many in the crowd noted that Antonelli, accompanied by three other Cardinals, remained on the loggia of the Quirinale after Pius had withdrawn and enthusiastically applauded the hymn written by Pietro Sterbini for the occasion. This contributed to his new, liberal image. Thus, when the Cardinal Secretary of State Gizzi called for an end to the noisy demonstrations in the capital, critics saw this as the work of conservative clerics, but did not include Antonelli in their circle.[34]

In Rome, the champions of reform aroused the masses because the newly instituted Council was composed entirely of ecclesiastics. Meanwhile, in the provinces, the news that Antonelli was to be sent as Cardinal Legate to Ravenna led to widespread disturbances, for the conservative image of Antonelli still prevailed there. Giacomo, who had left a disagreeable impression in Viterbo for his political condemnations, was denounced as a persecutor of the liberals and deemed persona non grata. Pius, already under considerable pressure as a result of the resignation of his Secretary of State, Cardinal Gizzi, who opposed the authorization of a civic guard in early July, relented, and did not send Antonelli to Ravenna. Instead, he appointed the Cardinal to the Commission created to elaborate the Consulta di Stato he had earlier promised his people.[35] Thus, rather than leaving Rome for Ravenna, Antonelli was made President of the Commission to determine the character and functions of the Consulta, which was proclaimed by the Motu Proprio of October 14, 1847.[36] Circumstances had contrived to award him prematurely the rank of Cardinal, while leaving him in Rome, which he preferred to the provinces.

The Consulta, or Council of State, was divided into four sections which dealt respectively with legislative, financial, administrative, and military matters.[37] Its members, called to Rome from the various provinces, were entrusted with the responsibility of deliberating, discussing, and offering advice upon all questions of a governmental nature. It was conceived as a deliberative rather than a legislative body. It had no power of initiative and its sessions were closed.[38] Indeed, the Pope made it clear that he reserved the right, after hearing the opinion of the Consulta and the Council of Ministers, to consult the College of Cardinals. Reformers in Rome envisioned a broader role for the assembly. In light of the conflicting views of this body held by the Pontiff and liberals, its President had to be acceptable to both. Pius nominated Giacomo Antonelli to the position.[39] His brothers prayed that God would enable Giacomo to meet this new responsibility by satisfying the Pontiff and the people.[40] It would not prove an easy task.

Early in November 1847, Antonelli was formally notified of his appointment as President of the Consulta and informed that the Pope desired it to meet in the Apostolic Palace of the Vatican.[41] When its members assembled before the Pope on November 15, he reminded them of his need to transmit his authority in its entirety to his successor. Pius proclaimed that he had created the Consulta to aid him in his sovereign resolutions and that it was not to become "the germ of an institution incompatible with the Pontifical sovereignty."[42] Thus forewarned, the members of the Consulta, led by Antonelli, proceeded to their chamber in the Vatican to commence their tasks.

From the first, Antonelli found himself between a Pontiff who had a very restricted view of the Consulta's role, and a group of liberals who hoped to see it evolve into a legislative assembly. The Cardinal, who had never presided over such a body, sought to have it focus upon the administrative and technical matters he knew best. During the discussions of the body he revealed himself as an empirical and astute minister, anxious to defend the temporal power by promoting positive reforms that fell within the Pope's guidelines. Consequently, various projects were brought forward to improve the Papal States' financial position.[43]

Although Antonelli preferred to concentrate upon technical matters, others in the Chamber saw its political potential and pressed for change. The Cardinal was thus constrained to deal with the thorny issues that paved the way for his stormy political career that would last for three decades. Presiding over the Consulta, the Cardinal found himself mediating between the Pope and the liberals. Soon after the Consulta opened, Pius made it clear to Marco Minghetti, one of the leaders of the reformers, that he did not intend to accept all of the advice of the consultative Chamber, once again citing his obligation to transmit to his successors all of the rights of the Holy See.[44] This angered and aroused the liberals, who would not accept the limited role outlined by the Pope. The confrontation between the Chamber and the Sovereign exploded early.

In its initial session, the members of the Consulta, rather than issuing a simple note of thanks to the Pontiff, evolved a program more appropriate for a legislative body than a consultative chamber. Antonelli, perplexed for a moment, concurred with the members in order to avoid a confrontation. No sooner had that crisis subsided than another potential one arose over the question of preserving the secrecy of the proceedings of the Consulta, as the Pope desired, or publishing its deliberations, as called for by the majority. Finally, as if to decide the issue, Antonelli indicated that one of the councillors, Minghetti, knew the opinion of the Pope on the matter. The latter admitted as much, but added that Pio Nono had not assumed an adamant stand. At any rate, since the Consulta was a consultative Chamber, its function was to give advice rather than serve as an obsequious mouthpiece. The Cardinal awoke to the reality that he was now in an entirely different situation, accountable not only to the Pope, but to a political body.

Immediately perceiving his error and concluding that Minghetti's analysis was accurate, Antonelli secured a compromise solution: most of the proceedings of the body were to be published while only a small part would remain classified. In evaluating Antonelli's performance as President of the Consulta, Marco Minghetti wrote:

> I must say that Antonelli was a very able president and that was, as far as I can remember, the only blunder he made. It was understandable in light of the fact that he was almost totally ignorant of

the procedures of deliberative assemblies when he undertook the task, and had never read any theoretical book on, nor read the proceedings of, such assemblies. However only two or three sessions were all that the Cardinal needed to learn the technique of directing the discussion with great wisdom, influencing the proceedings as much as a president could without infringing upon the rights of its members, or in any manner appearing to do so.[45]

Thereafter, the Consulta operated smoothly under Antonelli's direction and showed itself indefatigable in tackling the problems of the Papal States.[46] As before, Antonelli displayed competence in economic matters, although he met with the heads of the various sections of the Consulta, dealing with all sorts of problems.[47] Pellegrino Rossi, the French Ambassador, praised Antonelli's role in effecting enlightened change. Sensitive to the will of the Pope and the needs of the times, Antonelli sought to reconcile the two.[48]

The Pope was not disappointed in the performance of his new Cardinal. His pragmatism and *sang-froid* led him to consider alternatives and solutions which frightened the timid. He was quick, for example, to appreciate the political and economic advantages of maintaining good relations with the Kingdom of Sardinia. Word reached him that Carlo Alberto was affected by the upsurge of enthusiasm that had followed the election and reformism of Pius, as the Piedmontese Monarch sensed that the Pope's policy was the equivalent of a campaign against Austria.[49] Thus soon after the Pope's election, Carlo Alberto took advantage of the presence of his Minister Count Solaro della Margarita in Rome to express his devotion to the Holy Father, congratulating him on his liberal policies and placing himself at the Pope's disposal.[50] While the Piedmontese very likely looked forward to an eventual national crusade against Austria, Antonelli sought to interest Piedmont in a commercial union that would bind the various states in the peninsula.

As early as January 1847, Antonelli had indicated the advantages of an economic union in Italy to the Sardinian Minister in Rome, Domenico Pareto. Later, in August 1847, during the meeting of the commission to study Papal policy in Italy, one of the Cardinals, most likely Antonelli, championed the tariff union as a means of fortifying the Italian states against internal disturbances and foreign invasion.[51]

In August 1847, the Pope sent Monsignor Corboli Bussi to Turin and Florence to persuade the Piedmontese King and the Tuscan Grand Duke to join with Rome in a commercial union.

Antonelli, who played a major part in bringing about the mission, supervised the negotiations from Rome. From the first he deplored the slow pace of the talks, charging that the Piedmontese placed unnecessary impediments in the way of an agreement.[52] His analysis proved accurate, as the Turin government hesitated implementing the limited commercial agreement sought by Rome. In October, the Pope personally wrote to Carlo Alberto about the importance of the league for the peace and prosperity of the peninsula, hoping that his intervention would finally move the Piedmontese.

The Pope and Antonelli were seconded by Monsignor Corboli-Bussi, who urged Rome to press the Piedmontese to hasten the conclusion of the League. Their efforts proved abortive. On October 16, 1847 the Piedmontese Minister of Finance addressed a note, full of reservations, to the Papal representative in Turin, insisting that all the conditions of the Turin cabinet be met. At best, it represented a tentative and conditional adherence to the tariff league.[53] This proved but one of the many problems that burdened the Pope, who increasingly looked to Antonelli for support.

Pius, lacking political experience and economic judgment, had reason to rely on Antonelli, who possessed the two in good measure. Resisting the call for laicization of the regime, the Pope perceived another advantage in advancing Antonelli, who was a Cardinal though not a priest. Pius considered the entry of laymen into the government a weakening of his religious authority, and therefore moved slowly, ceding more to the pressure of events than the advice of the French Ambassador, Rossi. The Cardinal, who understood the Pope's fears, was a key figure in the Cabinet and in the Curia.

As 1847 came to a close, much of Italy, including the Papal States, fell into turmoil. Pius awoke to the gravity of the situation. "The police no longer exist," he wrote his brother, "I have the need to create it."[54] Metternich believed that the Pope was the cause of much of his suffering insofar as he failed to realize that the parties did not want reform but the overthrow of the existing legal and political order. The Austrian Chancellor warned:

> The Pope daily shows himself to be lacking in all practical sense. Born and raised in a liberal family, he has been formed in a bad school; a good priest, he has never turned his ability towards governmental affairs. Warm of heart and weak in conception, he has allowed himself to be drawn into a bind since his assumption of

the tiara from which he no longer knows how to emerge, and if things follow their natural course, he will be chased out of Rome.[55]

The moderate liberals, Antonelli, and the English, disagreed, insisting that the best means of dealing with the revolutionaries was by timely reform. Pius concurred, and at the end of the year agreed to revise the Council of Ministers. By a decree of December 29, 1847, he liberalized the Papal government, and for the first time stipulated that ministers were responsible for their acts. In addition, the decree provided that vital issues would not be forwarded for the Pope's approval until discussed in the Council.[56] Antonelli helped effect this change, which represented an important concession on the part of the Pope.[57] Unfortunately it was poorly understood, and little appreciated, by most Romans. By this time only a constitution would satisfy those who longed to modernize the Papal government.

Pius, confused and uncertain, did not know how far he could, or should, go in pleasing his subjects. Antonelli could not provide much help until he had perceived how far his volatile sovereign was willing to proceed. He dared not surge too far ahead or linger too far behind Pius. While the Pope prayed and procrastinated, and Antonelli attempted to assess the path Pius would pursue, the situation in Rome deteriorated. Although the Eternal city remained on the margins of European developments, it was increasingly buffeted by ideological and political concepts that crossed the frontier, combining with internal frustrations, to provoke a revolutionary atmosphere.

Chapter Five

The Antonelli Government: The First Constitutional Ministry of the Papal States

Eighteen forty-eight opened with the cry for further change in the Papal States as agitators and admirers shadowed the Pope. Angelo Brunetti, called Ciceruacchio by the Romans, proved most pressing and persistent in demanding additional changes. When Pius ventured out of the Quirinale Palace on January 2, Ciceruacchio waved a banner which read "Justice for the People."[1] The Pope, still anxious to please the Romans, responded by creating a new ministry which included a number of popular laymen. Guiseppe Pasolini was designated Minister of Commerce, Francesco Sturbineti Minister of Public Works, while Michelangelo Caetani was made Minister of Police.[2]

The Consulta, presided over by Antonelli, was barraged with requests for domestic reforms, and above all, beseeched to provide for an adequate defense of the state in light of the agitation that threatened the peninsula. Under the Cardinal's leadership the assembly seconded the plea for a reorganization of the Papal army, calling for an increase in its size, inviting a distinguished Italian officer to assume command, mobilizing part of the civic guard, and organizing a reserve force.[3] Subsequently, the Pontifical government asked Carlo Alberto of Piedmont to provide Rome with a military man of distinction to create and lead a viable Papal army. In mid-February 1948, as revolution erupted in Palermo and Paris, and the clamor for a constitution in Rome continued, Pius created a special commission of Cardinals to examine the prospect of moving towards constitutionalism. The commission, which included Cardinal Antonelli as well as Monsignor Corboli-Bussi, was to coordinate existing institutions, while at the same time proposing others compatible with the authority of the Supreme Pontiff.[4] Most important, it was to determine whether the granting of a constitution would violate the nature of Papal authority. These responsibilities were grave, and Giacomo's brothers feared that his participation in the decision-making process jeopardized his future career. Filippo and Gregorio urged Giacomo to withdraw from the presidency of the Consulta, but the Cardinal refused to shirk his obligations.[5] Indeed, he assumed new ones.

In the ecclesiastical commission created to develop new, and coordinate old, institutions, Antonelli adopted a commanding and pragmatic stance, considering the granting of a constitution less dangerous than other alternatives. The commission espoused his position, finding no theological hindrance to the introduction of constitutionalism in the political realm, and citing the danger of revolution or foreign intervention. Despite the pleas of Marco Minghetti, the Pope would not permit laymen to take part in the deliberations of the committee, which began to draft the Statuto or constitution for the Papal States.[6]

Antonelli, with the help of Corboli-Bussi, was largely responsible for the document which emerged. Pellegrino Rossi, the French Ambassador, noted that they were participating in the funeral of the temporal power of the Papacy, led by a Cardinal with the absolution of the Pope. He charged that the draft of the Papal constitution, drawn up by Antonelli and Corboli Bussi, established legal warfare between the Sovereign and his subjects.[7] His assessment proved accurate.

There was talk that Antonelli, highly praised by some members of the Consulta, would be made President of the new Council of Ministers provided by the constitutional regime. Luigi Carlo Farini, for one, had reservations, observing that the people of Rome did not love him, while those of the provinces did not esteem him.[8] Nonetheless, on March 10, 1848, Cardinal Bofondi notified Giacomo that the Pope had nominated him Secretary of State and President of the new, constitutional Council of Ministers.[9] The Cardinal's appointment to the highest political position in the government created dissension in the Antonelli family. His brothers, foreseeing a stormy road ahead, questioned Giacomo's decision to preside-over this government, convinced that he would find himself in an untenable position. Giacomo remained optimistic, certain that the conflicts between the various groups could be minimized and the numerous problems plaguing the Papal States, resolved.

The Antonelli Ministry was by far the most liberal and capable that the Pope had sanctioned to date. This cabinet reflected the popular demand for lay ministers and included Gaetano Recchi, Minister of the Interior, Luigi Carlo Farini, Undersecretary of the Interior, Marco Minghetti, Minister of Public Works, Guiseppe Pasolini, Minister of Commerce, Prince Aldobrandini, Minister of War, Guiseppe Galletti, Minister of Police, and Francesco Sturbinetti, Minister of Justice. Cardinal Mezzofanti was made Minister of Public Instruction and Monsignor Morichini, Minister of Finance. It was hoped that these men would satisfy the liberals, the aristocracy, the capital, and the provinces. At this juncture, Antonelli, assigned the portfolio of Secretary of State, resigned from the Consulta, as did Minghetti and Recchi, who entered his cabinet. Thus, the Consulta lost three of its original members.[10]

In the first meeting of the Council of Ministers, as in subsequent ones, Antonelli found himself in agreement with the moderates of Farini's and Minghetti's stamp. Like them, he supported constitutional government and hoped that the ties which bound the Pontifical State to the other constitutional regimes in the peninsula would become closer for their individual benefit, as well as for that of the common fatherland. His attitude reflected pragmatic rather than theoretical considerations, and did not flow from the study of contemporary political problems. Nor did Antonelli wish to diminish the power and privileges of the ecclesiastical caste in Rome. It was the sight of so many thrones overturned in Europe that led him to suggest a moderate course, which he hoped would spare the Papal States the violence erupting elsewhere.[11]

The address of the Antonelli Ministry to the Pope on March 11 informed the authorities of the principles and beliefs which animated the new government. It stressed the need to follow the suggestions of the Consulta and to provide for the country's defense, calling for a solution to the pressing financial situation. Concerning the critical fiscal issue, the Cardinal adhered to his earlier position, considering it imprudent to raise taxes at that juncture.[12] Antonelli's Ministry assumed a patriotic stance as it expressed the hope "that the ties of friendship which already exist between the Papal Government and the other constitutional Governments of Italy will be ever more tightened for the benefit of our common country."[13]

The first constitutional Ministry awaited the promulgation of the fundamental law promised by the Pope. It was proclaimed on

March 14.[14] Under its terms the Sacred College of Cardinals was invested with the functions of a Senate, inseparable from the Pope. However two deliberative councils were now created for the formation of law. To preserve the position of the Pope and the Church, it was specified that the councils could not propose any legislation which appertained to ecclesiastical or "mixed matters," or that was contrary to the canons or discipline of the Church. Article thirty-eight prohibited even the discussion of the diplomatic-religious relations of the Holy See. Since the Pope could not separate his Principality and temporal power from his independence as head of the Church, he reserved to himself and his successors the right to approve all the laws deliberated by the councils he had conceded, and determined to preserve his influence in all religious and moral matters.[15] The Statuto thus specified that for the security of all Christianity the new governmental form must not limit the rights of the Church or the Holy See. Pius felt that this was all he could concede, but the Antonelli constitution failed to satisfy those who wanted to remake the Papal States along modern, parliamentary lines.[16]

The institution of a Council of State was provided for in two articles of the March 14 *Statuto*. Article 62 declared that this body would be composed of ten councilors, and a group of auditors not to exceed twenty-four, all to be nominated by the Pope. Article 63 prescribed its functions. The Council was entrusted with the task of drafting law projects, the regulation of public administration, and was to offer its opinion on matters of procedure.[17]

Once established, the Council sought to interject its voice in the country's economic and political life. It drafted projects for the reorganization of the administration, sought to clarify penal and civil legislation, as well as streamline administrative procedures. One of the problems it attacked was the position of the Jews in Rome. Until the promulgation of the constitution, Jews had been shut in the ghetto and were frequently persecuted by the populace. The Council determined that they should enjoy full civil, if not political, rights; the constitution stipulated that one had to be a Catholic to enjoy the latter.[18] This led some to criticize the new regime.

Antonelli was caught in a dilemma from the start, finding it difficult if not impossible to conciliate the will of the Pope and the needs of the Papacy with his responsibility to execute the constitution and follow the directives of the cabinet. Giacomo and his brothers prayed for deliverance from this dilemma.[19] For the moment, all exits seemed barred. The financial situation continued to deteriorate, and could not easily be reversed. A more immediate problem was the growing clamor for the expulsion of the Jesuits, who were identified with a reactionary course, from Rome. The lay members of the Cabinet conceded that the government had the responsibility of protecting the rights of all its citizens, but feared that unless some steps were taken to quiet the outcry against the Jesuits, it would be impossible to preserve domestic order and tranquility. Pius, for his part, considered the polemics and demonstrations against the Order a scandal and an outrage.[20]

Antonelli, who confessed to the Ministers of Russia and Spain that the government no longer had any authority,[21] understood the need for some compromise. Given the sentiments of the Pope on the one hand, and the passion of the demonstrators on the other, any solution required great tact and diplomacy. The Cardinal rose to the occasion, meeting with the General of the Order, Father Johann Roothaan, persuading him that it would be best if the Jesuits left the capital of their own accord, lest their presence be made the pretext of grave disorders and the shedding of blood. Antonelli thus resolved the issue by urging the fathers to leave, observing that they were not legally constrained to do so, but were simply ceding to the present agitation.[22] Under the circumstances it was a prudent solution, but one that troubled the heart of Pius. He regretted the "shameful misfortune" which had befallen these "workers in the vineyards of the Lord." At the same time he grew increasingly suspicious that his subjects were seeking not only self-government, but the right to dictate the affairs of the universal Church. The latter prospect troubled Pius.

Antonelli sought to calm and reassure the Pope on the matter of the Jesuits, and seconded his efforts to provide moral support for the much-maligned Order. At the Pope's request, Antonelli wrote to the Archbishop of Cambray urging him to do all within his means to persuade the Abbe Vincenzo Gioberti, author of *The Modern Jesuit*, to revise his book and retract his errors against both Catholic doctrine and the Company of Jesus.[23] His efforts proved fruitless.

Even more troublesome for Antonelli was the question of Papal participation in the war of national liberation initiated by the resistance of the Milanese against the Austrians on March 18, 1848, and broadened by the decision of the Piedmontese to lend their support. On March 23, Carlo Alberto donned the revolutionary tricolor and went to the aid of the Lombards. As the cry *"Fuori*

I Barbari!" (Throw the Barbarians out!) swept from the Alps to Sicily, the Cardinal joined his Cabinet in urging the Pope to send his army northward. Pressured by his Cabinet, and frightened by the consequences of non-compliance, Pius finally consented, but from the start meant for his forces to assume a purely defensive posture. At the end of March, when the Pope learned that Carlo Alberto's forces had entered Lombardy, Antonelli wrote to Cardinal Amat, Delegate at Bologna, that the Papal troops were to mass at the frontier, as the Piedmontese desired.

Antonelli, who appreciated that the Pope's position was governed by religious scruples, sent instructions to the troops which had been allowed to march north, not to cross the Po River, warning that Pius would denounce the move.[24] The Cardinal's lay colleagues, less constrained by the Pope's religious principles, called upon their sovereign to declare war upon Austria. The Pope doubted he could take such a step. On the evening of April 17, Pius convoked an extraordinary commission of Cardinals, which included Cardinals Lambruschini, Castracane, Orioli, Altieri, Vizzardelli, Bernetti, Bofondi and Antonelli, with Monsignor Bedini as secretary. The Cardinals were asked, could the Papal States participate in the war against Austria? If so, how were they to do so? If not, how could they cope with the expected reaction? The Cardinals responded "no" to the first question, and therefore found "no need" to reply to the second. To the third query they responded, *"Deus providebit."*[25]

Antonelli had earlier counselled the Pope that the way out of this maze was for the Papal States to join an Italian League. This would satisfy the Roman desire to participate in the national war, while sparing the Pope the odium of declaring or waging it.[26]

Pio Nono followed Antonelli's advice and favored the formation of an Italian federation, explaining that while he could not declare war, he might be dragged in by the needs of a pre-established union.[27] Such a federation hinged upon the cooperation of the Turin government, but Carlo Alberto, who wanted Papal support for his war against Austria, was little inclined to purchase it by limiting his own sovereignty.[28] Meanwhile, General Giovanni Durando, the Piedmontese commander of the Pope's troops, sought to utilize the great moral influence of the Pontiff against the Austrians. Anticipating a Papal pronouncement against the enemy, the General told the Papal forces he commanded that they had Pius' support in their struggle against the enemies of God and Italy, so their crusade was not only national, but eminently Christian.

When Pius learned of Durando's message, he was furious. Not only were his troops passing the Po against his express prohibition, he was presented as the principal author of the war, causing consternation among German Catholics and raising the spectre of a new schism. Only the intervention of the Antonelli Cabinet prevented Pius from lashing out against the scandal and denouncing Durando. Cautioned against provoking an outburst that would have unforeseen consequences, the Pope's response was limited to an article in the *Gazzetta Ufficiale* which noted that when the Pope wished to express a sentiment, he did so directly, rather than through subordinates. To the pleas of his ministers that he enter the conflict, Pius counterposed the need for a League, which would absolve him of the responsibility of waging war upon part of his flock.[29]

Although the Pope had not eliminated altogether the possibility of being dragged into the war, he openly revealed his reluctance to declare it. "Italian nationalism is overrunning the whole of Italy and it is a natural sentiment," he wrote on April 25, 1848, "but my position is such that I cannot declare war against anyone."[30] Since his troops on their own initiative had joined with those of Carlo Alberto in fighting the Austrians, the Antonelli Cabinet implored the Pope to legitimize their action by a declaration of war.

In a memorandum of April 25, the Ministry indicated that the war issue could be resolved in one of three ways. The first was for the Pope to permit his subjects to wage war. The second was to have the Pope declare openly and clearly that he would not wage war. The third possible solution was for the Pope to assert that while he favored peace, he could not prevent his subjects from joining the conflict. The Cabinet unanimously concluded that the waging of war was called for by the needs of the time, and believed that it would strengthen the moral and material standing of the government. The refusal to enter the war, the Ministers concluded, would gravely compromise the temporal power, while the third solution would announce to the world that the Pope had lost control of events and would annul the remaining authority of the government.[31]

Pius found himself in a bind, pressured by his Cabinet to wage a war he felt he could not, and should not, declare, fearing catastrophic consequences. He confided to Corboli-Bussi that he intended to inform the Cardinals in Council that his government could not declare war against anyone, but at the same time acknowledge that he could not prevent his troops, inspired by an ardent nationalism, from pushing beyond the Po, and attacking the Austrians.[32] These ideas were included in the Papal Allocution of April 29, 1848, which precluded any declaration of war.[33] The Pope's statement against intervention in the war galvanized the general unease and mood of malaise, creating an outbreak of discontent which disrupted the peace of both the countryside and the capital. The state veered on the brink of total anarchy.

Antonelli, who had joined the Cabinet in calling for war, claimed that he was not privy to the Pope's message, and was as surprised and disappointed as his lay colleagues.[34] Some considered the Cardinal's explanation poorly contrived, suggesting that he had written the controversial Allocution—although there is a copy of the message among Pio Nono's papers in his own hand.[35] Meanwhile public criticism of the Antonelli ministry mounted, condemned for the failure to implement its program and fulfill its priorities, and above all its inability to bring the Papal States into the national crusade against Austria.

When the Cabinet received a translation of the Allocution against the war it resigned. "But why? What is it?" Pio Nono repeated, stunned and saddened by the crisis his Allocution had provoked as he sought to mitigate its significance. The Cabinet members, in turn, indicated that in light of the public sentiment and popular agitation aroused by the Allocution, they could no longer assure the public order of which they were the custodians. "Very well," Pius interjected, perturbed by their response, "I see that the Romans do not understand Latin, therefore I shall speak in Italian. Remain tranquil, stay at your posts, and tomorrow I shall reassure you completely."[36] On the basis of Pio Nono's promise that he would issue a clarification of the Allocution that would satisfy the public, the Cabinet temporarily remained in office.

Pius immediately commenced work on the statement that was to pacify the public and please his government. "I shall make you happy," he told Pasolini and Recchi the evening of May 1, "in fact, I want to show you the galleys (of the proposed proclamation) so there will no longer be any misunderstanding between us."[37] At this point Pius ordered one of his servants to bring him the galleys, but the latter returned empty-handed, reporting that they were not ready. Pasolini recounts that the Pope threatened to remain in the garden until the galleys were brought to him, and waited impatiently for them to appear. When his servant did not return, Pasolini persuaded Pius to retire for the evening, observing that the galleys could be read in the morning. The next day the Pope's proclamation, which was plastered upon the walls of Rome, completely confirmed the basic points of the Allocution. Why did the Pope fail to keep his promise and satisfy his Ministers? Did Antonelli play a part in this episode?

According to Monsignor Francesco Pentini, who revealed the story only years later, Antonelli was the villain in the drama. Pentini claimed that a chastened Pius had asked him to produce a statement in favor of the war, or at least one that would quiet the outcry of his subjects, and he had complied, asserting in his draft that the Pope had the duty of defending his people and seconding their interests. The Pope allegedly approved the contents of the Pentini message, and then sent it to the press of the Secretariate of State to be typeset. If printed as written, Pentini maintained, there would have been no rift between the Pope and his subjects, but Antonelli entered the press room and revised the proclamation.[38]

Pentini's story has never been substantiated and is contradicted by all the available evidence, as well as common sense. Why would a Pope, who was jealous of his authority, allow Antonelli to violate his orders and alter his words and intent? Also, if the Secretary of State had dared to unilaterally edit the Pope's message, what prevented him from setting the matter straight? These unanswered questions, plus the fact that the Pope had indicated to friends and diplomats alike that he could not declare war, negate the story that the shadow of the Cardinal intervened to prevent a conciliation between the sovereign and his subjects.

Pius repeatedly affirmed the content of his Allocution in a consistent and clear manner. "No one is ignorant of the words pronounced by us in the last Allocution, that we were adverse to a declaration of war," the Pope explained in his letter of May 11, 1848 to the people of Rome, "but at the same time we averred that we were incapable of restraining the ardor of that portion of our subjects who were animated by the same spirit of nationality as other Italians . . ."[39] He hoped this would satisfy his subjects, but it did not. Years later in 1855, Pius criticized Guiseppe Pasolini for his opposition to the Allocution of 1848, noting that "the Pope could not have spoken otherwise." Interestingly enough, the same Pasolini who sought to blame Antonelli for the Allocution, when face to face with the Pope, denied attacking the Pope's message.[40]

There was some criticism of Antonelli by his colleagues for refusing to sign the letter of resignation of the Cabinet. The Cardinal cited his ecclesiastical allegiance to the Pope, openly admitting his disappointment with the Pontiff who had placed them in such a perplexing situation. Pointing to his vestment, Antonelli allegedly decried that he was not free to leave as they were. "If he commands me as Pontiff I shall obey because my ecclesiastical oath binds me," Antonelli reportedly told his lay ministers, "but as a prince, no, he shall never have my services again."[41] This promise, if made, was not kept. In light of the Cardinal's subsequent actions it appears that his departure was the result of his inability to govern without the moderates who had resigned, rather than any moral revulsion against the Pope's Allocution. Whatever his motivation, one period of service had closed for Antonelli, and another was about to begin.

Chapter Six

The Cardinal Confronts the
Revolution and the Roman Republic

Following the Allocution of April 29, 1848, the love the Romans had showered upon the Pope turned to hate. There were charges of betrayal and criticism of the reactionary role played by the Cardinals who diverted the once popular monarch from the path of reform. Conservatives in the curia were accused of having made the Pontiff cold to the national cause and hiding the truth from his eyes. The civic guard, reflecting popular fears and suspicions, occupied the gates of the capital, arresting all couriers and intercepting correspondence with the outside world. There were outbreaks of disorder in Bologna and elsewhere in the Papal States.[1] A perplexed Pius found himself in a virtual snakepit, while his ministers watched helplessly, paralyzed by fear.

In the capital, where unrest and dissatisfaction combined with confusion, Antonelli immediately grasped the gravity of the situation. Giacomo's brothers, relieved that Giacomo no longer presided over the Cabinet, believed he remained cloistered in the Quirinale Palace for quiet and safety.[2] Giacomo shared their concern for the future, praying that the soul of Gregorio's young daughter, who had recently died, would serve as their protector in heaven.[3] The Cardinal did more than pray, remaining in close contact with liberals such as Minghetti and Pasolini, entertaining them by showing his collection of precious gems. He did not wish to be associated with the reactionaries.[4]

Cardinal Soglia, the new Secretary of State, inept, weak, and inexperienced, proved incapable of confronting the crisis. He encouraged Pius to consult regularly with Antonelli, whom the Pope named to the Congregation for Extraordinary Ecclesiastical Affairs. Although no longer part of the government, Antonelli retained the confidence of Pius who continued to seek his advice on the elaboration of various projects. Thus, it was the Cardinal who asked Carlo Alberto of Piedmont to assume command of the Papal forces that had crossed the Po River against the Pope's orders. Luigi Carlo Farini, entrusted with a special mission to Turin, succeeded in persuading the Piedmontese King to honor Antonelli's request. Farini argued that Pius would do all he could to protect the nation, so long as it did not interfere with his obligations as spiritual leader of the Church.[5] Nationalists in Rome were not mollified, however, so the Pontiff once again sought Antonelli's assistance.

Unexpectedly, Antonelli's position as private counsellor made him more powerful than he had been while head of the constitutional ministry. Very likely it was at his suggestion that Terenzio Mamiani replaced him as effective head of the Papal government on May 3, 1848.[6] Likewise, it was the Cardinal who encouraged the Pope to write to the Austrian Emperor on May 3, 1848, calling upon that ruler to recognize the national existence of the Italian people and proposing that the Papacy mediate a peace between Austria and the Kingdom of Sardinia. Thus, though the new ministry was in place by May 12, 1848, the Pope relied on Antonelli to inform Farini and the Piedmontese of the Papal initiative to Vienna.[7] Antonelli explained that the Pope still did not comprehend why his Allocution had been misconstrued as anti-Italian. The fact that he could not participate in the war did not mean that Pius opposed Italian aspirations, Antonelli continued, noting that the Pope had called upon Austria to give up a domination which could be neither noble nor happy when based solely on force.[8]

News of the Pope's letter to Vienna, and his selection of a new, liberal ministry, quieted the outcry in Rome for the moment, but problems persisted. Those close to Pius knew that he did not appreciate the program of the Mamiani Ministry, which called for war against Austria, and secularization of the Papal government. Furthermore, Pius did not accept Mamiani's contention that while the Pope "blessed, prayed, and pardoned," his Chamber and Ministers were responsible for temporal affairs. The Pope and Cardinal Altieri soon revealed their reluctance to accept Mamiani's stance, with unfortunate consequences for the public tranquility.[9] Nonetheless, Antonelli remained in the Quirinale, by the Pope's side, at a time when most of the other Cardinals, fearing for their safety, had left.[10] Minghetti, among others, recognized the great influence Antonelli continued to exercise from the sidelines.[11] His perception was confirmed by the fact that it was Antonelli, and not the Secretary of State, who was entrusted with formulating the Papal protest against Piedmont's actions vis-a-vis the Duchies of Parma and Piacenza in June 1848.[12]

The quiet diplomacy of Antonelli could not keep Rome from the brink of revolution as relations between Pius IX and Mamiani steadily deteriorated.[13] The Pope believed that Italian affairs were complicated by the intrigues of the party that desired to see the entire peninsula unified, and warned of the consequences flowing from their policy.[14] He openly refused to sanction Mamiani's plan to separate the temporal from the spiritual power, and on July 10, responded to the Ministry's proposals by insisting on his full liberty of action in the interests of religion and society.

> If the Pope prays, blesses and pardons, he also has the obligation to loose and tie. If as a Prince, he desires to safeguard and reinforce public affairs and calls the two councils to cooperate with him, the Priest-Prince requires all that liberty which does not paralyze his actions in the affairs of religion and the state. And that liberty remains intact notwithstanding the fact that the Law on the Council of Ministers and the Statuto, which he granted, also remain intact.[15]

Relations between Pius and the Ministry were also strained by the failure of the Pope's mediation with Austria,[16] while the lay ministers still insisted on bringing the Papal States into the war against Austria. Pius let it be known that the fulfillment of Italian national aims—as far as he was concerned—could not be achieved by the waging of war. Disagreement over the civic guard, as well as the Pope's refusal to sanction war against Austria, led to outbursts of disorder in the capital and the resignation of the Mamiani Ministry at the end of July 1848.[17]

The Ministry of Count Eduardo Fabbri, which succeeded, proved no more successful in resolving the war issue and lasted less than two months. Rome remained in a state of agitation, and those around the Pope felt the tension. Giacomo longed to return to the quiet of his family in Terracina and soothe his frayed nerves by bathing in the blue-green waters of the Mediterranean. He had planned to return South in August, but an attack of gout at the beginning of the month kept him in Rome, to the evident satisfaction of the Pope who relied upon his common sense and sang froid.[18] His difficulty in walking flowed from the gout rather than venereal disease, as later charged.

On the advice of Antonelli and Antonio Rosmini, among others, Pius named Pellegrino Rossi, the former French Ambassador to Rome, Minister of the Interior and Finance, as well as effective head of the government.[19] Shortly thereafter, Antonelli was confirmed in the position of Prefect of Pontifical Residences, with apartments in the Vatican and Quirinal Palaces. This was a new position created specifically for the Cardinal, who could thus remain by the Pope's side and provide him with counsel. It was not, as some supposed, simply a sinecure. Rossi officially, Antonelli unofficially, provided Pius with the support and confidence he needed. Both favored resolving the war-issue by means of the Italian Confederation the Cardinal had earlier proposed.

Pius was encouraged to write to Carlo Alberto stipulating that the need for the Italian Confederation was greater than ever.[20] Once again, however, negotiations led nowhere, and Rossi enraged the nationalists by holding the Piedmontese responsible for the failure.[21] Even Rosmini grew disenchanted with the man he had earlier championed, denouncing him as a dictator. Rossi's assertions that France was not a "corporal in the service of Italy," and could not be expected to fight the Austrians, as well as his determination to uphold the Pope's prohibition against a unilateral intervention in the war, precipitated his murder on November 15, 1848, and the revolutionary events of November 16. Both the assassination and the tempestuous aftermath were planned and coordinated.

The morning after Rossi was struck down by the dagger of an assailant, a large crowd, with the deputies of the Chamber at its head, marched upon the Quirinal Palace, demanding a democratic Ministry that would declare war on Austria. While the diplomatic corps in Rome hastened to the Pope's side, including the representatives of France, Spain, Bavaria, Brazil, Holland, and Russia, members of the Ministry, and even the Curia, fled in terror. Only a single company of Swiss troops, less than one-hundred strong, remained to protect the Pope. "You see," Pius told the foreign representatives, "the Quirinal is deserted and almost all have abandoned me. If you were not with me, I would be alone with the swords of the brave men who will defend me."[22]

At this hazardous juncture Antonelli demonstrated his loyalty by remaining by the Pope's side. Only he and Cardinal Soglia did not abandon Pius to his fate. Antonelli acted with resolution and courage, meeting with the Captain of the Swiss guard and having all the approaches to the Quirinal hastily barricaded by placing the few troops to the best advantage. The Cardinal ordered these men to remain at their posts, but instructed them to rally at the entrance of the Pope's chamber, should the crowd break into the Palace. The Prefect of Pontifical Residences perceived the dangerous position that he and the Pope confronted.[23] Antonelli preferred some sort of accommodation, but Pius' refusal to compromise his dignity rendered a confrontation inevitable.

When the Pope informed a delegation of the protesters that he would consider their demands for a democratic ministry, but would not be pressured, insisting that the crowd disband before any action on his part, the siege of the Quirinal commenced, resulting in the death of the Secretary of Latin Letters, Monsignor Giovan Battista Palma.[24] Pius was warned that if he did not accept the ministry demanded by the "people," the Palace would be stormed, and all destroyed save the Pope. Faced with this prospect, Pius reluctantly submitted, making it clear that he yielded only to the threat of force.[25] Rosmini refused to serve in this government imposed upon the Pope, fleeing first to the French Embassy, and then a Palazzo outside of Rome. On November 17, the *Gazzetta di Roma* published the names of the members of the "democratic" ministry. Soon thereafter, the Pope was forced to disband his Swiss troops, which were replaced by the Civic Guard, which Pius and Antonelli considered a warden more than a protector.[26]

From the moment of the formation of the new Ministry in mid-November 1848, Antonelli and Pius concurred that the position of the Pope was deplorable. The Cardinal was warned that an attempt would be made to destroy the temporal power, and every available means should be employed to frustrate that "devilish scheme."[27] It was a concern shared by the Pope. Pius feared that his actions would no longer be free, and he would be constrained to sanction measures which violated his conscience. Above all, he suspected that this anti-Austrian government might provoke a schism in the Church and sought to avoid that eventuality. In the presence of Antonelli he confessed to the diplomatic corps that the steps taken by his government were against his will, refusing to accept responsibility for them.[28] Pius was in an untenable position. Antonelli, who remained by the Pope's side as Prefect of Holy Palaces, recommended flight. The Pope remained uncertain, fearing the consequences of such a step. The aristocrats of the former royal guard were not encouraging, citing their personal safety, and that of their families, if they helped the Pope escape. Antonelli, however, saw no other alternative and commenced to make preparations for the flight. He did so quietly, keeping his plans even from his brothers.[29]

Preparations for the Pope's flight were left in Antonelli's hands not only because he was Prefect of Papal Palaces, but also because Pius had confidence in him and few others. The Cardinal proved equal to the task, meeting with the representatives of the Catholic powers, especially France, Spain, and Bavaria to coordinate their efforts. Count Spaur, the Bavarian representative, was most cooperative, and shared Antonelli's conviction that the Pope had to be removed from the perilous Roman situation. Antonelli met with Martinez de la Rosa of Spain, and the Duke d'Harcourt of France, winning their support.

Antonelli also confided in those constitutionalists who had proved their loyalty to the Pope, understanding their desire to follow the Pope to make clear that Pius's departure was not prompted by a revulsion against constitutionalism, but by the excesses of the "democratic" ministry. This was not simply a ploy to reassure the moderates, but the Cardinal's true assessment of the situation. Actually, Pio Nono's disillusionment with constitutionalism had commenced, but Antonelli did not know, because this sentiment had not yet trickled from the Pope's subconscious to his conscious mind. The Pope still proclaimed his adherence to constitutionalism, but his actions betrayed his reluctance to accept its implications. Only the aristocratic members of the guard refused to lend their support to the flight, concerned about the consequences should the plan fail, while fearing for the safety of their wives and children should it succeed with their assistance.[30] Pius, despite his confidence in Antonelli, remained perplexed and uncertain.

The logic of Antonelli's arguments for flight were influential but not decisive in determining the Pope's decision to flee from his capital. Only the receipt of a letter and present from Monsignor Chatrouse, Bishop of Valence, on November 17, proved decisive. The Monsignor included a small silver case, the very one in which Pius VI had carried the Eucharist with him into exile, and the Pope interpreted this as a sign from heaven to leave his capital. Pius made the decision on November 17, and informed the relieved Cardinal.

From the first, Antonelli orchestrated all the details of the flight, including the eventual destination. Initially he favored Majorca both because it was easily reached by sea, and because the

Spanish ambassador had recently offered the Pope hospitality on that island. Since Pius was pleased by the proposal, all that remained was for the Spanish ship to appear along the coast and transport him there. When Antonelli informed the French ambassador of their plans, D'Harcourt, acting on his own initiative, offered the Pope hospitality in France. The French suggestion was bolstered by the fact that the French steamboat Tenare had been at Civitavecchia since mid-October, and was immediately available, while the Spanish ship which would bring Pius to Majorca had not yet been sighted in the waters off the Papal States.

The French proposal created complications for Antonelli, who knew that the Pope did not place great confidence in the country where a few months ago a revolution had led to the creation of a provisional republic. The memory of two other Pope's exile in France, suspicion of Louis Napoleon, as well as the part played by Charles Lucien Bonaparte in the events of November in Rome, increased Pius's apprehensions. Antonelli saved the Pope from this dilemma by pointing to Gaeta in the Kingdom of Naples as a possible refuge, confident that King Ferdinando could be persuaded to offer the Pontiff hospitality. Since Antonelli required the assistance of both the Spanish and French ambassadors, and did not wish to prematurely close any doors, he insisted that no one be told of their preferred destination. Pius left matters entirely to the Cardinal, who alone was entrusted with his safety.

The manner in which Antonelli arranged, and then executed, the flight from Rome demonstrates both his diplomacy and duplicity. Having set the escape for the evening of November 24, and established the manner by which Benedetto Filippani, a trusted agent of the Pope, was to get him out of the Quirinal Palace, Antonelli had to deal with the Spanish and French Ambassadors, each of which insisted on his homeland as the Pope's destination. His difficult task was to prevent the Spanish ambassador from directing the Papal coach to the coast, where the Spanish ship was expected, which planned to sail the Pope to Majorca. At the same time he had to prevent the French ambassador from directing the Pope's coach to Civitavecchia, where the French steamship was waiting to transport the Pope to France. The Cardinal was to succeed, with the help of the Bavarian Ambassador and his Roman wife, Teresa Giraud, in deceiving both.

The negotiations to arrange a marriage between a princess of Bavaria, and the older son of Ferdinando II of the Kingdom of the Two Sicilies, offered the Bavarian Ambassador and his wife the opportunity to journey to Naples, and Antonelli determined that the Pope, in disguise, would accompany them. His strategy was not revealed to his other co-conspirators. In order to reassure the suspicious Gallic minister, he entrusted some of the Pope's personal belongings to D'Harcourt to transfer to Civitavecchia and the Tenare. Furthermore, two important ecclesiastics, Monsignor Stella, the confessor of the Pope, and Monsignor Della Porta, his private secretary, remained with D'Harcourt and were to accompany him to Civitavecchia, where the Pope was expected. So certain was D'Harcourt that the Pope was going to France that he agreed to provide the Pope with the opportunity to escape by arranging for an interview the evening of the departure, thus removing the suspicion that the Pope would abandon the Palace at that time.

The Spanish ambassador was likewise misled by Antonelli, who told him that if the Spanish ship that was to transport him to Majorca was not sighted, the Pope would go to Gaeta and await it there. As proof of his commitment, Antonelli would proceed to Gaeta in the company of the Secretary of the Spanish Ambassador, Gonzalez del Arnao.[31] Both De La Rosa and D'Harcourt were in for a surprise when they arrived at Civitavecchia: the first for not finding the Spanish ship that was to proceed to Gaeta, the latter for first learning of the Pope's change of plan. D'Harcourt ordered the Tenare to proceed to Gaeta in the expectation that it would pick up the Pope and bring him to Marseilles. Antonelli had other plans.

On the morning of November 25 Pius, dressed as a simple priest and sporting large spectacles, arrived with the Bavarian Ambassador's coach at Mola di Gaeta, some six miles from Gaeta proper. Shortly thereafter the carriage stopped at Fondi to pick up Gonzales D'Arnao and Antonelli, who was wearing ill-fitting clothes, a three-cornered hat, and a red scarf wrapped about his neck and chin. Pius smiled at the latter's appearance. "I thank thee, my God," the Pope exclaimed, "for having preserved me my dear Cardinal Antonelli."[32] He had liberated the Pope from an "imprisonment" which endangered his policies and violated his principles. The next day Pius showed his gratitude by naming him head of the Pontifical government in exile and soon, thereafter, news of the appointment reached Rome.[33]

Antonelli, in Gaeta, feared that the French and Spanish ambassadors would attempt to bring Pius to their respective countries. He preferred that the Pope remain where he was, freeing him of the protection of the great powers and from the stigma of exile in a far-away, non-Italian land. The Cardinal hoped that at Gaeta, near the confines of his state, the Pope could more effectively maintain relations with the moderate element in his territory interested in returning the state to calm, while keeping it free and constitutional. A protracted stay in the Neapolitan Kingdom required an invitation from Ferdinando II, which Antonelli believed would be forthcoming once the Pope's plight became known. He, therefore, had Pius write to Ferdinando informing him of his arrival at Gaeta, and instructed Spaur to deliver it personally to the King. Privately Spaur was to encourage Ferdinando to offer Pius asylum at Gaeta, freeing him of the danger of being brought to France. The Pope's letter, drafted by Antonelli, read:

> The Roman Pontiff, the Vicar of Jesus Christ, the sovereign of the States of the Holy See, has found himself in the circumstances of having to abandon the capital of his dominions in order not to compromise his dignity, and in order not to show support by his silence of the enormous excesses that have been committed in Rome. He is in Gaeta, but he is there for a short time, since he does not intend to compromise in any manner Your Majesty or the quiet of his people, if this presence might possibly compromise them.
>
> Count Spaur will have the honor of presenting this letter to Your Majesty and will tell you more which for lack of time he cannot now express about the place where in a short while the Pope intends to go.
>
> With a tranquility of spirit, with a resignation to the devine design, he transmits to Your Majesty, the Royal Consort, and finally to all his people, the Apostolic Benediction.[34]

Upon receipt of the letter, Ferdinando and his family determined to sail to Gaeta personally to invite the Pope to remain within the Kingdom. D'Harcourt, who arrived in Gaeta on the Tenare at four o'clock the morning of November 26, witnessed the arrival of the three royal ships from Naples, and learned of Ferdinando's invitation to the Pope to remain in his realm. The French ambassador sought to persuade Pius to adhere to his "original" plan, and depart for Marseilles. Only with difficulty did Antonelli persuade him to permit the two ecclesiastics to disembark, and to return the Pope's luggage. Two considerations influenced D'Harcourt's determination to bring Pius to France: national pride, and the desire to keep the Pope on the path of liberal reform. When the French ambassador saw Pius harden his heart against liberalism, he reluctantly left Gaeta.

The Pope's flight from Rome, engineered by Antonelli, was unexpected, and disturbed most Romans. Word of the escape spread throughout the Papal States, so that by December 1, Gregorio, in Terracina, was certain that Giacomo was by the Holy Father's side in Gaeta. Angelo, in Rome, knew less, and was upset by the stories circulating in the capital which held Giacomo responsible for the Pope's precipitous flight and other "crimes." Although some twenty-seven Cardinals eventually found their way to Gaeta, Pius relied upon Antonelli, who was there from the first. At Gaeta, Antonelli was not only the "soul" of the Pontifical Government, he was the cabinet. In December, the Pope appointed him Secretary of State, acknowledging the prominence the Cardinal exercised. The fact that he was named acting Secretary of State did not indicate that the appointment was temporary, but reflected the fact that Pius was in exile, and therefore lacked a government with effective control over the state.[35]

Giacomo confided to his brothers that at Gaeta he enjoyed not only access to, but influence with, the Pontiff.[36] With his support, on November 27, Pius issued a statement describing the deplorable conditions in Rome which had constrained him to abandon the capital, citing the need to enjoy full liberty in the exercise of the supreme power of the Holy See.[37] Political power in Rome was entrusted to a commission consisting of Cardinal Castracane, Monsignor Roberto Roberti, the Prince of Rovino, Prince Barberini, the Marquis Bevilacqua of Bologna, the Marquis Ricci of Macerata, and Lieutenant-General Zucchi. Democrats in the capital, however, were little inclined to accept their mandate, suggesting that since the Pope had left he had abdicated, and the creation of an entirely new government was in order.[38]

On December 7, 1848, Pius prorogued both of the Roman Chambers, but proved unable to implement his mandate. In fact, the Chambers met, set aside the governmental commission created by the Pope, and by joint resolution established its own supreme committee to exercise the executive power. Plans were also made to convoke a constituent assembly for the Papal States to provide a permanent alternative to Papal rule. These steps provoked the Cardinals in Rome to urge Antonelli to denounce the outrage. Pius complied on December 17, by condemning the illegitimate government created in Rome.[39] On December 29, 1848, when the Roman Junta issued the call for the election of the constituent assembly, Pius unleashed another denunciation.[40] He considered the situation in Rome deplorable.[41] These developments, plus the re-establishment of amicable relations with Austria[42], led Pius, and therefore Antonelli, his agent, to abandon constitutionalism, and to seek to restore the Pope without incumbrance.

Pius resolved not to negotiate with rebels, demanding a restoration without conditions. He thus refused the offers of political asylum in constitutional Piedmont, as he had in Republican France.[43] The Pope thanked the Savoyard King for his offer of hospitality, but preferred to remain at Gaeta awaiting the repentance of his subjects, as well as the response of the Catholic powers to his appeals. Antonelli, who had agonized over the best means to effect a restoration, on December 4, 1848, issued a call to France, Spain, Naples and Austria to restore the Pontiff to his Kingdom. The Pope and Antonelli were disappointed by the evasive answers and vague offers of hospitality provided by the powers. Spain, alone, suggested a concrete plan when Juan Donoso Cortes argued that the Catholic states had to take action to restore the Pope to Rome and called for the opening of a congress of these states to coordinate the action.

Father Antonio Rosmini, sent to Gaeta by the Piedmontese government with the mission of persuading the Holy Father to remain a constitutional monarch, found his views and his presence less than welcome. He blamed both developments on the Cardinal, whom he distrusted.[44] Rosmini, who remained at the Pope's residence at Gaeta from November 26, 1848 to January 22, 1849, accused Antonelli of charting the Pope's conservative course, as well as creating a rift between Pius and himself. Rosmini's bitter denunciations of the Cardinal are confused and contradictory. The Barnabite priest erred in focusing all of his anger on Antonelli; others in the court and the curia wanted Rosmini removed and his works condemned. No sooner had Rosmini left than the conservative Cardinal Lambruschini confided that his arrival at Gaeta had created tensions, but these had been dissipated, thanks to the wise conduct the Pope had pursued towards him. Later, when Lambruschini was asked about the priest, he bitterly replied, "I do not know him."[45]

The events of 1848 turned the Pope, and therefore Antonelli, against reformism. Subconsciously, Pius deemed his earlier flirtation with liberalism partly responsible for the outbreak of disorder in Italy. He suffered exile as a result. They were living in dangerous times he wrote while abroad, where he believed he had been sent by divine providence, and warned of the grave consequences risked by those ecclesiastics who courted the popularity of the masses, as he had in the first years of his pontificate. In his view this justified his refusal to assume the leadership of the national movement noting, "With what conscience could the Pope have supported such a movement, knowing that for certain it would lead to . . . religious incredulity and social dissolution?"[46] While Pius was willing to provide assistance to various individuals and charities in his capital, he refused to negotiate with the leaders of the revolution.[47]

Some sought to blame Antonelli for the Pope's disillusionment with constitutionalism, and his deep suspicion of Piedmont. Giacomo wrote his brother Gregorio that only the worst scoundrels could accuse him of following his own policy, separate from the wishes of his Prince, the Pope.[48] The available evidence corroborates his position, suggesting that the Cardinal pandered to the Pope's change of heart rather than provoking it.

Pius' distrust of the Piedmontese stemmed from their relations with the rebels in Rome. When the diplomatic corps followed Pius to Gaeta, the Piedmontese representative, Domenico Pareto, remained behind. Pius was also scandalized by the unilateral Piedmontese effort to alter Church-State relations in their realm.[49] Constitutionalism, it appeared to Pius, promoted not only revolution but a sacrilegious attack upon the Church. Indeed the Pope had entered the constitutional course reluctantly, and never fully accepted its implications even before the revolution had forced him to flee his state. Antonelli had early let it be known that though the Pope had granted a Statuto, he did not realize this restricted his sovereignty and sought to rule as he did previously. Pius would not sacrifice the interests of the universal church to advance Italian national interests, the Cardinal continued.[50] While Antonelli accepted the Pope's decision, his rebellious subjects in the abandoned capital did not.

On February 9, 1849, the constituent assembly proclaimed the Roman Republic, prompting Pio Nono to issue yet another protest from Gaeta.[51] On February 18, Antonelli issued a second call for the armed intervention of Austria, France, Spain and the Kingdom of the Two Sicilies, proclaiming they were in the best position to restore order to the Pope's state. The next day, the Secretary of State condemned the confiscation of ecclesiastical property in the Papal States, branding this and all other actions undertaken since the Pope's departure null and void.[52] The Piedmontese energetically opposed foreign intervention, and resented their own exclusion from the call for help. They were especially upset since they had decided to renew the war against Austria, and in March, were routed by the forces of General Radetzky at Novara. The road was now open for the Austrians to occupy Rome.

At the end of March 1849, the Conference of Catholic Powers opened at Gaeta under the presidency of Antonelli, the Pope's plenipotentiary. The suggestion that the two Italian states of Naples and Piedmont undertake the restoration of the Pope received only the approval of the French. Antonelli indicated that such an intervention was unacceptable to Pius, citing the Piedmontese fraternization with the rebellious faction in Rome hostile to the temporal power. Acknowledging that the Pope's own forces could not effect a restoration, he called upon the support of the four Catholic powers. The Cardinal looked to the Catholic party in France to assure the participation of the Republic in the restoration.[53]

The Cardinal Secretary of State, acting upon the Pope's instructions, demanded the reestablishment of the temporal power, without any conditions or reservations. The representatives of Austria (Esterhazy), Spain (Martinez De La Rosa) and Naples (Ludolf) concurred, and were inclined to provide immediate assistance. The French envoy, the Duke D'Harcourt, sought some assurances from Antonelli about the nature of the restored regime. He urged the creation of a constitutional regime to assure the peace, and prevent the outbreak of a new revolution. The French sought to reconcile what was increasingly difficult if not impossible: restoration of the temporal power and preservation of the constitutional guarantees of 1848.[54]

Despite the Pope's reluctance to make any constitutional commitments, the French decided in mid-April to send an expedition to Rome. The French Foreign Minister wrote D'Harcourt that Cardinal Antonelli had to be made to understand that to take advantage of the French expedition, the Pope had to publish a manifesto to his people, guaranteeing free institutions. Such a step would decrease resistance in Rome, and render the French conquest easier. In response to D'Harcourt's pleas, Antonelli commented that the Pope would make his intentions known, once restored.

The French landing at the port of Civitavecchia was not resisted. This was in marked contrast to their attempt to enter Rome, a week later, which was repulsed. As the French prepared to undertake the siege in earnest, Antonelli urged the other Catholic powers to participate in the invasion, so the Pope would not have to be obligated to Paris alone. In the interim, the ministry of Massimo D'Azeglio in Turin decided to send the scrupulously Catholic Count Cesare Balbo to Gaeta to combat the Spanish and Austrian representatives, who were seen to lead Pius in an autocratic, unconstitutional direction. Once again the Piedmontese request to participate in the armed intervention to restore the Pope was rejected. The Nuncio claimed their request had arrived too late. Concerning the institutions the Pope intended to grant his subjects, Antonelli informed Balbo that the Pope could make no pledge at the moment.

Count Balbo found Antonelli both courteous and affable, noting that the Cardinal listened eagerly to all he had to say, indeed, sought out his opinion. Nonetheless, he was little inclined to follow his suggestions and remained obstinate in his opposition to retention of the Statuto of 1848. Conscience, honor, the well-being of the Pope's subjects, were among the reasons Antonelli cited for abandoning constitutionalism. His litany of complaints against constitutionalism echoed the Pope's.

In a frank and forthright manner, Antonelli told Balbo that the Pope's subjects and indeed all Italians were not prepared or educated for the institutions granted in 1848. This was Pio Nono's conclusion. Above all, Antonelli observed, the conscience of the Pope would not permit him to establish anything that impeded his spiritual authority, and he regarded the temporal power as essential for the exercise of the spiritual dominion. Furthermore, he claimed that the Pope had regained his liberty of action as a result of his subjects' rebellion against his authority. This had freed Pius, Antonelli argued, from his obligation to retain the constitution. Balbo appreciated the importance of these words because he regarded Antonelli as the really important personage at Gaeta, the only figure who knew the mind and heart of the Pope. Without his approval, noted the Piedmontese envoy, nothing was approved.

Balbo observed that Antonelli and Pio Nono were in complete accord. Their arguments against constitutionalism and the reformism of 1848 included: the lack of parliamentary education of the populations, as shown by the deplorable facts, the desire of his loyal subjects that the Pope not return to the constitution, considered the cause of so many ills, and the incompatibility, or quasi-incompatibility, of the constitution with the free exercise of the Pope's spiritual power.[55]

These same reasons were given to the French, who also urged the Pope to preserve liberal institutions in Rome. Antonelli told D'Harcourt that the Holy Father was determined to take no step which would compromise his temporal power, essential for the preservation of his spiritual authority. Pius personally explained his position to Father Rosmini, who still sought to keep the States of the Church constitutional. After long prayer, the Pope explained to the theologian he had understood the incompatibility between the governance of the Church and constititionalism.[56] The Cardinal Secretary of State hastened to convert to the new orthodoxy.

Pius turned his back not only on parliamentary government, which he regarded as unsuitable for his subjects, but freedom of the press and liberty of association, which he considered subversive of religion and faith.[57] This condemnation of modern political institutions disturbed Rosmini, but not Antonelli. The Cardinal, whose position depended on the Pope's approval, had reason to bolster that absolutism which kept him in power. He pledged his diplomatic expertise to implement the conservative policy flowing from the Pope's religious convictions.[58]

At the beginning of July 1848, Antonelli received word that a French entry into Rome was imminent.[59] He continued to rail against the excesses in the Eternal City, waiting for the collapse of the "sacrilegious regime." On July 4, the French entered the capital and the Tricolor flew over the Castel Sant' Angelo. Neither he, nor Pius, were pleased by the conduct of the French, resenting the pressure placed upon the Pope to grant reforms, and the tolerance shown the republicans in Rome, where Mazzini remained until July 16. Only at the end of July did Pius formally thank the French President for re-establishing the authority of the Holy See in the Papal States.[60]

On July 17 Pius wrote his subjects from Gaeta that the Lord had raised his hand and stilled the anarchy, guaranteeing the liberty and independence of the Pontiff necessary for the tranquility of the Catholic world.[61] Nothing was said of the political rights or reforms for the Pope's subjects, while a commission of Cardinals composed of Gabriele Della Genga, Ludovico Altieri, and Luigi Vannicelli Casoni, all of a conservative bent, was entrusted with the Pope's temporal sovereignty in Rome, pending his return. Known as the "Red Triumvirate" in opposition to the Republican Triumvirate of Armellini, Mazzini, and Saffi, who had directed the Roman Republic, it was deemed hopelessly reactionary by liberals and nationalists. Papal officials in French-occupied Rome sought directions from the Secretary of State, and inquired who exercised control in the capital. To assert Papal sovereignty, Antonelli insisted that the commission of Cardinals immediately enter the Papal States.[62]

At the beginning of August, the triumvirate of Cardinals, the Commissione Governative di Stato, sought to obliterate the recent unpleasant memories in Rome, and in the remainder of the State. On August 3, the three Cardinals wrote Antonelli that they had assumed their position in the capital and found the citizens of Rome tranquil.[63] By their first decree, that of August 2, the commission, housed in the Quirinal Palace, annulled all that had been passed in the Papal States since November 16, 1848. At the same time a special committee of censure was created to determine the fate of public employees in Rome. Similar councils were created in every province of the state.[64] These actions provoked an outburst of indignation against the commission, to which the French had transferred a part of the power until then exercised by the military. The reactionary commission was a portent of things to come.

On August 11, 1849, during the course of the twelfth session of the conference of Catholic powers meeting at Gaeta, Antonelli explained that the Pope had invoked the help of France, Austria, Spain, and Naples to help him re-establish the independence needed in the exercise of his apostolic mandate, but would not permit these powers to impose the criteria his government should pursue. Still, the Pope was prepared to introduce a number of reforms in the administration of justice, and provide for elected municipal councils. Antonelli, however, knew that Pius opposed the laicization demanded by the French. For this, among other reasons, the Cardinal sought to move cautiously and diplomatically, to avoid provoking Napoleon unduly.

Chapter Seven

Architect of the
Conservative Restoration

Giacomo Antonelli, entrusted by the Pope with the task of re-structuring his government, found himself pressured by the forces of reform and reaction. While the former centered in France and Piedmont-Sardinia, which served as havens for Italian liberals and nationalists, the latter emanated from the conservative curia which surrounded the Pope in the illiberal Neapolitan ambience. The Cardinal sought a balance as he resisted extremist elements in the apostolic college, while integrating the Papal States into the European state system. He had to move cautiously, for the Pope feared the dangers of liberalism to the Church following the revolutionary experience of 1848.[1]

"You find me anticonstitutional," the Pope blurted out to Antonio Rosmini in June 1849.[2] The fact that Pius chose to have a picture painted of himself with the King of the Two Sicilies, Ferdinando II, labeled "Bomba" by his critics for his bombardment of Messina, seemed indicative of the path Pius had chosen.[3] Rather than returning home, early in September Antonelli and the Pope left with the Neapolitan Bourbons on the royal caravelle Cristina for Portici. For the moment the conservatives seemed to have triumphed, but Antonelli feared their victory almost as much as French and Piedmontese designs. Some conservatives had neither forgotten nor forgiven his liberal interlude, and resented his influence on the Pope.

In his conflict with liberals and conservatives Antonelli had one all-important asset, the confidence of the Pope, who had little respect for the cardinals left him by his predecessor. Thus it was Pius, rather than his Secretary of State, who distanced them. In contrast, Pius had great respect for the ability of Antonelli, and tended to pile all sorts of responsibilities upon his shoulders.

Thus, at Gaeta the Cardinal was in charge of the overall disburse-
ment of funds and the supervision of all expenses throughout the
Papal States.[4] It was he, rather than the Minister of Finance, who
negotiated with the Paris banks for the desperately needed state
loans.[5] Even the Pope's personal largesse and contributions to
charity were funneled through Antonelli, who always obtained receipts for funds distributed.[6] Drawing upon his financial expertise
and his experience at the Treasury, he kept concise records of the
monies spent by the distracted Pontiff for personal, spiritual, and
temporal matters.[7]

The Cardinal likewise oversaw the planning and execution of
all public works projects for which his approval was mandatory.[8]
The police in Rome were constrained to keep Antonelli abreast of
events in the capital, transmitting bi-weekly reports of political
bulletins to the Cardinal.[9] Antonelli also received reports on the
present and past conduct of all civil servants and ecclesiastics who
were under scrutiny.[10] Almost all matters, including the funding
of Christian education, fell within the Cardinal's purview at
Portici.[11] Small wonder that there were those who charged that
while abroad, Antonelli had absorbed most of the powers of the
Papacy.

The French and the Piedmontese did not decry the extent of
the Cardinal's influence, but the decidedly conservative course he
seemed to pursue.

The prospect of a conservative restoration in Rome disturbed
Louis Napoleon, who wished to be perceived as the champion of
Roman liberties rather than their executioner. He was denounced
by liberal republicans who deplored his spilling of French blood for
the Pope and absolutism. Napoleon sought to diffuse their criticism by pointing to the reforms granted by Pius, but found the
Cardinal determined to proceed along a cautious path. On August
11, 1849, with the support of the Austrian representative at the
twelfth session of the conference of powers, Antonelli revealed
what institutions the Pope planned to grant his subjects. Pius
would permit municipal councils, elected on the basis of tax payment, provincial councils, nominated by the sovereign, a Council of
State, with an essentially technical character, and a Consulta to
deal with the finances of state, without a deliberate vote. There
were no plans for further laicization of the administration.[12]

Napoleon, disturbed by the antics of the Commission of Cardinals, found Antonelli's program unacceptable. The irate French
President responded in August by writing to his friend Colonel Ed-

ouard Ney, who was in Rome, reminding the French commander that the French Republic did not dispatch an army to Rome to snuff-out Italian liberty, but to regulate it. The projected restoration of the Pope on the basis of tyranny and proscription dishonored the French intervention and undermined the stability of the Papal States, Napoleon complained. He proposed a general amnesty, secularization of the administration, the application of the Code Napoleon, and liberal institutions.[13]

Colonel Ney realized that Napoleon's message was not for him alone, and sought to have it published in the *Giornale di Roma,* the official government journal. General Louis de Rostolan wished to comply, but the Commission of Cardinals would not have it appear without the approval of the Secretary of State, and Antonelli refused the request. The Cardinal insisted that the letter was a private correspondence, lacking official character. By way of rejoinder to Napoleon, Antonelli informed the Commission that the Holy Father planned to grant his subjects reforms of a useful nature, discounting if not discrediting the President's letter. Nonetheless, the letter riled Pius and his entourage.[14] They had reason for concern, for while Antonelli could prevent its gracing the columns of the *Giornale di Roma,* he could not hinder publication in the September 6, 1849 *Moniteur* of Paris. Its appearance encouraged opponents of the Papal regime in Rome and outside.[15]

Antonelli, by the Pope's side at Portici, concentrated on Papal policy from morning to evening.[16] His social life, never rich, now atrophied to non-existence. He was particularly preoccupied with drafting Papal institutions and resisting French pressure for liberalization. Napoleon had suffered a setback in his attempt to influence Papal policy, but had not surrendered. Antonelli shared Lord Malmesbury's assessment that obstinancy remained the most remarkable feature of Louis Napoleon's character. "All projects once formed and matured in his head remain there perfectly uncommunicated in detail," wrote the Englishman, "but their practical attempts or fulfillment will be a mere question of time."[17] The Cardinal expected to hear more from Napoleon and did not have to wait long. The French minister dispatched a threatening letter, warning that reforms were essential. The French called for a general amnesty from which individuals, but not groups, might be excluded; the elimination of ecclesiastical tribunals for the lay population, and granting the Consulta a deliberative vote. If these concessions were not forthcoming, Paris would not relinquish the reins of government, preventing the Holy Father's return to Rome.[18]

The threat failed to intimidate Antonelli, who instructed the members of the Governing Commission in Rome that if anyone questioned their authority, they should alert him immediately.[19] To undermine the French contentions, he transmitted a note to the chief diplomatic legations, including two statistical tables which disproved the claims that ecclesiastics monopolized offices in the Papal States.[20] Although Antonelli had assumed the offensive, he found himself in a difficult predicament, caught between the desires of the French for reforms, and the determination of the Pope to resist such concessions. His power flowed from the Pontiff, but the pragmatic Cardinal understood the political importance of France. Above all, he recognized the need to preserve the goodwill of the French commander in Rome.[21] Then, too, economic realities had to be considered, since the Cardinal relied on Paris for the loans needed to reorganize his financially stricken state.[22]

Antonelli sought to accomodate the French without antagonizing the Pontiff. It was an effort which transcended the diplomatic finesse of the Cardinal, requiring the Pope's prayer. Acting on Pius's instructions, he elaborated governmental forms which did not compromise the temporal power. The Motu-Proprio of September 12, 1849, contained the Secretary of State's reorganization, which remained until the collapse of the Papal states in 1870. He hoped that its publication would resolve the issues raised by Napoleon, blocking further pressure from the Paris government.

Although the Motu-Proprio of September 1849 said little about specific political liberties, it did not represent a reversion to the conditions existing under Gregory XVI. It followed the Memorandum of the Powers of 1831, reflecting Pio Nono's original moderate reformism. Administrative and judicial reforms, a Council of State for administrative questions, a Consulta for financial matters, as well as a degree of administrative autonomy were provided.[23] Unable to grant a broad measure of political liberty, Antonelli understood the need for some measure of modernization as well as a touch of liberality, if not liberalism. Pius granted an amnesty to those who had taken part in the revolution, excluding former members of the Republican Government, its military chiefs, and those who had abused the amnesty of 1846.[24]

It represented the most that Pius would concede. The Cardinal, meanwhile, had learned that the Roman Question loomed large as an issue in France and influenced the conduct of its Catholic party. He surmised that Napoleon's prime concern was to remain in power, predicting he would not create difficulties that might alienate his Catholic supporters.[25] His analysis proved accurate; Napoleon wrote Pius that his letter to Colonel Ney sought only a more generous amnesty from the Pope, nothing else. The Secretary of State, delighted by the turn of events, wrote his Governing Commission in Rome that the President who had sought to pressure the Pope to grant the Consulta a deliberate vote had changed his tune. Napoleon, Antonelli continued, had solemnly proclaimed in the Chamber that he would never force the Holy Father to make such a concession. He was now less alarmed about the prospect of French interference in the internal affairs of the Papal government.[26]

The French hoped that the Pope would return to his capital, but Pius and his Minister hesitated. Antonelli feared the "sacriligious excesses" of the democratic party, determined to protect the "precious days of the Pontiff."[27] The attempt made upon the life of the priest Don Benedetto Devico, secretary of the Cardinal, on the Via del Corso in Rome, the evening of September 14, did not reassure the Cardinal. For the moment Antonelli and Pio Nono, always together, traveled as far as Benevento.[28] Pio Nono doubted that the moment was propitious for his return home, and Antonelli concurred. Another six months elapsed before the two felt sufficiently confident about returning to Rome.

The Pope's failure to return home, his retreat from constitutionalism, and the curia's intransigence on the Church-State issue in Piedmont, alarmed the Turin government. Count Camillo di Cavour, who emerged as Piedmont's leader, early favored a separation of Church and State. The Count explained his preference for the ecclesiastical freedom which prevailed in the United States, convinced that it would eventually take root in Italy. Such talk, and the subsequent ecclesiastical policy of the Piedmontese government, aroused the Pope, precipitating the protests of his Secretary of State.

In 1850, following Turin's unilateral emancipation of non-Catholics, relations between Piedmont and the Papacy remained strained. Pius resented the legislation which restricted ecclesiastical control over education, placing supervision of the curriculum in the hands of the state. His resentment was aggravated by the fact that the Archbishop of Turin, Luigi Fransoni, and the Bishop of Asti, Filippo Artico, had been compelled by popular pressure to leave their dioceses.

The Pope and Antonelli were little inclined to make concessons to Count Giuseppe Siccardi of Piedmont, who arrived in Portici in October 1849, seeking approval for projected changes in the country's ecclesiastical laws. Siccardi sought papal sanction for the suppression of religious orders, the introduction of civil matrimony, and the termination of the clergy's ecclesiastical jurisdiction, a program not palatable to Pius. Antonelli responded that the Pope could not remain indifferent to the harm done to the Church by a Catholic power, and threatened to issue a formal protest.[29] Irritated by the anti-Piedmontese sentiment in the curia, and convinced that no agreement could be reached at Portici, Siccardi returned home. Pius's religious principals prevented Antonelli from making any accomodation.

The Piedmontese government again decided to act unilaterally, presenting the Siccardi legislation before Parliament in early March 1850. The first five articles abrogated various forms of ecclesiastical jurisdiction. The sixth eliminated the Church's ancient right of asylum; the seventh limited the application of punishment for non-observance of religious solemnity to Sundays and six major holidays. Proposal eight provided for the suppression of mortmain, stipulating that ecclesiastical corporations could only acquire real property with the state's consent. The last provision sought to regulate marriage in relation to civil law.[30] On March 9, the Subalpine Parliament passed most of the package, antagonizing the Pope.

Pius had Antonelli protest to the Sardinian Minister, the Marquis Spinola, that the government of the Holy See, deferential towards the King of Piedmont, did not deserve such treatment. Antonelli claimed Rome had been prepared to negotiate, but the Sardinian envoy had been hastily recalled to Turin.[31] The Cardinal reiterated Pius's dictum that Piedmont's actions violated the concordat, arguing it was unacceptable for a Catholic State to introduce changes which might prove detrimental to the Church, without the consent of the Holy See. Although Cavour hoped for a truce with Rome, the tension between Piedmont and the Papacy mounted. Religious dissension aggravated the political division between the two.

The return of the Archbishop Fransoni in mid-March did not help matters, for he directed a circular to his clergy ordering them to procure permission from their superiors before appearing in state courts. He was supported by the Pope, who through Antonelli, claimed that the Archbishop had only asserted his rights. The State authorities disagreed, claiming that the Archbishop questioned the legality of the recent legislation, and had him imprisoned. Antonelli protested the arrest, calling for Fransoni's release. Not receiving satisfaction, the Cardinal issued a stronger protest, deploring Piedmontese actions.[32]

The Cardinal also denounced the government's seizure of a convent in Genoa, discounting the pretext that it was to be converted into a new, national college.[33] Antonelli insisted that the Holy See desired an accomodation with the Turin government, but could not achieve one when that government persisted in unilaterally abrogating the sacred rights of the Church.[34] So long as Piedmont provoked the religious scruples of Pius, Antonelli could not achieve a rapprochement.

In 1850, when Pietro di Santarosa, Minister of Agriculture, and a staunch supporter of the Siccardi Legislation, fell ill, Fransoni created further problems for Antonelli, aggravating Church-State relations in Piedmont. The inexorable Archbishop ordered his clergy to refuse the last rites to Santarosa, unless the Minister made a full and formal retraction of his part in the passage of the Siccardi Laws. Shocked by the intransigent attitude of Fransoni, and the obedience of the Servite priests who refused to administer the sacrament, the Piedmontese re-arrested Fransoni and expelled the Servites from the state. Pius had Antonelli protest once more.[35]

While the Pope had his Secretary of State hurl denunciations against the Piedmontese, he had only kind words for the Neapolitans, who had been generous hosts for over a year. Secure in the southern Kingdom, Pius insisted that he would not return home until tranquility prevailed. Some suspected that Antonelli needlessly prolonged the stay abroad to free Pius from possible liberal currents. The facts indicate otherwise. At the end of October, Giacomo wrote Filippo that he hoped the Pope would soon leave for Rome. In December he made arrangements for the Pope to spend an evening in Terracina on his way home. Only when Pius assured himself that all was well in Rome on March 9, did he call the Cardinals to Portici for a secret consistory, revealing his determination to return to his state in April.

On March 12, Antonelli informed France, Spain, Naples, and Austria of the Pope's decision. The news welcomed in the capital, which also cheered to hear that the Secretary of State had concluded a new loan that would enable the government to withdraw the paper money that had proved so detrimental to the country's commerce. The Cardinal, instrumental in securing the loan, supervised every aspect of the Pope's return home. Before the departure two ceremonies were held, one at Portici, to which the important personages of the Neapolitan Kingdom were invited, and the second at Caserta, restricted to the royal family. On the eve of the first celebration, according to an account by the Cardinal's nephew, Agostino, the Secretary of State was surprised by the Pope who visited him in his apartments. Pius confessed that while he owed much to the King of Naples, he owed more to Antonelli, who he would repay by keeping him minister for life.[36]

On April 4, Pius and Antonelli left Portici, spending the evening at the royal palace of Caserta. "I bless you, I bless your family, I bless your people," an emotional Pius exclaimed to Ferdinando at the frontier on April 6, as he crossed the border back into his own state.[37] Pius's appreciation of absolutist Naples contrasted with his resentment of constitutional Piedmont. Antonelli reflected this sentiment. Moving northward, the Pope and his Secretary of State stopped at Terracina, the latter's home, on April 9.[38] On April 11, Pius was in Velletri where he received a warm reception. By April 12, they were back in Rome.

Following their return, the triumvirate of Cardinals who had exercised authority was eliminated, and power was concentrated in the hands of Antonelli, the first and most powerful minister of state. The Cardinal would retain this preeminent position until his death in 1876. On May 3, Filippo Antonelli was elected governor of the Banca Romana with an influence transcending the banking sector. Gregorio, in Terracina, served as mayor from 1850 to 1857. Luigi Antonelli was nominated one of the eight conservators of Rome, and assigned the Annona for provisioning Rome, while Angelo Antonelli served as Giacomo's, Filippo's, and Gregorio's secretary abroad. The Cardinal made Monsignor Giuseppe Berardi, his closest friend, undersecretary of State.[39]

The Pope's return was greeted with brilliant and "spontaneous" illuminations throughout the capital.[40] April 12 would be celebrated annually in the Papal States. Antonelli claimed that these demonstrations disproved the lies about the Pope's unpopularity.[41] Shortly thereafter the Spaniards and Neapolitans withdrew, the French reduced their forces to one division in the vicinty of the capital, and the Austrians maintained one division in the Legations.

Antonelli remained as the Pope's political councilor and voice. In this dual capacity he proved intelligent and energetic, in overall control of the government and supervising the Pope's relations with other governments. "The government is, as formerly, purely clerical," Gladstone was informed, "for the Cardinal Secretary of State is the only real minister."[42] In light of Pio Nono's bitter experience with constitutional government, and his unwillingness to separate the temporal from his spiritual power, he shunned liberalization. The Pope rejected all reforms that seemed to undermine the Papal government. Antonelli was assigned the task of implementing this conservative course. Without hesitation, Antonelli sacrificed consistency for obedience.

The Pope increasingly turned his attention to religious matters and to his role as spiritual leader of the universal Church. In the capital, Pius chose to live in the Vatican, rather than the Quirinale, where he had spent the first two and half years of his reign, and where he had served more as a monarch than Pope. He went out among the people practically every day, visiting churches, hospitals, schools, workshops, prisons and convents. He left much of the day-to-day business and the execution of policies his principles inspired in the hands of his Secretary of State. The Cardinal proved skillful in both internal and foreign matters, despite the hostility he confronted from a number of Cardinals.[43] In the words of De Cesare:

> The cares of State were borne by Antonelli, the real arbiter, who managed everything without seeming to do so or raising any suspicions in the minds of the Pope. Knowing Pius IX's character intimately and able to measure his weaknesses and resisting power, he never came into collision with either, nor provoked his anger, no easy matter with such an impulsive nature as that of the Pope. This was indeed the Cardinal's great merit, that, in the midst of such surroundings, he presented the only stable point of that long and dramatic Pontificate, and that he calmly surveyed the fall of the temporal power, whose existence he knew not how to prolong. A man of moderate powers, devoid of passions or ideals, without even a semblance of culture, he nevertheless did not lack foresight.[44]

In 1851, when the acting Minister of Arms, Colonel Filippo Farini, died, Antonelli assumed his office. He was also nominated President of the Commission for Financial Reforms.

Antonelli, who rejected abstract theories and principles, did seek to modernize and render more efficient the state's mechanism, while shunning the constitution the Pope deemed unacceptable. The provincial administration was reorganized with the institution of lay councils and other functionaries that would work

with the Apostolic Delegates and Papal Legates. Under his leadership, control of the communes was entrusted to elected municipal
councils, the tariff was reformed, railroads were developed, and
agriculture stimulated. The Cardinal sought to preserve traditional practices by a system of rational reorganization. By an edict
of 1851, postage stamps were introduced into the Papal States and
Italy.[45]

Antonelli probably would have gone further had he not been
prevented by the Pope. "We moderate liberals cannot be con-
tented," he explained to Pasolini who had been his colleague in
1848, "but it is a question of opportunity."[46] The Cardinal joked
about the hesitations of his sovereign and his fear of innovation.
On one occasion when asked to implement a provision, Antonelli
responded that it would be done if the Pope "does not consult the
Holy Spirit."[47] His efforts to secure loans from the Paris Rothschild's were made difficult by the Pope's refusal to comply with
James Rothschild's request for an improvement of the position of
the Jews in the Papal States. Pius refused, exclaiming that he preferred martyrdom to submitting to such demands.[48] Nonetheless,
the Cardinal managed to set straight the financial chaos he inher-
ited from the revolutionary period, so that by the end of the 1850's
the state's finances were in order.

Antonelli was too perceptive and objective to delude himself
that the restored regime could rely solely on the loyalty of its subjects to preserve itself. The people of the provinces were not satisfied with the innovations in the administration or with their level
of participation in government, having already fallen under the
sway of the constitutional and national program.[49] In his inner
heart he seemed to recognize that the days of the Papal States
were numbered. This was confirmed by his reliance on foreign
forces to preserve the restored regime.

Only the most astute diplomacy could help preserve the temporal power, and Antonelli showed great affability in his relations
with the diplomatic corps. Despite shortcomings in his education,
Antonelli possessed considerable diplomatic skills. "Cardinal Antonelli has received the education of a Roman prelate. He has
never left Italy and is very lightly acquainted with the affairs of
other countries," Russell, the English representative in Rome,
wrote home. "But great natural parts, laborious habits, a logical
mind, insinuating manners, animated conversation and the experience of the drawing rooms amply supply the shortcomings of his
education."[50] Convinced that the Catholic powers could not aban-

don the Pope to his weakness, nor impose their will upon him, he accepted their support without following their suggestions. The Cardinal Secretary of State served as host for the first official dinner following the Pope's return to Rome, in honor of the consecration of Cardinal Vannicelli as Archbishop of Ferrara, and a number of other bishops. This and other official festivities dominated the Cardinal's social life which he subordinated to political and public needs. In an effort to improve the strained relations with the French, Antonelli invited the new Minister of the French Republic, Count de Rayneval, and the Commander in Chief of the expeditionary force, General Gemeau. The French still urged Rome to grant reforms, and even the Austrians indicated that some changes were in order. The Cardinal Secretary of State thus found himself caught between the repeated call of the powers for change, and the intransigence of the Pope against both liberalism and constitutionalism. His task was not an easy one.

The State Antonelli sought to defend was one of the oldest in Europe with a territory of some 41,400 square kilometers, divided into twenty districts following the second restoration, and a population of some three million.[51] It shared in the world-wide prosperity after 1850, but its government faced serious difficulties. The restricted amnesty had to be implemented in such a manner as to satisfy Pius without antagonizing the French. Indeed, all its governmental forms had to please the Pope without unduly upsetting Paris.[52] Antonelli's edict of September 10, 1850 put into effect the Motu Proprio issued earlier at Portici and instituted a Council of Ministers and a Council of State. Both were presided over by Antonelli, but powerless without the Pope's accord.[53] Likewise the Consulta di Stato, inaugurated at the end of October 1850, was headed by a Cardinal, but ultimately responsible to the Pope.[54] Despite Antonelli's efforts to create an enlightened administration, the regime was not constitutional, and out of harmony with the demands of the times.[55]

The Cardinal's edict of January 25, 1851 reconstituted the municipal body or senate of Rome, composed of forty-eight councilors.[56] It was not until March 12, however, that its members were selected, and this delay, like so much else, was placed at the doorstep of the Secretary of State, who was believed to control everything. Supposedly Antonelli, desirous of obtaining Roman citizenship and nobility for himself and his brothers, determined that this would more readily be granted by the provisional commission rather than by the Senate. Others criticized the Secretary of State for failing to place more power in the hands of the body, bemoaning that it was more or less limited to enacting provisions for the hygenic and elementary necessities of the city's life.[57]

The conservative, pro-Austrian position of the Papal States had wounded liberal and nationalist pride in the peninsula. Both inside the state and abroad, Antonelli the architect of the political structure, was held responsible. Patriots decried the fact that his government had signed a railroad convention with Modena, Parma, Tuscany, and Austria in 1851—all under Habsburg influence—as well as a concordat with Spain. Likewise the censorship and penalties for the publication of anti-governmental literature was traced to the Cardinal.[58] Few acknowledged that the inspiration for the censorship flowed from the religious scruples and political fears of the Pontiff. For example, Pius was intransigent on the matter of keeping books on the index, and forbidden to be read by Roman Catholics, his Minister only reflected his position.

The pragmatic Antonelli, conscious of French ascendancy in Europe, sought to preserve the friendship of her president, who became supreme head of state following the coup d'état of December 1851. "My foes had asserted that the whole population of France would rise up as one man to defend the constitution," noted Napoleon. "But when the time came to rise, the patriots numbered a baker's dozen."[59] Antonelli appreciated the significance of the event, understanding that henceforth Napoleon would have even greater influence. Pius, on the other hand, continued to emphasize the priority of principle over politics.

It was largely due to the Pope's principles rather than Antonelli's politics that negotiatons between Count Manfredo di Sambuy, the Piedmontese representative, and Vincenzo Santucci, Pius's plenipotentiary, came to naught. The Pope was incensed when he heard that negotiations would not affect things already accomplished, only future developments. An angry Pope let it be known that he was not prepared to sanction the unilateral reordering of ecclesiastical affairs in Piedmont.[60] He was further incensed by the attempt to introduce civil matrimony, complaining that the project was neither constitutional nor Catholic. At the same time he urged the King to curb the excesses of the press in his country, which he considered a scandal.[61] The Pope's political intransigence rested upon religious convictions, which he found impossible to compromise.

Pius looked to Antonelli to implement the conservative decisions he made. On March 18, 1852, he appointed the Cardinal his permanent Secretary of State, indicating that Antonelli had exercised the affairs entrusted to him to his full satisfaction. He had neither contradicted nor challenged Papal directives as had his constitutional ministers. Praising his "zeal, sagacity, and wisdom," Pius was convinced that the "Holy See would receive new proofs of his affection and faith in the defense of its prerogatives, and the sustaining of its rights."[62] Delighted by this vote of confidence, Antonelli despatched a circular note to the powers announcing his permanent appointment.[63] At the end of that same 1852, Cavour assumed the Presidency of the Council of Ministers in Piedmont, rendering the Cardinal's work as Secretary of State all the more difficult.

Turin created political and religious difficulties for Rome, and Antonelli had to confront them both. The Secretary knew that emigrants from all over Italy continued to pour into Piedmont, which preserved its constitution and protected the liberal party.[64] The Cardinal also realized that Turin was emboldened by the tacit support of the French President, who talked about the desirability of reorganizing the peninsula, with a consequent decrease in the size of the Papal State. Antonelli sought to determine if Napoleon was prepared to act upon this program. The Nuncio in Paris reported that the Italian situation might change with conditions in the rest of Europe, but there was nothing to fear so long as the European situation remained stable. Nonetheless, he advised improving the administration of the Papal States as a useful precaution.[65] Louis Napoleon's proclamation as Emperor Napoleon III at the end of 1852 aroused concern in the Vatican, which sought to assess its implications for Italy.[66] "Some people say, the Empire means war," Napoleon reported at a banquet at Bordeaux. "I say, the Empire means peace. It means peace because France desires it, and when France is satisfied, the world is peaceful."[67] Antonelli was not so certain.

Caught between the French demand for change, and the Pope's determination not to tolerate innovations which violated his conscience and endangered public tranquility, Antonelli looked to the Hapsburg Empire for support. Austria was relied upon to defend healthy political principles in Europe. News from Vienna was gratifying to the Cardinal. In May 1852, he was assured that Austria would preserve the best of relations with the Holy See. In June, word reached him that Austria would allow the Jesuits to return. Confronted with a new French regime, and the threat this might pose for the peace of Europe, the Nuncio in Vienna and Antonelli sought the cooperation of the conservative states: Austria, Prussia and Russia.[68]

While Antonelli used diplomacy to safeguard the state from external danger, other means had to be employed for internal security. A number of individuals were hired by the government as informants on the various revolutionary and liberal sects within the Papal States.[69] The revolutionaries were divided into fusionists and republicans in the early 1850's.[70] Perhaps because the dissatisfied emigrated or were forced into exile, the statistics for the 1850's indicate a steady decrease in crime in the state governed by Antonelli.[71] Rome in 1853, according to the last census before its incorporation into the Kingdom of Italy, had a population of 176,002 inhabitants, half of whom lived on some form of public charity.

To improve the country's economic life and commerce, a maritime agreement was signed with England, while a telegraph convention was signed with the Kingdom of the Two Sicilies. To reduce discontent in the provinces of Bologna, Ravenna, and Forli, the price of salt was reduced and the export of common wines and grains was forbidden. A new gold coin was minted in Rome and Bologna, having the value of a scudo, which helped to restore confidence in the currency.[72] Antonelli instituted a series of modifications of the tariffs and tolls of the state, in order to further the development of commerce and protect home industries. Meanwhile, Rome was swarmed by a host of visitors from abroad, from which its residents benefited. In 1853 Verdi's "Il Trovatore" was performed there for the first time; early the next year, the main street in the capital, the Corso, was illuminated by gas to the delight of the Romans who broke out in spontaneous applause.

The Pope turned his attention to religious issues and from the first had a precise program for the Church. He sought to increase the concordats with Catholic countries, and had Antonelli negotiate some eleven of them between 1851 and 1859. In 1854 Pius summoned the bishops to Rome to discuss paragraph by paragraph, the solemn dogmatic bull defining the Immaculate Conception. Asssisted by the Jesuit fathers Giovanni Perrone and Carlo Passaglia, the bull Ineffabilis Deus defined Mary's special position, and was promulgated on December 8, 1854 in St. Peter's. That evening the capital was illuminated, and the cupola of St. Peter's basillica was lit by thousands of lights. In many ways this was the light, and the quiet, before the storm.

Chapter Eight

The Quiet Before the Storm

Although tranquility had been restored in Rome, and the provinces remained restive, Antonelli feared that a spark from abroad might have incendiary consequences. He had cause for concern. At the beginning of 1853 the indefatigable Mazzini, who had played a key role in the Roman Republic, called for the national party to transform itself into a party of action. In February his attempts to direct a revolutionary outburst in Austrian controlled Milan troubled the Vatican as well as Austria. A week later Rome received word of the attempted assassination of Emperor Franz Josef, causing further consternation in the Holy City.[1] At the same time, the political and religious policies of Piedmont angered the Pope, who protested against the Protestant influence there, arguing that schools, bookshops, and churches of the reformed faith should not be tolerated in an eminently Catholic country.[2] Furthermore, relations with France were not good, as Pius refused the request of Eugenie, Napoleon's intended, to venture to Paris to perform the marriage, citing his advanced age and infirmities.[3]

Events in Europe conspired to undermine the diplomatic structure and balance of power that had preserved the status quo in Italy in general, and the position of the Papal States in particular. The Russian pressure on Constantinople, English determination to preserve the integrity of the Ottoman Empire, and the bad blood between the Russian Tsar and the French ruler did not bode well for the peace of Europe. The Vatican knew that the French were upset since the Tsar had refused to refer to Louis Napoleon as his brother in their correspondence, but did not expect the discourtesy to lead to war.[4] Other issues were more explosive, notably Russian ambitions vis-a-vis Turkey, and the Anglo-French pledge to prevent their realization. Austria, likewise, seemed determined to prevent Russian expansion into the Balkans and the dissolution of the Ottoman Empire.[5] Antonelli recognized that a conflict between France, England and Austria on the one hand, and Russia on the other, was a matter which affected the interests of all the powers, including the Papal States.[6]

The Cardinal's concerns were mirrored in his correspondence with Michele Viale Prela, the Nuncio in Vienna. The two concurred that the peninsula was threatened by revolutionry upheaval, reinforced by supplies from Piedmont, and they shared the belief that an Austrian involvement in war elsewhere would lead to a relaxation of her vigilance in Italy.[7] Viale Prela warned that, should Austria become embroiled in the conflict in the near east, they could expect new, revolutionary attempts in the Italian peninsula.[7] Antonelli also feared Piedmont's actions as news spread that Marco Minghetti had visited Palmerston to win English support for Sardinia, while discrediting the temporal power.[8] Once England and France had declared war against Russia in 1854, these powers sought to draw the Piedmontese into the conflict, to the dismay of Rome and Vienna.

Early in 1855 the alliance for war with England and France against Russia was concluded by Piedmont, which dispatched 10,000 troops to the Crimea.[9] Cavour, no less than Antonelli, foresaw the importance of Piedmontese participation in the Crimean War. "If Piedmont performs well, as I believe it will," he noted, "it will see its authority and credit grow and its allies will be obliged to support and second its aims. If instead—and this I do not believe—Piedmont should not do its share, all the conditions, all the promises, will remain a dead letter."[10] The Holy See recognized the significance of this "unholy" alliance and watched developments closely.[11]

The events of 1855, as well as the Vatican's religious mission, brought the Vatican into a closer relationship with Vienna. Pius was grateful that Napoleon kept a force of some 3,500 men divided between Rome and Civitavecchia, for the protection of his State, and also appreciated the protection accorded the Catholic faith in France.[12] Nonetheless, he remained suspicious of the Emperor and questioned his friendship with the Piedmontese. He had few doubts about Franz Josef, and during the course of the year was confirmed in his pro-Austrian convictions.

In August 1855 a concordat was concluded by the representatives of the Holy See and the Empire which guaranteed the Church the rights and privileges of divine and canon law. This was but one of the eleven concordats that Antonelli negotiated between

1851 and 1859.[13] In the Austrian agreement, both public and private education was placed under the scrutiny of the Church, which guaranteed that it remained in accordance with Catholic doctrine. The agreement also assured the bishops freedom of communication with Rome, and complete liberty in Church administration. Cavour condemned the concordat, claiming it relegated Church-State relations to the medieval age. Nonetheless, to soothe the Pope and his resourceful Secretary of State, the Piedmontese Minister sent his parish priest, Father Giacomo da Poirino, to explain Piedmontese ecclesiastical policies.[14] It was a public relations gimmick rather than a serious attempt at reconciliation. Neither Pius nor Antonelli accepted the Piedmontese rationalizations and explanations.[15]

During the course of 1855 the Pope and Antonelli faced problems flowing from the European war, Piedmontese provocations, such as the Law of Convents, and personal danger and crises. On April 12, 1855, the two men traveled to the excavations of the tomb of Sant'Alessandro and stopped at the convent of Sant' Agnese. While there, Pius, with the Cardinal at his side, agreed to receive the students of the College of the Propoganda in one of the reception rooms. When the anxious students, who numbered well over a hundred, rushed in to pay their respect, the floor caved in, hurling Pius and Antonelli, and some hundred and thirty others, to the story below with a deafening crash. The entire party, including the Pope and Antonelli, escaped injury. Some considered this no less than a miracle, while others insisted that it was symbolic of the impending fall of the papacy.[16] Antonelli took the accident in stride.

On the evening of April 28, 1858, the Italian Giovanni Pianori, a shopkeeper by trade, shot point-blank at Napoleon III, as he rode along the Champs Elysees. This would-be-assassin, presumably sent by Mazzini from London, failed to hit the Emperor. Pianori was captured, condemned to death, and executed, and his family sought to strike back. It was only Cardinal Antonelli's information that Pianori's brother was on his way to Paris on a mission of revenge that enabled the French police to arrest him at the railway station. [17] Napoleon had reason to be grateful to the Cardinal.

Within a matter of months Antonelli again was to escape the jaws of death. At dusk, the evening of June 12, 1855, the Cardinal was descending the great staircase of the Vatican Palace for a visit to St. Paul's basilica. He was accompanied by the Cavaliere Minardi and two of his domestics, and he spotted a strange looking fellow on the landing below, obviously hiding something under his shirt. Although the man pretended to be a petitioner, Antonelli, always alert, grew suspicious as he sensed the stranger's nervousness and agitation. His fears proved warranted when the assailant produced a fork-like weapon. The Cardinal fled back up the steps, eluding the missile thrown at him. In response to his cries for help, Antonelli's servants seized the would-be assassin, who was later identified as Antonio De Felice, a thirty-five year old Roman hatmaker, who lived in the Via del Gesu. His peculiar weapon, lack of resistance during the arrest, strange appearance, and confused gaze, plus the fact that he had no relationship or special resentment for Antonelli, all suggest that he was mentally unstable. For this and other reasons, Antonelli urged that De Felice's life be spared, but Pius refused his request. Condemned to death, arrangements were made for his execution. Moved by the plight of his widow, Antonelli quietly arranged to provide a pension for her.[18]

Antonelli, some said, was haunted by the attempt on his life and always had before him the spectacle of the assassination of Pellegrino Rossi. The Cardinal, in fact, was no more affected by the assassination attempt than his earlier precipitous fall, failing to mention it in his subsequent correspondence and discussing it only with his brothers.[19] Those diplomatic representatives who visited the Cardinal the day after the abortive assassination were impressed by his calm and nonchalance, and lack of rancor. One of them noted that "his expression was not at all changed and he spoke of the events with a moderation that testified to his character."[20] Others seemed far more disturbed than he, conveying their sentiments to his brother Filippo. "I can imagine your anxiety and I share it. Because of his labors and zeal for the good of the Church and Europe he has earned the reputation of being a formidable enemy of the revolutionary sects," noted one of Filippo's correspondents. "This is an honor he shares with the sovereigns and this thought leads to the hope that Providence will not permit any difficulty to overtake him."[21] There would be no further danger, however, from De Felice, who was decapitated on the Piazza della Bocca della Verità, the morning of July 14, 1855. Paradoxically, Antonelli, who had pleaded for clemency, was branded vindictive.

The execution of De Felice was soon overshadowed by the preliminaries for peace in the Near East, and the talk of an impending congress. While the Catholic party in France approved of the Crimean War, in which it perceived Napoleon as defender of the faith,[22] Antonelli, from his perspective, had reservations. The Cardinal knew that Cavour, who accompanied Victor Emmanuel on his trip to London and Paris at the end of 1855, sought not only to consolidate the Crimean coalition, but to discredit the Papal regime. Word reached Rome that in Paris the Emperor had asked him what he could do for Italy, and in London, the Count had been hailed as the hero of a new reformation. Quite naturally Antonelli had severe misgivings about the Franco-Piedmontese cooperation in the Crimean War and awaited its end. When Pio Nono heard that peace had been attained, he had 101 cannon shots fired from the Castel Sant' Angelo. Rome's euphoria following the proclamation of peace proved to be short-lived.

The Pope and Antonelli were concerned that Piedmont, which had boldly assumed the leadership of the national movement in the peninsula, would be the only Italian state represented at the Congress of Paris. It was no secret that its government spread agitation throughout the peninsula, seeking to impose reforms on all the Italian states, and demanding a secularization of the Papal States.[23] Rome's suspicions were not without foundation, as Italians throughout the peninsula grouped together in Piedmont and formed the organization later called the National Society. Favoring unification, the Society looked to Piedmont and Cavour for leadership. Further alarming the Vatican was the news that Massimo D'Azeglio, who was to represent Piedmont at the Congress, had withdrawn at the eleventh hour, replaced by the wily Cavour.

Word soon filtered from Paris that Cavour had sent his "cousin", the Contessa di Castiglione, described by the French Foreign Minister as "the lovliest woman in Europe" to seduce Napoleon, and incite him to wage war against Austria. "A lovely countess," Cavour wrote Luigi Cibrario, charge d'affaires at the Foreign Office, "is now enrolled in the Diplomatic corps of Piedmont. I have asked her to flirt with—and if necessary, to seduce— the Emperor. I have promised, if she succeeds, to give her brother a secretaryship at St. Petersburg. She made her debut yesterday at the concert at the Tuileries."[24] Almost immediately Cavour's ward, who became the sensation of the social season, became the Emperor's mistress and used her influence to win the French ruler to the Italian cause. The Countess was not the only means Cavour utilized to persuade Napoleon to champion the Italian cause.[25]

The episode reveals the level to which the Piedmontese Prime Minister was willing to resort to achieve his ends.

Antonelli, entrusted with the task of counterbalancing Cavour's influence at the French court and the impending Congress, relied on reverence for the Pope to block the Piedmontese campaign. Pius with the encouragement of his Secretary of State, wrote a personal letter to the Catholic Emperor of Austria, Franz Josef, imploring him to protect the interests of the Church. The Austria Emperor promised to do all within his means.[26] Concomitantly, Pius wrote to Napoleon III, seeking his protection as well for the Church.[27] The Pope feared for his temporal as well as his spiritual power, and this was clearly expressed in his letter to the French Emperor. Charging that the temporal power of the Holy See was under assault from the incredulous and revolutionaries of the entire world, and especially from those who dreamed of Italian unification, Pius sought assurances that in the future Congress nothing be discussed pertaining to Papal affairs.[28] Cavour had other plans.

Although the Congress, which opened officially on February 25, 1856, was to settle the Eastern Question, Cavour sought to bring forward the Italian problem. Antonelli pressed to prevent it from being raised, but found himself at odds not only with the Piedmontese, but the English and French as well. On March 30, 1856, the Treaty ending the Crimean War was signed. Eight days later Count Alexander Walewski, at Napoleon's behest, brought up the Italian situation within the context of other matters that troubled the peace of the continent. This provided Lord Clarendon, the English representative, the opportunity to criticize both the Papal and Neapolitan governments, and led him to call for reforms. It bolstered Cavour's long-held conviction that a firmly knit Kingdom of Italy worked to England's advantage, and that she would therefore contribute to break the Austrian yoke on the peninsula. Convinced he enjoyed the sympathy of England as well as France, the Count criticized the Austrian presence in the Papal States. The Austrian Count Buol, acting in accordance with the wishes of the Emperor, who sought to honor his promise to Pius, announced that the subject of Italy transcended the competence of the Congress and that he would not discuss it. Buol regreted that the matter had been raised by others.

Antonelli understood that the Congress of Paris had been detrimental for Rome. In the French capital, Cavour had cemented his relations with Italian refugees living there, promising them unity, and winning over even his former adversary, Daniele Manin.[29] True enough, the wily Minister had obtained no new concessions for his country, but the fact that he had championed the cause of Italy in a public forum, increased its prestige, while the Holy See faced increased isolation and an uncertain future. The Cardinal sought to mend his state's diplomatic fences and with this thought in mind persuaded Pius to renounce his feudal suzerainty over the Kingdom of Naples. The Pope did so reluctantly, receiving 40,000 scudi as compensation, which was utilized for the construction of a column in honor of the Immaculate Conception in the Piazza di Spagna in Rome.[30]

Aware that Napoleon was more superstitious than religious, Antonelli played upon both sentiments when he had the Pope write him in February, 1856. "I believe that He wills that new bounties shall descend upon you, Sire, in the measure in which you fulfill your agreement to support and protect the Church in whose bosom you were born," wrote Pio Nono. "As for me, I have no other aim in my words and prayers than to bring about the glory of God, the salvation of souls, the propogation of the Faith, and the honoring of Catholic princes."[31]

On Palm Sunday, March 16, 1856, following the celebration of Mass, Pius heard of the birth of the Prince Imperial. In comemoration, he had the cannon of the Castel Sant' Angelo sound a one hundred and one gun salute. He pleased the Empress, whom he knew to favor the Papal cause, by sending her the Golden Rose which he had blessed during the Lenten festivities. To strengthen further the political and religious ties between Paris and Rome, Pius agreed to serve as the godfather of the child of Napoleon and Eugenie. Thus, on June 14, the Cardinal Vicar of Rome, Costantino Patrizi, served as his proxy during the course of the baptism ceremony in Paris. The Pope sent his godchild a golden rose tree resting on a lapis lazuli pedestal, as well as a reliquary, containing a piece of the holy manger.[32] This was perhaps the highpoint of the cordiality between Napoleon III and the Church.

Antonelli sought to capitalize upon this goodwill by introducing reforms with the parameters established by his sovereign. The provincial administration was improved, and financial disaster averted. Improvements were made in the railway system to dispell the contention that the Papal States were backward.[33] Finally, the Secretary of State sought to publicize the contents of the positive report of the French envoy, Count Alphonse de Rayneval, to his government in 1856. This report on the condition and society of the Papal States, and the character of its administration, was extremely favorable, in marked contrast to the denunciations of Clarendon at the Congress.

Cavour was shocked and scandalized by the Rayneval report, which described the Papal administration as one of the most benevolent and equitable in the whole of Europe; he suspected that Cardinal Antonelli had played a part in its composition. The Piedmontese Minister complained that Antonelli had persuaded the naive and gullible Rayneval, the French ambassador to Rome, that the Roman administration had but one fault—it was too secularized. Combining a vivid imagination with political deviousness, Cavour charged that the Secretary of State blocked real reform, because he sought to provoke disorders in the peninsula that would justify foreign intervention.[34] The plethora of accusations hurled by the Piedmontese Machiavelli against Antonelli often reflected the intrigues and schemes of the former, more than the policies of the latter. Nonetheless, the political attacks flowing from the fertile imagination of the political genius who governed in Turin were accepted by Piedmont's supporters and patriots in the peninsula, if not the diplomatic community at large.

Cavour had made it clear that odious methods might be necessary in politics, where one should not expect philanthropy or gratitude. Time and time again, he would take great pleasure in deceiving others, while being self-righteously indignant about the unprincipled conduct of those who opposed him. His reputation as a cunning though successful intriger led Petruccelli della Gattina to describe him as "a cross between Sir Robert Peel and Machiavelli."[35] In this instance his accusations had the desired effect, for Napoleon decided to bury the Rayneval report, thus preventing the Papal government from benefiting from its findings.

Antonelli sought other means of combatting the negative image burdening his state. Above all, he wished to disprove the accusation that the government was hated and kept in place only by the presence of French bayonets by having the Pope visit the most disaffected provinces. Pius and his Secretary of State sought to take advantage of the sympathy the population had for the Pope, if not their sovereign. While Antonelli stressed the political advantages to be derived, Pius was moved by religious considerations. He had promised to make a pilgrimage to the shrine of Loreto following his miraculous escape at Sant' Agnese, convinced that the protection of the Virgin had shielded those involved from certain death. The visit was postponed by the Crimean War and rescheduled for 1857 both for political and religious reasons.

On May 4, the Pope left the capital with a party of sixty, just as General Goyon commenced his inspection of the Pontifical troops. They planned to visit Imola, Foligno, Assisi, Perugia, Bologna, Ravenna, and Lugo.[36] The trip had two political aims. First the Holy Father wanted to see first hand the improvements his government had made, wishing to assess for himself what else was needed. Second, and more important, Pius sought to show himself in those parts of the state that were most agitated. Pius learned that his people were not completely satisfied as he moved through the provinces, beseiged by no less than 30,000 petitions.

Antonelli did not accompany Pius on the tour, and there were those who believed that this reflected a decline in the Cardinal's power and prestige. This, coupled with the fact that in 1857 Antonelli acquired the palace of the Duchess of Saxony in Via Magnapoli, which had a viletta on the grounds, and into which his brother Filippo moved, led some to conclude that Giacomo had fallen into disfavor. The opposite was the case. According to English press reports, the French commander General Goyon had warned Antonelli that if the entire court of the Pope should leave the capital, including the ministers, he would consider himself master of Rome, and would introduce the changes suggested by Napoleon in his letter to Ney. Perhaps to avoid any pretext that Rome had again been abandoned, Antonelli decided to remain in Rome while the Pope visited the northern provinces.[37] Pius agreed.

On April 24, 1857, Pius revealed the depth of his trust in Antonelli by formally conferring on him full power to preside over the government while he traveled. Antonelli, in turn, informed the other officials that under his direction, they retained complete authority to continue their work.[38] During his travel, the Pope kept in close contact with his Secretary of State by mail, informing him of the receptions he received, and of his observations on conditions in the northern reaches of his state, as well as transmitting summaries of the talks he had with various suppliants and political personalities.[39] The Cardinal, for his part, provided the Pope with a running account of the work of the various ministries.[40] Antonelli found that he had to spend most of his time in his Vatican apartments, consumed by affairs of state, but whenever an opportunity arose, he sought solace in the Villa Saxony. The Villa was a sanctuary to which few outside the family were granted access.

The absence of the Pope from Rome for over three months, reinforced Antonelli's privileged position, for as Prime Minister he exercised all the powers of government, and as Secretary of State, exercised considerable influence over the Church. When delegations present Pius with problems or possible projects, he responded that the seat of government remained in Rome, and petitioners should address their proposals or grievances to the Secretary of State.

In Imola, when the former Papal minister, Giuseppe Pasolini, called for reforms, the Pope indicated his disenchantment with liberal government. "If these liberal governments are going to resemble that of Piedmont," he complained, "they would be anti-Christian and thoroughly disgust a large part of the population." At the same time he revealed that it was he, rather than Antonelli, who opposed substantial changes in the government. "He who is scalded by hot water," Pius related, referring to the revolutionary upheaval of 1848–1849, "fears even the cold."[41]

When Pius reached Bologna he had a series of talks with yet another of his former ministers, Marco Minghetti, who also called for reforms and a reconciliation with Piedmont. The Pope acknowledged that his subjects had asked for local improvements that he was prepared to grant, but Minghetti was not satisfied and insisted that more had to be done. "I would not know what more to do," the perturbed Pontiff responded. "The demands are excessive and no one is ever satisfied." Refusing to remain silent, Minghetti complained that even concessions granted were not always honored, and pointed to the possible responsibility of the Cardinal Secretary of state. "I understand," said Pius, "you allude to the municipal elections that were not conducted as the law provides. That can be done in the future." Unwilling to allow Minghetti to hold his Secretary of State responsible, Pius added, "I want you to know that Antonelli wanted to follow the law; it was I who feared by so doing there might be disorders and tumults."[42]

Although the Pope assumed responsibility for the cautious policies of his government, Antonelli supported, if he did not inspire, the position Pius assumed towards his former ministers during the "grand tour." The Cardinal approved of his sovereign's attitude, assuring him that it was the only path possible. Antonelli wrote the Pope that the "notable progressives" to whom he had spoken—Minghetti and Pasolini included—would always be dissatisfied, because their ultimate aim was the destruction of the Pontifical government. Appealing to the Pope's religious sensibilities he concluded, "The Lord will defend us from their various projects, and will continue to protect the cause of justice, which is the cause of the Holy See."[43]

Unfortunately for Antonelli, the liberals had found a champion in Piedmont, which Pius denounced as anticlerical and expansionist. Worse still, from the Vatican's perspective, Piedmont found an ally in Napoleonic France, which continued to apply pressure upon Rome for reforms and "an end of abuses." It was reported that its Emperor sought to secularize the Papal government, without creating an outcry from the priests.[44] To counteract the negative picture of his regime emanating from Turin, the Pope wrote Napoleon of his splendid reception during the course of his visit to Bologna, negating the Piedmontese allegations that his subjects were dissatisfied. Pius revealed that he had been received with respect in all of his provinces, disproving the lies of the enemies of the Pontifical State who sought to discredit it. The Pope did not deny that there was room for improvement, but added that this could be best attained by funding practical programs rather than granting liberal institutions.[45] Unfortunately, the financial situation of the state precluded the expenditure of additional revenue in the provinces, while the prospect for new loans in 1857, was not good.

The French Emperor remained convinced that reform rather than revenue was central to solving the problems of the Papal States, and in August, as Pius prepared to return home, renewed his efforts to extract concessions. On August 16, 1857, Monsignor Sacconi, the Nuncio at Paris, informed Antonelli that the French government was determined to convince the Holy See to make changes, and with this aim in mind, had replaced the pro-Papal Rayneval, with the Duke de Gramont, as French ambassador to Rome. Shortly thereafter, Antonelli received the French project for the reform of the Papal government, with variations suggested by Austria. Arguing that the Pontifical government, in accordance with its special nature, had offered all the reforms it could legitimately grant, Antonelli rejected the call for additional changes. Pius concurred. On September 5, 1857, the conservative Pope returned to Rome, welcomed by Luigi Antonelli, one of the Cardinal's brothers, who was then head of the Roman municipality.[46]

The French did not relent in their determination to reorganize the Pope's state, and Filippo Antonelli's correspondents in France warned of that country's policies towards Piedmont and Naples.[47] Italian revolutionaries, and especially the Mazzinians, threatened the life of the Emperor when he failed to fulfill their national objectives. In 1857, Tibaldi, Bartolotti and Grilli were sent from London by Mazzini to assassinate Napoleon before the apartment of the Contessa di Castiglione, who Napoleon often visited at night.[48] In January 1858, Antonelli was alarmed by the attempt made by Felice Orsini on the life of Napoleon, and suspected that Cavour would use it as a pretext to persuade Napoleon to employ military means to resolve the Italian question.

Antonelli's concerns proved well founded when word leaked out of Cavour's visit to Napoleon at Plombieres. The Cardinal feared that the two conspired to reorder the Italian peninsula. His worst suspicions were confirmed when he received word from Paris that Napoleon had informed Palmerston that the present state of affairs in Italy could not endure. The Emperor expected a crisis that would probably end with great sacrifices on the part of Austria in Italy. Antonelli also learned that Paris was not well disposed towards the Papal States, and believed that the Pope should preside over a smaller territory that would prove less burdensome. It was a practical suggestion, but anathema to Pius, who insisted that the temporal power be preserved in its entirety, and trusted Antonelli to do so.

The task of the Cardinal was rendered difficult by the intransigent stance assumed by Pius in religious matters, including his unwillingness to relent in the Mortaro affair. This was a case where liberal Europe was scandalized by a young Jewish boy's removal from his parents home in Bologna, and his placement in the College of San Pietro in Vincoli, in Rome, because he had been secretly baptized by a domestic during an illness, years earlier. Despite the French warnings of the unfortunate consequences flowing from the Pope's refusal to return the child to his parents, Pius would not bend. Sacconi, from Paris, warned Antonelli of the Emperor's resentment at the papal intransigence.[49] The Secretary of State understood the ramifications of the Mortaro affair, but there was little he could do. He knew that the spiriting of the Jewish boy from his family, the Pope's failure to crown Napoleon, and his refusal to allow Monsignor Maclines, who Napoleon favored, into the curia, all angered the French ruler. These papal policies proved more detrimental to the temporal power than did the unflattering words of Edmund About or the sword of Garibaldi.[50] His intransigence in these, as in other matters, stemmed from the religious principles of the Pope rather than the political maneuvers of Antonelli. Those who knew the curia, as did Giuseppe Pasolini, considered Antonelli "the least bad of the Cardinals."[51]

Confronted with the charge that only French troops preserved the Roman regime, Antonelli sought to reduce the French force, and doubled his efforts to form a new Pontifical contingent to replace them. At the beginning of October 1858, the Cardinal, as acting Minister of Arms, published a new organic article on the administration of the army corps, that was to go into effect in January, 1859 and was modeled upon the French system. Ultimately, however, the Cardinal relied on the diplomacy rather than military means to preserve the Pope's state. This mission was a difficult one, swayed by the winds of change. Thus, on December 10, 1858, when the Cardinal wrote to his mother on the feast of Loreto, her name-day, wishing her many more of these days in the years ahead,[52] he might well have pondered how many more years the Papal States could survive in their present form.

Chapter Nine

The Cardinal Between the Intrigues of Napoleon III and the Intransigence of Pio Nono

Eighteen fifty-nine did not open well for the Papal States or its Secretary of State. Although the Cardinal relied upon French bayonets for the preservation of order in Rome, he knew the French Emperor was no friend, and virtually constrained to keep his troops in the Eternal City. Napoleon did nothing to discourage Edmund About from producing a series of derogatory articles about Papal Rome, and the effective head of its government, Cardinal Giacomo Antonelli. These blatantly anti-clerical pieces appeared originally in *Le Moniteur,* the official journal, and later in 1859, published in book form. There were those who believed that the French ruler virtually commissioned the production of this scathing denunciation of the temporal power and its chief champion.[1]

About, following Napoleon, tended to reproach Antonelli for all the ills and evils that afflicted the Papal States the past ten years, and above all, for failing to follow the French suggestions for change. The scourge of the foreign occupation, About wrote, fell upon the Cardinal's head, for he alone, was responsible.

> Has he, at least, served usefully, the reactionist party? I doubt it. What factions has he suppressed in the interior? What complaints has he silenced without? Europe complains unanimously, and daily lifts her voice higher. He was not reconciled to the Holy Father one party or one power. In ten years of dictatorship, he has gained neither the esteem of the foreigner, nor the confidence of the Roman; he has gained time—and nothing more. His pretended capacity is only knavery. He has the art of the peasant, the cunning of the Indian; he has not those lofty views

which lay a solid foundation for the oppression of a nation. No one better than himself knows how to prolong an affair of business, beat about the bush, weary diplomatists, but it is not by games of this sort that one confirms a tottering tyranny. He has all the tricks of a bad policy—I am not sure he has the talent for it.[2]

Napoleon, frustrated by Antonelli's diplomatic maneuvering and political procrastination, had come to the conclusion that action was necessary to nudge Rome from its policy of *Non Possumus*. The war in northern Italy would at once remove Austria from the peninsula and resolve the problem of the Papal States. Napoleon heralded its outbreak during the course of his reception for the diplomatic corps when he expressed regrets, with some severity of tone, to the Austrian representative, Baron Hubner, that relations between their governments had become strained. Fearing that this bombshell portended Franco-Austrian hostilities, and the removal of the Habsburgs from the peninsula, Sacconi, the Papal Nuncio, left the reception "pale as death."[3]

Although Napoleon tried to soothe the Austrian representative during the reception at the Tuilleries the next evening, and the French Foreign Minister sought to reassure diplomatic Europe that no belligerent intent lurked behind the Emperor's remarks, both Vienna and the Vatican were alarmed. In the French Court, Eugenie alone remained unswervingly devoted to the Pope, but found herself increasingly isolated and condemned by Italophiles such as Prince Jerome Napoleon, for her unbending ultramontanism.[4] Antonelli remained calm, despite the ominous news he received from various sources.[5]

There were those who wondered whether it was coincidental that the Piedmontese Prime Minister had met with Giuseppe Garibaldi a week before Napoleon III had sounded his warning. From Florence, the Nuncio reported to Antonelli that the Piedmontese were scheming with the revolutionaries, charging that the chief instigator was Giuseppe La Farina, who served as Cavour's agent.[6] Victor Emmanuel's speech opening the Parliament in Turin provided further proof that the European peace was fragile at best. The King's assertion that he could not remain insensitive to the cries of anguish arising from all over Italy electrified revolutionaries throughout the penisula, and led the English to fear for the preservation of the treaties.[7] "Evil spirits are at work even in my dominions," the Pope confided to Russell, the unofficial English representative at Rome, "and the late speech of the King of Sardinia is calculated to inflame the minds of all the revolutionary men of Europe."

Napoleon sought to reassure the Pope that no matter what happened, he had no cause for concern. Pius remained skeptical. For one thing, he heard from Antonelli that the French urged him to make additional concessions to his people, and had not abandoned their campaign to laicize the Papal States. "It is called States of the Church (Etats de L'Eglise) and that is what it must remain," the Holy Father protested, adding "should governments and events turn against me they cannot make me yield."[8] The Secretary of State thus found himself caught between his sovereign, who was determined to follow his conscience and preserve the traditional order, and the French Emperor, who continued to insist on the need for change. The Piedmontese Representative at Rome, Di Minerva, observed that as a consequence Antonelli was found wanting by both the obstinate, retrograde clerical wing, as well as the progressives in the capital. Pius knew that many spoke ill of his Secretary of State, but noted that this did not keep visitors away. He concluded that men were crazy, as well as bad.[9]

The difficulties of the Cardinal were compounded in early February 1859, with the publication of the pamphlet *L'Empereur Napoleon III et L'Italie.* Credited to the Viscount Arthur de La Guerroniere, it was inspired by Napoleon's criticism of the clerical character of the Papal States and his determination to free Italy of Papal supremacy. Among other things, it argued that the union in one person of religious and political power was at the base of all the problems of Rome, and proposed the federal union of the Italian states as the only way to resolve the problems of the peninsula. Shortly after its appearance on February 7, the French Emperor, in a speech to the Chamber, reiterated one of the main points contained in the pamphlet—namely the abnormal condition of the dominions of the Pope and the need for some solution.

An outraged Sacconi immediately reported to Antonelli.[10] At a reception at the Chateau of Princess Mathilde the distressed Nuncio, most likely with Antonelli's consent, announced that he could not understand why France was willing to risk waging a war in northern Italy that was only in the interest of revolutionaries. Aware that the French Emperor was unhappy with the minimal reforms of Pio Nono, the Nuncio indicated that the Holy Father was not absolutely opposed to a constitution, and under the right circumstances might grant one. The Nuncio proved unable to glean Napoleon's intentions, knowing that the cabinet was divided on the Italian Question. On Saturday, February 12, 1859, Count Walewski and Prince Napoleon had a lively altercation over the course to pursue in the peninsula.[11] However, several days later, on February 20, Napoleon revealed his sentiments by receiving a delegation of eight Italians, six of whom were Papal subjects, relating his support and sympathy for the Italian cause.[12] Antonelli concluded that the Emperor meant to provide the national cause support by waging a war against Austria in Italy.

Distressed by the criticism of the foreign occupation of his state, and fearful of a possible clash between French and Austrian forces on Papal territory, Antonelli was determined to ask the foreign troops to leave. In March, Antonelli called for their complete evacuation within the year.[13] It was a dangerous move which carried great risk. Nonetheless, the Cardinal Secretary of State did not share the conviction of those who argued that the Papal States could rely on volunteers drawn from the Catholic world to protect the Pope's territory. He noted that while the notion appeared plausible on paper, in practice innumerable obstacles prevented its implementation. Pius, who felt foresaken by France, placed his trust in God.[14]

The English and Russians sought a diplomatic rather than a divine solution, and called for a European Congress to settle the Italian problem. Russia's proposal of a Congress of the Five Great Powers, announced in the *Moniteur* of March 23, 1859, sought to settle the Italian Question, as well as the critical overall European situation. It provided the Emperor Napoleon both an honorable means of quieting the fears of the allies, as well as a means of freeing him of his commitment to Cavour. Prospects for such a congress depended on the attitude of the Turin and Rome governments, neither of which looked kindly upon the intervention of the powers. Piedmont, under Cavour, was determined to wage the war of liberation planned at Plombieres.

Rome, likewise, responded less than enthusiastically to the call for the congress. Antonelli indicated that the Holy See could not look kindly upon a congress of the five great European powers making proposals for the Italian states, which in turn, would only be granted a consultative vote. The Secretary of State insisted that the Holy See could not accept conditions which might compromise its independence, and the liberal exercise of its authority. "There are incontestable and sacrosanct rights which the Holy See has always sustained even in its most difficult times," he wrote the Nuncio in France, Sacconi. "If the other Italian sovereigns must certainly refuse such an invitation, even more so must the Supreme Head of the Church, who in his double role could never permit other governments, and especially non-Catholic ones, to call him as if before a tribunal, for questioning and explanations while they sit in judgment."[15] He also opposed the congress as a meddling of the great powers in the internal affairs of the little ones.

Although Rome would not sanction a congress to settle their affairs, the English and Russians persisted in their efforts. Lord John Russell was known to be pro-Italian to the point of carrying on a considerable correspondence with Italian patriots both in France and Italy. Palmerston, in turn, believed that both the French and Austrians ought to evacuate the Roman States, leaving the Pope to settle matters with his own subjects.[16] From Paris the Cardinal learned that the French government was prepared to champion an Italian Confederation, even though the Pope had made known his reservations. In the face of English, French, and even Russian pressure to agree to the congress, Antonelli maintained his opposition, but kept his composure. His firmness in political and diplomatic matters contrasted sharply with his friendliness on the personal plane, as his magnetic powers of attraction worked magic on those around him.[17]

By the spring of 1859 Antonelli realized that a war in Italy was unavoidable. Walewski confessed to the English ambassador that the situation was "très grave." His prediction materialized on April 21, when the Vienna government sent Turin an ultimatum, demanding Sardinian disarmament. The demand was refused by Count Cavour on April 26, the very day that Cardinal Antonelli sent a note to the ambassadors of France and Austria asking that should a conflict erupt, the neutrality of the Papal States be respected by all combatants. The prospect of warring armies on Papal soil distressed Antonelli as much as the precipitous French withdrawal from the capital at a time when passions were aroused by the Piedmontese-Austrian war, and the Papal army remained under-staffed. Following the Papal benediction after the solemn festivities on Easter, April 27, the Roman crowd, on seeing the French ambassador and General Goyon, began to shout "long live the Emperor," "long live France," and "long live Italy."

Antonelli feared the worst, uncertain of Napoleon's intentions and actions. Having little else to rely upon but these promises, Antonelli hoped that Napoleon could be counted upon to preserve the tranquility of the Papal States.[18] Napoleon's policies did not inspire Antonelli's confidence. The French had not lifted a finger to help the Grand Duke Leopold II of Tuscany, who was forced to abdicate in the face of an insurrection. Paris simply watched as the Grand Duke and his family fled for Mantua, while the King of Piedmont was named dictator of Tuscany. It was expected that when the war erupted, Parma and Modena would follow suit.[19]

Despite the fact that Paris had made promises and commitments to Rome it had not made to Florence, the Papal States fared little better in securing French assistance. Napoleon proved unable or unwilling to fulfill his promises to the Pope and Antonelli. The Franco-Piedmontese war against Austria was perceived as one of national liberation, and served as a signal to undermine the established order throughout Italy. Thus, following the April 27 revolution, which forced the Grand Duke Leopold II to flee, the insurrection spread to the various duchies and the northern tier of the Papal States. Antonelli complained that the Piedmontese, who had unleashed Garibaldi, instigated the rebellion throughout the peninsula, and encouraged the enemies of the Pontifical Regime. "Now I cannot conceal from you that all this is evidently a preconceived plan between Sardinia and France," Antonelli told Odo Russell. "The former takes the lead, the latter follows to establish an excuse and very shortly Prince Napoleon will occupy Bologna, and then our Austrian troops in the Legations will simply become a large body of French prisoners."[20] Gustavo Cavour, the elder brother of the Piedmontese Prime Minister, acknowledged that Antonelli's complaints were not without foundation.

In June, the departure of the Austrians from the Legations provoked the disorders the Cardinal feared. Although the Legate, in a proclamation, implored the population to preserve law and order and the sovereign rights of the Pope, insurrections erupted in Bologna, Ravenna, and Perugia, followed by the establishment of provisional governments. This was followed by disturbances elsewhere, while the Cardinal Secretary of State received daily reports of Piedmontese revolutionary activities in the Papal provinces.[21] To cope with the disastrous turn of events, Antonelli asked the French to extend their occupation of these parts of the Papal States evacuated by the Austrians, but his request was refused. Other means were therefore needed to protect the Pope's territory, and the failure of diplomacy led to the exercise of military means as Swiss regiments were ordered to Perugia and Ancona. Then on June 18, 1859, the Holy Father in an encyclical stressed the Church's need for the temporal power, and two days later on June 20, condemned the attempt to undermine it.[22] The

Pope personally wrote to Napoleon, expressing his disappointment in Paris' policy towards Piedmont.[23]

Antonelli also denounced Piedmontese actions and was critical of the French for not restraining their "treacherous" allies. Nonetheless, still relying on diplomacy in general, and the French in particular, Antonelli was more restrained in his criticism. Early in July he complained to the Paris government that, despite their assurances that Victor Emanuel would not accept control of the Marches, Piedmontese officials had been sent to Bologna, and were expected to move against those provinces in which Papal authority had been reestablished. Shortly thereafter, he sent a circular to the diplomatic corps decrying the Piedmontese intervention in the Papal provinces, and their attempts to usurp the temporal dominion.[24] While Antonelli had recourse to diplomatic measures to preserve the Pope's sovereignty, Pius prayed for deliverance.

On July 11, following the defeat of the Austrians at Magenta and Solferino, the Pope's prayers seemed to be answered when Napoleon concluded an armistice with the Austrians at Villafranca. Eugenie, disturbed by the impact of the war of 1859 upon the Papal States, apparently played a crucial role in bringing it to a speedy conclusion. The Villafranca agreement proposed the creation of an Italian confederation under the honorary presidency of the Pope; called for the Austrian cession of Lombardy to France, which would in turn transmit it to Sardinia; and provided that the Emperor of Austria would keep Venetia, but would permit it to take part in the Italian Confederation. On July 14, Napoleon wrote Pius, confirming the terms earlier transmitted by the Nuncio, and adding that the various sovereigns who had been pushed off their thrones in Italy would be allowed to return. The restored sovereigns were to promote needed reforms, and a general amnesty would be granted. The Emperor also revealed his views on how best to reorganize the Papal States to assure a solid peace and the future tranquility.[25] Pius thanked God for the peace, but doubted it would endure, for its enemies were, in his words, "insane" and "evil."[26]

Antonelli also feared the peace would not last. True enough, he welcomed the unexpected end of hostilities in northern Italy, and hoped that the revolutionary movement and Piedmont's influence in the Romagna would now end. In practice, however, the Piedmontese seemed to continue their usurping "actions" in the Papal provinces. The Cardinal was likewise distressed by the French suggestions for reform and their insistence on secularization, a new law code, a constitution, and liberty of the press. Antonelli knew that Pius was adamantly opposed to such concessions, just as he refused Napoleon's suggestion that he entrust the governance of the Romagna to a deputy.[27] Confronted with these demands, the Secretary of State remarked to the French Ambassador, " . . . the French people are enjoying so many liberties that they feel the need of exporting them?"[28]

Once again Antonelli found himself between Scylla and Charybdis. On the one hand he knew that the call for reform originated from Napoleon, and believed that some concessions were needed to avoid a complete break with the French, which might lead to unfortunate consequences. On the other hand, he realized that the Pope was little inclined to bow to pressure. Pius, in fact, continued to vehemently insist that the Papal States had to be administered by men of the Church; he preferred to go to the catacombs rather than yield on the issue.[29] Thus the Cardinal had to reject the French call for reform and the creation of a separate administration for the Marches and the Romagna. Concerning the Pope's assumption of the presidency of the Italian Confederation, he responded that the Pope could not make a decision until he knew all the conditions. In fact, Pius, who had initially displayed some interest in the confederation, changed his mind and rejected the notion when he learned of Napoleon's terms. Antonelli concluded that in light of Piedmontese actions, which the Holy Father deemed eminently evil, Rome found it difficult, if not impossible to enter any alliance with it.[30]

The Cardinal Secretary of State sought Austrian intervention against the rebels and the Piedmontese in the Papal States, but the Habsburg State made it clear that it would only act in conjunction with France and Spain.[31] With Austrian inability to act unilaterally, and the French unwillingness to do so, Antonelli had to rely on the papal forces, which numbered about 5,500. He defended this reliance on armed mercenaries to protect his state, observing that it was a common custom throughout Europe even for rulers who did not have an international status and a Church to protect.[32] These forces proved efficient, and brought Ancona, Fano, Urbino, Fossombrone and Perugia back under Papal control. It proved move than a local military success, for in addition to the immediate submission of Umbria, it paved the way for the submission of the Marches and showed that the Pontifical State could defend itself.

Antonelli's victory was short lived, for even though the losses in Perugia were light, Cavour denounced the siege by the Papal forces as "brutal" and launched an effective propaganda campaign to undermine the moral position of the Papacy. Cavour's campaign was supported by the French press which branded the Pope's suppression of the revolt in his provinces a crime.[33] From Paris, Napoleon urged the Pope to dismiss Antonelli, whom he deemed responsible for the "outrage."[34] The Secretary of State, in turn, countered that the stories had been exaggerated by the Piedmontese, whom he held responsible for the insurrection in the Papal States. In response to the English complaints about events in Perugia, Antonelli asked "What did you do in the Indies?"[35] Still, the efforts were not sufficient to pacify the Romagna, and the French returned to Napoleon's scheme to secularize the Legations of Bologna, Ferrara, Ravenna and Forli, which would remain the dominion of the Pope, but administratively, judicially, and militarily separate.

In light of the critical situation, Antonelli did not wish to antagonize the French any further by immediately rejecting the project he knew his sovereign found intolerable. Instead, he responded that the suggestion was so far-reaching, he could not provide an immediate reply. In fact, the Secretary of State knew that Pius was inflexible in his determination not to permit the institution of a vice-realm in the Romagna under the control of a lieutenant-governor.[36]

There was speculation of considerable disagreement between Antonelli and Pius, which supposedly provoked the Pope to ask for his Secretary of State's resignation.[37] In reality, Pius questioned neither the loyalty nor the effectiveness of the Cardinal, who continued to serve him well. Hoping for some solution that would extricate him from his difficult situation, Antonelli stalled for time, informing the English representative that the Holy Father had an ulcer on his leg which kept him bed-ridden, adding that "nothing could be done so long as the Pope was unable to attend to business." Meanwhile Antonelli informed the French that the Pope was willing to consider all reforms which did not threaten his liberty, claiming that no steps had been taken because of the Pope's poor health.

The Secretary of State, who promised that Pius would seriously consider additional reforms as soon as he fully recovered, did not disguise the fact that the Pope's illness was in part provoked by the rebellion in his provinces. "Until the Pope's health is sufficiently restored to admit of his attending to business no answer will be returned to the French propositions," Russell wrote to Lord

John, adding "the Duc [Duke de Gramont] has declined any argumentative or speculative conversation with Cardinal Antonelli on the subject until the Pope is prepared to return a positive and definitive answer to the French Government."[38]

Odo Russell found the Pope ill disposed towards the Emperor and his ambassador, the Duke de Gramont, and determined to refuse the reforms they sought. Nonetheless, Antonelli informed the French that the Pope had committed himself to certain reforms, noting that the present situation in the Papal States did not encourage him to announce them while some of his subjects remained in a state of rebellion. Victor Emmanuel's request that he be allowed to annex the Marches and Umbria aroused Pius against both the French and the Piedmontese. The Nuncio in Paris, Sacconi, was more upset and violent than Antonelli, and did much to inflame the anger of the Pontiff.[39] The Pope's position was hardened, and the pretense of concessions was eliminated, by the vote of the Romagna assembly for annexation to Piedmont, and Victor Emmanuel's formal extension of his protection to that area. Pius responded by a consistorial allocution in which he warned that all those who by their aid or advice took part in, or approved of, the seizure of the Romagna, were subject to ecclesiastical censure.[40] Antonelli now had no room to maneuver between Napoleon and Pio Nono.

Early in October 1859, the Cardinal sent a dispatch to the Minister of Sardinia in Rome, Count della Minerva, at once condemming Piedmontese actions in the Romagna and presenting him his passport, observing that the dignity of the Holy Father would not permit a representative of the Sardinian King to reside in the Eternal City. On October 9, Count della Minerva was quietly ushered out of Rome.[41] At the same time, a number of prominent French clergyman protested the spoliation of the Pope, but received no support from Napoleon who responded that "Europe cannot permit the occupation of Rome, which has existed more than ten years to continue indefinitely."[42] Meanwhile, the French continued to press their demands for reforms, warning that if they were not forthcoming their troops would withdraw from Rome, leaving the Pope at the mercy of the revolution. Antonelli refused to be intimidated, convinced that the threat was simply a ploy, rather than a plan they intended to implement.

The Duke de Gramont, who called for an end to the procrastination, now received a straight-forward answer from Antonelli on the issue of reforms. The Cardinal observed that until the Legations returned to their rightful sovereign, there would be no administrative reforms in Rome, or the rest of the Papal territory. This upset the French, who directed their anger against Antonelli, seeking his dismissal. The Secretary of State reportedly sought to resign but Pius would not let him do so, imploring, "You have been with me during easy times, now that troublesome times are upon us, you must remain."[43] Pius appreciated that he rather than Antonelli inspired the intransigent policy, and that the removal of his minister would only expose his personal responsibility, rendering all the more difficult the course he had charted.

The French, unable to secure Antonelli's dismissal, persisted in their determination to impose reforms on the Pope. In article 18 of the Treaty of Zurich, establishing peace between the French and Austrians, the two signatory parties stressed their determination to induce the Holy Father to make reforms in the administration of his state. The Cardinal still claimed that the Pope wished to grant reforms, but was impeded first by the ingratitude of his subjects, and subsequently by the prolonged occupation of the States of the Church by foreign troops. On the issue of secularization, he provided statistics demonstrating the lay predominance in the administration. It was a quantiative rather than qualitative account, which failed to quiet the criticism. Given the Pope's determination to reserve certain positions for clerics, it was the best defense the Cardinal could mount.

Antonelli was not particularly pleased with the French proposal to convoke a European Congress to settle affairs, but accepted the invitation to attend the Congress in Paris at the end of 1859. It was expected that the Pope's representative would occupy the same position he had at the Congress of Troppau, the presidency. Giacomo made plans to leave Rome at the end of December, accompanied by his brother, Angelo. In his fifty-third year, he was now at the height of his career, and expected to play an important role at the impending Congress, over which he would preside.[44]

In the interim Pius wrote to Victor Emmanuel, complaining that all sorts of illegalities were occurring in the Legations in the King's name, and called upon him to repudiate these iniquities.[45] The Pope also wrote the Emperor of Austria, and the Queen of Spain, invoking their assistance in defense of the rights of the Holy See, and the temporal power he deemed indispensable.[46] Finally, Pius wrote Napoleon, explaining that the Roman Pontiffs were not at liberty to dispose of their territories, noting that each Pope received the State as the patrimony of the Church, which his coronation oath bound him to preserve and transmit to his successor, in its entirety.[47] Pius expected little help from the English and surmised that Palmerston and Lord John Russell favored the Italian cause, as did the English press. The Pope also sensed that Queen Victoria had little sympathy for him, and favored the creation of a large kingdom in northern Italy under Sardinian leadership.

Antonelli, for his part, appreciated the profound changes in society and diplomacy which rendered the future of the Papal States precarious. Nonetheless, he was determined to prolong its life, doing all within his means to frustrate the designs of its enemies.[48] Selected to represent the Pope's interests at the impending Congress, the Secretary of State realized that his position was not strong, but he invoked the protection of God, and the blessed Virgin, to protect the cause of the Holy Father.[49] He revealed his fears to his brother, Gregorio, imploring his wife to seek the intercession of the Madonna. He also conveyed his concerns to Count Luigi Mastai, the Pope's nephew. Antonelli prayed that the Lord would assist him and enable the Holy See to triumph over its enemies. The task was not an easy one, and the Cardinal predicted that circumstances would not allow him to see much of the French capital.[50] His prediction materialized, as events conspired to bring about a cancellation of the Congress.

On December 22, 1859, there appeared in Paris a pamphlet entitled *Le Pape et le congres*. Word soon spread that though written by La Gueronniere, it too, was inspired by Napoleon, who had previously argued that the Pope should consider the advantages of relinquishing all of his territory but the Patrimony of St. Peter. La Gueronniere, maintaining the Emperor's position, suggested that Pius could hold Rome and the immediate surroundings, giving up the rest. He urged Pius to reject the greater part of his state at the forthcoming Congress. This provoked a violent reaction in Rome, where contrary to the advice of Antonelli, Pius assumed a hostile attitude towards Napoleon. The *Giornale di Roma* charged that the brochure paid homage to revolution and troubled all good Catholics by regurgitating the old arguments and cliches hurled against the Holy See.[51] One casualty in the ensuing cold war between Rome and Paris was the Congress, which France had proposed to deal with the Italian question. Pius wrote Napoleon explaining that he could not cede the rebellious provinces because the rights he exercised were not his alone, but were the common patrimony of all Catholics and the Church. He condemned *Le Pape et le Congres* as a "remarkable monument of hypocrisy" and "a vile tissue of contradictions."[52]

Eugenie, who opposed the pro-Italian policies of her husband, openly admitted that "the Emperor's politics in Italy lacks loyalty and good faith."[53] Both Antonelli and Pius had seen proof of that bad faith. Pius, more than Antonelli, resented the duplicity and was incensed by the fact that while Walewski, and the French Foreign Office, warned Cavour against the annexation of Central Italy, Napoleon privately assured the Piedmontese Minister that he approved and supported his ambitious policy.[54] Despite Antonelli's call for moderation, Napoleon's deceptions aroused the Pope, and played a part in the drafting of his encyclical letter of January 29, 1860, which threw down the gauntlet between Rome and the French Empire.

Chapter Ten

Antonelli Confronts
Italian Unification

Although Pius repeatedly rejected the French suggestion that he content himself with a truncated state, at the opening of the new year Napoleon continued to badger him to cede the insurgent provinces. The Pope, supported by Antonelli, would not be intimidated. Abandoning himself to a complete faith in providence, the tormented Pontiff found solace. His Minister's anxieties were not as easily alleviated. Seeking to mitigate the political cost and the diplomatic consequences of the policy which provided Pius consolation, Antonelli urged his sovereign to explain his position.

On January 8, Pius again repeated his refusal to cede part of his territory.

> I am writing to declare openly to your majesty that I cannot cede the Legations without violating the solemn vows I have obliged myself to uphold, without producing a lament and a shock in the remaining provinces, without bringing shame and wrong to all Catholics, without weakening the rights not only of the sovereigns of Italy, unjustly despoiled of their dominions, but the sovereigns of the entire Catholic world, who cannot remain indifferent to the actualization of certain principles.[1]

Napoleon, convinced that the occupation of Rome was at the root of most of his troubles, was not appeased. He sought to remove his troops from the Eternal City, but realized that this would provoke Catholic France.[2] Furthermore, the Emperor knew that the Pope and his "troublesome" Secretary of State would encourage, if not orchestrate, an outbreak of discontent in France. Incensed by the conduct of the French Emperor, Pius wanted to excommunicate him, but was dissuaded from so doing by the more cautious Cardinal Antonelli. Nonetheless, on January 19, 1860, the Pope issued an encyclical to the bishops openly attacking Napoleon's scheme to have the Papacy abandon the Romagna.[3] The Secretary of State rationalized that the Pontiff viewed the cession of the Romagna as a religious rather than a political issue.[4] This accounted for Pio Nono's strident tone and uncompromising stance.

Count Cavour, who returned to Power in January, 1860, understood that the intransigence of Rome stemmed from the religious principles of the Pope rather than the political machinations of Antonelli.[5] This rendered more difficult the task of the Minister who had to defend Rome's actions. Although Antonelli relied on the French military to preserve the remnant of the Papal States, he knew that many in the Tuileries had little sympathy for Rome. The French Minister in Turin proved to be no less anti-Papal than his English counterpart, describing the Papacy as an "anachronism" while denouncing the temporal power as a "monstrosity" which France should terminate. In the circle of the Italophile Princess Mathilde the prospect that the Pope might abandon Rome was welcomed in the hope that this would condone the fait accompli in the Romagna and elsewhere. As for the Emperor's plans, Antonelli concurred in the assessment of the English and Austrian representatives in Paris, that the French ruler was an opportunist who left as many doors open as possible.[6]

Antonelli, at the Pope's behest, was constrained to close some avenues of escape and paths of appeasement. He rejected the contentions of the Piedmontese and their French allies that the revolt in the Legations was provoked by the discontent of the population rather than by outside agitation. His assessment proved accurate. He also questioned the political wisdom of ceding the Romagana, predicting that this would establish a precedent which could be applied to the remaining Papal territory, a prospect which horrified him.[7] Cavour, in fact, recognized the validity of Antonelli's concerns, confessing that the Pontifical government could not make political concessions without committing suicide.[8] For these reasons, Rome refused to follow Napoleon's suggestions. "The Church can never cede any portion of her states," Antonelli informed Odo Russell. "The Pope for one can never give way, he will let himself be persecuted, martyrized, and will die for the glory of God, but mortal man shall not make him give way."[9] Antonelli confided to a traveler in Rome in February 1860 that whoever followed him as Minister would not be able to change the policy of Rome, which was based on the needs and traditions of the Church.[10]

By the beginning of March 1860, the pro-Italian French Foreign Minister, Edouard-Antoine Thouvenel, had reluctantly come to the conclusion that no concession on the Legations could be extracted from the Pope. The Emperor, distressed by Rome's obstinancy, threatened to pull his troops out of the Papal States, allowing the Piedmontese to do as they pleased in the Romagna. The French Minister in Rome, the Duke de Gramont, who affected the greatest contempt for Italian aspirations, found Antonelli cooperative but described the Pope as difficult. Gramont complained that the excitable Pius talked too much, and to all and sundry. The patrician Ambassador noted that when the Portuguese Minister said a few words in favor of conciliation, the enraged Pius muttered that this was "the advice of a small man representing a small country."[11] Gramont concluded that Antonelli was not responsible for the policy of *non possumus,* convinced that the stubborness and blindness resided in Pius, who spearheaded the opposition to every concession.[12]

Unable to convince Rome to compromise, Napoleon advised Cavour to accede to the petitions of the population of Central Italy regarding their union with Piedmont, respecting in principle the rights of the Holy See. Consequently, on March 11 and 12, 1860, the Piedmontese conducted plebiscites prior to their annexation of the area as provided by the Franco-Piedmontese agreement. The French and Piedmontese, in Cavour's words, were accomplices once again.

In Bologna, Papal authorities acknowledged considerable enthusiasm for union, as almost all windows displayed the Piedmontese flag. The evening of the twentieth there was a general illumination, in anticipation of a positive vote. These reports of pro-Italian sentiments did not prevent Antonelli from protesting the harm done to the Vicar of Christ, by depriving him of a substantial part of his temporal authority. Citing the violence and arbitrary actions employed to obtain the Romagna, the Secretary of State denounced the usurpation as null and void. Toward the end of March, Pius launched a major excommunication against the authors, counsellors, and adherents of the invasion and usurpation. The Holy Father, insisting God created the temporal power to assure the spiritual power of the Church, argued those who harmed the first, undermined the latter.[13]

Rome's position was precarious. Pius included Napoleon in the excommunication, even though Antonelli still relied upon the French to protect what remained of the Pope's territory.[14] For this reason, as well as the fact that the Pope placed more trust in the Neapolitans, the Cardinal was not adverse to Thouvenel's suggestion that French troops in Rome be replaced by those of the King of Naples. Antonelli discussed the possibility with De Martino, the Neapolitan Minister to the Holy See, who urged him to persuade his government to assume the responsibility.

The Pope, however, once again created difficulties as the French Minister in Rome noted Pius's mood swings, his locquaciousness, and his indiscretion.[15] The Pontiff reportedly boasted to General Charles Goyon, the French commander in Rome, "I have never asked anything of the Emperor and I want never to ask him for anything."[16] To pacify the French, Antonelli assured Gramont that Pius had been misquoted. His attempts to retain the goodwill of the French were little appreciated by conservatives in the curia, who demanded a more militant stance. Although the Cardinal devoted most of his time to the Papal cause, conservatives denounced his efforts as half-hearted.

The Pope mirrored their sentiment to the extent of abandoning the diplomatic solution sought by Antonelli, showing himself attentive to those who called upon the Church to rely on clerical resources and military means to save the temporal power. Monsignor Francois-Xavier De Merode clamored for a universal crusade in defense of the Papal States, while the Secretary of State catalogued the financial and political obstacles in the way of implementing the scheme. His objections were shunted aside. Early in April the Legitimist French General Lamoriciere was summoned to Rome and given the title of Generalissimo of the Pontifical Army, despite Antonelli's misgivings and warnings that this would alienate Napoleon III. De Merode, seeking eventually to replace Antonelli, for the moment sought the Ministry of War.[17]

De Merode's triumph was achieved at a price, for the French reacted precisely as the Secretary of State had foreseen. Gramont, their ambassador in Rome, complained that Lamoriciere had shown himself incontestably hostile to the French government, drawing a circle of men notorious for their Legitimist and Orleanist views. Paris protested the encouragement accorded this anti-Napoleonic coterie by important individuals in the Papal court. Antonelli was one of the few who disapproved of this militant course of action, but was not heeded. Indeed for a time the Cardinal's position was vulnerable. The English representative in Rome wrote home that the ultras urged the ouster of Antonelli, whose religious and political moderation, they contended, hindered the conquest of the Romagna. These men looked to De Merode to salvage the situation.[18]

On April 18, 1860, the *Giornale di Roma* announced the appointment of Monsignor De Merode as acting Minister of Arms. Gramont contended the announcement was greeted with hilarity by the public in Rome, but neither Napoleon nor Antonelli considered it a laughing matter. The Cardinal sought to limit the damage by urging Lamoriciere to focus upon the internal revolutionary movements, but his suggestion was rudely rejected by the General, who responded with a series of vicious personal attacks.[19] Gregorovius, in Rome, commented that Lamoriciere and De Merode plotted the downfall of Antonelli, and their campaign took its toll. During the reception at the Palazzo Venezia on April 25, the Cardinal, who had not been seen in public for some time, appeared pale and frazzled.[20] Matters were not going well for him.

The French Minister in Rome believed that the Antonelli-Merode conflict provided a pretext for the French withdrawal. Antonelli, Gramont noted, assumed a friendly stance, in contrast to the obvious opposition of De Merode and Lamoriciere. Antonelli and his Under Secretary of State, Monsignor Giuseppe Berardi, also manifested interest in the Italian Confederation proposed by Napoleon, but were frustrated by the opposition of Pius IX. The French likewise knew that the Secretary of State disagreed with the extremist position of De Merode, which called for the Pope to abandon Rome to provoke foreign intervention.[21] Finally, Antonelli continued to question the wisdom of the military program of the Lamoriciere-De Merode faction. He deemed the native military force unreliable and discontented because of its hostility to the Pope's Swiss Guard.[22]

Although the Italians in the Papal Army numbered some 6,500 and the French less than 600,[23] Paris feared the Legitimist and anti-Imperial sentiments of the Gallic contingent. The Secretary of State alerted the Pope to the unfortunate consequences of arousing the suspicions of Napoleon, but was overruled by the enthusiasm of De Merode and Lamoriciere, who enlarged the Papal Army under the auspicies of men hostile to the Second Empire. This served the interests of the Turin Government, which knew how to play upon the Emperor's fears to its own advantage. The wily Cavour, called "Papa Camille" by the common folk of Turin, found difficult situations stimulating.[24] Cavour recognized that Napoleon feared the Legitimists in the Papal forces as much as he did Garibaldi and his men, who eleven hundred strong had embarked from Quarto, southeast of Genoa, with little, if any, opposition from the Sardinian State. In fact, the Piedmontese government tolerated public subscriptions and enrollments against the Papal States and the Kingdom of the Two Sicilies, in Genoa, Milan, and even Turin.[25]

The expedition landed at Talamone on May 7, and from this small Tuscan port a force was launched under Callimico Zambianchini against what remained of the Papal States. The attack was easily repulsed by the Papal forces. The main body of Garibaldi's followers fared better, landing at Marsala on May 11, entering Palermo in June. They reached the mainland in August, and once on the continent commenced a march towards Naples, and beyond that Rome. Pius, branding the expedition a "pernicious scheme by dispicable men," feared Cavour as much as Garibaldi.[26] His fears were not unfounded. In Paris Napoleon expressed alarm at Garibaldi's daring antics, criticizing Turin for failing to restrain him, but proved unwilling to intervene either against the guerrilla chieftain or his Piedmontese ally.[27] The crisis reached Rome when Cavour secured French approval for the Piedmontese invasion of the Marches and Umbria by convincing Napoleon that this would avert a confrontation between the French and the Garibaldini, while destroying the Orleanist conspiracy by crushing Lamoriciere's army.[28] Napoleon bestowed his blessing, asserting, "*bonne chance, et faites vites.*"[29] Thus, it is not surprising that Cavour's ultimatum of September 7, 1860, called for the dissolution of the Pope's mercenary troops, insisting that the conscience of Victor Emmanuel would not permit these foreigners from repressing the national sentiment.[30]

The Piedmontese threat did not alarm De Merode, who believed that the Papal Army, under the leadership of Lamoriciere, could confront all the enemies of the Papal States.[31] Events were to prove otherwise.

Following the rejection of Turin's ultimatum, the Piedmontese army invaded the Marches and Umbria and subsequently absorbed most of the Papal States, with the exception of Rome and its immediate environs protected by French bayonets. The Pope's State was reduced from its four regions to one; from 41,000 square kilometers to 12,000; from the remaining 2.5 million inhabitants to 700,000 in the five provinces of Rome, Frosinone, Viterbo, Velletri and Civita Vecchia. The rump state was but an enclave within the emerging Italian Kingdom. On September 18, 1860, Lamoriciere's army was dispersed near the small town of Castelfidardo, near the shrine of Loreto. On September 21 the Piedmontese overran the province and city of Fermo.[32] The fiasco highlighted the superiority of Antonelli's diplomatic measures over De Merode's military means.

The Cardinal Secretary of State hoped the Empress Eugenie, who still had the Pope's interests at heart, might counterbalance the Italophile party and curb Turin's ambitions. The Cardinal's "queen" was checkmated by Cavour's "Queen of Hearts", the Contessa di Castiglione, who reemerged in Paris, placing her figure behind the Italian cause. The reappearance of this "fatal beauty", coupled to Napoleon's approval of a policy which sanctioned the spoliation of the "seamless robe", upset Eugenie, leading to her abrupt departure for Scotland.[33] "The Pope thought he could better his own affairs by upsetting my house," an angry Napoleon remarked about the affair, "but he has made a mistake."[34] "In truth, Eugenie, you forget two things," the Emperor reprimanded his consort for her criticism of his Italian policy, "that you are French, and you have married a Bonaparte!"[35]

Antonelli was left with the responsibility of salvaging what he could from the wreckage. In a note of September 13 to Cavour, the Cardinal complained that it was a pretense to attribute to the Pontifical troops the cause of the deplorable disorders in the Papal States. He placed the blame on the Piedmontese who had provided the money, the arms, as well as the instructions to the insurgents.[36] This was followed by a circular note of September 18, which protested the invasion of the Papal States by the so-called volunteers, who acted in concert with Turin. Then, in a consistorial allocution, Pius decried the "hostile" and "horrendous" occupation of the Papal States by the forces of the King of Piedmont. The Holy Father raised his voice against the spoliation of Victor Emmanuel and his government, declaring their actions null and void.[37] The scathing allocution denounced the French as well as the Piedmontese.

France's failure to prevent the Piedmontese invasion led to a paroxysm of anti-French sentiment in Rome. The curia, scandalized by the French suggestion that a Sardinian garrison replace theirs, encouraged the French clergy to oppose the Emperor.[38] Gramont complained that with the exception of Antonelli, everyone in the Pontifical government had lost his head. Pius denounced the Emperor's policies before General Goyon, much to the chagrin of the Cardinal Secretary of State who realized that the survival of the remnant of the Papal State rested on the good will of the French. To mitigate the damage, Antonelli explained that the Pope still suffered from epilepsy, and when an attack was imminent could not be held responsible for all he said. The English representative reported that a large party of foreign prelates urged Pius to leave Rome, and appeal to the Catholic world for protection, but Russell did not believe that Antonelli shared their sentiment. This was confirmed by the French Minister in Rome who wrote that Antonelli, unlike others around the Pope, continued to place his trust in France and advised his sovereign not to abandon the capital.[39] The Cardinal realized, as the ultras in the Curia did not, that the political climate had changed drastically since 1848. Austria had been defeated, the Kingdom of Naples had virtually disintegrated, Spain was in shambles, and France conspired with the usurpers. The "Catholic Coalition" no longer existed, and the diplomatic situation did not favor a "third restoration" if Pius fled Rome.

Early in November the Cardinal Secretary of State transmitted a note to the diplomatic corps, denouncing the plebescite by which the Turin government sought to justify its annexation of Papal territory.[40] Nonetheless, he continued to oppose the Pope's flight from Rome, knowing that the French Emperor had guaranteed his Holiness the undisputed possession of Rome and Civita Vecchia. Pragmatic to the core, Antonelli sought to salvage what remained of the Papal States. "The enemies of Antonelli would be willing for the Pope to leave Rome I think as they have no other hope of his separation from the Secretary of State," wrote John P. Stockton, the American Minister in Rome. "But while there are many to attack, find fault, and embarrass his policy, there is not one fit to take his place."[41] It was known in Rome that Antonelli represented the moderate party, while the fanatical De Merode led the ultras, who called for the Pope to flee. The Belgian prelate contended that affairs would be in much better condition but for six people in the Vatican, and above all the Cardinal Secretary of State.[42] De Merode, never one for mincing his words, also heaped verbal abuse upon the French, insulting General Goyon by charging "You are the last tinsel that your master employs to cover his infamy."[43]

The defeat of the Papal forces at Castelfidardo did not teach Antonelli's rival any lessons nor did it diminish his enthusiasm for military measures. Convinced that the best defense was an offense, he charged that the Secretary of State was responsible for the calamity for not informing the military of the intentions and whereabouts of the Piedmontese. Intolerant of the views of others, and easily agitated, De Merode did not limit his attacks to Antonelli; he only reserved the strongest barrage for him. The "crazy one", as the War Minister was dubbed, still sought to energize the Pope, calling upon Rome to assume a more forceful stance, rather than meekly relying upon diplomacy.[44]

Antonelli, steadfastly refused to second the military policy of the Pope and opposed the formation of a new army.[45] The Cardinal Secretary of State pleaded with Pius to accept his resignation, but the Pope refused. "My position," Antonelli explained to Gramont, "differs from that of another minister, because I am, by my religious oath forced to remain in office despite my wishes, if the Holy Father commands, as he has in this moment."[46] He repeated the excuse he had employed in 1848 to explain his service to the Pope after Pius' allocution and his abandonment of constitutionalism. Perhaps he believed it.

The Pope trusted Antonelli, and never seriously considered giving his post to another, least of all the less-than-diplomatic De Merode. Pius relied upon the Cardinal's political and economic experience, his skill in the management of affairs, and above all his realism. The Cardinal, no less than Cavour, realized that Napoleon pursued a double policy and warranted close watching. He was willing to duel diplomatically with his Piedmontese rival to preserve his French connection. Napoleon, in fact, was influenced by both, admitting that he could not be seen in Piedmont as acting on behalf of the Pope, but found himself unable to abandon Pio Nono.[47] "If the Pope abandoned Rome, it would be said that France was not powerful enough to protect him, when she had promised to do so;" complained Napoleon, "if he remained, France would be accused of being the obstacle to Italian liberty."[48] Having concluded that the Pope owed his present existence in Rome to the protection of the French, the crafty Cardinal regarded as imbeciles those who provoked and denigrated them. He complained of the stupidity of Monsignor De Merode, but allowed him to maneuver in the slush, fully confident that he would eventually tire and drown himself.[49]

Following Piedmont's absorption of the greater part of the Papal States, Cavour sought some accomodation with Rome in order to quiet internal opposition and to satisfy his French ally. Napoleon advised Pius to reach an agreement with Turin, leading the Pope to exclaim, "My goodness! I can do that whenever I wish, and without the help of foreigners. When all is said and done, we are

Italian."[50] Negotiation was not the course which Pius intended to pursue, except on his own terms. The Piedmontese Prime Minister supported the solution provided in the memorandum of the liberal Catholic physician Diomede Pantaleoni, and the ex-Jesuit Father Carlo Passaglia, which called for "a free Church in a free State." Cardinal Vincenzo Santucci showed the draft proposal to Pius, who consulted Antonelli for a confirmation of his own reservations. The departure of Passaglia for Turin created a sensation in Rome, and led some credence to the assertions of the Piedmontese and the Italian party that secret negotiations were underway to resolve the Roman Question. Such talk was premature.

Antonelli had met with Pantaleoni, and spoke with Passaglia on a number of occasions, but the Cardinal no more than the Pope seriously considered Cavour's condition that they totally renounce the temporal power. Small wonder that both the Sovereign and his Secretary of State regarded the Count's emissaries with diffidence. Rumors of official talks were flatly denied by Antonelli, who explained that Passaglia had undertaken the journey on his own initiative. It was absurd, the Cardinal continued, to suppose that Rome would negotiate with Turin. The Cardinal's stance was confirmed by Gramont who wrote to his foreign minister on January 26 that there was no truth to the rumor of the so-called negotiations between the Holy See and the Sardinian government through the intermediaries of Cardinal Santucci and Father Passaglia; the rumor was born following the interview of Odo Russell with the Pope.[51]

The failure to secure a negotiated settlement disturbed both Paris and Turin and pundits in these capitals sought a scapegoat. Antonelli emerged as the villain for the belief persisted in France and Piedmont that if he had favored negotiations, his influence would have swayed the Pope.[52] In fact, some in both capitals were convinced that money was the surest means of winning the goodwill of the Secretary of State, who was allegedly venal to the core. They were inebriated by the rhetoric of their own press. Cavour thus instructed Passaglia to spend as much as necessary to win the subalterns in the curia round to a settlement, and to do so on a larger scale for the "bigger fish." To facilitate an accord the Cardinal was promised that the Italian government would confirm all the contracts held by his family, while the Secretary of State would personally receive three million lire.[53] It is not known if these offers were transmitted to the Cardinal; it is a fact that Antonelli rejected the Passaglia proposal which had been approved by Cavour and Napoleon.

In Piedmont and Italy, abuse was heaped upon Antonelli for his refusal to compromise and his rejection of further reform. The Cardinal, it was claimed, scoffed that reform in Rome was as ridiculous as wanting to wash a pyramid with a toothbrush.[54] The French, too, were critical of the Pope's Minister, but in Rome, Gramont sang his praises. The Ambassador noted that Antonelli remained immune to the frequent changes in opinion and proved constant in his support of French positions. Gramont maintained that Antonelli alone, in Rome, had real political sense. Pius, rather than the Cardinal, blocked negotiations. Antonelli made this clear to the Austrians as well as the French. The Holy Father would have to renounce rights the Papacy had enjoyed for centuries, he explained to the Austrian Ambassador Bach, a renunciation he could not make since he considered himself the depository of such rights. There were other reasons for the Pope's intransigence. Pius feared that Cavour's state jeopardized the "eternal salvation" of millions of his former subjects. The Pope, Antonelli explained to the Nuncio in Paris, could not remain indifferent to such an "iniquity" by abandoning his people to a regime that threatened to undermine their faith and corrupt their morals.[55]

The French Ambassador informed his government that there were no negotiations between the Pope and the King of Sardinia, predicting that the Papacy would not accept any settlement that included its acceptance of the spoliation of the Papal States. Pius complained that the Piedmontese wanted the world to believe that Rome was engaged in secret negotiations, which he vehemently denied. Antonelli, meanwhile, reiterated that the Pope could not receive Pantaleoni as a public person, certified for official negotiations, alerting Father Passaglia that the Pope wanted him out of Rome.[56] Subsequently, Pantaleoni was given his passport and ordered out of the capital so that even unofficial talks came to an abrupt end. They could not cede to unjust demands, Pius wrote Francesco II, the last King of Naples, because to cede to them would be tantamount to cooperating with their evil and would thus be an implication in the crime.[57] In February 1861 Gaeta fell and the King of Naples, the royal family, and the court left for Civita Vecchia on route to Rome.[58]

On March 17, 1861, Victor Emmanuel was proclaimed King of Italy. The next day Pius issued a consistorial allocution, *Jam dudum cernimus*, which condemned both liberalism and its representatives, barring the way to any negotiations with the new Kingdom so long as it remained in possession of Papal territory.

Pius cited the incompatibility of antagonistic principles, the impossibility of reconciling virtue and vice as the struggle continued between the rights of holy religion, and the notions of "modern civilization."[59] The allocution provided yet another proof that it was the needs of the Papacy rather than the politics of the Secretary of State that put Rome at variance with liberalism, progress, and the contemporary world. In the Pope's view this "modern civilization" could not be tolerated because it sanctioned spoliation of the Church, heresy, the admission of non-Catholics to all offices of the state, persecution of believers, and the abolition of the legitimate rights of the bishops. Pantaleoni wrote Cavour on March 19, 1861, that the Pope had finally burnt all of his bridges, and left himself no room for maneuver or negotiation. Pius, for his part, believed that he had performed his sacred duty as pastor and head of the Church.[60] Once again political considerations were subordinated to spiritual concerns.

The French Emperor harped upon the need for direct negotiations between Rome and Turin, suggesting that the cession of the island of Sardinia to the Pope would remove him from the mainland and resolve the thorny Roman Question.[61] Antonelli had to convince Paris as well as Turin that Pius would not compromise or negotiate on the matter of the temporal power, observing that he had bound himself to the Catholic world by his encyclical letter.[62] He informed Passaglia that the Holy See was prepared to endure all sacrifices rather than negotiate with the government of the King of Sardinia. The issue of the temporal power, Antonelli observed, was not only a national one, but an international and Catholic issue as well, and therefore required the input of the Catholic powers.[63] Cavour's proclamation at the end of March that Rome was to be the capital of Italy did not help matters, and convinced Pius that he was dealing not only with evil, but insatiable forces. He was incensed that a petition was circulated in Rome which called upon Victor Emmanuel to take possession of the eternal city and gathered 10,000 signatures before the police stopped its circulation.[64]

By 1861 Cavour in Turin and Antonelli in Rome agreed on one thing—the key to the Roman Question rested in the Tuileries with Napoleon III. Cavour believed that if the Emperor withdrew his forces Pius would be forced to compromise, knowing that the Emperor sought desparately to extricate himself. Napoleon sought an honest way of abandoning the Pope without arousing the Catholic world in general and French Catholics in particular.[65] His aspiration for liberation was frustrated by the Papal Secretary of State. Antonelli, who endured the French occupation as a necessary evil, orchestrated the policy which bound Napoleon to preserve Rome for the Pope. Architect of the diplomacy which barred the Italian entry into the Eternal City, the Cardinal remained indispensable to Pius. Baron Bettino Ricasoli, who succeeded Cavour in power following the Count's death on June 6, 1861, recognized Antonelli's importance in the attempt to resolve the Church-State conflict.[66] Napoleon also urged the Secretary of State to come to terms with the new Italy. Neither was to have any success in persuading the Papal Minister to violate the trust of his sovereign and negotiate a settlement. "If the Turin government had not wounded Pius' conscience as head of the Church," Antonelli confided to Bach, the Austrian representative, "God only knows what he would have conceded and where we would find ourselves today."[57]

Chapter Eleven

The Troubled 1860s

Following the creation of the Kingdom of Italy, and the loss of the greater part of the Papal States, Antonelli's main political task was the preservation of the Pope's remaining temporal power. Deprived of fifteen of its twenty provinces, and retaining only some 700,000 inhabitants out of an original population of three million, the Papal States were truncated just as Napoleon had suggested all along. The rump state faced financial ruin. In 1863 income was 5,319,910.42 scudi and expenses totalled 10,728,123.06, leading to a deficit of 5,408,212.64—a difficult situation that threatened bankruptcy and political collapse.[1] Once again it was the Cardinal, assisted by his brother Filippo, who saved the day. The two reorganized Peter's Pence, the contributions of the faithful worldwide, on a professional basis so that between 1859 and 1864, it brought in some 7,500,000.00 scudi and eased the financial problems of Rome.[2]

Social problems also loomed large as the aristocracy of the truncated state split in two with the "black" aristocracy remaining faithful to the Pope, while the "blue" championed the cause of the Kingdom of Italy. Those remaining in the Pope's camp were the Borghese, Salviatti, Massimo, Aldobrandini, Patrizzi, Altieri, and Rospigliosi, among others. The princes Doria, Colonna, Pallavicini, the dukes of Fiano, Sermonetta and the marquises Calbrini, Trogli, and Cavolti revealed their national sentiments.[3]

The political problems confronting the state were more serious than the social and economic ones, for the Secretary of State had few cards to play following Austria's defeat in northern Italy, and its increasing preoccupation with German affairs. Having few options, Antonelli relied on the French Emperor's commitment to protect what was left of the papal provinces against the Turin government and Garibaldi's encroachments. The Cardinal's hope of retaining the goodwill and support of the French was menaced by the Pope's bitterness and intransigence, the ploys of the De Merode faction to have Pius abandon the French connection, the intrigues of the Italians, as well as Napoleon's desire to rid himself of the pressure of the Italian cauldron. Antonelli's determination to keep the French in Rome dominated Papal diplomacy during the decade of the troubled 1860s.

The cardinal had first to deal with his own sovereign and the Italian bishops, who remained unreconciled to the loss of any part of the papal territory, and resented the French failure to prevent the Piedmontese usurpation. This prompted Antonelli to warn Passaglia that Rome could not negotiate on the basis of renouncing any part of its state. Such a renunciation, he explained, exceeded the authority of the Secretary of State, and even the Pope himself, and perhaps required the convoking of a council. He therefore could not trade territory lost to secure what remained, the sacred college would not allow it. Antonelli's options were limited; the advisability of negotiation had been discussed by an extraordinary congregation meeting before the Pope, and the commission had discouraged such talks.

Antonelli represented a sovereign and an episcopacy unwilling to reach an accomodation with the Italian state. Napoleon sought to conciliate the independence of the Holy See with the liberty of Italy, but Pius made his task arduous and created headaches for Antonelli, who sought cordial relations with the French. The Secretary of State found himself in an embarrassing position when Monsignor Talbot, the Pope's Chamberlain, charged that Napoleon had made a pact with the devil, whom he frequently consulted.[4]

The Italian bishops, in turn, were almost unanimous in their support of the Pope's contention that the *dominum temporale* was essential for the independence of the Holy See.[5] There was thus little prospect of convincing the bishops and the Pope that they should recognize the fait accompli, and normalize relations with the Italians, as the French government urged. Paris offered the Holy See a guarantee of what remained of its temporal power if it came to terms with Italy, but Pius absolutely rejected these conditions. Confronted with this inflexibility, Napoleon confided to a visiting Nassau Senior, "We cannot remain the supporters of that odious tyranny, and the obstacle to Italian unity. Every motive requires us to escape such a situation."[6] The 1860s, more than the preceding decade, saw the dominance of Pio Nono's religious outlook in determining papal policy. Antonelli remained what he had always been, a necessary figure, perhaps now more important than ever, in executing the decisions inspired by the Pope.[7]

Antonelli, rather than the Pope, had to explain the Papal position to the French ambassador in Rome. The Cardinal denied that there was discord between the Pontiff and Italy, arguing that while the Holy Father had ruptured relations with the cabinet of Turin, it had excellent rapport with the people of the peninsula. Italian himself, Antonelli continued, the Pope suffered with his country, and was pained by the grave difficulties burdening the Church in Italy. One of the profound reasons for Pius IX's opposition to the *Risorgimento* transcended the loss of the temporal power or the reorganization of the peninsula, and flowed from the Church's loss of its special position in Italy. The Pope feared that the new lay state jeopardized the spiritual salvation of millions of its inhabitants and would not cooperate in the "crime." For this among other reasons, Pius would not negotiate with the spoliators. Antonelli's hands were tied.

The French found the papal position frustrating, and this undermined their resolve to uphold the temporal power. The Pope's attacks on the policy and person of the Emperor did not help matters, creating diplomatic nightmares for his Secretary of State. Napoleon resented both the Pope's recriminations and the fact that he made Rome a haven for the discontented from Parma, Modena, Lucca, Tuscany, and above all the former Kingdom of the Two Sicilies. The Emperor cautioned the Pope against providing refuge for Francesco II and the Neapolitan royal family, but Pius, who felt obligated to them for the hospitality offered him during the revolutionary upheaval of 1848, had Antonelli invite them to Rome.[8] The decision aroused the Italians and their French allies. Although Francesco promised not to promote agitation in his former realm, the deposed monarch soon became the center of opposition to the Italian regime in Naples. Despite considerable French pressure, Pius refused to expel Francesco and his exiled court from the city protected from the Italians by French soldiers.[9]

The French Foreign Minister urged an accomodation between Rome and Turin. He sought to persuade Antonelli and the Pope to negotiate, promising that the signatories of the Treaty of Vienna would all guarantee what remained of the Papal State, and a civil list would be assured the Holy See, to which France would contribute an annual sum of three million francs. These inducements did not budge Pius, who was determined to remain faithful to the oath taken upon his election in which he promised to preserve intact the territory of the Church.[10] Consequently, Antonelli was forced to reiterate that the Pope would only negotiate on the basis of the restoration of his entire state.[11]

In October 1862 Edouard-Antoine Thouvenel, who had pledged to remove French troops from Rome if he could not get Pius to achieve a reconciliation with the Turin government, was replaced by Edouard Drouyn de Lhuys, who posed no such condition. Among the first steps taken by the new Foreign Minister was to recall Benedetti from Turin and La Valette from Rome, replacing the latter with the pro-Papal Prince de la Tour d'Auvergne, with Henry D'Ideville serving as his undersecretary. Emile Olliver, in Rome at the time, commented to Antonelli that he must be happy to see the anti-papal Thouvenel leave. "No," responded the Cardinal, "it is now that we tremble, they will entrust our friends to execute us."[12] Pius proved less astute, placing too great a political significance on the appointment of the Prince and the removal of the troublesome La Valette, who had been hostile to Papal interests.[13] The Secretary of State placed no greater trust in Napoleon than did De Merode, but unlike the latter, Antonelli realized that French opinion did not favor Italian unification. When Prince Jerome Napoleon, the Emperor's cousin, had denounced Rome in the Senate as an anachronism, few echoed his sentiment. The Duke de Persigny was practically alone among the ministers in support of Italian national goals. Jules Favre's proposal for the evacuation of Rome in the Corps Legislatif was defeated by a vote of 246 to 5. To be sure, Napoleon was sympathetic to the Italian cause, but he needed the support of French Catholics at home, and the defense of Rome was the price of their support. Rumor had it that when the Cardinal was asked "When will the French garrison be withdrawn from Rome?" he had replied, "when I withdraw my garrison from Paris."[14]

Antonelli realized that Napoleon's Roman policy was motivated by fear rather than love; he was politically constrained to protect the Pope. He had few illusions about the Emperor, whom he characterized as an opportunist prepared to take advantage of difficulties and blunders of states and statesmen. While the Cardinal was seldom surprised by the enigmatic Emperor's twists and turns, others in and out of the diplomatic service were both surprised and upset. "I have an idea in my head. I hardly know whether it is practicable or not. I only throw it out as a notion which crosses me," the French ruler told the new Nuncio in 1862. "Suppose the Pope were to leave Rome, just to show the impossibility of Italian unity!"[15] The Nuncio was flabbergasted, knowing this was the ultra and legitimist position, which the Cardinal Secretary of State, in conjunction with the French Ambassador, had fought. He did not know if his own loyalty was being tested, or if this was simply some fleeting scheme of the Emperor. Napoleon, sensing the Nuncio's discomfort, reassured him that it was only an idea, and he would do all within his means to meet the Pope's wishes. Antonelli had good reason to monitor Napoleon's mood swings and policy changes.

Antonelli was equally critical of England, whom he accused of having grown great by feeding on the miseries of others.[16] His conviction that the English sought an end to the temporal power was accurate. "If the Pope is driven from Rome," the English Ambassador to France wrote his Foreign Minister, "I for one, shall not care to criticize the manner in which it is done. The blessing to mankind will overrule everything else in the situation."[17]

Antonelli courted the goodwill of the remaining great powers, seeking a rapprochement with Russia. In anticipation of a mission to this eastern power, Antonelli's friend and close collaborator, Giuseppe Berardi, who had served him as undersecretary of State since 1859, in 1862 was hastily ordained a priest. Just when it appeared that a nuncio might be accepted in St. Petersburg, Pius was aroused by new Russian persecutions against the Catholic Poles. The Pope denounced the Russian repression of the Polish revolution, undermining the goodwill which his Minister had cultivated.[18] The disaffection was compounded by the Russian recognition of Italy. Antonelli was particularly upset, for he had received assurances that the Russians would not recognize the Kingdom.[19]

Despite his problems with the great powers, and above all the vacillations of Napoleon III, the Cardinal did not believe that the Papacy had a viable alternative in the military measures suggested by De Merode, Montalembert's brother-in-law, and Lamoriciere. That the danger was real, he had no doubt. The aim of Urbano Rattazzi, who succeeded Bettino Ricasoli as Italian Prime Minister in March 1862, was known to all—to overthrow the temporal power and complete Italian unity with the consent of France.[20] In the summer of 1862, when Giuseppe Garibaldi took up the cry "*O Roma O morte!*" (Either Rome or Death!), and was encouraged more than hindered by the Rattazzi government in Turin, Antonelli again relied on diplomacy rather than military measures to deal with the threat. He had the Pope decline the of-

fer of General Lamoriciere to go to Rome to defend the Holy Father, menaced by the revolution. The Cardinal preferred to rely on
the pressure of conservative Catholics to assure that Napoleon
would restrain the Garibaldini, and the Italian authorities who
encouraged them. His policy succeeded as Napoleon rejected the
Italian contention that Garibaldi could only be stopped if they occupied Rome. Napoleon insisted that the Italian government act
against the Volunteers.[21] Responding to the pressure from Paris,
on August 29 Italian troops fired on Garibaldi and his followers at
Aspromonte, in Calabria, wounding the General and scattering his
"Roman Legion." Napoleon had forced the Italians to protect Rome
from Garibaldi, who became disenchanted with the Rattazzi government that had earlier encouraged him. The duplicity of the
government in the Aspromonte affair contributed to its fall at the
end of 1862.

Aspromonte revealed the wisdom of Antonelli's diplomatic
course, for it had been the French presence in Rome, and Napoleon's ability to coerce his Italian ally, that had saved what remained of the temporal power rather than De Merode's military
force. Nonetheless, the Minister of War continued to oppose Antonelli and proposed an alternative course. "De Merode wants me
to fire Antonelli," the Pope confided to Dupanloup in 1862, adding,
"but I won't do it: he is not worth much on the offensive, but is
without equal in a defense."[22] Pius belatedly acknowledged the importance of Antonelli's policy of preserving good relations with the
French. Thus New Year's day, 1863, when the Pope received the
French officers, he expressed his heartfelt gratitude for their protection, clearly seeking to mend relations between Rome and
Paris.

De Merode refused to concede the contest to Antonelli, and
continued to attack his person and policies. On February 22, 1862,
Ludovico Fausti, apostolic despatcher and a gentleman belonging
to Cardinal Antonelli's household as Chamberlain to his Eminence, was arrested on the charge of having betrayed the cause of
the Pope, and accused of having acted in concert with the national
committee to provoke a revolution in Rome. Fausti was taken into
custody on the basis of flimsy evidence and questionable wit-
nesses, chief of whom was Costanza Diotallevi, who was released
from prison to testify. She proceeded to denounce almost half of
Rome as participants in the conspiracy to turn the Eternal City
over to the Italians. Princes, prelates, cardinals, military men as
well as public officials were accused by this imaginative criminal,

whose accusations were accepted as truth by the political and judicial authorities.

Contemporaries clearly understood that the case against Fausti was aimed to discredit Antonelli, who was implicated by his close association with Fausti. Rumors spread of Piedmontese money having been showered on the Secretary of State, and Antonelli found himself in a quagmire. If he did nothing to assist his chamberlain, he would be condemned, making it appear that the actions taken against him were justified, and the Cardinal, by association, shared his guilt. If, on the other hand, Antonelli took steps to defend his servant, De Merode was prepared to charge that the Secretary of State was abusing his power.[23] The Cardinal appealed privately to Pius, who retorted that the Minister of the Interior could arrest whomever he pleased, without requiring the approval of the Secretary of State. Pius further embarrassed Antonelli by letting it be known that he had personally sanctioned Fausti's arrest.[24] Unable to set the matter straight, Antonelli tended his resignation, but the Holy Father refused to accept it. [25] De Merode and the ultras had been sufficiently strong to humiliate the Cardinal, but had not succeeded in removing him from office.[26] This was only one battle in a protracted war between De Merode and Antonelli; Pius, for the moment, remained neutral.

The Cardinal Secretary of State, angered by the actions against Fausti and the innuendos against his person, called for the ouster of Monsignor Pisa, Minister of the Interior, who had collaborated with De Merode against him. However, he steadfastly refused to interfere in the trial, allowing justice, or as he claimed, injustice, to take its course. The only assistance Antonelli lent his servant during the "processo Fausti" was to provide meals while he was imprisoned. Without Antonelli's assistance, Fausti was condemned to twenty years in prison. Ultimately Antonelli's studied inactivity and nonintervention proved effective, for public opinion in Rome was outraged both by the severity of the sentence and the nature of the evidence against Fausti. Antonelli would eventually triumph, as the Pope, on his own initiative, pardoned Fausti who served only four years in prison.[27]

"The growing influence of Merode, the declining power of Antonelli, the false position of France, the increasing strength of United Italy, the follies of the Bourbons, and the illness of the Pope are undoubtedly producing more distinct parties in the Church," Odo Russell wrote Earl Russell on April 22, 1863, "and these parties may sooner or later exercise some influence on the solution of the Roman Question."[28] Russell's assessment was premature, for the attempt to discredit Antonelli had backfired, and the Secretary of State became the rallying point for moderates in the curia as well as those who sought to restrict the influence of the intransigent party. The Cardinal emerged from the ordeal stronger than he had been before; there were those who insisted that he alone could save the Papacy.[29]

The Duke de Gramont, the former French ambassador to Rome, remained devoted to Antonelli. He did not forget that it was in Rome that his wife converted to Catholicism, nor the role played in the conversion by the Cardinal.[30] Antonelli also maintained cordial relations with various individuals in France, and the other European countries. In April 1863 he was honored with the Grand Cross of Prussia in appreciation for the many courtesies he had extended to the royal family.[31] Outside of his family and close circle of associates, Antonelli's social life was confined to the diplomatic community where he had many acquaintances but few friends. The Cardinal was kept in office by Pius not only because of his many contacts abroad, but also for his tact and ability to define and describe the papal position to others. He converted the Pope's emotional response into a rational policy. Furthermore, his decision to seek the support of the European chancelleries, and above all that of France, seemed the only viable one.

The supple Minister, seeking to disprove the assertion that the Papal regime survived only by means of French bayonets, encouraged the Pope to visit his southern provinces and show the world that he was loved and esteemed by his subjects. This would complement, in part, the visit made by Pius to his northern provinces in 1857. Pius followed Antonelli's suggestion, and from May 11 to May 20, 1863 visited the campagna by train. In the southern provinces, Pius received touching and popular ovations.[32] The official journals such as *Civiltà Cattolica* noted the evident enthusiasm with which the Pope was greeted, the inauguration of public works initiated by the Holy Father, and the pomp and ceremony with which he was received upon his return to the Eternal City. The visit of 1863, more restricted and shorter than that of 1857, revealed that the Pontiff was still popular and sensitive to some of the needs of his people. This popularity, while real, did not enable him to solve the political problems which threatened the state and distressed the French.[33]

In October 1863, the Prince de la Tour was replaced by the Comte de Sartiges, which was not a good signal for the Papacy.

While in Washington, the French Count had confided to Odo Russell that the Catholic Church would endure forever, because it was based on the absurd. In Rome, he had no new instructions, beyond inviting Pio Nono to visit Paris. Early in 1864 the Count told Antonelli that it would be advantageous to the Pope if Francesco II could be induced to depart from Rome, suggesting that the Turin government might offer concessions to get him out. Antonelli, aware of the Pope's eternal gratitude to the Neapolitans, responded that he could not listen to such propositions. In late April the Pope fell ill, and in May there was speculation about a possible succession, but Pius recovered despite the predictions left at the statue of Pasquino that he would be followed by Victor Emmanuel II.[34]

In June 1864, negotiations resumed between the Italians and the French, with the aim of ending the French occupation of Rome and entrusting the Pope's security to the Italians. On many occasions, according to Costantino Nigra, the Italian Minister plenipotentiary sent to Paris, Napoleon repeated "I wish for nothing better than to evacuate, but I cannot allow either the King or Garibaldi to enter Rome: give me securities that this will not occur and I withdraw the troops."[35] Antonelli, aware that Napoleon prevented Garibaldi and the Italians from seizing Rome, sought to placate him to the extent that Pius would allow. The Pope did not make matters easy for his Secretary of State, who knew that the conversion and forced removal of another child of Jewish ancestry, Joseph Cohen, angered the Emperor and a good part of European opinion. Pius, however, refused to compromise on the matter, announcing that as a spiritual Pontiff he was responsible to his Christian conscience. Only God could judge him.[36] Relations between Paris and Rome suffered as a result.

On September 15, 1864, the Minghetti government of Italy and the French Empire signed an agreement to regulate the Roman Question. Rome had been kept in the dark during the negotiations and only learned of the terms of the accord on September 17, when Antonelli was informed by the French ambassador, Sartiges. According to some, when the Secretary of State received word of the September Convention, he quickly ended the interview. The generally accepted account relates that the Cardinal allowed Sartiges to deliver his message, responding that the Pope would assure his own defense.

The terms of the Convention provided that France would withdraw its troops from Rome within two years, in return for a pledge from the Italian government to respect and protect what remained of the temporal power from outside incursions. As a sign that the Italians abandoned the scheme to make Rome their capital, the Minghetti government promised to transfer the capital from Turin to another city within six months. Eventually the Italians opted for Florence, which became capital of the Kingdom in 1865. In addition, the Italians withdrew their opposition to the formation and maintenance of a papal army of volunteers drawn worldwide, so long as the force remained defensive and did not threaten the Kingdom of Italy. Finally, the Italian government promised to pay part of the debt of the Papal territory, which had been earlier incorporated into Italy.

From the first, Antonelli saw the problems posed by the September Convention. The Minister of the Italian King at the French Court, Nigra, did not hide the fact that his government considered the shift of their capital an expedient pending the eventual acquisition of Rome.[37] Since Napoleon, alone, could block the ambitious schemes of Victor Emmanuel, the Cardinal deemed it essential to preserve his goodwill. Pius, on the other hand, considered the Convention just another proof of the decadence and malaise which afflicted the world and undermined the good and just. The Pope was convinced that the moral climate had been deteriorating for some time, and had long felt the need to speak out. He desired to condemn *en bloc* the present theological and moral errors, as well as the political ones. His resolve was strengthened by the publication of the Convention. Pius complained that the French treated him like a child, or someone under interdict. "They have not consulted me," he grumbled, "they did everything in Paris."[38] When Monsignor Place, a close friend of the French Foreign Minister, visited Rome to reassure Pius regarding the September Convention, he found the Pope skeptical. This skepticism remained. When the French Ambassador was instructed to confide to him that more than ever he had to have confidence in the Emperor, Pius responded, "Yes I have confidence, but only in God, he alone never deceives."[39]

The Pope had his Secretary of State denounce the Convention in a circular note to the powers. Angered by the French betrayal and abandonment, Piedmontese aggression, and the writings of those in the liberal Catholic movement, Pius took the occasion to strike back. He did so in the encyclical *Quanta cura* promulgated on December 8, 1864, to which was appended a catalog of erroneous propositions previously condemned by the Pope or his predecessors. While Mazzini, sheltered in London, reportedly the paymaster for the assassination attempt on Napoleon in 1864, sought to alter the course of events by actions, the Pope hoped his words would be equally influential.

There had been talk in Rome of the need for a condemnation of modern errors since the revolutionary upheaval of 1848, and the restoration of 1849. Initially there was some thought of linking this condemnation to the proclamation of the dogma of the Immaculate Conception in 1854, but this was deemed inappropriate.[40] The condemnation was temporarily shelved, but was resurrected following the seizure of the greater part of the Papal States in 1859, deemed a new assault upon the Church, and perceived as the consequences of the new doctrines. Pius thus placed before the cardinal inquisitors of the Supreme Congregation of the Holy Office a list of seventy errors for their scrutiny and condemnation.[41]

The notion of issuing a condemnation of modern errors was also presented to the bishops who had congregated in Rome on the occasion of the canonization of the Japanese martyrs, an event of political as well as religious significance. The allocution *Maxima quidem* of June 9, 1862, was of notable importance both for the variety of errors condemned and later repeated in the Syllabus, as well as the solemnity of the occasion. Although the invitations to the bishops to participate focused on the religious motivation for their attendance, the European governments, and above all the Italian one, feared a hidden political agenda. Antonelli, therefore, found it necessary to reassure the ambassadors of France and Austria.[42] The Cardinal Secretary of State, whose policy rested upon the support of the European chancellories, and above all that of France, recognized the political ramifications of the condemnation of the principal errors of the time, and did not encourage it. Indeed he sought to reassure the Catholic powers that the Holy See would proceed with all the necessary prudence. The Pope's disillusionment with France, following the September Convention, made the publication of the Syllabus drafted by the Piedmontese Barbabite Luigi Bilio, inevitable.[43]

On December 8, 1864 Pius IX's encyclical *Quanta Cura* appeared accompanied by a list of 80 errors drawn from previous papal documents, condemning various movements and beliefs. The encyclical contained six major points: three negative and three positive. On the one hand it struck out against the notions that [1] society should be constituted and governed with no more regard to religion than if it did not exist [2] the sovereignty of the people should be seen as a supreme law independent of human and divine rights and, finally [3] the absolute principle of freedom of conscience and worship. While these principles were condemned there followed three affirmations: [1] the absolute independence of the Church vis a vis civil authority [2] the Church's right to educate consciences, particularly those of the young and [3] the plenitude of papal authority even in spheres outside the area of faith and morals.

The "Syllabus of the Principal Errors of our Times" passed through at least eight different versions and was in many ways confusing.[44] Sent out by Antonelli, it did not bear Pio Nono's signature, but his imprint was there. The first clue to its origins and the Pope's responsibility was provided by the Cardinal in the Introduction:

> Our Holy Father, Pius IX, Sovereign Pontiff, being profoundly anxious for the salvation of souls and of sound doctrine, has never ceased from the commencement of his pontificate to proscribe and condemn the chief errors and false doctrines of our most unhappy age, by his published Encyclicals, and Consistorial Allocutions and other Apostolic Letters. But as it may happen that all the Pontifical Acts do not reach each one of the ordinaries, the same Sovereign Pontiff has willed that a Syllabus of the same errors should be compiled, to be sent to all the Bishops of the Catholic world, in order that these Bishops may have before their eyes all the errors and pernicious doctrines which he has reprobated and condemned.[45]

The unequivocal condemnation of contemporary political movements and thought systems made the Syllabus perhaps the most controversial doctrinal statement of the Pontificate. De Merode was very satisfied with the Encyclical.[46] Not so Antonelli, who sought to mitigate its political damage by noting that it was a declaration of abstract principles which did not call into the question the concrete political institutions upon which the greater part of European constitutions were then based. The Cardinal assured the various ambassadors that the anathemas of the Vatican were directed against the spirit of socialism, and the evil passions of the century, rather than against any specific state, adding that the Syllabus represented the thesis, the ideal of the Church, rather than the hypothesis, the norm of conduct which had to take cognizance of circumstances.[47] Noting the Cardinal's efforts to explain it away, Odo Russell thought that Antonelli had opposed publication of the Encyclical, but had been overruled by the Pope, and the Jesuits.[48]

Antonelli apparently had reservations about the Syllabus, which he feared might undermine the diplomatic position of Rome, and remained preoccupied by the maneuvers of De Merode. Throughout this tumultuous period the cold war between Antonelli and the Belgian prelate simmered, with the Minister of Arms critical of Napoleon, claiming he had ambitions in Italy.[49] The Cardinal was helped by the fact that the Minister of Arms was stricken by a bout of malaria, which kept him away from the Pope at Castel Gondolfo. When he recovered and returned, however, he showed himself as insulting as ever, and even the Pope's pleas that he moderate his language went unheeded. When Pius heard that the caustic minister had broken his leg he retorted, "It would have been better if he had broken his tongue."[50] In October 1865, when De Merode least expected it, he was summoned to the Pope who announced that because of his illness and fatigue, he was being relieved of his post. At the same time, Matteucci, the Governor of Rome, who had also crossed Antonelli, was replaced.[51] On October 21 the *Giornale di Roma* announced the removal of the Minister of the Interior and Justice, Monsignor Andrea Pila, the major supporter of De Merode in the government, and Monsignor Matteucci was removed as Director General of the Police. Antonelli's triumph was complete. A few days afterwards Antonelli had dinner at the French Embassy and appeared "rejuvenated."[52]

The Cardinal did not gloat over his victory, comporting himself with restraint and dignity in the face of his rival's defeat. Indeed when Henry D'Ideville and his wife went to see the Cardinal early in 1866, the conversation turned to De Merode, and Antonelli had only good things to say about the former Minister. Antonelli admitted that he and De Merode did not always see eye to eye, but never doubted that the Minister of War was devoted to the Holy Father, and had the interests of the Church at heart.[53] His behavior touched even the usually insensitive prelate, who believed his fall was due to the vagaries of Pio Nono, rather than the intrigues of Antonelli, with whom he remained on good terms. He attributed the Secretary of State's benevolence to the fact that he, too, had suffered heartaches because of the arbitrary behavior of the Pope, claiming that in this regard the two were kindred spirits in suffering. Thus De Merode's anger with Pius led him to forget his rivalry with Antonelli, whom he now saw in a far better light.[54]

The Papal army, under the command of General Hermann Kanzler from 1865 to 1870, remained, but the military policy of De Merode and Lamoriciere was abandoned. "The Pope was not a military prince," Antonelli told Russell in Rome. "It would be folly to renew an experiment which recent experience taught could end so fatally, and the Pope was therefore resolved not to add a soldier to his present army."[55] On October 22, 1865 Gregorovius commented on the fall of De Merode in his diary:

> Rome is full of the event; everyone rejoices. With Merode the Jesuit-legitimist faction is suppressed, and the national party under Antonelli has returned to the helm. It cost a great effort to set aside the fanatic. It was represented to the Pope that owing to Merode's action the Maritima and Campagna would be lost, like Umbria and the Marches. This took effect. The fall of the favorite was also demanded by France. They are convinced at the Vatican that Austria cannot go to war.[56]

Antonelli, above all, realized that there was little that Austria could do at present on behalf of Rome. The Hapsburg state faced dangers of its own stemming from its long rivalry with Prussia, which seemed bent on some form of German unification. In fact in April 1866, La Marmora, the Prime Minister of Italy, and Bismarck signed an Italian-Prussian alliance whose object was to wage war against Austria within three months. As the clouds of war spread over Europe in June, Antonelli fell ill, distressing the Pope, who daily asked for reports on his Secretary of State's health.[57] Because he was not seen in public for some time, reports circulated that the Pope had dismissed the Cardinal and sought a successor.[58] Amidst the speculation, Prussia declared war on Austria on June 16, and Italy followed suit four days later. While Antonelli favored the Austrian cause, neither he nor Pius would second the plea of Franz Josef that Rome declare the cause of Austria was that of justice. The Cardinal Secretary of State counselled a strict neutrality, spiritual and temporal.[59]

Although the Italians suffered defeat, both on land (Custozza) and on sea (Lissa), the Prussians decisively defeated the Austrians at Sadowa on July 3. Napoleon belatedly expressed concern and sought some means to save Austria.[60] It was too late. When Antonelli received the news of Sadowa he cried out, *"Casca il mondo"* (the world is collapsing).[61] "Good God," the Cardinal exclaimed as he struck his forehead with the palm of his hands, "what is to become of us?"[62] The defeat and withdrawal of pro-Papal Austria from Venetia rendered its influence in Italy minimal, making Antonelli's task of preserving what was left of the temporal power virtually impossible.

The French Empress, disturbed by the consequences of her husband's policies, believed that the Pope had a right to complain.

> What has the protection of France wrought? Had the Emperor left the Pope to his national friends, Austria, Naples and Tuscany, his rights would have been secure, but having deprived him of these friends, the Emperor now withdraws his own protection, and leaves the Pope to his fate.[63]

The situation was not as bleak as Eugenie painted it. Although the French troops were withdrawn from Rome, Napoleon promised that should disturbances erupt he would again provide protection. To provide further assurances to the Secretary of State, while limiting his own liability, Napoleon sought to conclude a convention with Prussia, providing for their joint guarantee of the temporal power. Bismarck, however, courteously but definitely rejected the proposal.[64] Antonelli did not have the same leverage with Protestant Prussia that he had with Catholic France.

The Cardinal's policies were criticized in Paris and Turin, and there were those in Rome who continued to find fault even after the fall of De Merode. The American wife of La Valette went to see the Secretary of State to lecture him on politics and the dangers facing the Pontifical government, suggesting paths he should pursue to improve their position. She was neither the first nor the last to offer advice, without considering what was possible. As usual the Cardinal showed patience and restraint. He listened attentively to her recommendations, and when she finished replied, "I believe Madame Marchessa, that you would like to look at my collection of precious stones; these always interest the ladies."[65] The angry Madame La Valette stormed out without comment, leaving Antonelli to confront the many problems undermining the regime.

Antonelli sought to improve relations with the Italians on an unofficial basis. One year earlier, in 1865, both he and the Pope received the moderate deputy Boggio, who wanted Papal support against the brigandage which plagued the Italian *mezzogiorno*. Pius confessed that he was hurt to think that there were those in the peninsula who believed him an accomplice of that pernicious movement, and Antonelli added that his brother in Terracina was constantly menaced by the brigands. "Gasperone cost us twenty years and twenty million," the Cardinal told one of the ambassadors to underscore the difficulty Rome faced in suppressing brigandage.[66]

In 1867 the Antonelli government signed an agreement with the Italians at Casino, which led the two to cooperate in the fight against brigandage. Meanwhile, with an edict of June 1866, Antonelli created a new pontifical "lira" which was the equal of the Italian one, and he allowed various Italian officials, senators, and deputies to visit Rome. These measures of the Cardinal represented de facto if not de jure recognition of the status quo, pressing to the limit of Pio Nono's restrictions. Despite the limitations posed by his sovereign, under the Cardinal's direction the truncated Papal State was well-run, and in some respects progressive. This did not satisfy Italian liberals and nationalists, who sought its incorporation rather than its reform.[67]

Chapter Twelve

The Infallible Pope and His Fallible Minister

In 1866, as the Romans prepared for Christmas, the French executed the September Convention and evacuated the Castel Sant' Angelo and the fortresses of Civita Vecchia, turning them over to the Papal army. The departure was not marred by incident or violence.[1] The calm of Rome was in marked contrast to the turmoil in Turin, following the announcement of the transfer of the Italian capital to Florence. Victor Emmanuel had to call out the troops to restrain the riots, at the cost of some two hundred lives and hundreds others wounded. The King dismissed Marco Minghetti, who had negotiated the Convention, but he knew that the price of French withdrawal had been the transfer of the capital. If the Torinesi and some in the Papal court were outraged by the Convention and its consequences, Napoleon was satisfied. He had finally extricated himself from the Roman imbroglio.

At the opening of the National Assembly in February, Napoleon commented that the government of the Holy Father had entered a new phase, and was now maintained by its own strength, the veneration it inspired, and the loyal protection of the Italian government. "But if democratic conspiracies should seek audaciously to threaten the temporal power of the Holy See," the Emperor warned, "Europe . . . would not allow the accomplishment of an event which would throw such great trouble on the Catholic World."[2] Neither the Pope nor his Secretary of State was reassured by these vague words. They knew that the ardor and audacity of nationalists was not curbed by the Emperor's veiled threats and that their determination to acquire Rome remained. The day that General Montebello and his officers took leave of the Holy Father, Eugenie, in Paris, observed a day of mourning.[3]

145

The Italian government considered Papal Rome a perilous thorn in its side. Its walls sheltered the head of the Catholic Church, who steadfastly refused to recognize the new Kingdom, calling its validity and viability into question. "Without honesty, without ability, and that which is most important, without God, societies cannot be formed," wrote Pius, predicting that "only chaos results."[4] The Holy Father was seconded and supported by disgruntled aristocrats from Tuscany, Parma, Modena and Lucca and the Court of the King of Naples, which plotted to undermine the authority of the new unitary state in the South. Pius feared that the revolutionaries would try to enter Rome, but was determined to die rather than be implicated in his ruin by negotiating with the enemy.[5] For the moment the spectre of invasion did not materialize. The French withdrawal was followed neither by violence in Rome nor by any attempt on the part of the Pope to abandon his capital as in 1848. Antonelli remained permanently in Rome, no matter what the season.[6] His private life was consumed by his public service. Antonelli, like Cavour, was married to his office, and if the life of the "Piedmontese Machiavelli" formed a chapter in the history of the *Risorgimento,* that of his opponent forms one, if not several, in the annals of the counter-*Risorgimento*. The Rome Antonelli served remained expectant, if quiet, in a lull before a storm.

Early in 1867 the trouble that Antonelli foresaw and feared began to brew. The Italian government, humiliated by the defeats of Lissa and Custozza in the 1867 war against Austria, won only by Prussian arms, sought solace in the acquisition of Rome. In light of their commitment to the September Convention, the Italians could not act openly and directly. Not surprisingly, Victor Emmanuel turned to his confidant Urbano Rattazzi, to form a government, and this, in turn, encouraged Garibaldi to initiate another move against Rome. Despite the warnings of the French, the General openly recruited men for his campaign to "Reedeem Italy or die." The Italian authorities showed themselves both unwilling and unable to protect the patrimony of St. Peter as provided by the terms of the September Convention. Under pressure from Paris, Garibaldi was finally arrested by the Italian authorities on September 24 at Sanalunga, close to the border of the Papal States, and returned to his home on the island of Caprera, treated more like a hero than a revolutionary and conspirator. Rome soon had more cause for complaint.

In mid October Garibaldi easily eluded the royal ships that were to have kept him on Caprera, and rejoined his volunteers, who had already crossed the Italian border into the Papal States. Antonelli grumbled that if the Rattazzi government did not openly assist the invading forces which threatened the Holy City, it encouraged them.[7] Napoleon shared the Cardinal's assessment. Victor Emmanuel's belated pronouncement of his adherence to the September Convention and disavowal of the Garibaldini fooled neither Antonelli nor Napoleon.[8] The Emperor, embarrassed by Antonelli's complaints, and convinced that the Italians were not fulfilling their commitment to protect Rome, abandoned the Convention and returned his troops to what remained of the Papal States. On October 30, a new French expeditionary force under General Failly landed at Civita Vecchia.[9] "Romans! The Emperor Napoleon once more sends an Expeditionary Force to Rome to protect the Holy Father and the Pontifical throne against armed attacks of revolutionary bands," read the proclamation of the Commander-in-Chief. "You know us well. We come, as before, to fulfill a purely moral and disinterested mission."[10] To the pawky Cardinal it all seemed like a pre-arranged comedy, whose consequences he had predicted.[11]

On November 3, 1867, Garibaldi was defeated by a Franco-Papal military force at Mentana on the outskirts of Rome. Despite the heroism of the General and his followers, they were outnumbered and outgunned. The Garibaldini were some four thousand strong, while the Pontifical Zouaves and French had twice their number. Furthermore the volunteers, with their muzzle loading muskets or rifles, were easy targets for the French with their new breech loading rifle, which fired twelve times a minute and could be loaded lying down.[12] The *chassepots* took their toll. Gregorovius commented that it was easier for Garibaldi to overturn the rotten Kingdom of Naples than to defeat the Papal army, in which there had not been one single case of desertion.[13] Among the Pope's troops, devotion rather than desertion was the rule. Still, Garibaldi neither lost heart nor abandoned his hope of seeing Rome liberated from the clutches of the "Papal monstrosity."[14] Antonelli hindered his efforts.

Rome's victory flowed from the Cardinal's diplomacy which enjoyed another success when the new French Minister of State, Eugene Rouher, declared in the Chamber on December 5, 1867, that the Emperor would maintain the Papacy in full posession of its present dominion. At home, too, Antonelli's government proved successful, for Garibaldi's call for a general uprising among the Romans had gone unanswered.

The Cardinal remained vigilant, and following Mentana, had
to confront other dangers. At the Pope's behest, Antonelli resolutely denounced the Austrian marriage and education laws, and
Franz Josef's violation of the concordat. Asserting that the Holy
See respected the right of every sovereign to adopt the institutions
and the form of government that he found most convenient for the
welfare of his subjects, Antonelli admonished that it always had,
and would always, condemn those principles that were in opposition to the maxims of the Church.[15] Vienna, as well as Paris, created problems for the Holy See.

On November 8, 1867, Napoleon suggested the calling of an
international conference to resolve the troublesome question of the
temporal power. The Pope and his Secretary of State proved unwilling to entrust this sensitive mission to a congress, in which the
non-Catholic powers played a prominent part. On the other hand,
Antonelli recognized it was dangerous to reject outright the Emperor's proposal, lest he withdraw the troops that kept the Italians
out of Rome. The Cardinal sought to placate Napoleon by accepting the conference in principle, but posing so many conditions, including the restoration of the provinces already lost by the Holy
See, as to render its implementation impossible.[16]

Antonelli's diplomacy, which salvaged what remained of the
Papal States, pleased the Pope.[17] It depressed others, including
the unofficial English representative in Rome, who decried that
French arms had saved the Papal dominions from annexation to
Italy. To make matters worse in English eyes, the Cardinal's "le-
gions" in France were seen to extract additional concessions.

> The next achievement of the clerical party was to compel M. Rou-
> her to declare, in the name of the Emperor's government, that the
> French protectorate of Rome would 'never' cease. Having thus se-
> cured the existence of the temporal power, the influence of the
> clergy was successfully exerted all over the Catholic world to com-
> mand unlimited supply of Catholic crusaders for the Papal army,
> and an unlimited supply of Peter's Pence for the Papal
> Exchequer . . .[18]

The prospects for a change in the status quo were slight. Following the failure to rouse Rome to revolution, the city wafted
back to its old routine and seemed unchanged to Henry Wads-
worth Longfellow, who revisited after a lapse of forty years. When
he mentioned this observation to Antonelli, the Cardinal replied,
"Yes, thank God."[19] Antonelli recognized what his sovereign did

not like to acknowledge, that the French presence in the capital prevented the Italian seizure of the Holy City. How long the French would remain this time was uncertain. The occupation of Rome was motivated by French fears and interests. "I indulge in no illusions on the subject, the Emperor does not hold Rome and protect the Pope for our sake *(pour nos beaux yeux)* or because he has the interests of religion at heart," Antonelli confided. "No, he holds Rome because its serves his own personal and dynastic interests to do so . . ."[20]

Antonelli's analysis of French interests and policy was accurate for the early half of the decade, but less so for the second half, when France was confronted with the spectre of Prussian expansion and sought allies. The commitment to protect Rome frustrated his scheme to conclude a triple alliance of France, Austria, and Italy to prevent German unification. Indeed, following Mentana, the French representative in Rome, the Count de Sartiges, received an ominous engraving of Germany in the act of advancing towards France. The caption read: "The first day of the New Year, 1868: to His Majesty Napoleon III, in the name of the patriots massacred in Rome and at Mentana."[21]

Victor Emmanuel also indicated his displeasure with the French presence in Rome, revealing that the evacuation of the city was the *sine qua non* for his government's participation in the alliance which would have brought the French, Austrian and Italian support. "I cannot undertake any formal engagement in the matter until the September Convention, as relates to the state of the Holy See, shall have been once more on both sides fully and completely carried out," Victor Emmanuel wrote Napoleon.[22] The Emperor knew that the formation of the anti-Prussian alliance hinged upon the evacuation of Rome, but could not extricate himself before the opening of the Vatican Council.

As early as the secret consistory of December 6, 1864, Pius had revealed his determination to convoke an ecumenical council. Antonelli had not been present on that occasion, suffering from the gout which periodically plagued him. Nonetheless, he was privy to his sovereign's intentions. The idea of calling a council gained momentum, and in June, 1867, this was announced in the bull *Aeterni Patris,* with the council formally opening December 8, 1869. There had not been a council of the whole Church since Trent (1545–1563).

Cardinal Antonelli, involved in the technical and economic preparations for the gathering, was also charged with the respon-

sibility of quieting the fears that the calling of the council had provoked among the powers, and the alarm generated by the talk of a
proclamation of papal infallibility. On the issue of infallibility the
Cardinal saw no need for such a proclamation, believing that a
definition by acclamation would not be in keeping with councilliar
tradition.[23] He dismissed as misinformed the newspaper accounts
which claimed that the bishops would discuss the *ex cathedra* infallibility of the Pope. "The *ex cathedra* infallibility of the Pope has
ever been an article of faith with every true Catholic," Antonelli
informed Russell, "and therefore admits of no discussion."[24] His
conspicuous lack of enthusiasm for a public pronouncement of the
dogma was not based on any conviction that it was theologically in
error, but flowed from the fact that he considered a proclamation
unnecessary and inopportune.

Insofar as the convoking of the Council rendered embarrassing and difficult a French withdrawal, it met the approval of Antonelli. However, he feared the adverse political consequences.[25]
From Florence he received word of the concerns of the Italian
government.[26] There was also alarm in Paris, especially when
word began to circulate that one of the aims of the fathers was a
pronouncement on papal infallibility. Later, in January 1870 a liberal cabinet presided over by Emile Ollivier assumed power with
Count Napoleon Daru, who was known to be hostile to the Council, holding the post of Minister of Foreign Affairs. The news from
Germany was equally distressing, with the Nuncio in Munich
warning that there was the prospect of a schism if the Council
should define infallibility.[27]

The suspicion of the monarchs of Europe was compounded by
their failure to receive invitations to the council. Since this represented a departure from custom, Antonelli was pressed for an explanation. The Cardinal responded that since one of the monarchs
had been excommunicated and could not be invited (an obvious
reference to Victor Emmanuel), the Pope believed it best not to
send invitations to any of them.[28] Nonetheless, Antonelli informed
the princes that they could send a representative if they chose, so
long as they announced their intention three months before the
assembling of the body. Both he and his sovereign were relieved
when the French Emperor decided not to send a plenipotentiary,
and the other Catholic powers followed suit. Initially Antonelli
sought to minimize the impact and importance of the Council, dis-
avowing the columns of the *Civiltà Cattolica* that hinted there
might be a definition of Papal infallibility, and suggesting that the

fear had been founded on phantoms.[29] Antonelli later proved more forthright, explaining to the Ambassador of Portugal that since the Catholic governments had all withdrawn their political and religious protection from the Holy See, Rome perforce had to rely upon its own actions and resources.[30]

The Council, which held its first solemn session on December 8, 1869, preoccupied the Cardinal who received the bishops and other Church fathers as early as eight in the morning, and hosted a number of dinners in their honor.[31] He, like others, worried that the Council might drag on for years.[32] He was particularly distressed by the long and repetitive speeches, noting that if they continued, the Council would last at least a decade. Nonetheless, he opposed closure, arguing that any limitation of discussion would lead to the charge that the Council's freedom of action had been curtailed.[33] The Cardinal Secretary of State sought to avoid all acrimony, and to limit as far as possible the hostility engendered by the Council.

First and foremost, Antonelli sought to allay the fears of the various statesmen that the schemata under consideration in Rome might impinge upon the domain of the civil power. He explained that the principles under consideration were not new, and the Council was simply expressing them in a more concise and accessible format.[34]

Although Antonelli defended the actions of the Pope and the Church fathers, he remained aloof from the partisans of Papal infallibility, and even more so from those who championed the rights of the Church against the temporal power. Thus the Cardinal Secretary of State did not second the intolerance of Cardinal Henry Edward Manning, head of the infallibilist majority, who sought to exclude from the Commission on Faith all those who opposed infallibility, arguing that heretics had to be condemned, not followed.[35] Cardinal Bonnechose noted that Antonelli did not want new dogmas but sought a declaration interpreting the Council of Florence, with a canon against Jansenism and extreme Gallicanism. His plan did not please the balky Pius, who complained that the draft Antonelli had apparently approved made no mention of the words dogma or infallibility.

Pius assumed a partisan stance on the issue of infallibility. Antonelli, on the other hand, believed that as Secretary of State, his task was to remain equidistant from the majority and minority into which the Council had early divided.[36] Keeping his distance from the prevailing party, he surrounded himself with prelates not in this ruling faction. While accepting the truth of the dogma of Papal infallibility, he foresaw that its porclamation would wreak dreadful havoc, fearing its publication would unleash the turmoil and tribulations which had marked the opening of the Pontificate. Since he was not esteemed as a theologian, nor consulted on questions of doctrine, he had little say in the matter. The Cardinal's role remained restricted to the political and diplomatic realm where he was expected to ward off the inevitable political complications. He did so with unflinching skill.[37] The Cardinal unequivocally stated that the Papal government, over which he presided, had not countenanced the definition of infallibility, adding that the Bishops could not be prevented from taking it into consideration.[38]

A number of politicians and diplomats had spread the rumor that the Pope claimed the right to depose sovereigns, arousing fear and provoking increased opposition to infallibility.[39] The Cardinal faced considerable pressure from the Vienna government, which sought to use his influence to denounce the definition.[40] The French foreign minister likewise sought to influence Antonelli by making it clear that the policy of the Holy See rendered difficult the retention of French troops in the Eternal City.[41]

Non-Catholic countries were also concerned. In Prussia Bismarck was disturbed by the events in Rome, although he instructed his representative to the Holy See, Baron von Arnim, to move cautiously. Above all, the Prussian chancellor cautioned that though he was to give his moral support to the bishops who were in a minority and opposed infallibility, the opposition should appear to come from within the Church rather than from the various states.[42] This opposition to infallibility, both veiled and open, kept the Cardinal so busy that he found it difficult, if not impossible, to write to his brothers with whom he ordinarily remained in close and cordial contact.[43] More than ever his public service overwhelmed and dominated his private life.

Odo Russell wrote home that Monsignor Lavigerie, Archbishop of Algiers, warned Antonelli that Napoleon was determined to withdraw his troops from Rome if the Council proclaimed the personal infallibility of the Pope. The Cardinal Secretary of State was grieved by the message.[44] In Rome the story circulated that Antonelli, uneasy about the unfortunate political repercussions of the definition of infallibility, led a group of Cardinals to implore the Pope to withdraw it from the agenda. Supposedly Pius responded, "I have the Blessed Virgin on my side; I will go ahead."[45]

It is an unlikely story. Antonelli may have lamented the political consequences of the proclamation, but he knew that the Pope was committed to it, and saw it as a religious rather than a political move. Under these circumstances the Cardinal did not dare to intervene and place politics above religion.[46] The Cardinal consistently accepted Pio Nono's subordination of the political to the spiritual order; it was this acceptance, among other things, which inspired the Pope's confidence in him.

"Earlier, before becoming Pope, I believed in infallibility," Pius exclaimed, "now, however, I feel it."[47] His view was bound to carry great weight not only because of his office, but also because of his influence with the bishops, most of whom had been consecrated during Pio Nono's long pontificate. "The question of majorities was one that had been mis-represented by the Press, and bishops were quite right to say that majorities could not decide questions of faith in the Council, because no decision of a Council was binding on the conscience of the faithful until it had the sanction of the Pope," Antonelli explained to the Protestant Russell.[48]

Aware of the Pope's determination to have the doctrine of infallibility proclaimed, his Secretary of State did not believe it could be prevented. The most that the Cardinal could do was to allay the fears of the French and Austrians concerning its effects, informing them that the definition of infallibility would alter neither the relations between the rights of the state vis-a-vis the Church nor the relations between the bishops and the Pope.[49] Likewise he informed the Austrian Ambassador that the definition would deal only with religious questions and matters of faith, and would not encroach upon the political realm.[50]

In response to the proposition that the decisions of the Council might influence the future of the French garrison in Rome, Antonelli retorted that the presence of French troops there depended on treaty engagements between France and Italy to which the Holy See was not a party. The French apparently saw things otherwise. On April 15, 1870, the French Ambassador to the Holy See, the Marquis de Banneville, presented the memorandum of Count Daru, which asked the Pope and the Council to set aside everything in the schema *De Ecclesia*, which might have disastrous consequences for the legal and social order and the European state system. Russell, in Rome, did not believe that this note would fulfill its purpose and advised his government not to support it. Nonetheless, on April 12, he verbally advised Antonelli that his government shared the apprehension of the French government that the schema *De Ecclesia* might create conflict between the civil and religious powers.[51]

Antonelli insisted that the apprehensions of the French government were without foundation, arguing that the Church restrained from interference in matters relating to the constitutive principles of government, their civic institutions, and the political rights of its citizens. Before the Daru memorandum was transmitted to the Pope, word reached the Cardinal that Daru had resigned and Ollivier had assumed his place. The role of the memorandum in Daru's replacement is still being debated, but Antonelli believed that Daru had been ill advised in interfering with the Council.[52] His sources led Antonelli to conclude that most Frenchmen did not appreciate their government's intervention in Church matters and forced Daru's resignation. The Secretary of State believed that as a consequence there would be no further interference with the Council from the French government. A smiling Cardinal informed Russell of this development. The powers had no cause for concern; Antonelli reassured them that the proposals in *De Ecclesia* did not threaten the authority of the bishops or the civil power.[53]

Although Antonelli frustrated the attempts of the French and the other powers to interfere with the work of the Council in general, and the proclamation of infallibility in particular, in his own quiet way the Secretary of State expressed his opposition to the proclamation. On July 13, when the Congregation secretly voted on the *schema* of infallibility proposed by the doctrinal commission, the Cardinal chose not to attend the session and vote. Having privately made his point, on July 18 he attended the public session and voted in favor of infallibility. He minimized the significance of that vote, arguing that the Council had merely confirmed what existed rather than introducing anything new.[54]

The outbreak of the Franco-Prussian War on July 18, the day the Council approved the definition of Papal infallibility, more than anything else diverted the attention of the French government from the issue. Graver problems now confronted both Paris and Rome. On July 20, the fathers of the Council were authorized to return to their Sees. Antonelli worried about the impact of the war upon the temporal power and the Papacy. He had cause for concern.

Chapter Thirteen

The Fall of Rome and After

Antonelli feared new disasters for Papal Rome from the moment that France declared war on Prussia and the North German Confederation on July 18, 1870. The Vatican's attempted mediation proved fruitless. The Cardinal's worst anxieties materialized as France suffered a number of catastrophic defeats. Antonelli realized that the fortune of the Second Empire and the temporal power were inextricably tied. He placed little trust in the statement made by Costantino Nigra in Paris on July 22, that the Kingdom of Italy would in no manner take advantage of France's involvement in the war to create embarrassment for Napoleon as regards the Roman Question. The Secretary of State suspected that these words were prompted by the Italian desire to reassure, not to say lull, the French regarding the consequences of their departure from the Eternal City, which was currently being debated in the French capital.[1] The reassurance proved useful to the Italians, for on July 26 the decision was reached in Paris to withdraw the French garrison from Rome.

At the end of July 1870, the French formally informed Antonelli of their resolution to depart, and the Cardinal Secretary of State, in turn, apprised the Pope. "Now is the time for prayer," Pius responded calmly, "but everything will end well."[2] The afternoon of July 30, when the French commander Dumont bade Antonelli farewell, he sought to inspire the Cardinal with confidence by referring to the good faith of the cabinet in Florence and listed numerous reasons why he expected the Italians to honor the September Convention. "All this is very fine," Antonelli responded, "but I must tell you there are three men, and three men in a good position to judge of the situation, who do not share in the confidence with which you wish to inspire me, the first is yourself, the second Victor Emmanuel, the third myself!"[3]

The French government officially notified the Florence government that in withdrawing from Rome, it was reverting to the September Convention, trusting that the Italian State would honor it and guarantee the Pope his possession of Rome as stipulated. The Italians promised to do so, but Rome placed little confidence in their guarantees. Antonelli realized that with the French troops gone, Paris could exercise precious little restraint upon the Italians.[4] Could the wolves be expected to guard the sheep? At the end of July the Pope called a meeting of his most trusted Cardinals to discuss the critical situation precipitated by the Franco-Prussian War, and the real prospect of further Piedmontese aggression.

During the course of this and subsequent meetings, the Secretary of State, whose image abroad always reflected the Pope's intransigence, assumed a moderate stance and advised political realism. Thus Antonelli did not support the posture of those who advised the Pope to flee abroad. The Cardinal was even more insistent than he had been in 1865 that the Pope not abandon the capital. In the end his counsel prevailed over that of the General of the Jesuits. However, Pius was not prepared to accept his Minister's suggestion that contact with the Italians was the only means of redress.[5]

The urgency of the situation was aggravated by the fact that, on August 5, French forces abandoned the Holy City, and shortly thereafter these troops left Civita Vecchia on the French ship Cayenne, removing the Papacy's last protective wall. Rumors circulated that the Pope had been given assurances that Bismarck would protect Papal Rome, and Pius supposedly had exclaimed in appreciation, "Prussia will be our salvation." This, however, was born of wishful thinking, for the Pope had not requested, nor had Prussia offered, any assistance.[6] Defense of the rump Papal State rested on the two brigades of Pontifical forces, which numbered some 13,000, under the command of General Hermann Kanzler.[7] They were clearly unable to deal with the Italian force of 60,000 poised on the frontier, prepared to overrun Rome.[8]

Events conspired to hasten the Italian march to Rome. On August 4 the French suffered a disastrous defeat at Weizenburg, followed by their rout at Worth two days later. The French, fighting for survival, clearly had matters other than the Roman Question on their mind. This encouraged the Italian Foreign Minister, Emilio Visconti-Venosta, to prepare the way for Italian action vis-a-vis Rome. He sent a circular note to the powers citing the dangerous situation in the Holy City that called for remedy. Actually the Italians represented the sole threat to the tranquility of Rome.

The French defeat at Sedan, and the capture of the Emperor on September 2, 1870, led to the fall of the Empire and the proclamation of a provisional Republic in France, and at the same time precipitated the Italian operation against the Eternal City. "I am charged to tell you that my government can no longer maintain the status quo as regards Rome," the Italian Ambassador in Paris informed Jules Favre, of the new provisional government. "Count Ponza di San Martino is to be sent to his Holiness to make an amicable arrangement. If these propositions fall through we shall be under the necessity of occupying Rome."[9] The French posed no obstacle to the Italian action, nor did Prussia, England, Austria-Hungary, or Spain.

Victor Emmanuel's envoy, Count Gustavo Ponza di San Martino, left for Rome on a special train the afternoon of September 9, 1870, and met with Cardinal Antonelli that same evening. The Count, who had anticipated an icy reception, was surprised by the courtesy extended to him by the Secretary of State, who quietly exposed the hypocrisy of the Italian position.[10] San Martino informed the Cardinal that Italian troops had already received orders to enter the Pope's territory, arguing that the Italian public demanded that chaos be averted in Rome, and if the King did not comply, he would be overturned by a "red republic." Antonelli was not persuaded by the envoy's logic, responding that the Italian action was a pure and simple aggression, which could not be justified on the grounds of averting revolution, for Rome was perfectly tranquil.[11] His assessment was accurate. Nor was Antonelli reassured by the Count's affirmation that his mission was above all designed to guarantee the independence of the Holy See by the Italian government. The only redeeming fact, retorted the Cardinal, was that the Italian government recognized the need for independence for the Holy Father. To San Martino's rejoinder that his government meant spiritual liberty, Antonelli answered that, too, was necessary for the Papacy to fulfill its mission.[12]

Although the Cardinal Secretary of State had reservations about Italian intentions, he pragmatically inquired about the terms of its government's guarantees. He revealed that he wanted to place his trust in San Martino's loyalty and that of the Italians, and asked in whose name the promises were being made. The Secretary of State was assured that these promises and guarantees were put forward on behalf of the government of the King. At this juncture Antonelli questioned the permanence, and therefore the security, of such an arrangement, expressing the reservation that the Papacy would adhere to until 1929. The Cardinal reminded the Count that the Italian government was constitutional, so the Ministry presently in power might tomorrow be replaced by one whose views were diametrically opposed. One government could not bind its successor, so the so-called guarantees depended on the whim and will of future regimes. Furthermore, Antonelli continued, there was the Parliament which claimed the right of revision and approval, and might even reject the terms transmitted to the Holy See. Therefore, how could San Martino assure that the Parliament or whatever ministry followed the present one, would sanction and preserve in its entirety any convention or agreement concluded between the parties? In fine, Antonelli did not see how any simple agreement could be made with the Italian government that would assure the independence of the Holy See.[13]

The Pope assumed the same stance as his Secretary of State, but proved less patient and diplomatic in listening to the King's envoy. Count Ponza di San Martino reported that he found the Pope "calm and serene but absolutely and inflexibly resolved not to make any accommodation whatsoever."[14] Pius was outraged by the King's letter whose message claimed it was written with the affection of a son, the faith of a Catholic, and the loyalty of a King. "Nice words, but ugly deeds," the Pope muttered as he read the thinly disguised ultimatum. The Pope did not consider it worthy of an affectionate son who glorifies in the profession of the Catholic faith.[15] Enclosed with the King's letter of September 8 was the draft of an agreement, which San Martino had already discussed with Antonelli, proposing a solution to the Roman Question of the basis of its ten articles.

The provisions of the draft agreement provided:

1. the Pontiff would preserve the dignity and inviolability as well as all the other prerogatives of sovereignty;

2. the Leonine City, that part of Rome, including the Vatican, the Castel Sant´ Angelo, and the borgo, which Pope Leo IV (847–855) surrounded with a defensive wall after the Saracen raid of 846, would remain under the full jurisdiction of the Pontiff;

3. the Italian government would guarantee the full liberty of communication of the Pontiff with foreign powers, the dip-

lomatic immunity of its nuncios and legates towards foreign powers, and representatives attached to the Holy See;

4. the Italian government would preserve all the institutions, ecclesiastical entities, and their administration presently in Rome, but would not recognize their civil and penal jurisdiction;

5. the Italian government would not interfere in the internal affairs of ecclesiastical institutes in Rome;

6. the bishops and parish priests of the entire realm would be free of all government interference in their ministry;

7. Victor Emmanuel would renounce to the Church all rights of royal patronage upon ecclesiastical benefices in the city of Rome;

8. the Italian government would provide for the Holy See, by fixed endowment to the Pontiff and the Sacred College, a sum not less than that assigned them by the budget of the Pontifical State;

9. the government would preserve the existing rank, stipends, and pensions of civil and military employees of the Pontifical State who are Italian;

10. the present terms are to be considered a bilateral treaty, and would form the object of an accord with the Catholic powers, who wish to adhere to it.[16]

The Holy See rejected the draft proposal citing Antonelli's objections to San Martino that the agreement, while similar to a treaty, was not really a treaty between two equally sovereign entities. Pius dismissed both the projected agreement, and the Italian request to enter his Capital. "If we are unable to prevent the thief from entering," he responded, "let it at least be known that he enters only by means of violence."[17]

On September 11, Antonelli received word that the Italian army, 60,000 strong under General Raffaele Cadorna, had crossed the Papal frontier, and a state of siege was proclaimed in Rome. A deep trench was dug outside the Porta Pia while the gate itself packed with sandbags in anticipation of the onslaught. By September 19 the Italians stood poised outside the capital ready for the entry, which could not be prevented by Kanzler's force of

13,000. Antonelli, wishing to avoid bloodshed, which he feared would only aggravate an already difficult situation, suggested that it would be best to let the "Piedmontese" into the city, finding the Zouaves standing at attention, with their firearms at their feet.[18]

The Cardinal openly and decisively opposed any attempt at resistance. He believed that spilling blood would only arouse the animosity of the invaders, rendering more precarious the position of the Holy See. A part of the College of Cardinals concurred with Antonelli, as did most of the diplomatic corps. Pius disagreed, insisting that the Zouaves should be allowed to defend the walls of the city. Pius was determined to show the entire world that he was the victim of an unwarranted aggression, though he concurred with his Secretary of State that a prolonged and bloody defense, that was bound to fail, would have only unfortunate consequences. His will naturally prevailed. Rome remained in a state of quiet expectancy, with most of its shops closed and its postal and telegraphic communications cut off.[19]

On September 20 at five in the morning, the attack commenced along a line extending from the Porta del Popolo to the Porta San Giovanni. Under fire from heavy artillery, the old walls proved utterly useless, crumbling completely in places. As per Antonelli's arrangements, the diplomatic representatives remained by the Pope's side during the invasion. These numbered seventeen, but only Prussia, Bolivia, the Netherlands, Belgium, Portugal, and Brazil sent their ranking ministers. The Austrian, French, and Spanish ministers were not present. When the Italian forces breached the walls near Porta Pia and Italian soldiers swarmed into the city, Pius ordered a capitulation, indicating that a further defense would be useless. Only Garcia Moreno of Ecuador protested the Italian action.[20]

In the late afternoon of September 20, following the departure of the diplomatic corps, the Cardinal Secretary of State, awaiting the terms of surrender from the Italians, had a long talk with the Pope. He had been unable to stop the enemy from entering and taking Rome, and in the eyes of many had failed the Pontiff and the Church. The Cardinal frankly examined his position in the administration, indicating that Pius should not feel bound by the promise made at Gaeta to retain him permanently as Secretary of State, in light of the changed conditions. Antonelli, who had dedicated his life to the service of the Papal State, recognized that many held him responsible for the loss of the temporal power, which they saw as the culmination of two decades of misrule. Perhaps it would be best, the Cardinal suggested, for the Pope to select a new figure to lead, a man who would not be compromised by past policy and who could develop a new strategy? Some have questioned the sincerity of Antonelli's suggestions in light of the fact that he knew that Pius would find it difficult if not impossible, to renounce the policies he himself had inspired. To dismiss Antonelli would have been tantamount to repudiating his own political conduct as much as the man who executed it, and this the Pope was not prepared to do. Furthermore, Pius required his diplomatic expertise more than ever. Not surprisingly, Pius determined that it would be imprudent to separate himself from his Secretary of State at this critical juncture.[21]

Pio Nono's rejection of Antonelli's tentative resignation was very likely precisely what the Cardinal had anticipated. The Pope insisted that Antonelli remain at his post. In return, the Cardinal offered to follow His Holiness in considering himself a fellow-"prisoner" in the Vatican, until such time as the temporal power should be restored. Antonelli, if not the Pope, knew this was a life sentence; but he recognized that Pius would not budge on the matter. Indeed as early as 1860, when the threat of losing Rome first loomed on the horizon, Pius had embraced the notion of a self imposed imprisonment. "The Pope in Rome could only be sovereign or prisoner: sovereign if independent, prisoner if he was not."[22] In his meeting with the Cardinals, Pius first confirmed Antonelli's position, and then considered the defense of the Vatican compound against possible factious incursions, now that Rome was occupied by the enemy, who had dissolved the Papal forces and thus deprived the Pope of the means of self defense. Pio Nono's dilemma, and indirectly Antonelli's responsibility, was pinpointed by the United States Consul at Rome, David Maitland Armstrong, reporting to the American Secretary of State, Hamilton Fish.[23]

General Kanzler, after consultation with the Pope and his Secretary of State, signed the capitulation drawn up by General Cadorna, the afternoon of September 20, effectively eliminating the longest existing European state. The capitulation, signed at the Villa Albani, provided that the Leonine City should remain in Papal hands. Evidently the Italian government sought to leave the Pope a mini-state, so that his condition would not be perceived as desperate. The subsequent occupation by the Italians had been placed on Antonelli's shoulders. Critics intimated that the Cardinal called in Italian troops because he was less than loyal to the

Pope; others have characterized his action as a Machiavellian maneuver geared to provoke foreign intervention on behalf of the Papacy.[24]

Antonelli's decision to call for an Italian occupation of the Leonine City followed the news that a number of agitators had already burst-in, and posed a potential hazard for the Pope. The Cardinal and the Pope both vividly recalled being besieged in the Quirinal Palace; they were not going to experience the same terror in the Vatican. Since there were no troops to protect the Pope's person, Antonelli, after consultation with Pius, called for Italian intervention the evening of September 20. When the disturbances and agitation failed to materialize, the Secretary of State did not deliver the call for assistance to General Cadorna. However, the following day there were new rumors and threats that a popular demonstration against Pius was imminent. This prompted the drafting of a second note calling for Italian assistance; the latter was signed by the Papal commander Kanzler, rather than Antonelli. "His Holiness entrusts me to inform you that he desires you to take efficient and energetic steps to safeguard the Vatican," Kanzler wrote, "since his troops have been dissolved, he does not have the means to stop the disturbances and disorders under his sovereign residence."[25]

Depressed that his troops had been disarmed, the Papal flag had been lowered at Castel Sant' Angelo, and his army no longer existed, Pius wrote his nephew on September 21, "All is over. Without liberty it is impossible to govern the Church."[26] He likewise lamented to the Cardinals that he could not freely exercise his spiritual powers now that his temporal power had been eliminated.[27] This sentiment was echoed by the Cardinal Secretary of State. "The Church has only right on her side," he told an Italian journalist, "there is no middle ground between respect for and violation of right. If one renounced it in part it would be the same as renouncing it entirely."[28] Reflecting the thought and position of his sovereign, Antonelli occasionally resorted to violent language and claimed that the editors of the Italian press sprang from the pits of hell.[29]

Antonelli was more circumspect in his circular note to the powers protesting the seizure of September 20, 1870:

> Your Excellency is well acquainted with the fact that the violent seizure of the greater part of the States of the Church made in June 1859, and in September of the following year by the Gov-

ernment now installed at Florence. Equally matter of notoriety are the solemn reclamations and protests of the Holy See against that sacrilegious spoliation; reclamations and protests made either by allocutions pronounced in consistory and published in due course, or else by notes addressed in the name of the Sovereign Pontiff or the undersigned Cardinal Secretary of State to the diplomatic body accredited to the Holy See.

The invading Government would assuredly not have failed to complete its sacrilegious spoliation if the French Government well informed as to its ambitious projects, had not arrested them by taking under its protection the City of Rome and the territory still remaining by keeping a garrison there. But, as a consequence of certain compacts entered into between the French Government and that of Florence, compacts by which it was supposed that the conservation and tranquility of the dominions yet left to the Holy See would be secured, the French troops were withdrawn. These Conventions, however, were not respected and in September 1867, some irregular bodies of men, urged forward by secret impulses, threw themselves upon the Pontifical territory with the perverse design of surprising and occupying Rome. Then it was that the French troops returned, and lending a strong-handed succor to our faithful soldiers, who had already fought successfully against the invasion, they achieved on the plains of Mentana the repression of the audacious invaders and caused the complete failure of their iniquitous design.

Subsequently, however, the French Government having withdrawn its troops on the occasion of the declaration of war against Prussia, did not neglect to remind the Government of Florence of the engagement which it had contracted by the Convention specified above, and to obtain from that Government the most formal assurances on the subject. But the fortune of War having been unfavorable to France, the Government of Florence, taking advantage of these reverses to the prejudice of the agreement it had entered into, took the disloyal resolution to send an overpowering army to complete the spoliation of the dominions of the Holy See; although perfect tranquility reigned throughout them in spite of very active instigation made from within and in spite of the spontaneous and continual demonstrations of fidelity, attachment and filial affection to the august person of the Holy Father that were made in all parts, and especially at Rome.

Before perpetrating this last act of terrible injustice, the Count Ponsa di San Martino was sent to Rome as the bearer of a letter written by King Victor Emmanuel to the Holy Father. That letter stated that the Government of Florence, not being able to restrain the ardor of the national aspirations nor the agitation of the "party of action," as it is called found itself forced to occupy Rome and the territory yet remaining annexed to it. Your Excellency can easily imagine the profound grief and indignation which filled the heart of the Holy Father when this startling declaration was made to him. Nevertheless, unshaken in the fulfillment of his agreed duties, and fully trusting in Divine Providence, he resolutely rejected every proposal for accommodation, forasmuch as he is bound to preserve intact his sovereign powers as it was transmitted to him by his predecessors.

In view of this fact, which has been brought to pass under the eyes of all Europe, and by which the most sacred principles of law and especially those of the law of nations, are trampled underfoot, His Holiness has commanded the undersigned Cardinal Secretary of State to remonstrate and protest loudly, and the undersigned does hereby, in the sacred name of His Holiness, remonstrate and protest against the unworthy and sacrilegious spoliation of the dominions of the Holy See, which has lately been brought to pass; and he at the same time declares the King and his Government to be responsible for all the mischiefs that have resulted or shall result to the Holy See, and to the subjects of the Pontifical Power, from that violent and sacrilegious usurpation.

In conclusion, I have the command from His Holiness to declare, and the undersigned does hereby declare in the name of His Holiness, that such usurpation is devoid of all effect, is null and invalid, and that it can never convey any prejudice to the indisputable and lawful rights of dominion and of possession whether of the Holy Father himself or of his successors in perpetuity; and although the exercise of these rights may be forcibly prevented and hindered, yet His Holiness both knows his rights, and intends to conserve them intact, and re-enter at the proper time into their actual possession.

In apprising your Excellency officially, by command of the Holy Father, of the deplorable event that has just taken place, and of the protests and remonstrances which necessarily follow it, in order that your Excellency may be enabled to bring the whole matter to the knowledge of your Government, the undersigned Cardinal Secretary cherishes the persuasion that your Government will be pleased to take into its earnest consideration the interests of the Supreme Head of the Church, now and henceforth placed in such circumstances that he is unable to exercise his spiritual authority with that full liberty and entire independence which are indispensable for it.

Having now carried into effect the commands of the Supreme Pontiff, it only remains that I subscribe myself, etc.

J. Cardinal Antonelli[30]

When Italy made Rome its capital, a palace was needed for the royal residence, and the Italians sought the Quirinale Palace from the Pope. The Pope refused to relinquish it. Cardinal Antonelli tried to prevent its seizure by arguing that the funds for its upkeep came from the Pope's private purse rather than state revenues, but this nicety did not persuade the Italians who insisted on its possession.[31] When Pius was asked for the keys he refused to turn them over. "I'm sure they'll find a way to get in without the keys," he responded, not wishing to implicate himself by indirectly legitimizing the action by any sort of co-operation, "I have nothing more to say."[32] The Italians lived up to his expectations, bursting open the main gates and requisitioning the Palace in preparation for the royal arrival. Early in October the Romans were belatedly asked to sanction the seizure of Rome by voting for union with the constitutional Kingdom of Italy. The resulting vote was overwhelmingly favorable to the Italian cause.[33]

Pius had his Secretary of State transmit another note to the diplomatic community, protesting the actions of the Italians. The Pope instructed Antonelli to alert the courts of Europe that the Italian takeover of Rome deprived him of the right "to exercise his spiritual authority with that full liberty and entire independence which are indispensable to him."[34] With these notes the Cardinal Secretary of State resumed the diplomatic defense he had been waging against the Italians for the past eleven years. Subsequently Antonelli protested the transfer of the Society of Freethinkers to Rome, as well as Victor Emmanuel's visit at the end of December, when the city endured a severe flood. On that occasion, Antonelli transmitted another circular letter to the diplomatic representatives of the Holy See, noting that the visit lasted only thirteen hours and the reception the King received in Rome was colder than had been anticipated.[35]

The Cardinal Secretary of State also protested against the Royal Prince's move into the Quirinal Palace, the irreligious demonstrations and offensive parodies encouraged during carnival festivities, the solemn entry of the King into the capital in July 1871, and the inauguration of the Italian Parliament in the Montecitorio Palace, November, 1871. At the same time Antonelli condemned the abuses of the press and the isolation in which the

Pope was placed, having neither postal nor telegraph contact with the outside world. The last condemnation was not entirely fair for the cutting of communication was not only the fault of the Italian Government. General Cadorna had actually offered the Cardinal the opportunity to set up a post office in the Vatican as well as a telegraph office for his exclusive use. The offer was rejected by Pius, who was determined to demonstrate to the Catholic world his desperate situation. Word spread in Rome that the Pope planned to flee the capital for Corsica. A contemporary cartoon plastered on walls and poles of the metropolis portrayed Antonelli on an ass holding a large umbrella over Pius, who had shrunk to the dimensions of a child, while the Jesuit Carlo Curci pulled the beast by a rope[36] The cartoon was wrong on both accounts. The Cardinal did not overshadow or dominate the Pope; and neither intended to abandon Rome.

On November 1, Pius issued the major excommunication against the invaders of his capital. "We declare before God and the entire Catholic world, " he wrote, "that we find ourselves in such an imprisonment, that we are unable to exercise securely, promptly, and freely our supreme pastoral authority."[37] Relations between the Holy See and Italy went from bad to worse, and there were those who feared that this might prompt the intervention of the Catholic powers to preserve the spiritual independence of the Pontiff. Very likely this is what the Pope and Antonelli intended, and the Cardinal had been seen as the architect of this *politique du pire*. It is possible, though it is unlikely, that the Pope would have made claims about the weakening of his spiritual powers if he did not believe such was the case, no matter what his Secretary of State suggested.

The Italians sought to reassure the powers as well as the Pope by their unilateral guarantee, which was designed to regulate relations between the Kingdom of Italy and the Holy See after Rome's incorporation into Italy. Composed of two parts, the Law of Papal Guarantees defined the prerogatives of the Pope and the Holy See on the one hand, while spelling out the relationship between Church and State on the other. The projected legislation accorded the Pope royal status, assuring him full freedom to exercise his prerogatives as head of the Church, full sovereignty in diplomacy, as well as extraterritoriality for the Vatican and other apostolic palaces. As compensation for the loss of his territories he was to receive annually the sum of 3,222,000 lire free of taxation. As regards relations between Church and State, the *exequatur* and *placet* were abolished, as well as other government mechanisms for controlling the publication and execution of ecclesiastical acts.[38] An attempt was made to implement Cavour's notion of "a free Church in a free State."

The Law of Papal Guarantees proposed to maintain the Pope in a condition of absolute independence as regards all powers, Luigi Corti, the Italian Minister to the United States, assured Hamilton Fish, the American Secretary of State. "Finally this law, by recognizing a diplomatic corps accredited near the Holy Father, as well as the right of sending nuncios to the heads of other governments, leaves intact the high position which public law has recognized as belonging to the Pope, as regards the exercise of his spiritual mission."[39] If the Americans were convinced that the Italian legislation fully protected the Pope's spiritual mission, Pio Nono did not share their confidence, and this was reflected in his Secretary of State's criticism of the law.

Nonetheless, the Italian Government persevered in the hope that the Holy See would accept the Law of Papal Guarantees. Reports were rife that while Antonelli launched a war of words against the Italian spoliation, he maintained relations with the "usurpers" by letter as well as personal contact. In fact, Antonelli had contact with Cadorna, the Italian Commander in Rome, only through an exchange of correspondence, which focused upon the preservation of order under difficult conditions. Indeed the Cardinal made it clear that the Pope would not meet with the Italians under any circumstances in the near future. After 1870 the Pontiff and almost the entire Roman world tied to the Vatican deluded themselves on the possibility of a second intervention of the Catholic powers to rescue the Pope and restore his control of Rome.[40] Antonelli knew better, convinced that the Pope's flight would not provoke intervention. The Cardinal knew that the Catholic powers of 1849 were no longer available. France and Austria had been defeated by Prussia, Naples had been incorporated into Italy, and Spain veered on the brink of anarchy.

Following the fall of Rome, Antonelli joined Pio Nono as a fellow-"prisoner" in the Vatican. The Pope, trusting to providence to provide for his needs and those of the Church, assumed an intransigent stance towards the Kingdom of Italy, refusing to sanction any negotiations. His Secretary of State, less religious and far more practical, recognized that some sort of accommodation, however limited, had to be reached with the "usurpers." There were those who criticized Antonelli's dealing with the enemy, but the Cardinal's efforts assured that the Vatican complex remained in Papal control.[41]

Chapter Fourteen

Last Years: "Prisoner" In The Vatican

Following the Italian seizure of Rome, Antonelli met with Baron Alberto Blanc, the Italian Ambassador, to discuss administrative matters, but would not discuss political issues. The Cardinal, whose astounding flexibility and resiliency was the mark of a fine mind, if not a fixed character, had reason to keep open some channel of communication. During the course of his conversations with Blanc, Antonelli disclosed that a good part of the funds of Peter's Pence had been left in various institutes now controlled by the Italians, and that these monies were the exclusive property of the Apostolic See. He produced receipts for the deposit of these funds amounting to five and a half million lire. In order to placate the Pope and his Minister, the Italian government quietly turned over 4,952,021 lire to the Cardinal. Antonelli accepted this money, which he argued in no way compromised the opposition of the Papacy to Italian actions, nor legitimized the Italian presence in Rome.

In another gesture of goodwill, at the beginning of 1871 the Minister of Finance, Quintino Sella, and the Government decided to relinquish the Palace of the Chancery to the Pope, in the hope that it might incline Pio Nono to accept the Law of Papal Guarantees, then before the Italian Chamber. Meanwhile, the Baron Blanc promised Antonelli that his government was prepared to award the Holy See concessions which no other government had conceded in order to assure its spiritual independence. The Cardinal showed great interest in the project, pledging to bring it immediately to the Pope's attention. Pio Nono did not share his enthusiasm. Antonelli later reported that the Pope was skeptical about the project, citing the instability of Italian ministries and placing little faith in the permanence of any law whose passage they secured.[1] In truth, neither the Pope nor the Cardinal was prepared to com-

promise the independence of the Papacy, which might have occurred as a result of their acceptance of the Law of Guarantees.
While Antonelli sought some accommodation, his Sovereign made
it clear that it could not be at the expense of Papacy, which he
believed would follow a sanctioning of the pending legislation. Indeed the Pope branded it a monument of barbarous ignorance and
a ghastly joke.[2] His opposition was vocal and found expression in a
series of letters and pronouncements in which he repudiated and
condemned the "so-called" Law of Guarantees.[3] Horrified by the
enormity of the crime and the blatant lack of repentance, the Pope
called upon Jesus Christ to have mercy on the "perverted and adulterous" generation that had committed the sacrilegious spoliation.[4]
His verbal infelicity complicated the Cardinal's diplomacy.

Antonelli, who was more measured and moderate in his language, supported Pio Nono's position and was assigned the task of
informing Sella that the Pope would do nothing to prejudice his
inalienable rights.[5] "I am loath to suspect the good intentions of
your King or even of his Ministry," he explained to a member of the
Italian parliament, "but how long are these men likely to remain
in office? Who can answer for their successors?"[6] Always reasonable and understanding of political and practical realities, the
Cardinal recognized that the "Piedmontese" government was
sometimes constrained to do things against its own wishes "to prevent worse things from happening." Nonetheless, he insisted on
the Pope's right and indeed his responsibility to refuse to condone
such actions.[7] Unable to undo what the Italians had accomplished,
the Cardinal could only protest and wait. He hoped God would
provide better days and frequently invoked the intercession of the
blessed Virgin, claiming that he more than anyone else had the
need for her protection.[8] He had little social interaction outside
the corridors of the Vatican.

Pius proved less resigned and restrained in his opposition. He
refused the annuity assigned him under the terms of the Law of
Papal Guarantees, denouncing the attempt to return part of what
the "Piedmontese" had stolen from him. When Sella informed Antonelli that the annual payment of 3,225,000 lire had been set
aside for the Holy See in the Register of the Public Debt, the Cardinal had once again to explain why he could not collect it. He
wrote the Minister of Finance on November 13, 1872:

> Your Excellency's letter of the 12 inst.,No.1526, has had my
> attention, and I do not hesitate in stating to Your Excellency that

the provisions of the law which you mention cannot be accepted by the Holy Father, who issued his judgment upon the law and brought it to the knowledge of the Catholic world with the Encyclical letter of May 15 last year, addressed to the Catholic Episcopate, and with his allocution of October 27 of last year. Your Excellency will readily understand how the Holy Father, after the violent occupation of his state and capital, cannot recognize any certificate issued by those who committed this spoliation. Whatever may be the consequences that may follow upon this fact for his August Person, he will never take any action which may prejudice the unalienable rights of the Holy See, which he has the obligation to preserve intact. He will therefore always prefer to live with the aid of the generous charity of the faithful than to receive under any form whatsoever an allowance from the government to which Your Excellency belongs.

Accordingly, Your Excellency will see that it is impossible for me to delegate any person to withdraw the certificate of income of 3,225,000 lire as a dotation reserved to the Holy See.

I beg to thank Your Excellency for the communication you addressed to me, and I am, with sentiments of esteem,

G. Card. Antonelli[9]

Pio Nono could scorn the offer of Italian financial assistance because his Secretary of State, with the assistance of his brother Filippo, had revised the collection and investment of the monies that flowed from Peter's Pence, making it one of the primary sources of Papal income.[10] In his quest to place the Holy See on a sound financial basis, Antonelli asked Pius to end the division that had hitherto existed between the Cardinal Secretary of State and the Prefect of Sacred Palaces, the first having the various ministries under its jurisdiction including the ministry of finance, the second answering only to the Pope and a commission of Cardinals. Following the occupation of Rome, Antonelli insisted this division no longer was viable, and the function of the prefect of Papal Palaces was placed in the Secretary of State's hands, so he was now responsible for the policy, administration, and finance of the Holy See.[11] Having limited social intercourse and denied even the occasional walks he once relished in the capital, Antonelli willingly assumed new burdens.

In 1872 Pius charged Antonelli with the task of keeping before the eyes of the European powers the deplorable position he endured as a result of the Italian seizure of Rome. In his formal letter to his Secretary of State, he instructed his minister to alert the diplomatic community that the Italian crimes threatened not only the Papacy but the whole of Catholicism. Pius explained that there could not be a reconciliation between the Pontiff and the usurping government, for he could not abandon to the caprice of this unreliable regime his sublime mission of preserving the independence of the Church.[12] He deemed the *Risorgimento* a "moral, civil, and religious oppression."[13] The Pope perceived it within the broader context of the "fierce and obstinate war" that he saw launched upon the Church by her enemies.[14]

The contrast between the language of the Pontiff and his Secretary led to the speculation that the latter did not approve of his Sovereign's speeches, which only antagonized the Italians and rendered Antonelli's task all the more difficult. During the course of 1872 it was rumored in Rome that the Cardinal sought to limit the damage done by Pio Nono by preventing his speeches from appearing in print, asserting that so much talking in the Vatican did not have positive effects abroad. This alleged attempt to silence the Pope supposedly aroused Pius, who in turn grew angry with his Minister and give him a "severe scolding and made . . . to understand that he must keep his place."[15] The story is apocryphal. Antonelli may well have questioned in private the wisdom of Pio Nono speaking out in such strong terms, but he did not issue orders to the clerical journals to ignore the Pontiff's speeches. Furthermore, the journals would have followed the Pope's directives rather than those of his Minister. At any rate, such orders were never given and the so-called breach between Antonelli and Pius was imaginary.

The Pope and his Secretary of State were united in protesting the seizure of Rome and the loss of the temporal power. "The Church alone has right on her side," the Cardinal posited, parroting the argument of his sovereign. "Between respect for and violation of right there is no middle path."[16] Nevertheless, the points each used in their denunciations tended to differ in emphasis. The Pope saw the seizure as an attack upon the Church and religion and did not hesitate to claim that the disasters experienced by the Italians in 1872 and 1873 were punishments inflicted by God upon the people for the sins and transgressions of their government. He therefore catalogued the disasters that struck the peninsula since the breach of Porta Pia: the overflowing of the Tiber, the volcanic eruptions in southern Italy, and the spread of disease, among others, arguing that perhaps a just God had taken these lives to spare them the ills of moral corruption.[17] Antonelli's contentions were by contrast political and diplomatic as he defended the legitimacy of the Pope's temporal power and cited the violation of international law. In this manner the Cardinal kept the Roman Question alive, affirming that the Papacy would not accept the fait accompli until its status was clarified and its independence fully secured. The positions of the Pope and the Secretary of State were not contradictory but complementary, with the first appealing to the faithful and the Catholic powers while the latter focused on the diplomatic community and international law.

Although Antonelli no longer bore the burdens of governing a state, he had little time for leisure, for his duties and responsibilities remained onerous to the point that he found little time to write to his family, to which he remained closely attached.[18] Younger than the Holy Father, and only in his sixties, the work load and worries imposed on his shoulders took a toll on his health. Little was known about Antonelli's maladies because the Secretary of State was taciturn and stoic, and kept health problems even from members of his family. Those about him were not so quiet, and there were those in the Vatican who did not wish him well.

During the course of 1874 there were frequent reports of his physical difficulties which temporarily incapacitated him. Antonelli endured crippling attacks of gout which were accompanied by intense pain and severe inflammation. Nonetheless the Cardinal never allowed his illness to long interfere with his work, which increasingly served as his sole diversion from the constant pain. In January, and again in June, of that year, the press indicated that Antonelli was seriously ill with gout, stories that the Vatican denied.[19] Despite these denials, eyewitnesses confirmed that the Cardinal had recurring attacks of gout which made his life difficult, particularly during the steamy summer months. Antonelli responded by simply withdrawing further from any social intercourse, spending most of his time in his apartments working. Always aloof about his private affairs, the Cardinal was more than ever a shadowy figure behind the walls of the Vatican.

Despite some loss of vigor, the Cardinal did not become dispirited, finding both meaning and mission in his service to the Pope. He joined Pius in decrying the plight of the Papacy and in demanding redress. The Pope set the tone and his Minister followed. Pio Nono would not hear of any accommodation with the "enemy." To the many requests from Italians who sought guidance on whether it was proper to sit in the Italian Chamber of Deputies, the Pope's response was an unequivocal no. An angry Pope observed that the selection of deputies was not really free, but even if elections were honest, there remained the obstacle of the oath required of every deputy. It committed deputies to swear to the observance, the safeguarding, and the maintenance of the laws of the state, and thus Pius concluded they had to sanction the spoliation of the Church, the anti-Catholic teaching, and the numerous outrages perpetrated against religion.[20] The Pontiff made it clear that he could not even approve of Catholics going to the polls to vote for such a sacrilegious legislative assembly.[21] Antonelli concurred, insofar as it was another means for the Holy See to call into question the legitimacy of the Italian Kingdom's absorption of Rome. Both men encouraged Italian Catholics to participate in politics on the local level and involve themselves in the provincial administration, while strenuously opposing participation on the national plane.

The bitter struggle between the papacy and Italy perforce influenced the relations of the Holy See with the other powers, particularly the Catholic ones. This is apparent in the case of Spain, where the removal of Queen Isabella II displeased Pius. Pius' concern was increased when Amadeus of Savoy, Duke of Aosta, son of Victor Emmanuel II, was placed upon the Spanish throne. Pio Nono's opposition emboldened the Carlists and contributed to the break in relations between the Holy See and Spain, and the eventual abdication of Amadeus in the face of Papal hostility.[22] It also explains Antonelli's support of Don Carlos, darling of the clericals, whom the Secretary of State deemed the rightful sovereign.[23]

The last years of Antonelli and Pius IX were further embittered by the outbreak of the *Kulturkampf* in Prussia and Germany, and the failure of Republican France to champion the rights of the Papacy. Adolph Thiers explained his position to a militant French Catholic who deplored the plight of the Pope.

> My opinion is not changed. I am not the author of the policy which has made policy the unity of Italy, and with the unity of Italy that of Germany. I have thought in the past, and I still think, that France has a great moral and political interest in the protection of Catholics, just as Great Britain everywhere protects the Protestants and Russia the members of the Orthodox church. But the physiognomy of Europe is changed, all the Catholic powers saw the entrance of the King of Italy in Rome, but I cannot remain isolated, separating myself from Italy, and I cannot compromise our foreign policy. While recommending to the Italians the *menag-*

ements due to the Holy See, I cannot change the relations of France with the Italian monarchy. Visconti-Venosta, a wise man who understands the dignity of others, *parce qu'il en a beaucoup lui-meme,* has felt that France had a special position at this time . . . All that we can do to insure a bearable position for Pius, with the respect due to his personal virtues and to the Holy See, will be done by us; but we shall succeed more easily through the influence of friendly relations with Italy than with inopportune threats, which would constitute a double error against the interests of France.[24]

The Pope found the French "indifference" to the plight of the Church deplorable in the face of the hostility of the *Risorgimento* and the *Kulturkampf's* attempt to subordinate Catholicism to state regimentation. While Antonelli sought to avoid a conflict with Bismarck's Germany, his sovereign remained determined to frustrate all attempts to destroy the Church and undermine religion. Bismarck, for his part, had his own fears and paranoia. Thus despite the Cardinal's attempts at mediation, a clash was almost inevitable.

The appearance of the German Center Party in the new Empire distressed the Iron Chancellor, who claimed that this party sought a restoration of the temporal power and proved more sensitive to the moods of the Vatican than the needs of Berlin. Furthermore, the architect of German unity resented Pio Nono's refusal to influence the Center Party, discounting his claim that the Pope did not involve himself in the affairs of a state when Church interests were not involved.[25] The Imperial Chancellor, perhaps hoping to compromise the Center Party or at least outskirt it, named Cardinal Gustav zu Hohenlohe as the representative of the German Empire to the Holy See. The scheme did not work, for Pius opposed the appointment of the Cardinal, who had been a thorn in his side during the Vatican Council, and had been receptive to the anti-infallibilist views of Johan Josepf Ignaz von Dollinger, who had inspired the Old Catholic movement.[26] Following the presentation of his name, Antonelli laconically responded that considering the present relations between the Holy See and Germany, the Vatican could not permit a cardinal to occupy so delicate and important a post. A few days later he explained to Count Gustav von Kalnoky, the Austrian Minister plenipotentiary, who was a conservative and confirmed clerical, that Prussia, almost entirely a Protestant power, could not have its policies represented by a cardinal of the Church.[27] Bismarck, despairing of the "fanaticism" of Pius, hoped to convince Antonelli of the need for compromise. The Chancellor appreciated that, at the beginning of the conflict, the Cardinal Secretary of state, anxious not to alienate the most important power on the continent, criticized the actions of the Catholic Center.[28] The Secretary of State was also willing to listen to what the Imperial Chancellor had to say through his representative Count Karl von Tauffkirchen, the Bavarian who had succeeded Count Harry von Arnim as Minister to the Vatican.

In response to Bismarck's request that the Pope moderate the Center's opposition to the policies of the German Chancellor, Antonelli, always the diplomat, gave the impression that something might be done by uttering a few, well-chosen statements. Clearly the Cardinal sought to avoid embittering Church-State relations in Germany and antagonizing the Empire. However following the visit of Bishop von Ketteler to Rome, and his explanation of the position of the Center, the Pope professed that he would support rather than silence the Party.

Once Pio Nono revealed his determination to uphold the Center Party, regardless of the consequences, Antonelli, perforce, had to follow suit. Subsequently, the Cardinal issued a statement of support for the Party, assuring it the full moral backing of the Holy See in the defense of rights and religion.[29] During the course of the attack upon the position of the Church in the Empire and Prussia, Antonelli assumed the defense of the rights of the Holy See, relying on the major authorities, political and theological, in drafting his responses. Still, Bismarck found Antonelli far more understanding and accommodating than his master, if less powerful. The German Chancellor hoped to find another Antonelli who was intelligent enough to meet the secular power halfway in peace.[30]

The Cardinal Secretary of State, who had devoted himself to the cause of the Papacy, found less and less time for personal matters. His socialization was now restricted to a limited clerical circle and an occasional correspondence with family members. Burdened with the cares of diplomacy as well as of administration, and restricted to the Vatican compound, the isolation weighed heavily upon the Cardinal, especially after the death of his confidant and collaborator, Filippo Antonelli. There was absolutely no one that Giacomo could talk to about personal and political matters as he had to his older brother. The bond between Giacomo and Filippo had been special; none of the Cardinal's other brothers could take his place.

During the last years of his life while he remained by Pius's side and shared his imprisonment in the Vatican, the Cardinal wrote only a few letters to his family, to whom he remained devoted. Only fourteen of the more than three hundred letters in the family archive are from the period 1871–1876[31] In part this was due to the awesome responsibilities still resting on his shoulders; in part to the fact that by this time the Cardinal had trouble reading print and script.[32] The loss of his mother in 1862, followed by the loss of Filippo at the end of 1873, troubled Antonelli, who did not express his sorrow or pain in his correspondence. Rather in his letters to his remaining family he sought to provide psychological support, and he inquired about their health and economic well-being.[33] He was most appreciative of even the small gestures and kindness shown by his relatives and profusely thanked his nephew Agostino for the flowers he sent for Easter.[34] Like the great Napoleon, Antonelli believed that blood was thicker than water and trusted few outside his family.

In his correspondence with both friends and family, Antonelli rarely mentioned the gout with which he had been afflicted for some time. The attacks he endured in his last years were aggravated by the fact that ever since his return from Naples he had spent little time outdoors and had precious few opportunities to walk or exercise. He spent most of his days and nights within the confines of his apartment, a situation which worsened after 1870, when he chose to remain by Pio Nono as a fellow-"prisoner" in the Vatican. To complicate matters, the Cardinal disliked seeing physicians and shunned their advice and prescriptions. Above all, he refused to lighten his work-load and lead a more relaxed, restful life.[35] Limited leisure, restricted space, and the ravages of his illness combined to deprive Antonelli of the opportunity to stroll, formerly his chief pastime. During the past decade this life-style had contributed to the onset of a number of attacks of gout, from which his recovery was, at best, partial. In 1866 he suffered an attack which began in May and lasted until August. The illness repeatedly struck with particular vilulence between July and August, and during these months in 1871, the Cardinal was again stricken. With the passage of years both the frequency of attacks and the severity of symptoms, increased.

The year 1876 was an ominous one for the Cardinal, who suffered an attack of gout in January. Just before his relapse, he had instructed the Nuncio in Madrid to keep the Spanish government loyal to the Church "in view of the tendencies revealed by the

178 CARDINAL GIACOMO ANTONELLI AND PAPAL POLITICS

elections."[36] This time the Vatican could not conceal the health problems of the Secretary of State. "Despite numerous denials," *The Morning Standard* of London reported, "Cardinal Antonelli is seriously ill."[37] Still, having a great will power and determination, and considerable character and courage, Antonelli continued to function as the chief figure in the Vatican. He suffered for months, with only intervals of tolerable health, revealing an indefatigability and force of soul which allowed him to transcend his bodily ills.[38] There was no miraculous cure, however, and a price had to be paid for his exertions. His forced activity proved counterproductive, for the Cardinal suffered a relapse at the beginning of the summer.

On June 25 the Cardinal commented on his general health and the most recent bout with his recurring illness, observing, "my health is alright, however, I cannot free myself of this blessed gout, which does not allow me to walk and forces me to rely on a cane. I hope that the heat will help rid me of this affliction . . ."[39] Antonelli, did in fact, witness something of a temporary improvement, but suffered a setback in September. In October his condition deteriorated, and by the beginning of November had spread from the joints to the vital organs.[40]

There are innumerable, fictitious tales about the last days and hours of the Cardinal. Among other things it is claimed that Pius showed little concern for his minister during the course of his malady, and even less at the time of his death. It has even been reported that the Pope refused to visit the Cardinal, who died without repenting and without confession. These stories were circulated by those who did not have access to either the Pope or Antonelli. The accounts given by those close to the two men, who had worked together for three decades, present a different picture. Monsignor Adriano Zecchini, chaplain of the Cardinal, Monsignor Giuseppe De Bisogno, who also had ready access to the Pope and his Minister, and Cardinal Vincenzo Vannutelli, then Deputy Secretary of State, who was by the Cardinal's side during the last hours, reveal that Giacomo was concerned about the state of his soul during this time, as he had always been.[41]

These figures also concur in their conclusion that the Pope was both preoccupied and concerned about the Cardinal's condition, sending his own private doctor to examine and treat his Minister. When he received the medical prognosis that Antonelli's situation was grave, Pio Nono advised his Secretary of State to receive the Last Sacrament. This surprised the Cardinal, who knew he was not well but did not suspect he was at death's door. Indeed the morning of November 5, the day before his death, the Cardinal had insisted on being carried to the Pope's apartments in Pius's sedan chair, so he could conduct his usual conference. While there, providing the Pope an accounting of the sums received from Spanish pilgrims, he felt worse, and was immediately taken to his apartments in the Vatican.[42] By this time, he recognized the need for confession and asked his chaplain Monsignor Zecchini to call his Jesuit confessor, Father Rossi. Pio Nono, worried about the Cardinal's condition, visited him that evening, expressing satisfaction that he had received the Holy Sacrament.[43]

During the course of his last hours Giacomo wrote his brother Gregorio, "I see that my days are being shortened; my only regret is that I must leave this poor old Pope, and God alone knows where those voracious wolves of the revolution will drag him."[44] He left instructions to inform the Pope that in the morning he would have one less faithful servant. Late that evening as his health failed, Antonelli sent a prelate to the Pope asking pardon for any involuntary offense he might have committed, placing himself at the Pope's feet and invoking his apostolic benediction.[45] He then spent a difficult night, suffering in intense agony. In the morning he heard mass and at seven he received Extreme Unction and died. Upon receiving the news, Pius said mass for the repose of his soul.[46]

The Cardinal was buried quietly, almost clandestinely, at five in the morning, on November 8, in a simple manner without pomp or ceremony. Thus the Cardinal, who had borne the responsibilities of state for more than two decades, was carried to his resting place in a second class hearse. In light of the prevailing prejudice in the capital against his Minister, Pius sought to avoid publicity, fearing demonstrations in the capital against Antonelli and Papal policy during the *Risorgimento*. Nonetheless, the Pope was criticized by some for the simplicity of the funeral.[47] Others asserted that this "shabby treatment" provided positive proof that Pius had long resented his Secretary of State, whom he had been afraid to dismiss. Supposedly the Pope had finally taken his revenge.

The Account of Antonelli's death in the *London Times* combined fact and fiction. It read:

> Cardinal Antonelli, Pontifical Secretary of State, died at the Vatican this morning at 5 o'clock in the 71st year of his life. For some years the Cardinal has suffered severely from gout, and dur-

ing the last few weeks the attacks have greatly increased in severity. Unwilling to recognize the gravity of his case, he insisted on
continuing the performance of the duties of his office. Acting contrary to the advice of his physicians, he not only refused to (slow
his pace) but persevered in paying his daily visit to the Pope, remaining with His Holiness for some time for the disposal of business. The day before yesterday he gave an audience to Baron
Baude, the new French Ambassador. Yesterday his Eminence was
with the Pope, giving him an account of some of the sums of money
received from Spanish Pilgrims, when he was suddenly taken with
severe attacks of his malady in the chest, and had to be carried
back to his apartment. The Pope was so much alarmed that he
immediately dispatched messengers for his own physician and sur-
geon, doctors Peragalli and Ceccarelli, and after holding a conversation they informed the Cardinal that he was at the point of
death. At first he would not give credence to what they told him,
but afterwards he consented to receive the final sacraments.
When these were administered he was already too far gone to
swallow the water. Notwithstanding the many warnings lately
given him, Cardinal Antonelli placed so little belief in his ap-
proaching end that he was occupied, among other things, in preparing a handsome present he intended to offer personally to the
Pope on his next name-day, the Festival of St. John the Evangelist.
Just before his death, he sent to beg the Pope's last blessing, imploring his pardon for all faults he may have committed during
his long administration of the affairs of the Pontifical States. It is
affirmed that he never went outside the walls of the Vatican Palace since September 1870. His colossal fortune, it is said, will be
divided equally among his brother Count Angelo Antonelli and
three other members of his family, and he left his valuable collection of precious stones and rare marbles to the Vatican Museum.[48]

Antonelli's foes pursued him to the grave, criticizing the will
he had made in January 1871, shortly after the Italian occupation
of Rome. The will, divided into two parts, deals first with spiritual
matters, and secondly, with material considerations. This document, lucid, exact, clear, and concise, reflects the character of the
Cardinal. He begins by expressing his gratitude to God, invoking
the intercession of Mary and his protector saints, Peter, Paul, Giacomo, and Luigi. The Cardinal, ever diplomatic, left it to the Pope
to decide in which church to hold his funeral mass. However, he
left precise instructions that he be neither cut nor embalmed, asking to be buried in the chapel of the Church of Santa Agata alla
Suburra, next to his mother.

The Cardinal named his four remaining brothers and two male nephews, Agostino and Paolo, as his heirs. He had purposely excluded his nephew Pietro, the second son of his brother Luigi, who was the only family member to go over to the Italian side, becoming not only an Italian nationalist but an anticleric as well. On the other hand, the Cardinal made special provision for his brother Angelo, who served as his secretary for the last twenty-five years, and for Agostino, son of Gregorio, to whom he left his beloved palace in Via Magnapoli. Sums were also bequeathed to his assistants for years of loyal service.

Aware of the Pope's religious nature and disdain for material possessions, Antonelli left Pius his desk crucifix, which he hoped would remind his sovereign of his years of service and dedication. He also left small sums and sacred vestments to a number of churches under his protection, provoking an outburst of indignation. Opponents of the Cardinal claimed he left the fantastic and fraudulently acquired fortune of seven million gold francs to his family and practically nothing to the Church. In fact the sum the Secretary of State left to his relatives and charitable organizations came closer to 623,341 gold francs and was derived from his family patrimony. Nor is it true that he left little to his Church, bequeathing his collection of precious gems, which had long been criticized, to the Vatican museum.[49] "I declare that I do not possess any other capital beyond that which comes from the heritage of my excellent father, or which I have been able to acquire through the means left me by him," he explained in his will. "I protest therefore, against all calumnies which on that or any other account whatsoever have been in so many ways circulated through the world, before God who is to judge me and before Him, I forgive from my heart all those who have tried to do me evil."[50]

The Cardinal would very likely have even forgiven the young countess Loreta Lambertini, who belatedly and mysteriously materialized, insisting that she was his daughter and claiming his estate for herself. Her appearance provoked a judicial conflict, which further defamed the Cardinal.[51] The Italian courts, less than friendly to the man who was perceived as the villain of unification, proved unable to decide the issue of paternity, although they let stand the Cardinal's will which provided for his brothers and nephews as beneficiaries.[52] The inconclusiveness of the patrimony suit convinced many that Lambertini was in fact Giacomo's daughter and this has persisted in the historiography.[53]

Those who wished to believe the worst of the Cardinal conveniently forgot the fact that the cause of the countess was advanced by her guardian, the Piedmontese yellow journalist Costanzo Chauvet, who introduced an anticlerical and pornographic press to Rome.[54] The case against Antonelli was political rather than legal, with opinions on this issue, as on many others, formed not on the basis of evidence but prejudice, and the polemical literature of the last two decades. The paternity suit therefore provided a convenient mechanism for rehashing many of the older accusations against Antonelli, at once defaming his character as well as the cause he served.

Chapter Fifteen

Conclusion: Villain of the *Risorgimento* or Hero of the Counter-*Risorgimento*?

Cardinal Antonelli remained by the Pope's side during the revolutionary upheaval of 1848, planned and provided for his flight from Rome, and executed the conservative policy of the Papacy following the restoration of 1849. Charged by the Pontiff with spearheading the counter-Risorgimento, he fought to prevent the nationalists from absorbing the Papal States into the Kingdom of Italy. The most powerful political figure in Rome until its capture by the Italians in 1870, he supervised the Pope's relations with other governments until his death in 1876. He confounded those who believed that the collapse of the temporal power, of which he had been the most decisive and strenuous defender, would lead to his dismissal. Following the fall of Rome, Antonelli remained as indispensable as ever to Pio Nono.

The biography of Cardinal Giacomo Antonelli to date has been shaped by the role he played in the counter-Risorgimento. His pro-Papal, anti-national stance understandably played a part in the construction of the *leyenda negra,* surrounding his person and policies. Occupying the most prominent and conspicuous position in the government that worked to block the creation of United Italy, and undeniably the most capable adversary of the national movement, the Secretary of State inevitably became the *bete noir* of liberals and nationalists alike. "The disappointment and discontent which a long political crisis inevitably breeds are all vented upon him, because respect enshrines the sacred person of the Pontiff," Odo Russell in Rome wrote to his uncle Lord John in 1860. In explaining the almost universal enmity Antonelli inspired, Russell added, "His youth irritates the venerable members of the Sacred

College, his low origin the patrician families, his firmness exasperates the liberal party, his commanding position excites the envy of all."[1]

At his death Antonelli was remembered for "battling with the Revolution, sharing the Pope's exile, maneuvering with Napoleon, defying the astute Cavour, snapping his fingers at Great Britain, now bullying and then lavishing his blandishments on Austria, and ruling the pontifical states with a rod of iron . . ."[2] While some maligned him for opposing Italian unification, others did so for failing to prevent the emergence of the Kingdom of Italy and the ensuing loss of the temporal power. There were even those who suggested that this Minister betrayed his sovereign's trust and cause. In 1859 the press reported that the Cardinal, by means of his brother Filippo, had provided 400,000 lire for the Piedmontese loan.[3] The most calumnious anecdotes were repeated and readily believed about the Cardinal. With the passage of time these stories and charges increased both in intensity and frequency. As private in his personal life as he was public in his protests, little was known about the life of this chief minister of the Pope.

If the Cardinal had died before 1870, and the loss of Rome, very likely the judgment of him would have been less severe. It was only after 1870 that all seemed to turn against Antonelli. Even a number of the friends of the regime, assuming that the fall of the Pontifical Government was an act of God, sought to determine who had provoked the divine wrath. Instinctively they shied away from any criticism of Pius, whom they revered as a saint. The attempt to preserve unsullied the figure of Pius led writers to heap responsibility upon the shoulders of his Secretary of State.[4] Ruggero Bonghi, a contemporary, concluded that upon Antonelli had fallen all the opposition and condemnation of the policies pursued since 1848, all the anger with, and resentment of, the bizarre conduct of the old Pope, although in many cases the Cardinal's greatest fault was his inability to prevent these policies.[5]

Since responsibility for the failure of papal policy had to be placed somewhere, the "Red Pope" as Antonelli was dubbed, became the convenient scapegoat, providing Pius both deniability and credibility. Thus, by the time of his death his enemies, as well as many friends of the Pope, burdened him with the responsibility for all of the errors of Papal Rome. Italians were convinced that his counsel, more than any other, influenced the conduct of Pio Nono.[6] The Cardinal's personal conduct as well as his policies were bitterly criticized.

All sorts of accusations, many of them confusing and contradictory, were made about Antonelli's private life. Political animosity combined with fertile imagination to transform the bland existence of the Cardinal to the libertine one depicted in the press and polemical literature. His religious convictions were called into question, and it was suggested that he was a mason and nonbeliever. Actually, the Cardinal attended mass daily at six in the morning, a service at which he frequently assisted. In his last years he went to confession and received communion weekly.[7] Giacomo, like his mother and brothers, contributed to a wide number of charities.[8] In Rome, Antonelli was the protector of numerous monasteries and confraternities, especially favoring the work of Don Giovanni Bosco, who ministered to abandoned children.[9] The Cardinal provided both gifts and encouragement.

Those who discounted the Cardinal's contributions and were prepared to believe the worst of him, have never adequately explained why Pio Nono, acknowledged by almost all to lead a saintly life, kept a "libertine" in his service. We know that the Pope was aware of the stories which circulated about his Minister. Indeed a series of anonymous letters were sent to the Pontiff, recounting the Cardinal's alleged escapades, lurid sex life, and disloyalty, calling for Antonelli's removal. Pius, distressed by these letters, discounted them. He followed the advice of Cardinal Costantino Patrizi, who counselled, "Pay no attention, Holy Father, to such voices, they are rivals, who resent the fact that he enjoys the confidence of your Holiness; he is completely faithful to you and deserves your complete confidence." In response to those in the college of Cardinals who urged the Pope to dismiss Antonelli, Pius inevitably asked, "Do you believe that you could replace him?"[10] They always admitted they could not.

The relationship between Antonelli and Pio Nono is important and merits further study, including the accusation that the Cardinal deliberately kept potential rivals from the Pope's side, virtually banishing them from Rome in some cases. It has been charged, for example, that the source of much of Pius's hostility to Antonio Rosmini, founder of the still active institute of priests of charity known as the Rosminians, can be traced to the jealousy and rivalry of the Secretary of State.[11] In reality Rosmini had early aroused the anger and suspicion of the Jesuits and certain conservative cardinals, above all Luigi Lambruschini, who accused him of doctrinal errors.[12] Pius, himself, deemed unorthodox a number of this theologian's views on God, the Trinity, and Christology. Both his *Delle cinque piaghe della santa chiesa* and his *La costituzione secondo la giustizia sociale* were placed on the Index of books forbidden to Catholics. Furthermore, Rosmini's politics of accommodation with the Italian national cause, and his failure to preside over a government in November 1848, at a time of crisis for the State and the Church, may have also influenced the Pope, who preferred the man who stood by his side and pursued his policies, rather than the one who sought to impose a national policy, and failing to do so, deserted his cause.[13]

Likewise, one might call into question the generally accepted notion that it was Antonelli's hostility that kept Gioacchino Pecci, the future Leo XIII, away from Rome, and delayed his becoming a cardinal.[14] The historian Giuseppe Clementi has concluded that there were other reasons for the Pope's aloofness towards Pecci, including the fact that his mission to Belgium had not been as successful as some have supposed, and the fact that while serving as archbishop of Perugia he had difficulties with Girolamo D'Andrea, the Apostolic Commissioner for Umbria. Furthermore, Pecci, considered imprudently liberal, had been opposed almost until the end to the proclamation of the Dogma of the Immaculate Conception, so dear to the heart of the Pope. When it became clear that the dogma would be proclaimed, Pecci pleaded that those who believed otherwise not be branded heretical. Small wonder that Pius, and therefore Antonelli, kept Pecci at a distance.[15]

The Cardinal's part in shaping papal political policy is still being debated.[16] According to Raffaele De Cesare who focused on *The Last Days of Papal Rome:*

> The cares of State were borne by Antonelli, the real master and arbiter, who managed everything without seeming to do so or raising any suspicions in the mind of the Pope. Knowing Pius IX's character intimately and able to measure his weaknesses and resisting power, he never came into collision with either, nor provoked his anger, no easy matter with such an impulsive nature as that of the Pope. This was indeed the cardinal's great merit that, in the midst of such surroundings, he presented the only stable point of that long and dramatic Pontificate, and that he calmly surveyed the fall of the temporal power, whose existence he knew not how to prolong. A man of moderate powers, devoid of passions or ideals, without even a semblance of culture, he nevertheless did not lack foresight. He realised that the political Papacy was doomed, and was therefore quite convinced that nothing could avert the catastrophe due to the changes and conditions. He there-

fore left a free hand to the Ultramontanes after he saw that Pius IX took their follies seriously. Perhaps he, too, had some illusions; but that touch of Roman skepticism which endowed the race as a whole with a substratum of good sense, convinced him that resistance was useless, wherefore he let events take their course, not feeling assured like Pius IX, that the Divinity would interfere.[17]

De Cesare combines fact and fiction in his analysis of Antonelli's role in Rome. Like so many others he tends to exaggerate the Cardinal's influence in shaping policy, and fails to differentiate the Minister's role in the inspiration and execution of papal policies. Unquestionably, the Secretary of State played a key role in the latter, but his part in initiating and making policy was always subordinate to that of the Pontiff. From the moment that Antonelli was first appointed Secretary of State, and given the charge of presiding over the constitutional cabinet in March 1848, the Cardinal found he could not conciliate the Pope's position with constitutional government.[18] Terenzio Mamiani had the same experience, although the Pope refused openly to admit his unwillingness to operate within a constitutional framework. Only after the revolutionary events of 1848–1849 was Pius forced to conclude that constitutional government was incompatible with the government of the Church.[19]

It is inaccurate to depict Pius as a *roi faineant* while Antonelli is portrayed as the prime mover and inspirer of all temporal decisions.[20] The Cardinal served Pius, he did not lead him, even in political matters. He had grave reservations about the organization and leadership of the Papal Army proposed by De Merode, but proved unable to frustrate the plans of the Minister of Arms. Only a train of unfortunate consequences led the Pope to abandon this policy. Likewise, the Pope's tendency to speak out in the strongest language did not always have Antonelli's approval, but there was little the Minister could do to curb the tongue of his sovereign. On one occasion, when he again criticized Russia's conduct in Poland to the minister of the Tsar, he knew that his protest displeased Antonelli. "That which had to be said, I said," he confided to Cardinal Patrizi, adding, "this evening, however, I expect a reprimand from the Secretary of State."[21]

In an article of December 9, 1876, in *L'Univers*, Louis Veuillot wrote, "while Pius IX heroically pursued his course through this chaos, his minister inspired by considerations of prudence, at times counselled retreat *(donna des conseils recalcitrants)*."[22] Veuillot added:

He had only feet of a man with which to tread a path marked out for the footsteps of an angel. It is to his credit that he gave expression to the fears, and at the same time it is to his credit that he remained besides his master, who, without disregarding them, nonetheless refused to yield. He spoke as a Minister of State whose duty it was to follow the guidance of human reason. But as a deacon he obeyed and followed his bishop . . . Minister and sovereign were alike faithful each to his post and faithful to one another. But these are things which our age will not understand.[23]

Although Antonelli was blamed for much of what was done in Rome, the inspiration for his actions usually flowed from the Pope, who feared the detrimental consequences of liberalism and nationalism upon the Church. Thus, when Antonelli was compared to Cardinal Richelieu, he rejected the comparison. "Richelieu served a king who was simply a man and ruled only a kingdom," he replied, "but I serve the Pontiff, the vicar of Christ, who governs the Christian world."[24]

Responsible to Catholics throughout the world, Pius, who had taken an oath to uphold the apostolic constitutions which forbade the alienation in any manner of the territories belonging to the Roman Catholic Church, refused to compromise or jeopardize the temporal authority.[25] The Pope admitted that he had shown himself naive and inexperienced when he dabbled with liberalism in the first days of his pontificate by telling the story of a child who had witnessed a magician make appear and then disappear a demon, and imitating him had succeeded in evoking the terrible apparition, but had forgotten the charm for exorcism. That child, Pius revealed, was none other than himself.[26]

The two men responsible for Papal policy, Pius and Antonelli, dubbed respectively the "white Pope" and the "red Pope," had quite different characters. Personality-wise, the Pope was an outer-directed extrovert, who was warm and spontaneous, although he did not have a particularly close relationship to his family. Antonelli, on the other hand, was inner-directed, closed and controlled, and remained closely tied to his family, which served as the focus of his universe. He had no circle of friends to provide diversion or consolation. Even in his family, the Cardinal was referred to as "His Eminence" and addressed as Monsignore by his parents and brothers.[27] He lived for decades in the Vatican without ever giving a party, and only rarely gave a dinner for the diplomatic corps or a visiting prince. Despite the persistent rumors of his frolicking lifestyle, he appeared infrequently in society and

Notes

Chapter One

1. Federico Sclopis di Salerano, *Diario segreto (1859–1878)*, ed. by Pietro Pirri (Turin: Deputazione subalpina di storia patria, 1959), p. 222; Giacomo Martina, *Pio IX* (1851–1866) (Rome: Università Gregoriana Editrice, 1986), p. 38.

2. *Archivio di Stato di Roma. Fondo Famiglia Antonelli, busta 2, fascicolo* 13.

3. American Catholic Historical Association, *United States Ministers to the Papal States: Instructions and Despatches 1848–1868*. Edited for the American Catholic Historical Association by Leo Francis Stock (Washington, D.C.: Catholic University Press, 1933), I, 262, 288, 307, 340.

4. *The New York Times*, November 7, 1876.

5. The recent biography by the journalist Carlo Falconi contains a treasure trove of information and is far more objective than most previous volumes on the Cardinal. Unfortunately, Falconi has not provided notes. This omission is serious, for most readers will not know if the author's findings are based on the available primary source material, which Falconi often puts to good use, or the dubious secondary sources into which he has also dipped. Carlo Falconi, *Il Cardinale Antonelli. Vita e carriera del Richelieu Italiano nella chiesa di Pio IX* (Milan: Mondadori, 1983).

6. Lillian Browne-Olf, *Their Name is Pius* (Milwaukee: Bruce Publishing Company, 1941), p. 201.

7. Paolo Dalla Torre, "Il Cardinale Giacomo Antonelli fra carte d'archivio ed atti processuali," *Pio Nono* 8 (1979) 144.

8. R. Aubert, "Giacomo Antonelli," *Dizionario Biografico degli Italiani* (Rome: Istituto della Enciclopedia Italiana, 1961), III, 493.

9. Edmond About, *The Roman Question*, trans. H. C. Coape (New York: Appleton and Co., 1859), p. 102.

197

198   NOTES

10. *The Roman Journals of Ferdinand Gregorovius, 1852–1874,* ed. Friedrich Althaus, trans. Mrs. Gustavus W. Hamilton (London: George Bell and Sons, 1907), p. 202.

11. Wiliam Roscoe Thayer, *The Life and Times of Cavour* (New York: Houghton-Mifflin Co., 1911), I, 179–181; George Martin, *The Red Shirt and the Cross of Savoy* (New York: Dodd, Mead and Co., 1969), p. 402; A. Bianchi-Giovini, *Quadro dei costumi della corte di Roma* (3rd. ed. Rome: Libreria speciale della novità, 1861), p. 75; *L'Osservatore Cattolico,* November 8, 1876.

12. John Francis Maguire, *Rome: Its Rulers and Institutions* (London: Longmans, Brown, Green and Roberts, 1857), p. 13.

13. Robert Sencourt, *Napoleon III: The Modern Emperor* (New York: Appleton-Century Co., 193), p. 237.

14. Raffaele de Cesare, *Roma e lo Stato del Papa dal ritorno di Pio IX al XX Settembre* (Rome: Forzani, 1907), I, 140–147); Giuseppe Leti, *Roma e lo Stato Pontificio dal 1849 al 1870. Note di storia politica* (2nd ed.; Ascoli Piceno: Giuseppe Cesari Editore, 1911), I, 16; Martina, *Pio IX (1851–1866),* pp. 39–40.

15. Thayer, I, 180–181.

16. *The New York Times,* August 30, 1873; Leti, I, 317.

17. Bianchi-Giovini, pp. 75–78; Leti, I, 16; *The Roman Journals of Ferdinand Gregorovius,* p. 27; Thayer, I, 180.

18. Pietro Pirri, "Il Cardinale Antonelli tra il mito e la storia," *Rivista di Storia della Chiesa in Italia,* XII (1958), 119–120.

19. A. J. Whyte, *The Political Life and Letters of Cavour, 1848–1861* (London: Milford, 1930) p. 156; About, p. 107; Bianchi-Giovini, p. 80.

20. "Un Infame Proceso in Roma," *Archivio di Stato di Roma, Miscellanea di Carte Politiche O Riservate, busta,* 124, *numero* 4344; Monsignor Baudard, *Ozanam in his Correspondence* (New York: Benzinger Brothers, 1925), p. 241; Thayer, I, 180.

21. Edmond About, *The Roman Question,* ed. E. N. Kirk, trans. Annie T. Wood (Boston: J. E. Tilton and Co., 1859), p. 143.

22. Raymond Corrigan, *The Church and the Nineteenth Century* (Milwaukee: Bruce Publishing Co., 1938), p. 61.
Quattro parole D'Un Sacerdote ai popoli dell'Umbria e delle Marche (Asisi: Tipografia Scariglia, 1860), p. 27.

23. R. De Cesare, *The Last Days of Papal Rome,* 1859–1870, trans. Helen Zimmern (London: A. Constable and Co., 1909), p. 89.

24. *The Making of Italy, 1796–1870,* ed. Denis Mack Smith (New York: Harper, 1968), p. 406.

25. *The New York Times,* November 7, 1876.

26. Giuseppe Masari, *Diario dalle cento voci* (Bologna: Cappelli, 1959), p. 79.

27. "Un Infame Processo in Roma," *Archivio di Stato di Roma, Miscellanea di Carte Politiche O Riservate, busta* 124, *numero* 4344.

28. Hippolyte Castille, *Le Cardinal Antonelli* (Paris: E. Dentu, 1859), pp. 11, 31; Leti, II, 276; Thayer, I, 179.

29. Carlo Falconi, *The Popes in the Twentieth Century: From Pius X to John XXII,* trans. Muriel Grinrod (Boston: Little, Brown and Co., 1967), pp. 49, 147.

30. *Il Progresso Italo-Americano,* September 17, 1970; Falconi, *Il Cardinale Antonelli,* pp. 250–251.

31. *United States Ministers to the Papal States,* I, 244.

32. *Scribner's Magazine,* XXXVII (April 1905), 431; Martina, *Pio IX (1851–1866),* p. 42.

Chapter Two

1. Carlo Falconi, *Il Cardinale Antonelli. Vita e carriera del Richelieu Italiano nella chiesa di Pio IX* (Milan: Mondadori, 1983), pp. 10–14, 21–27.

2. Correspondence between Cardinal Albani and Domenico Antonelli. *Archivio di Stato di Roma. Fondo Famiglia Antonelli, busta* 4.

3. Noel Blakiston (ed.), *The Roman Question: Extracts from the Despatches of Odo Russell from Rome 1858–1870* (London: Chapman and Hall, 1962), p. 78; Falconi, pp. 27–28.

4. "Cardinal Antonelli," *Dublin Review,* XXVIII (January 1877), p. 75; Falconi, p. 29.

5. Project for a political treaty between the Holy See and Napoleon, *Archivio Segreto del Vaticano, Archivio Particolare Pio IX, Oggetti Vari, n.* 909, *fascicoli* 4 and 5.

6. Napoleon's Decree of April 1808, *Archivio Segreto del Vaticano, Archivio Particolare Pio IX, Oggetti Vari, n.* 909, *fascicolo* 1.

7. *Archivio Segreto del Vaticano, Archivio Particolare Pio IX, Oggetti Vari, n. 909, fascicolo* 16.

8. Falconi, pp. 15–22, 41.

9. David Silvagni, *La corte e la società romana nei secoli XVIII e XIX* (Naples: Arturo Berisio Editore, 1967), III, 496; *Dublin Review*, XXVIII (January 1877), 76.

10. Letters of Domenico Antonelli 1814–23 and account of his administration of the affairs of Terracina, *Archivio di Stato di Roma, Fondo Famiglia Antonelli, buste* 4 and 5.

11. Armando Lodolini, "Un archivio segreto del Cardinale Antonelli-I," *Studi Romani* (July–August 1953), 411.

12. Account of expenses sustained by Domenico Antonelli in providing for the education of his sons Giacomo and Luigi, 1817–1830. *Archivio di Stato di Roma, Fondo Famiglia Antonelli, busta 6, fascicolo* 1.

13. Falconi, pp. 23–24, 35–39, 41–43, 52–53; Frank J. Coppa, "Rome and Revolution: From Pius VI to Pius IX," *Proceedings of the Consortium on Revolutionary Europe* (1984). Athens, Georgia, 1986, pp. 268–269.

14. Teacher's report of March 5, 1830, *Archivio di Stato di Roma. Fondo Famiglia Antonelli, busta,* 2.

15. Fiorella Bartocinni, *Roma nell'Ottocento* (Bologna: Cappelli Editore, 1985), p. 26.

16. Falconi, pp. 54–55; 59–68.

17. Domenico Antonelli assigns 1500 *scudi* a year for Giacomo's natural life for his service in the prelatura. *Archivio di Stato di Roma. Fondo Famiglia Antonelli, busta,* 6, *fascicolo* 1.

18. Blakiston, p. 78.

19. Boyhood friend to Giacomo congratulating him on entering the prelatura, August 8, 1830, *Archivio di Stato di Roma. Fondo Famiglia Antonelli, busta,* 1.

20. Series of letters to Domenico Antonelli congratulating him and the family on Giacomo's entry into the prelatura, *Archivio di Stato di Roma. Fondo Famiglia Antonelli, busta,* 1.

21. Letter of Giacomo to Gregorio Antonelli telling him of the gifts he is sending, December 24, 1831, *Archivio di Stato di Roma. Fondo Famiglia Antonelli, busta,* 1.

Notes 201

22. Complaints of Count Pompeo Dandini to his mother the Countess about the Antonelli's unwillingness to lend him additional sums, August 18, 1832, *Archivio di Stato di Roma. Fondo Famiglia Antonelli, busta,* 1.

23. Angelo Filipuzzi, *Pio IX e la politica austriaca in Italia dal 1815 al 1848 nella relazione di Riccardo Weiss di Starkenfels* (Florence: Felice Le Monnier, 1953), p. 98.

24. Henri Daniel-Rops, *The Church in an Age of Revolution 1769–1846*, trans., John Warrington (Garden City, N.Y.: Image Books, 1967), I, 241–252; E. E. Y. Hales, *Revolution and Papacy, 1769–1846* (Notre Dame: University of Notre Dame Press, 1966), p. 282.

25. Antonio Monti, *Pio IX nel Risorgimento Italiano con Documenti Inediti* (Bari: Laterza, 1928), pp. 40–41; Pierre Fernessole, *Pie IX Pape* (Paris: Lethielleux, 1960), I, 66–68.

26. A. C. Jemolo, *Church and State in Italy 1850–1950*, trans. David Moore (Oxford: Blackwell, 1960), p. 2; Fernessole, I, 27; Angelo Filipuzzi, *Pio IX e la politica Austriaca in Italia dal 1815 al 1848* (Florence: Felice Le Monnier, 1958), p. 10.

27. Bernetti who was named a Cardinal in 1827, and served as Secretary of State under Leo XII (1828–29), and under Gregory XVI (1831–36), remained a deacon and never became a priest.

28. Lodolini, *Studi Romani* (July–August 1953), 412.

29. Falconi, pp. 66–68; Frank J. Coppa, "Cardinal Giacomo Antonelli: An Accommodating Personality in the Politics of Confrontation," *Biography,* II (Fall 1979), 85.

Chapter Three

1. Carlo Falconi, *Il Cardinale Antonelli. Vita e carriera del Richelieu Italiano nella chiesa di Pio IX* (Milan: Mondadori, 1983), pp. 74–79.

2. Armando Lodolini, "Un archivio segreto del Cardinale Antonelli-I," *Studi Romani* (July-August 1953), 414.

3. Giacomo to Gregorio Antonelli, July 21, 1830, *Archivio di Stato di Roma. Fondo Famiglia Antonelli, busta* 1.

4. Lodolini, *Studi Romani* (July-August 1953), 413; Falconi, p. 70.

5. Ibid.

6. Falconi, p. 80.

7. Lodolini, *Studi Romani* (July-August 1953), 414–415.

8. Domenico to Filippo Antonelli, Letters of April 4 and April 27, 1836, *Archivio di Stato di Roma. Fondo Famiglia Antonelli, busta 7, fascicolo* 13.

9. Giacomo to Gregorio Antonelli, October 5, 1836, *Archivio di Stato di Roma. Fondo Famiglia Antonelli, busta* 1.

10. Ladolini, *Studi Romani* (July-August 1953), 414; Falconi, pp. 80–82.

11. Letters signed by Giacomo Antonelli, 1824–1876, *Archivio di Stato di Roma. Fondo Famiglia Antonelli, busta* 1.

12. Lodolini, *Studi Romani* (July-August 1953), 415; Falconi, pp. 83–84.

13. Domenico to Filippo Antonelli, April 4, 1836, *Archivio di Stato di Roma. Fondo Famiglia Antonelli, busta 7, fascicolo* 13.

14. Falconi, p. 78.

15. Domenico to Filippo Antonelli, January 13, 1836, *Archivio di Stato di Roma. Fondo Famiglia Antonelli, busta 7, fascicolo* 13.

16. Letter of the Secretary of State to Giacomo Antonelli informing him of his transfer from Orvieto to Viterbo, July 4, 1836, *Archivio di Stato di Roma. Fondo Famiglia Antonelli, busta* 3.

17. Giacomo to Filippo Antonelli, August 13, 1837, *Archivio di Stato di Roma. Fondo Famiglia Antonelli, busta* 1, n. 116.

18. Giacomo to Domenico Antonelli, April 28, 1837, *Archivio di Stato di Roma. Fondo Famiglia Antonelli, busta* 1, n. 84.

19. Giacomo to Filippo Antonelli, September 22, 1837, *Archivio di Stato di Roma. Fondo Famiglia Antonelli, busta* 1.

20. Falconi, pp. 97–105.

21. *Catechismo Sulle Rivoluzioni* (1832), *Archivio Segreto del Vaticano. Fondo Particolare Pio IX, cassetta* 5, *busta* 4.

22. Domenico to Filippo Antonelli, June 9, 1837, *Archivio di Stato di Roma. Fondo Famiglia Antonelli, busta 7, fascicolo* 13.

23. Cardinal Mattei to Giacomo Antonelli, July 12, 1841, *Archivio di Stato di Roma. Fondo Famiglia Antonelli, busta 2, fascicolo* 1.

24. Cardinal Mattei to Giacomo Antonelli, August 18, 1841, *Archivio di Stato di Roma. Fondo Famiglia Antonelli, busta 2, fascicolo* 1.

25. Cardinal Mattei to Giacomo Antonelli, July 12, 1841, *Archivio di Stato di Roma. Fondo Famiglia Antonelli, busta 2, fascicolo* 1.

26. Falconi, p. 111.

27. Ibid., pp. 112–113.

28. Giacomo to Gregorio Antonelli, April 15, 1841, *Archivio di Stato di Roma. Fondo Famiglia Antonelli, busta* 1, *numero* 147.

29. Domenico to Filippo Antonelli, March 1, 1842, *Archivio di Stato di Roma. Fondo Famiglia Antonelli, busta* 7, *fascicolo* 13; Falconi, pp. 114–119, 134.

30. Cardinal Mattei to Giacomo Antonelli announcing his appointment as Treasurer-General, April 21, 1845, *Archivio di Stato di Roma. Fondo Famiglia Antonelli, busta* 2, *fascicolo* 1; Falconi, p. 121.

31. George F. Berkeley and J. Berkeley, *Italy in the Making: January 1st 1848 to November 16, 1848* (Cambridge: University Press, 1940), p. 63.

32. Giacomo to Gregorio, 1845, *Archivio di Stato di Roma. Fondo Famiglia Antonelli, busta* 1, *numero* 185.

33. Domenico Antonelli to Cardinal Lambruschini and Cardinal Mattei, January 1845, *Archivio di Stato di Roma. Fondo Famiglia Antonelli, busta* 7, *fascicolo* 13.

34. Domenico to Filippo Antonelli, February 1, 1845, *Archivio di Stato di Roma. Fondo Famiglia Antonelli, busta* 7, *fascicolo* 13.

35. Domenico to Filippo Antonelli, January 6, 1844, *Archivio di Stato di Roma. Fondo Famiglia Antonelli, busta* 7, *fascicolo* 13.

36. Domenico to Filippo Antonelli, January 30, 1845, *Archivio di Stato di Roma. Fondo Famiglia Antonelli, busta* 7, *fascicolo* 15.

37. Armando Lodolini, "Un Archivio Segreto del Cardinale Antonelli-II," *Studi Romani* (September-October 1953), 511–512.

38. Falconi, pp. 131–133.

39. Giovanni Maioli (ed.), *Pio IX da vescovo a pontifice. Lettere al Card. Luigi Amat. Agosto 1839–Luglio 1848* (Modena: Società Tipografica Modenese, 1943), p. 101.

40. Metternich to Count Lutzow, June 9, 1846, *Mémoires, Documents et Écrits Divers laissés par le Prince de Metternich*. ed. by Prince Richard Metternich with papers being arranged and classified by M. A. de Klinkowstroem (Paris: 1880–84), VII, 246.

Chapter Four

1. Carlo Falconi, *Il Cardinale Antonelli. Vita e carriera del Richelieu Italiano nella chiesa di Pio IX* (Milan: Mondadori, 1983), p. 141.

2. Filippo to Gregorio Antonelli, October 22, 1847, *Archivio di Stato di Roma, Fondo Famiglia Antonelli, busta* 12; Noel Blakiston (ed.), *The Roman Question: Extracts from the Despatches of Odo Russell from Rome 1858–1870* (London: Chapman and Hall, 1962), p. 79.

3. Giuseppe Pasolini, *Memorie, 1815–1876,* ed. Pietro Desiderio Pasolini (3rd. ed.; Turin: Bocca, 1887), p. 57.

4. Armando Lodolini, "Un Archivio segreto del Cardinale Antonelli— I," *Studi Romani* (July-August 1953), 416.

5. Falconi, p. 142.

6. Marco Minghetti, *Miei Ricordi* (3rd. ed.; Turin: Roux, 1888), I, 219; Frank J. Coppa, *Pope Pius IX. Crusader in a Secular Age* (Boston: Twayne Publishers, 1979), p. 44.

7. Report on the Debt and the Financial Condition of the Papal States, August, 1846, *Archivio Segreto del Vaticano, Archivio Particolare Pio IX, Stato Pontificio.*

8. Discourse of Treasurer-General on Papal Finances, *Archivio di Stato di Roma. Fondo Famiglia Antonelli, busta* 9.

9. *Archivio Segreto del Vaticano, Fondo Paricolare Pio IX, cassetta X, busta* 2.

10. "Pensieri relativi all' amministrazione pubblica dello Stato Pontificio," in Alberto Serafini, *Pio IX. Giovanni Maria Mastai Ferretti dalla giovinezza alla morte nei suoi scritti e discorsi editi e inediti.* Volume I: *Le vie della Divina Provvidenza (1792–1846)* (Vatican City: Poliglotta Vaticana, 1958), pp. 1397–1406.

11. Pierre Fernessole, *Pie IX Pape* (Paris: P. Lethielleux, 1960), I, 106; Carlo Ghisalberti, "Il Consiglio di Stato di Pio IX," *Studi Romani,* II (1954), p. 58.

12. Count C. A. De Goddes De Liancourt and James A. Manning, *Pius the Ninth: The First Year of his Pontificate* (London: Thomas Newby Publishers, 1847), I, 282.

13. Carlo Minnocci, *Pietro Sterbini e la Rivoluzione Romana (1846–1849)* (Rome: Edizione "La Diana"), 1967.

14. Bernard O'Reilly, *A Life of Pius IX Down to the Episcopal Jubilee of 1877* (8th ed.; New York: P. F. Collier, 1878), p. 69; Pasolini, p. 57; Fernessole, p. 90.

15. "Amnistia accordata dalla Santità di Nostro Signore Pio IX nella Sua esaltazione al Pontificato," July 16, 1846, *Atti del Sommo Pontefice Pio Nono Felicemente Regnante. Parte seconda che comprende i moti pro-*

prii, chirografi, editi, notifacazioni, ec. per lo stato pontificio. Rome: Tipografia delle Belle Arti, 1857.

16. List of individuals who took advantage of the amnesty of 1846 and returned to their old revolutionary habits, *Archivio di Stato di Roma, Carte Miscellanea Politiche o Riservate, busta* 121, *fascicolo* 4246.

17. Antonio Monti, *Pio IX nel Risorgimento Italiano con Documenti Inediti* (Bari: Laterza, 1928), p. 70; Giacomo Martina, *Pio IX (1846–1850)* (Rome: Università Gregoriana Editrice, 1974), pp. 113–114.

18. "Disposizioni riguardanti la execuzione delle strade ferrate nello Stato pontificio," (November 7, 1846) *Atti del Sommo Pontefice Pio Nono Felicemente Regnante. Parte seconda,* I, 15–16.

19. Filippo Antonelli made a member of the National Society for Railroads in Pontifical States, *Archivio di Stato di Roma, Fondo Famiglia Antonelli, busta* 10, *fascicolo* 1.

20. Luigi Carlo Farini, *Lo Stato Romano dall'anno 1815 al 1850* (2nd. ed.; Florence: Felice Le Monnier, 1853), I, 190–191; Hippolyte Castile, *Le Cardinal Antonelli* (Paris: E. Dentu, 1859), p. 24; Louis Jourdan and Taxile Delord, *Les Celebrants du jour, 1860–61* (Paris: Aux bureau du journal *Le Siecle*, n.d.), p. 180.

21. Great Britain, *British and Foreign State Papers,* XXXVI (1847–48), 1881; Domenico Demarco, *Una rivoluzione sociale. La Repubblica Romana del 1849* (Naples: Mario Fiorentino Editore, 1944), p. 14.

22. "Disposisione tendente a rimuovere l'ozio come ordinaria sorgente di deletti che accadono in alcune provincie dello Stato ed a procciare una utile e religiosa educazione nella gioventù," *Atti del Sommo Pontefice Pio Nono Felicemente Regnante. Parte Seconda,* I, 8–10.

23. Report of Monsignor Corboli-Bussi to Pius on Third Session of the Congregation of State, July 15, 1846, *Archivio Segreto del Vaticano, Archivio Particolare Pio IX, Sovrani, Stato Pontificio, n.* 3.

24. Report of Monsignor Coboli-Bussi to Pius on Fourth session of the Congregation of State, August 26, 1846, *Archivio Segreto del Vaticano, Archivio Particolare Pio IX, Sovrani, Stato Pontificio, n.* 4.

25. *Archivio di Stato di Roma, Fondo Famiglia Antonelli, busta* 9.

26. De Goddes de Liancourt and Manning, II, 29.

27. Motu-proprio della Santità di Nostro Signore concernente la istituzione del Consiglio dei Ministri, *Atti del Sommo Pontefice Pio IX Felicemente Regnante. Parte Seconda,* I, 54.

28. Jourdan, p. 180; Falconi, p. 148.

29. "Cardinal Antonelli," *Dublin Review,* XVIII (January 1977), 78.

30. Louis Philippe to Giacomo Antonelli, June 30, 1847, *Archivio di Stato di Roma, Fondo Famiglia Antonelli, busta 2, fascicolo 2.*

31. Fredrich August from Dresden to Giacomo Antonelli, August 2, 1847, *Archivio di Stato di Roma, Fondo Famiglia Antonelli, busta 2, fascicolo 3.*

32. Romolo Quazza, *Pio IX e Massimo D'Azeglio nelle vicende romane del 1847,* Volume I: *Dalle questioni interne al problema nazionale* (Modena: Società Tipografica Editrice Modenese, 1954), I, 87.

33. Falconi, p. 148. *Archivio di Stato di Roma, Fondo Famiglia Antonelli, busta 2, fascicolo 1.*

34. "Desiderio di Sua Santità che sia posto termine alle insolite popolari riunioni e straordinarie manifestazioni per qualsivoglia occasione e motivo," *Atti del Sommo Pontefice Pio IX Felicemente Regnante. Parte Seconda,* I, 66–70; Quazza, I, pp. 168–169.

35. Filippo to Gregorio Antonelli, October 22, 1847, *Archivio di Stato di Roma, Fondo Famiglia Antonelli, busta 12;* Falconi, pp. 152–54.

36. "Motu-proprio della Santità di Nostro Signore sulla Consulta di Stato," *Atti del Sommo Pontefice Pio IX Felicemente Regnante. Parte Seconda.* I, 150–166.

37. Antonelli meets with the heads of the various sections of the Consulta di Stato, *Archivio di Stato di Roma, Consulta di Stato, busta 1, fascicolo 24.*

38. Angelo Filipuzzi, *Pio IX e la politica Austriaca in Italia dal 1815 al 1848* (Florence: Felice Le Monnier, 1958), p. 139; Luigi Rava (ed.), *Epistolario di Luigi Carlo Farini* (Bologna: Zanichelli, 1911), p. 731.

39. Filippo to Gregorio Antonelli, October 22, 1847, *Archivio di Stato di Roma, Fondo Famiglia Antonelli, busta 12.*

40. Gregorio to Giacomo Antonelli, October 24, 1847, *Archivio di Stato di Roma, Fondo Famiglia Antonelli, busta 12.*

41. Secretary of Stato to Giacomo Antonelli, November 3, 1847, *Archivio di Stato di Roma, Consulta di Stato, busta 1, fascicolo 5.*

42. Great Britain, *British and Foreign State Papers,* XXXVI (1847–48), 1348: John Francis Maguire, *Rome: Its Rulers and Institutions* (London: Longman, Brown, Green, 1857), p. 43.

43. Project to improve Papal State's financial position, *Archivio di Stato di Roma, Consulta di Stato, busta 1, fascicolo 19.*

44. Carlo Ghisalberti, "Il Consiglio di Stato di Pio IX. Nota storia-giuridica," *Studi Romani,* II (1954), 167; Minghetti, I, 297–300.

45. Minghetti, I, 300.

46. Rava, *Epistolario di Luigi Carlo Farini,* I, 780.

47. Giacomo Antonelli meets with the heads of the various subdivisions of the Consulta di Stato, *Archivio di Stato di Roma, Consulta di Stato, busta* 1, *fascicolo* 24.

48. Friedrich Engel-Janosi, "French and Austrian Political Advice to Pius IX, 1846–1848, *Catholic Historical Review,* XVIII (April 1952), 9: Farini, I, 191.

49. Emile Ollivier, *L'Empire Liberal* (Paris: Garnier Frerès, 1895), I, 380.

50. Carlo Alberto to Pius IX, August 19, 1846, *Archivio Segreto del Vaticano, Archivio Particolare Pio IX, Sovrani, Sardegna.*

51. Giacomo Martina, *Pio IX e Leopoldo II* (Rome: Pontifica Università Gregoriana, 1967), pp. 73–74.

52. Filippo to Gregorio Antonelli, *Archivio di Stato di Roma, Fondo Famiglia Antonelli, busta* 12.

53. Carboli-Bussi to Pius IX on Piedmont's tentative adherence to tariff league, October 17, 1847, *Archivio Segreto del Vaticano, Archivio Particolare Pio IX, Stato Pontifico.*

54. Minnocci, p. 58; Quazza, II, 31.

55. *Mémoires, Documents et Écrits Divers laissés par le Prince de Metternich* (Paris: 1880–84), VII, 342–43.

56. "Motu-proprio della Santità di Nostro Signore sul Consiglio dei Ministri," *Atti del Sommo Pontefice Pio IX Felicemente Regnante, Parte Seconda,* I, 204–05.

57. Giacomo to Gregorio Antonelli, December 30, 1847, *Archivio di Stato di Roma, Fondo Famiglia Antonelli, busta* 1, *sotto fascicolo,* 216.

Chapter Five

1. Breve racconto degli avvenimenti successi in Roma dall' esaltazione al trono del gloiorso Pontefice Papa Pio Nono, fino all' epoca in cui ebbe luogo l'intervento armato delle quattro potenze cattoliche, Austria, Francia, Spagna e Napoli, fatto da un suddito pontifice romano, *Archivio Segreto del Vaticano, Archivio Particolare Pio IX, Oggetti Vari,* n. 515.

2. Giuseppe Pasolini, *Memorie, 1815–1876,* ed. Pietro Desiderio Pasolini (3rd ed.; Turin: Bocca, 1887), p. 77.

3. Mr. Petre to Sir George Hamilton, January 18, 1848, *Great Britain, British and Foreign State Papers,* XXXVI (1848–49), 842.

4. Angelo Filipuzzi, *Pio IX e la politica Austriaca in Italia dal 1815 al 1848* (Florence: Felice Le Monnier, 1958), pp. 232–233.

5. Carlo Falconi, *Il Cardinale Antonelli. Vita e carriera del Richelieu Italiano nella chiesa di Pio IX* (Milan: Mondadori, 1983), pp. 160–61.

6. Giacomo Martina, *Pio IX (1846–1850).* (Rome: Università Gregoriana Editrice, 1974), pp. 209–212; Luigi Rodelli. *La Repubblica Romana del 1849* (Pisa: Domus Mazziniana, 1955), p. 44.

7. Pierre Fernessole, *Pie IX Pape* (Paris: P. Pethielleux, 1960), I, 195.

8. Luigi Carlo Farini to Leopoldo Galeotti, January 18, 1848, Luigi Rava (ed.), *Epistolario di Luigi Carlo Farini* (Bologna: Zanichelli, 1911), II, 38.

9. Cardinal Bofondi to Cardinal Antonelli, March 10, 1848, *Archivio di Stato di Roma, Fondo Famiglia Antonelli, busta 2, fascicolo 1.*

10. Luigi Armando Giovagnini, *Dalla elezione di Pio IX alla caduta della Repubblica Romana* (Genoa: Lanterna, n.d.), p. 21; Giuseppe Pasolini, *Memorie, 1815–1876,* p. 84.

11. Marco Minghetti, *Miei Ricordi* (3rd ed.; Turin: Roux, 1888), I, 339–340; Luigi Carlo Farini, *Lo Stato Romano dall anno 1815 al 1850* (2nd. ed.; Florence: Felice Le Monnier, 1853), II, 7.

12. Minister of Finance to Consulta di Stato, April 1, 1848, *Archivio di Stato di Roma, Consulta di Stato, busta 3, fascicolo 83.*

13. Address of Antonelli Ministry to the Pope, *Great Britain, British and Foreign State Papers,* XXXVII (1848–1849), 920.

14. For the text of the Statuto granted by Pio Nono see *Raccolta degli Statuti Politici proclamati in Italia e delle corrispondenti legge elettoriali* (Turin: Biblioteca dei communi italiani, 1852), I, 53–66.

15. "Statuto fondamentale del governo temporale degli Stati di S. Chiesa," *Atti del Sommo Pontefice Pio Nono Felicemente Regnante. Parte seconda,* I, 232; 223–224.

16. Leo Wollemborg, "Lo Statuto Pontificio nel quadro costituzionale del 1848," *Rassegna Storica del Risorgimento,* XXII (October 1935), 577.

17. *Atti del Sommo Pontefice Pio Nono Felicemente Regnante. Parte seconda,* I, 237.

18. Carlo Ghisalberti, "Il Consiglio di Stato di Pio IX," *Studi Romani,* II (1954), 165–166.

19. Gregorio to Filippo Antonelli, March 27, 1848, *Archivio di Stato di Roma, Fondo Famiglia Antonelli, busta 7, fascicolo 9.*

20. Minghetti, I, 353.

21. Giovagnini, p. 26.

22. Farini, II, 16; *Great Britain, British and Foreign State Papers,* XXXVII (1848–49), 918.

23. Cardinal Antonelli to Archbishop Cambray, March 6, 1848, *Archivio Segreto del Vaticano, Archivio Particolare Pio IX, Particolari, Francia, #2.*

24. G. F. Berkeley and J. Berkeley, *Italy in the Making: January 1st 1848 to November 16, 1848* (Cambridge: Cambridge University Press, 1940), III, 188–189.

25. Martina, *Pio IX,* pp. 232–233; Falconi, p. 170.

26. Giacomo Martina, *Pio IX e Leopoldo II* (Rome: Pontifica Università Gregoriana, 1967), pp. 73–74.

27. "Pier Silverio Leicht, Memorie di Michele Leicht," *Rassegna Storica del Risorgimento,* XXII (July 1935), II, 83.

28. Martina, *Pio IX e Leopoldo II,* pp. 112, 116.

29. Minghetti, I, 366–367.

30. Giovanni Maioli (ed), *Pio IX da vescovo a pontifice. Lettere al Card. Luigi Amat. Agosto 1839–Luglio 1848* (Modena: Società Tipografia Modenese, 1943), p. 117.

31. Minghetti, I, 370; Farini, II, 88–89.

32. Pio IX to Monsignor Corboli-Bussi, April 27, 1848, *Archivio Segreto del Vaticano, Archivio Particolare Pio IX, Particolari, Stato Pontificio.*

33. Allocution of Pope Pius IX, April 29, 1848, Great Britain, *British and Foreign State Papers,* XXXVII (1848–49), 1065.

34. Farini, II, 91.

35. Pio Nono's draft of the Allocution of April 29, 1848, *Archivio Segreto del Vaticano, Archivio Particolare Pio Nono, Oggetti Vari, n. 897.*

36. Pasolini, Memorie, p. 102.

37. Ibid.

210 NOTES

38. Ibid., p. 103.

39. Great Britain, *British and Foreign State Papers*, XXXVII (1848–49), 1071.

40. Guidi Pasolini (ed.), *Carteggio tra Marco Minghetti e Giuseppe Pasolini* (Turin: Bocca, 1924), I, 14.

41. Pasolini, *Memorie*, p. 106.

Chapter Six

1. Cardinal Amat to Pius IX, May 5 and 13, 1848, *Archivio Segreto del Vaticano, Archivio Particolare Pio IX, Sovrani, Stato Pontificio.*

2. Carlo Falconi, *Il Cardinale Antonelli. Vita e carriera del Richelieu Italiano nella chiesa di Pio IX* (Milan: Mondadori, 1983), pp. 174–175.

3. Giacomo to Gregorio Antonelli, May 16, 1848, *Archivio di Stato di Roma, Fondo Famiglia Antonelli, busta 1.*

4. Marco Minghetti, *Miei Ricordi* (3rd ed.; Turin: Roux, 1888), I, 219.

5. Luigi Carlo Farini to Pius IX, May 7, 1848, *Archivio Segreto del Vaticano, Archivio Particolare Pio IX, Sovrani, Stato Pontificio;* Luigi Rava (ed.), *Epistolario di Luigi Carlo Farini* (Bologna, Zanichelli, 1911), II, 220.

6. Cardinal Ciacchi was selected as President of the Council of Ministers and Minister of External Ecclesiastical Relations; Mamiani was Minister of the Interior; Count Marchelli, Minister of Secular Foreign Affairs, Pasquale De Rosa, Minister of Grace and Justice; Giuseppe Lunati, Minister of Finance; Prince D'Oria Panfili, Minister of Arms; Mario Massimo, Duke of Regnano, Minister of Public Works and Galletti, Minister of Police.

7. Pius IX to Carlo Alberto, May 12, 1848, *Archivio Segreto del Vaticano, Archivio Particolare Pio IX, Sovrani, Sardegna,* #13; R. M. Johnston, *The Roman Theocracy and the Republic, 1846–1848* (London: Macmillan and Co., 1901), p. 154.

8. Rava (ed.), *Epistolario di Luigi Carlo Farini*, II, 291; *Il Risorgimento,* May 31, 1848.

9. Arturo De Grandeffe, *Pio IX e L'Italia Libera* (Turin: Reviglio, 1859), p. 53; Luigi Rodelli, *La Repubblica Romana del 1849* (Pisa: Domus Mazziniana, 1955), p. 49; Mario Viana, *La Monarchia fra stato e Chiesa* (Turin: Seperga, 1962), p. 94.

10. Filippo to Gregorio Antonelli, August 4, 1848, *Archivio di Stato di Roma, Fondo Famiglia Antonelli, busta* 12.

11. Marco Minghetti to Cardinal Antonelli, May 13, 1848, *Archivio di Stato di Roma, Fondo Famiglia Antonelli, busta* 2, *fascicolo* 4.

12. Antonelli to Apostolic Nuncio in Turin, June 15, 1848, *Archivio di Stato di Roma, Fondo Famiglia Antonelli, busta* 1.

13. Mournier to Filippo Antonelli, June 11, 1848, *Archivio di Stato di Roma, Fondo Famiglia Antonelli, busta* 7.

14. Pius IX to Carlo Alberto, June 13, 1848, *Archivio Segreto del Vaticano, Archivio Particolare Pio IX, Sovrani, Sardenga.*

15. Rodelli, p. 50.

16. Emperor Ferdinand to Pius IX, July 2, 1848, *Archivio Segreto del Vaticano, Archivio Particolare Pio IX, Sovrani, Austria,* #4.

17. Filippo to Gregorio Antonelli, August 4, 1848, *Archivio di Stato di Roma, Fondo Famiglia Antonelli, busta* 12.

18. Giacomo to Gregorio Antonelli, August 7, 1848, *Archivio di Stato di Roma, Fondo Famiglia Antonelli, busta* 1.

19. Cardinal Soglia was named Minister of Foreign Affairs; Cardinal Vizzardelli, Minister of Public Instruction; Signor Cicognani, Minister of Justice; Signor Rignano Minister of Public Works and Signor Montanari, Minister of Commerce.

20. Pius to Carlo Alberto, October 1, 1848, *Archivio Segreto del Vaticano, Archivio Particolare Pio IX, Sovrani, Sardegna,* #16.

21. Frank J. Coppa, *Pope Pius IX: Crusader in a Secular Age* (Boston: Twayne Publishers, 1979), pp. 87–88.

22. Alexandre De Saint-Albin, *Pie IX* (Paris: E. Dentu, 1860), p. 250.

23. Filippo to Angelo Antonelli, November 19, 1848, *Archivio di Stato di Roma, Fondo Famiglia Antonelli, busta* 6, *fascicolo* 3.

24. *Archivio di Stato di Roma, Miscellanea di Carte Politiche O Riservate, busta* 124, *fascicolo* 4345.

25. Narration of Events of November 16, 1848, *Archivio Segreto del Vaticano, Archivio Particolare Pio IX, Stato Pontificio,* #19.

26. *Mémoires, Documents et Écrits Divers Laissés par le Prince de Metternich.* VII, 38.

27. Unsigned and undated letter to Giacomo Antonelli on conspiracy against Papacy, *Archivio di Stato di Roma*, Fondo *Famiglia Antonelli, busta* 1.

28. Narration of Events of November 16, 1848, *Archivio Segreto del Vaticano, Archivio Particolare Pio IX, Stato Pontificio,* #19.

29. Gianfranco Radice, *Pio IX e Antonio Rosmini* (Città del Vaticano: Libreria Editrice Vaticana, 1974), pp. 69–71; Giacomo to Gregorio Antonelli, November 9, 1848, *Archivio di Stato di Roma, Fondo Famiglia Antonelli, busta* 1, #228.

30. Luigi Francesco Berra, "La fuga di Pio IX a Gaeta e il raconto del suo scalso segreto," *Studi Romani.* V (1957), 674; Luigi Carlo Farini, *Lo Stato Romano dall' anno 1815 al 1850* (Paris: Dentù, 1859), III 29–30; Giuseppe Leti, *Roma e lo Stato Pontificio dal 1849 al 1870. Note di storia politica* (2nd ed.; Ascoli Piceno: Giuseppe Cesari Editore, 1911), I, 18.

31. Berra, *Studi Romani,* V, (1957), 672–79; 683–684; De Saint-Albin, 263–265.

32. Bernard O'Reilly, *A Life of Pius IX Down to the Episcopal Jubilee of 1877* (8th ed.; P. F. Collier, 1878), p. 239.

33. Antonio Sarti to Gregorio Antonelli, *Archivio di Stato di Roma, Fondo Famiglia Antonelli, busta* 7, *fascicolo* 1.

34. Pius IX (letter written by Antonelli) to Ferdinand of Naples, November 25, 1848, *Archivio di Stato di Roma, Fondo Famiglia Antonelli, busta* 1, *sotto fascicolo* 230.

35. Berra, *Studi Romani,* V (1957), 680–682; Falconi, pp. 190–196; 206.

36. *Giacomo to Gregorio Antonelli,* December 15, 1848, *Archivio di Stato di Roma, Fondo Famiglia Antonelli, busta* 1.

37. Allontanamento temporaneo del S. Padre dai suoi Stati, protesta per le violenze usate, e creazione di una commissione governativa ... , *Atti del Sommo Pontefice Pio Nono Felicemente Regnante,* I, 252.

38. Antonio Monti, *Pio IX nel Risorgimento Italiano con Documenti Inediti* (Bari: Laterza, 1928), p. 116.

39. Pius IX to Church Officials, December 17, 1848, *Archivio Segreto del Vaticano, Segreteria di Stato, Corrispondenza di Gaeta e Portici, anno 1848–50, Rubrica 3, fascicolo* 1, *sottofascicolo* 90.

40. "Ai Popoli Romani," December 29, 1848, *Archivio di Stato di Roma, Repubblica Romana, busta* 1, *fascicolo* 5.

41. Pius IX to Corboli-Bussi, December 28, 1848, *Archivio Segreto del Vaticano, Archivio Particolare Pio IX, Sovrani, Stato Pontificio.*

42. Apostolic Nuncio at Vienna to Antonelli, December 26, 1848, *Archivio Segreto del Vaticano, Segreteria di Stato, Corrispondenza da Gaeta e Portici, Rubrica 247, sottofascicolo 4.*

43. Pius IX to Carlo Alberto, December 28, 1848, *Archivio Segreto del Vaticano, Archivio Particolare Pio IX, Sovrani, Sardegna, #18.*

44. Radice, pp. 72–78.

45. Falconi, p. 202.

46. Pius to the Archbishop of Paris, September 17, 1849, *Archivio Segreto del Vaticano, Archivio Particolare Pio IX, Francia, Particolari, #30.*

47. *Archivio Segreto del Vaticano, Fondo Particolare Pio IX, cassetta 30.*

48. Giacomo to Gregorio Antonelli, December 15, 1848, *Archivio di Stato di Roma, Fondo Famiglia Antonelli, busta 1.*

49. Cardinal Antonelli to Apostolic Nuncio in Turin, June 8, 1849, *Archivio Segreto del Vaticano, Segreteria di Stato, Corrispondenza da Gaeta e Portici, 1848–1850, Rubrica 257, sottofascicolo 64.*

50. *L'Opinione*, June 5, 1849; Farini, *Lo Stato Romano dall' anno 1815 al 1850*, III, 183.

51. Protesta fatta in Gaeta da Sua Santità Pio PP. IX. contro l'atto della sedicente Assemblea costitutente romana in data 9 Febraja corrente, *Atti del Sommo Pontefice Pio Nono Felicemente Regnate*, I, 262–264.

52. Monti, p. 120; *Atti del Sommo Pontefice Pio Nono Felicemente Regnante*, I, 264–266.

53. Giacomo to Gregorio Antonelli, May 22, 1849, *Archivio di Stato di Roma, Fondo Famiglia Antonelli, busta 1, #231.*

54. Giacomo Martina, *Pio IX (1846–1850)* (Rome: Università Gregoriana Editrice, 1974), p. 339.

55. Nicomede Bianchi, *La politica di Massimo D'Azeglio dal 1848 al 1859. Documenti* (Turin: Roux e Favale, 1884), pp. 72–75; 82–86.

56. A. Rosmini, *Della Missione a Roma* (Turin: Paravia, 1881), pp. 143–144.

57. Pius IX to Dupont, Archbishop of Bourges, June 10, 1849, *Archivio Segreto del Vaticano, Archivio Partiolare Pio IX, Francia, Particolari, #18.*

58. Pietro Pirri, "Il Cardinale Antonelli tra il mito e la storia," *Rivista di storia della Chiesa in Italia*, XII (1958), 81–82.

59. Giacomo to Gregorio Antonelli, July 1, 1849, *Archivio di Stato di Roma, Fondo Famiglia Antonelli, busta* 1, #235.

60. Pius IX to Louis Napoleon, July 31, 1849, *Archivio Segreto del Vaticano, Archivio Particolare Pio IX, Sovrani, Francia,* #7.

61. *Il Risorgimento,* July 27, 1849.

62. Cardinal Antonelli to the Commission of Cardinals in Rome, 1849, *Archivio di Stato di Roma, Fondo Famiglia Antonelli, busta* 1.

63. Cardinals of the Commission to Antonelli, August 3, 1849, *Archivio Segreto del Vaticano, Archivio Paricolare Pio IX, Francia, Particolari,* #25.

64. *Atti del Sommo Ponterice Pio Nono Felicemente Regnante,* I, 272, 279–280.

Chapter Seven

1. Lajos Lukacs, *The Vatican and Hungary 1846–1878: Reports and Correspondence of the Apostolic Nuncios in Vienna* (Budapest: Akademiai Kiado, 1981), p. 40; E. Ollivier, *L'Empire Liberal* (Paris: Garnier, 1897), II, 334–337.

2. Carlo Falconi, *Il Cardinale Antonelli. Vita e carriera del Richelieu Italiano nella chiesa di Pio IX* (Milan: Mondadori, 1983), p. 210.

3. *Archivio di Stato di Roma, Fondo Famiglia Antonelli, busta* 1.

4. Monthly reports of expenses sent by the Consul General of Pontifical States to Antonelli, *Archivio Segreto del Vaticano, Segretaria di Stato Esteri, Corrispondenza da Gaeta e Portici, Rubrica* 258, *sottofascicoli* 36, 38, 39.

5. Antonelli arranges loans in Paris, *Archivio Segreto del Vaticano, Segretaria di Stato Esteri, Corrispondenza da Gaeta e Portici, Rubrica* 248. *fascicolo* 1, *sottofascicoli* 148–152.

6. Conta di cassa fatto da Antonelli, *Archivio Segreto del Vaticano, Fondo Particolare Pio IX, cassetta* 29, nn. 334–400; 402–465.

7. Ibid. December 5, 1849–June 19, 1850.

8. Minister of Public Works to Antonelli, January 3, 1850, *Archivio Segreto del Vaticano, Segreteria di Stato Esteri, Corrispondenza da Gaeta e Portici, Rubrica* 58, *sottofasicolo* 21.

9. Political Bulletins sent to Antonelli, *Archivio Segreto del Vaticano, Segreteria di Stato Esteri, Corrispondenza da Gaeta e Portici, Rubrica* 155, *fascicolo* 2, *sottofascioli* 2–33.

10. Antonelli inquires about conduct of ecclesiastics, January 3, 1850, *Archivio Segreto del Vaticano, Segreteria di Stato Esteri, Corrispondenza da Gaeta e Portici, Rubrica* 68, *fasciolo* 2, *sottofascicolo* 120.

11. Letter of Cardinal Antonelli to a number of priests in Bologna, February 2, 1850, *Archivio Segreto del Vaticano, Segreteria di Stato Esteri, Corrispondenza da Gaeta e Portici, Rubrica* 123, *sottofascicolo* 11.

12. Frank J. Coppa, *Pope Pius IX: Crusader in a Secular Age* (Boston: Twayne Publishers, 1979), p. 103; Andre Bellessort, *La Société francaise sous Napoleon III* (Paris: Librairie Academique Perrin Editeur, 1931), p. 143.

13. *Archivio Segreto del Vaticano, Segreteria di Stato Esteri, Corrispondenza da Gaeta e Portici,* 1849, *Rubrica* 242, *sottofascicolo* 57.

14. Gregorio to Filippo Antonelli, September 15, 1849, *Archivio di Stato di Roma, Fondo Famiglia Antonelli, busta* 7, *fascicolo* 9.

15. Consul General in Marseilles to Apostolic Nuncio in Paris, September 9, 1849, *Archivio Segreto del Vaticano, Archivio Nunziatura Parigi,* 1849, *n.* 77, *busta* 4.

16. Gregorio to Filippo Antonelli, September 5, 1849, *Archivio di Stato di Roma, Fondo Famiglia Antonelli, busta* 7, *fascicolo* 9.

17. Jasper Ridley, *Napleon III and Eugenie* (New York: Viking Press, 1979), p. 312.

18. Nuncio at Paris to Antonelli, August 30, 1849, *Archivio Segreto del Vaticano, Segreteria di Stato Esteri, Corrispondenza da Gaeta e Portici, Rubrica* 242, *sottofascicolo* 24.

19. Antonelli to the Governmental Commission in Rome, September 11, 1849, *Archivio Segreto del Vaticano, Segreteria di Stato Esteri, Corrispondenza da Gaeta e Portici, Rubrica* 242, *sottofascicolo* 66.

20. Antonelli to the Powers, September 30, 1849, *Archivio Segreto del Vaticano, Segreteria di Stato Esteri, Corrispondenza da Gaeta e Portici, Rubrica* 68, *Fascicolo* 1, *sottofascicoli* 167–174.

21. Antonelli to the Governmental Commission in Rome, September 3, 1849, *Archivio Segreto del Vaticano, Segreteria di Stato Esteri, Corrispondenza da Gaeta e Portici,* 1849, *Rubrica* 242, *sottofasciolo* 15.

22. *Archivio Segreto del Vaticano, Segreteria di Stato Esteri, Corrispondenza da Gaeta e Portici, Rubrica* 248, *fascicolo* 1, *sottofascicoli* 148–152.

23. "Moto-proprio di Sua Santità sulla istituzione del consiglio di Stato e della Consulta di Stato per le Finanze," *Atti del Sommo Pontefice Pio Nono Felicemente Regnante,* I, 287–289.

24. "Notiffacazione della Commissisione governativa di Stato colla quale si annuncia il perdone accordato da Sua Santità con alcune riserve a coloro che presero parte nella cessata rivoluzione negli Stati Pontifici," *Atti del Sommo Pontefice Pio IX,* I, 293.

25. Micaud to Antonelli, December 31, 1849, *Archivio Segreto del Vaticano, Segreteria di Stato Esteri, Corrispondenza da Gaeta e Portici, Rubrica* 248, *fascicolo* 2, *sottofascicolo* 133.

26. Antonelli to Governmental Commission in Rome, November 5, 1849, *Archivio Segreto del Vaticano, Segreteria di Stato Esteri, Corrispondenza da Gaeta e Portici, Rubrica* 242, *sottofascicoli* 101–103.

27. Antonelli to the Governmental Commission in Rome, November 17, 1849, *Archivio Segreto del Vaticano, Segreteria di Stato Esteri, Corrispondenza da Gaeta e Portici,* 1849, *Rubrica* 242, *sottofascicolo* 135.

28. Luigi Enrico Pennacchini, "Dopo la caduta della repubblica romana," *Rassegna Storica del Risorgimento,* XXII (July, 1935), II, 165; Gregorio to Filippo Antonelli, November 2, 1849, *Archivio di Stato di Roma, Fondo Famiglia Antonelli, busta* 7, *fascicolo* 9; Luigi Chiala (ed.), *Lettere edite ed inedite di Camillo Cavour* (Turin: Roux e Favale, 1883), I, 430.

29. Antonelli to Apostolic Nuncio in Turin, December 10, 1849, *Archivio Segreto del Vaticano, Segreteria di Stato Esteri, Corrispondenza da Gaeta e Portici, Rubrica* 257, *sottofascicoli* 181–182.

30. Vittorio Gorresio, *Risorgimento scomunicato* (Florence: Parenti Editore, 1958), p. 25.

31. *L'Opinione,* March 29, 1850.

32. Antonelli's note to the Charge' D'affaires of the Sardinian King, May 14, 1850 and Antonelli's note of June 26, 1850 to the Marquis Spinola, *Archivio Segreto del Vaticano, Archivio Nunziatura Parigi,* 1850, *n.* 78.

33. Antonelli to the Nuncio in Turin, June 29, 1850. *Archivio Segreto del Vaticano, Segreteria di Stato Esteri, Corrispondenza da Gaeta e Portici, Rubrica* 257, *sottofascicoli* 190–191.

34. Antonelli's Protest to the Charge' d'affaires of Sardinian King, July 19, 1850, *Archivio Segreto del Vaticano, Archivio Nunzitura Parigi,* 1850, *n.* 78.

35. Antonelli's Circular note to the powers, September 24, 1850, *Archivio Segreto del Vaticano, Archivio Nunziatura Parigi,* 1850, *n.* 78.

36. Falconi, pp. 232, 250.

37. Rafaelle De Cesare, *Roma e lo Stato del Papa* (Milan: 1970), p. 15.

38. Filippo to Angelo Antonelli, April 9, 1850, *Archivio di Stato di Roma, Fondo Famiglia Antonelli, busta 6, fascicolo 3.*

39. Lukacs, p. 41; Falconi, pp. 264–267.

40. Antonio Sarti to Gregorio Antonelli, April 13, 1850, *Archivio di Stato di Roma, Fondo Famiglia Antonelli, busta 7, fascicolo 1;* Henry D'Ideville, *Journal d'un diplomate en Italie. Notes intimes pour servir a l'histoire du Second Empire: Rome, 1862–1866* (Paris: Hachette, 1875), p. 153.

41. Antonelli to Nuncio in Paris, April 21, 1850, n. 78.

42. George Macaulay Trevelyan, *Garibaldi's Defense of the Roman Republic 1848–49* (London: Longman's, Green and Co., 1914), p. 236.

43. Mariano Gabriele (ed.), *Il Carteggio Antonelli-Sacconi (1850–1860)* (Rome: Istituto per la Storia del Risorgimento Italiano, 1962), I, xv.

44. R. De Cesare, *The Last Days of Papal Rome 1850–1870,* trans. Helen Zimmern (London: Archibald Constable, 1909), p. 124.

45. "Editto della Segreteria di Stato sulla tassa postale mediante l'opposizione de'segnale demoninanti bolli franchi," *Atti del Sommo Pontefice Pio Nono Felicemente Regnante,* II, 53.

46. Giuseppe Massari, *Diario dalle cento voci* (Bologna: Cappelli, 1959), p. 352.

47. Ibid., p. 45.

48. Falconi, pp. 239–240.

49. Fiorella Bartoccini, *Roma nell' Ottocento* (Bologna: Capelli Editore, 1985), p. 39.

50. Noel Blakiston (ed.), *The Roman Question: Extracts from the Despatches of Odo Russell from Rome 1858–1870* (London: Chapman and Hall, 1962), pp. 41, 178.

51. Lukacs, pp. 25, 82.

52. *Archivio di Stato di Roma, Miscellanea di Carte Politiche o Riservate, busta* 124, *fascicolo* 4345.

53. "Editto della Segreteria di Stato sulla istituzione di un consiglio di Stato," *Atti del Sommo Pontefice Pio Nono Felicemente Regnante,* I, 607–613.

54. "Editto della Segreteria di Stato sulla istituzione della consulta di Stato per le finanze," *Atti del Sommo Pontefice Felicemente Regnante,* I, 642–650.

55. Lukacs, pp. 25, 41.

56. "Editto della Segreteria di Stato sulla rappresentanza e sull' amministrazione del Comune di Roma," *Atti del Sommo Pontefice Pio Nono Felicemente Regnante,* II, 3–6.

57. Raffaele de Cesare, *Roma e lo Stato del Papa dal ritorno di Pio IX all' XX Settembre* (Rome: Forzani), I, 43, 57.

58. *Atti del Sommo Pontefice Pio Nono Felicmente Regnante,* II, 11–12; 21.

59. Comte Fleury, *Memoirs of the Empress Eugenie* (New York: D. Appleton and Co., 1920), I, 57.

60. Pius IX to Victor Emmanuel II, March 25, 1852, *Archivio Segreto del Vaticano, Archivio Particolare Pio IX, Sovrani, Sardegna,* #34.

61. Pius IX to Victor Emmanuel II, July 2, 1852 and September 19, 1852, *Archivio Segreto del Vaticano, Archivio Particolare Pio IX, Sovrani, Sardegna,* nn. 32 and 36.

62. Pius IX to Antonelli, March 18, 1852, *Archivio di Stato di Roma, Fondo Famiglia Antonelli, busta* 2, *fascicolo* 22.

63. Circular note of Cardinal Antonelli to the Powers, *Archivio di Stato di Roma, Miscellanea di Carte Politiche O Riservate, busta* 121, *fascicolo* 4269A.

64. Unsigned letter to Antonelli, June 23, 1852, *Archivio di stato di Roma, Miscellanea di Carte Politiche O Riservate, busta* 121, *fascicolo* 4213.

65. Nuncio in Paris to Antonelli, August 28, 1852, *Archivio Segreto del Vaticano, Segreteria di Stato, Rubrica* 242, *fascicolo* 6, *sottofascioli* 8–9.

66. De Rayneval to Antonelli, December 9, 1852, *Archivio Segreto del Vaticano, Segreteria di Stato, Rubrica* 242, *fascicolo* 6, *sottofascicoli* 196–197.

67. Ridley, p. 318.

68. Nuncio at Vienna to Antonelli, December 14, 1852, *Archivio Segreto del Vaticano, Segreteria di Stato, Rubrica* 242, *fascicolo* 6, *sottofascicoli* 106–109.

69. *Archivio di Stato di Roma, Miscellanea di Carte Politiche O Riservate, busta* 124, *fascicolo* 4370.

70. Division in the ranks of revolutionaries in Papal States in 1853, *Archivio di Stato di Roma, Miscellanea di Carte Politiche O Riservate, busta* 121, *fascicolo* 4234.

71. John Francis Maguire, *Rome: Its Rulers and Institutions* (London: Longmans, Green and Roberts, 1857), pp. 458–459.

72. *Atti del Sommo Pontefice Pio IX Felicemente Regnante*, II, 170, 206, 210–211, 219.

Chapter Eight

1. Frank J. Coppa, *Camillo di Cavour* (Boston: Twayne Publishers, 1973), p. 109; Lajos Lukacs, *The Vatican and Hungary 1846–1878: Reports and Correspondence of the Apostolic Nuncios in Vienna* (Budapest: Akademiai Kiado, 1981), pp. 440–444.

2. Pius IX to Queen of Sardinia, March 19, 1853, *Archivio Segreto del Vaticano, Archivio Particolare Pio IX, Sovrani, Sardegna,* #40.

3. Octave Aubry, *Eugenie Empress of the French,* trans. F. M. Atkinson (Philadelphia, Lippincott, 1931), p. 80; Alyn Brodsky, *Imperial Charade* (New York: The Bobbs-Merrill Company, Inc., 1978), 141, 147.

4. Nuncio at Vienna to Antonelli, January 10, 1853, *Archivio Segreto del Vaticano, Segreteria di Stato Esteri,* 1853, *Rubrica* 242, *fascicolo* 6.

5. Nuncio at Vienna to Antonelli, May 28, 1853, *Archivio Segreto del Vaticano, Segreteria di Stato Esteri,* 1853, *Rubrica* 242, *fascicolo* 3.

6. Antonelli to the Nuncio at Vienna, *Archivio Segreto del Vaticano, Segreteria di Stato Esteri,* 1853, *Rubrica* 242, *fascicolo* 3, *sottofascicolo* 23.

7. Letters of Nuncio in Vienna to Antonelli, June 9 and June 14, 1853, *Archivio Segreto del Vaticano, Segreteria di Stato Esteri, Rubrica* 242, *fascicolo* 3, *sottofascicoli* 19 and 24.

8. Marco Minghetti, *Miei Ricordi* (3rd. ed.; Turin: Roux, 1888), III, 26.

9. Giuseppe Massari, *Diario dalle cento voci* (Bologna: Cappelli, 1959), p. 112.

10. Leone Carpi (ed.), *Il Risorgimento Italiano Biografie storico-politico d'illustri Italiani contemporanei* (Milan: Antica Casa Editrice, 1886), II, 37.

11. Lukacs, p. 114.

12. Pius IX to Napoleon III, January 24, 1855, *Archivio Segreto del Vaticano, Archivio Particolare Pio IX, Sovrani, Francia,* #26.

13. These include the concordats with Tuscany (April 25, 1851), Spain (March 16, 1851), Bolivia (May 29, 1851), Costa Rica (October 7, 1852), Guatemala (October 7, 1852), Austria (August 18, 1855), Portugal (January 21, 1857), Wurtemberg (April 8, 1857), Modena (June 23, 1857), Baden (June 28, 1859) and Spain (August 25, 1859).

14. Lukacs, p. 111; Coppa, *Camillo di Cavour,* pp. 121–122.

15. Pius IX to Victor Emmanuel II, February 18, 1855, *Archivio Segreto del Vaticano, Archivio Particolare Pio IX, Sovrani, Sardegna,* #46.

16. Raffaele de Cesare, *Roma e lo Stato del Papa dal ritorno di Pio IX all XX Settembre* (Rome: Forzani, 1907), I, 143.

17. Comte Fleury, *Memoirs of the Empresss Eugenie* (New York: D. Appleton and Co., 1920), I, 415.

18. De Cesare, I, 178; Giuseppe Leti, *Roma e lo Stato Pontificio dal 1849 al 1870. Note di storia politica* (2nd ed.; Ascoli Piceno: Giuseppe Cesari Editore, 1911), I, 331–332; Armando Ladolini, "Un archivio segreto del Cardinale Antonelli-II," *Studi Romani* (September-October 1953), 515.

19. Ladolini, *Studi Romani,* II, 515.

20. Alberto M. Ghisalberti, "Appunti sull' attentato al Cardinale Antonelli," *Chiesa e Stato nell' ottocento. Miscellanea in onore di Pietro Pirri,* R. Aubert et al. eds., (Padua: Antenore, 1962), I, 302.

21. L. Mournier to Filippo Antonelli, April 24, 1855, *Archivio di Stato di Roma, Fondo Famiglia Antonelli, busta 7, fascicolo 6.*

22. Andre Bellesort, *La Societé francaise sous Napoleon III* (Paris: Librairie Academique Perrin Editeur, 1932), p. 150.

23. *Mémoirs du Comte Horace De Viel Castel sur le Regne de Napoleon III.* III–1854–1856 (2nd. ed.; Paris: Chez tous les Librairies, 1883), p. 237.

24. Federic Loliee, *Women of the Second Empire, Chronicles of the Court of Napoleon III* (London: John Lane, 1907), p. 16.

25. Abel Hermant, *La Castiglione: La Dame de coeur des Tuileries (1835–1899)* (Paris: Hachette, 1938), pp. 112–113.

26. Pius IX to Franz-Josef, February 8, 1856, *Archivio Segreto del Vaticano, Archivio Particolare Pio IX, Sovrani*, Austria, #19.

27. Pius IX to Napoleon III, February 8, 1856, *Archivio Segreto del Vaticano, Archivio Particolare Pio IX, Sovrani, Francia,* #30.

28. Pius IX to Napoleon III, December 19, 1855, *Archivio Segreto del Vaticano, Archivio Particolare Pio IX, Sovrani, Francia,* #32.

29. *Mémoires du Comte De Viel Castel,* III, 242.

30. Giacomo Martina, *Pio IX e Leopoldo II* (Rome: Pontifica Università Gregoriana, 1967), p. 92.

31. Comte Fleury, I, 86.

32. Ibid., I 87–88; 101–102.

33. "Editto della Segreteria di Stato con quale si stabiliscono leggi relative alle strade ferrate dello Stato Pontifico," *Atti del Sommo Pontefice Pio Nono Felicemente Regnante,* II, 338.

34. Edmondo Mayor (ed.), *Nuove lettere inedite del Conte Camillo di Cavour* (Turin: Roux, 1895), pp. 37, 352.

35. Denis Mack Smith, *Cavour* (New York: Knopf, 1985), pp. 196–197.

36. Notices and Political Bulletins, 1857, *Archivio Segreto del Vaticano, Segreteria di Stato, Rubrica* 1c, *fascicolo* 2, #6; Antonio Monti, *Pio IX nel Risorgimento Italiano con documenti inediti* (Bari: Laterza, 1928), pp. 132–134.

37. Notices and Political Bulletins, 1857, *Archivio Segreto del Vaticano, Segreteria di Stato, Rubrica* 1c, *fascicolo* 2, #124.

38. Pius IX to Cardinal Antonelli, April 24, 1857, *Archivio di Stato di Roma, Fondo Famiglia Antonelli, busta* 2, *fascicolo* 22.

39. Pius IX to Cardinal Antonelli, June 12, 1857, *Archivio di Stato di Roma, Fondo Famiglia Antonelli, Busta* 2, *fascicolo* 22.

40. Cardinal Antonelli to Pius IX, June 17, 1857, *Archivio Segreto del Vaticano, Archivio Particolare Pio IX, Sovrani, Stato Pontificio,* #19.

41. Raffaele De Cesare, *Roma e lo Stato del Papa dal ritorno di Pio IX al XX Settembre* (Rome: Forzani, 1907), I, 261.

42. Minghetti, III, 177, 181.

43. Cardinal Antonelli to Pius IX, July 11, 1857, *Archivio Segreto del Vaticano, Archivio Particolare Pio IX, Sovrani, Stato Pontifico.*

44. Minghetti, III, 165.

45. Pius IX to Napoleon III, July 29, 1857, *Archivio Segreto del Vaticano, Archivio Particolare Pio IX, Sovrani, Francia,* #38.

46. Breve cenni sul progetto di equilibrare le spese con l'introiti, 1857, *Archivio di Stato di Roma, Fondo Famiglia Antonelli, busta* 9; Leti, I, 354.

47. L. Mournier to Filippo Antonelli, June 5, 1858, *Archivio di Stato di Roma, Fondo Famiglia Antonelli, Busta 7, fascicolo* 6.

48. Joseph Ridley, *Napoleon III and Eugenie* (New York: Viking Press, 1979), p. 399.

49. Mariano Gabriele (ed.), *Il Cartegio Antonelli-Sacconi (1850–1860)* (Rome: Istituto per la Storia del Risorgimento Italiano, 1962), I, 5, 26; Comte Fleury, I, 417.

50. Bellessort, p. 155; Falconi, p. 283.

51. Leti, I, 362.

52. Giacomo Antonelli to Loreta Antonelli, December 10, 1858, *Archivio di Stato di Roma, Fondo Famiglia Antonelli, Busta 6, fascicolo* 2.

Chapter Nine

1. Andre Bellesort, *La Société française sous Napoleon III* (Paris: Librairie Academique Perrin Editeur, 1932), pp. 152–154; *Memoires du Comte Horace De Viel Castel sur le Regne de Napoleon III. VI–1860–1864* (2nd ed., Paris: Chez tous les Libraires, 1884), 59.

2. Edmond About, *The Roman Question,* trans. Annie T. Wood (Boston: J. E. Tilton and Co., 1859), pp. 149–150.

3. Giuseppe Massari, *Diario delle cento voci* (Bologna: Cappelli, 1959), p. 104.

4. Frank J. Coppa, *Camillo di Cavour* (Boston: Twayne Publishers, 1973), p. 152; Frederic Loliee, *The Life of an Empress (Eugenie de Montijo),* trans. Bryn O'Donnell (London: Eveleigh Nash, 1908), p. 84.

5. Giacomo to Gregorio Antonelli, January 27, 1859, *Archivio di Stato di Roma. Fondo Famiglia Antonelli, busta 1, fascicolo* 1; Noel Blakiston (ed.), *The Roman Question: Extracts from the Despatches of Odo Russell from Rome 1858–1870* (London: Chapman and Hall, 1962), p. 152.

6. Apostolic Nuncio at Florence to Antonelli, January 10, 1859, *Archivio di Stato di Roma, Miscellanea di Carte Politiche O Riservate, busta* 124, *numero 4344.*

7. Anna Maria Isastia, *Roma nel 1858* (Rome: Istituto per la Storia del Risorgimento, 1978), p. 21; Coppa, *Camillo di Cavour,* p. 153.

8. Blakiston, p. 2.

9. Massari, p. 112; Mariano Gabriele (ed.) *Il Carteggio Antonelli-Sacconi (1850–1860)* (Rome: Istituto per la Storia del Risorgimento, 1962), I, xi; Carlo Falconi, *Il Cardinale Antonelli. Vita e carriera del Richelieu Italiano nella chiesa di Pio IX* (Milan: Mondadori, 1983), p. 344.

10. Sacconi to Antonelli, February 12, 1859, Gabriele, I, 26.

11. *Mémoires du Comte Horace de Viel Castel,* V, 19, 24.

12. Isastia, p. 25.

13. Antonelli to Duke of Gramont, March 11, 1859, Gabriele, I, 44; Falconi, p. 331.

14. Antonelli to Sacconi, March 13, 1859, Gabriele, I, 45; Blakiston, p. 9.

15. Antonelli to Sacconi, March 31, 1859, Gabriele, I, 66.

16. *Secrets of the Second Empire . . . Selections from the Papers of 1st Earl Cowley* (New York: Harper and Brothers Publishers, 1929), pp. 171, 175.

17. Sacconi to Antonelli, April 1, 1859, Gabriele, I, 67.

18. Antonelli to Sacconi, May 14, 1859, Gabriele, I, 112; *Secrets of the Second Empire . . . Selections from the Papers of 1st Early Cowley,* p. 172.

19. *Mémoires du Comte Horace de Viel Castel,* V, 41.

20. Blakiston, p. 23.

21. Delegation of Fermo to Antonelli, 1859, *Archivio di Stato di Roma, Miscellanea di Carte Politiche O Riservate, busta 134, fascicolo 4859.*

22. Antonelli to Sacconi, June 25, 1859, Gabriele, I, 149.

23. Pius IX to Napoleon III, July 4, 1859, *Archivio Segreto del Vaticano, Archivio Particolare Pio IX, Sovrani, Francia.*

24. Antonelli to Sacconi, July 2, 1859; Antonelli's Circular Note to the Dipolmatic Corps, July 12, 1859, Gabriele, I, 158, 172–173.

25. Napoleon III to Pius IX, July 14, 1859, *Archivio Segreto del Vaticano, Archivio Particolare Pio IX, Sovrani, Francia, numero 44.*

26. Pius IX to Cardinal Vicar, July 15, 1859, *Archivio Segreto del Vaticano, Archivio Particolare Pio IX, Sovrani, Stato Pontificio, numero 120;*

Frank J. Coppa. *Pope Pius IX: Crusader in a Secular Age* (Boston: Twayne Publishers, 1979), p. 132.

27. Lajos Lukacs, *The Vatican and Hungary 1846–1878: Reports and Correspondence of the Apostolic Nuncios in Vienna* (Budapest: Akademiai Kiado, 1981); Antonelli to Sacconi, July 15, 1859, Gabriele, I, 169–170.

28. Roger L. Williams, *The World of Napoleon III, 1851–1870* (New York: Free Press, 1965), p. 88.

29. Blakiston, p. 2.

30. Pietro Pirri, *Pio IX e Vittorio Emanuele II dal loro carteggio privato. II: La questione romana, 1856–1864* (Rome: Università Gregoriana, 1951), pp. 103–104; Antonelli to Sacconi, July 23, 1859, Gabriele, I, 176; Antonio Monti, *Pio IX nel Risorgimento Italiano con documenti inediti* (Bari: Laterza, 1928), p. 146; Giacomo Martina, *Pio IX (1851–1866)* (Rome: Università Gregoriana Editrice, 1986), pp. 100–101.

31. Lukacs, pp. 516–517, 521.

32. G. F. Berkeley and H. Berkeley, *The Irish Battalion in the Papal Army of 1860* (Dublin: Talbot Press, 1929), p. 44; Blakiston, p. 40.

33. *Mémoires du Comte Horace de Viel Castel,* V, 83.

34. *New York Times,* February 6, 1860; Falconi, p. 334.

35. Massari, p. 344.

36. Pirri, II, 121–122; Antonelli to Sacconi, August 27, 1859, Gabriele, I, 214.

37. *New York Times,* August 31, 1859.

38. Blakiston, pp. 45, 47.

39. L. Thouvenel (ed.), *Le Secret de l'Empereur. Correspondance confidentielle et inedite exchangee entre M. Thouvenel, Le Duc de Gramont et Le General Comte de Flahault 1860–1863* (2nd. ed.; Paris: Calmann Levy, 1889), I, 38–40.

40. Arturo Carlo Jemolo, *La questione romana* (Milan: Istituto per gli studi di publica internazionale, 1938), pp. 132–133.

41. *Archivio di Stato di Roma, Miscellanea di Carte Politiche O Riservate, busta* 132; Giovanni Orioli (ed.), *Memoire romane dell' ottocento* (Rome, 1963), pp. 84–85.

42. *Mémoires du Comte Horace de Viel Castel,* V, 223; Gabriele, I, 239–240, 247.

43. Massari, p. 403.

44. Falconi, pp. 338–340.

45. Pius IX to Victor Emmanuel II, December 3, 1859, *Archivio Segreto del Vaticano, Archivio Particolare Pio IX, Sovrani, Sardegna, numero* 56.

46. Pius IX to Emperor Franz Joseph, December 1, 1859, *Archivio Segreto del Vaticano, Archivio Particolare Pio IX, Sovrani, Austria, numero* 27; Martina, *Pio IX (1851–1866)*, p. 580.

47. Bernard O'Reilly, *A Life of Pius IX Down to the Episcopal Jubilee of 1877* (8th ed.; New York: P. F. Collier, 1878), p. 363.

48. Isastia, p. 41.

49. Giacomo to Gregorio Antonelli, December 29, 1859, *Archivio di Stato di Roma, Fondo Famiglia Antonelli.*

50. Giacomo Antonelli to Count Luigi Mastai, December 24, 1859, Monti, p. 151.

51. Martina, *Pio IX (1851–1866)*, p. 102; *Memoires du Comte Horace de Viel Castel*, VI, 13.

52. Pius IX to Napoleon III, January 8, 1860, *Archivio Segreto del Vaticano, Archivio Particolare Pio IX, Sovrani, Francia, numero* 48; O'Reilly, p. 363.

53. Memoires du Comte Horace de Viel Castel, V, 56; VI, 28.

54. Henry D'Ideville, *Journal d'un Diplomate en Italie* (Paris: Hachette, 1875), pp. 20–22.

Chapter Ten

1. Pietro Pirri, *Pio IX e Vittorio Emanuele II dal loro carteggio privato, II; La questione romana, 1856–1864* (Rome: Università Gregoriana, 1951), p. 151.

2. *Conversations with Napoleon III: A Collection of Documents, mostly unpublished and almost entirely Diplomatic, Selected and arranged with Introduction by Sir Victor Wellesly and Robert Sencourt* (London: Ernest Benn, 1934), pp. 176–177.

3. Noel Blakiston (ed.), *The Roman Question: Extracts from the Despatches of Odo Russell from Rome 1858–1870* (London: Chapman and Hall, 1962), p. 77; Giuseppe Massari. *Diario dalle cento voci* (Bologna: Cappelli, 1959), p. 463. L. Thouvenel (ed.), *Le Secret de l'Empereur, Correspondance confidentielle ed inedite exchangee entre M. Thouvenel, Le Duc*

de Gramont et Le General Compte de Flahaut 1860–1863 (2nd ed.; Paris: Calmann Levy, 1889), I, xvi; The Roman Journals of Ferdinand Gregororovius, 1852–1874, p. 78.

4. Edgar Quinet, La question romaine devant l'histoire, 1848–1867 (Paris: Armand Le Chevalier, 1868), p. 323.

5. Pietro Pirri, "Il Cardinale Antonelli tra il mito e la storia," Rivista di Storia della Chiesa in Italia, XII (1958), 104.

6. Henry D'Ideville, Journal d'un diplomate en Italie. Notes intimes pour servir a l'histoire du Second Empire: Rome, 1862–1866 (Paris: Hachette, 1875), pp. 268–269; Memoires du Comte Horace de Viel Castel sur la Regne de Napoleon III. (1851–1864) (Paris: Chex tous Les Librairies, 1884), V, 94; Conversations with Napoleon III, p. 189.

7. "Un dispaccio del Cardinale Segretario di Stato a Mons. Nunzio in Parigi in risposta a due scritti del Ministro degli Affari Stranieri in Francia intorno alla quistione romana," Archivio Segreto del Vaticano, Segreteria di Stato, 1860, Rubrica, 165, fascicolo 70, sottofascicolo 85.

8. Rivista di Storia della Chiesa in Italia, XII (1958), 105.

9. Blakiston, p. 77.

10. E. Roux, "Le Cardinal Antonelli," Gazette du Midi, November 8, 1876.

11. L. Thouvene (ed.), Le Secret de l'Empereur. Correspondance confidentielle et inedite exchangee entre M. Thouvenel, Le Duc de Gramont et Le General Comte de Flahaut 1860–1863 (2nd ed.; Paris; Calmann Levy, 1889), I, 55.

12. Ibid.

13. Antonelli to the Diplomatic Corps, March 24, 1860, Archivio Segreto del Vatican, Segreteria di Stato, Rubrica 165, fascicolo 71, sottofascicoli 15–16; Giuseppe Leti, Roma e lo Stato Pontificio dal 1849 al 1870. Note di storia politica (2nd ed.; Ascoli Piceno: Giusepe Cesari Editore, 1911), I, 11; "F. Curci and the Roman Question," Dublin Review, XXX (1878), 15.

14. The Roman Journals of Ferdinand Gregorovius, 1852–1874, ed. Friedrich Althaus, trans. Mrs. Gustavus W. Hamilton (London: George Bell and Sons, 1907), p. 83.

15. Thouvenel, I, 79–83; Memoires du Comte Horace de Viel Castel, VI, 46.

16. Ibid., I, 169–170.

17. Ibid., I, 109; Carlo Falconi, *Il Cardinale Antonelli. Vita e carriera del Richelieu Italiano nella chiesa di Pio IX* (Milan: Mondadori, 1983), p. 348.

18. Blakiston, p. 99.

19. Thouvenel, I, 132; Pirri, *Rivista di Storia della Chiesa in Italia,* XII (1958), 92.

20. *The Roman Journals of Ferdinand Gregorovius, 1852–1874,* pp. 85, 91.

21. Thouvenel, I, 139, 165, 182.

22. *Conversations with Napoleon III,* p. 111.

23. G. F. Berkeley and H. Berkeley, *The Irish Battalion in the Papal Army of 1860* (Dublin: Talbot Press, 1929), p. 32.

24. D'Ideville, p. 163.

25. *Memoires du Comte Horace de Viel Castel,* VI, 60.

26. Giacomo Martina, *Pio IX (1851–1866)* (Rome: Università Gregoriana Editrice, 1986), p. 113.

27. *Conversations with Napoleon III,* p. 186.

28. Pirri, *Rivista di Storia della Chiesa in Italia,* XII (1958), 86.

29. Falconi, p. 351.

30. Cavour to Antonelli, September 7, 1860, *Archivio di Stato di Roma, Miscellanea di Carte Politiche O Riservate,* 1860, *busta* 134, *fascicolo* 4815.

31. De Merode to the Magistrates and Functionaries of Velletri and Frosinone, September 9, 1860, *Archivio di Stato di Roma, Miscellanea di Carte Politiche O Riservate, Busta* 134, *fascicolo* 4871.

32. Report on the Invasion of Province and Town of Fermo, *Archivio di Stato di Roma, Miscellanea di Carte Politiche O Riservate, Busta* 134; *New York Times,* October 5, 1860; Falconi, p. 351.

33. *Memoires du Comte Horace de Viel Castel,* VI, 97; Nancy Nichols Barker, *Distaff Diplomacy: The Empress Eugenie and the Foreign Policy of the Second Empire* (Austin: University of Texas Press, 1967), p. 75.

34. Barker, p. 75.

35. *Memoires du Comte Horace de Viel Castel,* VI, 132.

36. Cardinal Antonelli to the Prince of Carignano, September 13, 1860, *L'Archivio Centrale dello Stato, E.U.R. Archivio Fanti, Scatola* 1.

37. "L'Allocuzione del Papa," *Giornale Officiale di Sicilia,* October 11, 1860.

38. *Memoires du Comte Horace de Viel Castel,* VI, 192.

39. Thouvenel, I, 209, 228–229; Blakiston, pp. 129–130.

40. Antonelli's circular note to the diplomatic corps, November 4, 1860, *Archivio Segreto del Vaticano, Segreteria di Stato, Rubrica* 165, *fascicolo* 71, *sottofascicoli* 221–224.

41. John P. Stockton to Lewis Cass, November 15, 1860 in Leo Francis Stock, *United States Ministers to the Papal States: Instructions and Despatches, 1848–1868* (Washington, D.C.: Catholic University Press, 1933), p. 211.

42. *The Roman Journals of Ferdinand Gregorovius, 1852–1874,* pp. 109–116.

43. Thouvenel, p. 282.

44. Falconi, p. 355.

45. Thouvenel, I, 243.

46. Ibid., I, 305.

47. D'Ideville, pp. 305–306; *Conversations with Napoleon III,* p. 191.

48. *Conversations with Napoleon III,* p. 187.

49. Martina, *Pio IX (1851–1866),* p. 2; Thouvenel, I, 332.

50. Glorney Bolton, *Roman Century: A Portrait of Rome as the Capital of Italy, 1870–1970* (New York: The Viking Press, 1970), p. 42.

51. Martina, *Pio IX (1851–1866),* p. 115; Blakiston, p. 162; Thouvenel, I, 364.

52. Leti, II, 201.

53. Pirri, *Rivista di Storia della Chiesa in Italia,* XII (1958), 103; George Martin, *The Red Shirt and the Cross of Savoy* (New York: Dodd, Mead and Co., 1969), p. 639.

54. Fiorella Bartoccini, *Roma nell' Ottocento* (Bologna: Cappelli, 1985), p. 126.

55. Thouvenel, I, 459; Martina, *Pio IX (1851–1866),* p. 115.

56. Thouvenel, I, 395; Father Passaglia to Cavour, March 19, 1861, *Documenti Diplomatici Italiani, Prima Serie, 1861–1870,* I, 46.

57. Pius IX to Francesco II, November 13, 1860 and January 6, 1861, *Archivio Segreto del Vaticano, Archivio Particolare Pio IX, Sovrani, Napoli.*

58. *Memoires du Comte Horace de Viel Castel,* VI, 122.

59. "Allocuzione di N. S. Papa Pio IX, Marzo 18, 1861," *Civiltà Cattolica* Series IV, volume X, p. 5.

60. *The Roman Journals of Ferdinand Gregorovius, 1852–1874,* p. 130; Martina, *Pio IX (1851–1866),* pp. 118–119.

61. *Conversations with Napoleon III,* p. 194.

62. *The New York Times,* March 2, 1861.

63. Passaglia writes to Cavour about his talk with Antonelli on April 5, April 6, 1861, *Documenti Diplomatici Italiani, prima serie, 1861–1870,* volume I, 79.

64. *The Roman Journals of Ferdinand Gregorovius, 1852–1874,* p. 135.

65. *Conversations with Napoleon III,* p. 194; *Memoires du Comte Hourace de Viel Castel,* VI, 122.

66. Leti, II, 216.

67. Martina, *Pio IX, (1851–1866),* p. 146.

Chapter Eleven

1. *Consulta di Stato per le Finanze. Rapporto 5 marzo 1863, Archivio di Stato di Roma, Fondo Famiglia Antonelli, busta* 9.

2. Carlo Falconi, *Il Cardinale Antonelli. Vita e carriera del Richelieu Italiano nella chiese di Pio IX* (Milan: Mondadori, 1983), pp. 377–381.

3. Henry D'Ideville, *Journal d'un diplomate en Italie: Rome, 1862–1866* (Paris: Hachette, 1875), II, 61–62.

4. Andre Bellessort, *La Societe francaise sous Napoleon III* (Paris: Librarie Academique Perrin Editeur, 1932), pp. 161–164.

5. *The Roman Journals of Ferdinand Gregorovius, 1852–1874,* ed. Friedrich Althaus, trans. Mrs. Gustavus W. Hamilton (London: George Bell and Sons, 1907), pp. 152–155; Giacomo Martina, *Pio IX (1851–1866)* (Rome: Università Gregoriana Editrice, 1986), p. 125.

6. Nassau William Senior, *Conversations with Distinquished Persons During the Second Empire From 1860 to 1863,* ed. by M. C. M. Simpson (London: Hurst and Blackett, 1880), II, 28.

7. Falconi, pp. 391–92, 399.

8. Giacomo Antonelli to Francesco II, December 18, 1862, *Archivio di Stato di Roma, Fondo Famiglia Antonelli, busta* 1, *sotto fascicolo* 299.

9. Glorney Bolton, *Roman Century: A Portrait of Rome as the Capital of Italy, 1870–1970* (New York: Viking Press, 1970), pp. 45–46.

10. Martina, *Pio IX (1851–1866)*, p. 110.

11. Emile Bourgeois and E. Clermont, *Rome et Napoleon III (1849–1870)* (Paris: Libraire Armond Colen, 1907), p. 208.

12. D'Ideville, II, 211.

13. Ibid., II, 11–13.

14. George Macaulay Trevelyan, *Garibaldi and the Thousand* (London: Longmans Green, 1909).

15. *Conversations with Napoleon III: A Collection of Documents, mostly unpublished and almost entirely Diplomatic Selected and arranged with Introduction by Sir Victor Wellesly and Robert Sencourt* (London: Ernest Benn, 1934), p. 266.

16. W. J. Stillman to William H. Seward, January 3, 1862, in Leo Francis Stock, *Consular Relations between the United States and the Papal States: Instructions and Despatches* (Washington, D.C.: American Catholic Historical Association, 1945), p. 226.

17. *Conversations with Napoleon III*, p. 186.

18. Martina, *Pio IX (1851–1866)*, p. 258; D'Ideville, II, 268.

19. Odo Russell to Earl Russell, July 15, 1862 in Noel Blakiston (ed), *The Roman Question: Extracts from the Despatches of Odo Russell from Rome 1858–1870)* (London: Chapman and Hall, 1962), p. 232.

20. D'Ideville, II, 275.

21. George Martin, *The Red Shirt and the Cross of Savoy* (New York: Dodd, Mead and Co., 1969), p. 663.

22. Roger Aubert, "Giacomo Antonelli," *Dizionario Biografico degli Italiani* (Rome: Istituto della *Enciclopedia Italiana*, 1961), III, 489.

23. "Mezza citta' sotto accusa," *Il Progresso Italo-Americano*, September 21, 1970.

24. Odo Russell to Earl Russell, March 10, 1863, in Blakiston, p. 268.

25. Richard M. Blatchford to William H. Seward, March 7, 1863, in Stock (ed) *United States Ministers to the Papal States: Instructions and Despatches, 1848–1868.* (Washington, D.C., Catholic University Press, 1933), p. 273.

26. *The Roman Journals of Ferdinand Gregorovius,* p. 178.

27. *United States Ministers to the Papal States: Instructions and Despatches, 1848–1868,* p. 273.

28. Blakiston, pp. 271–272.

29. *The Roman Journals of Ferdinand Gregorovius,* pp. 175, 199.

30. Gramont to Antonelli, May 24, 1863, *Archivio di Stato di Roma, fondo famiglia Antonelli, busta 1, fascicolo 2.*

31. Frederick William, Prince of Prussia to Antonelli, April 10, 1863, *Archivio di Stato di Roma, Fondo Famiglia Antonelli, busta 2, fascicolo 20.*

32. D'Ideville, II, 82.

33. Martina, *Pio IX (1851–1866),* p. 144.

34. D'Ideville, II, 106–107, 164–167.

35. R. De Cesare, *The Last Days of Papal Rome, 1859–1870,* trans. Helen Zimmern (London: A. Constable and Co., 1909), p. 349.

36. D'Ideville, II, 205.

37. Comte Fleury, *Memoirs of the Empress Eugenie* (New York: D. Appleton and Co., 1920), I, 272.

38. D'Ideville, II, 214.

39. Ibid., I, 260.

40. Martina, *Pio IX (1851–1866),* p. 266.

41. Report of the Supreme Sacred Congregation of the Holy Office on the propositions containing the 70 principal errors of the time, *Archivio Segreto del Vaticano, Archivio Particolare Pio IX, Ogetti Vari n. 1779.*

42. Martina, *Pio IX (1851–1866),* pp. 108, 306.

43. Giacomo Martina, *Chiesa e mondo moderno* (Rome: Edizioni Studium, 1876), p. 75.

44. Martina, *Pio IX (1851–1866),* p. 288.

45. E. E. Y. Hales, *Pio Nono: A Study in European Politics and Religion in the Nineteenth Century* (Garden City, N.J.: Doubleday and Co., 1954), p. 267.

46. D'Ideville, II, 269.

47. Falconi, pp. 405–408.

48. Blakiston, p. 305.

49. D'Ideville, II, 222, 254.

50. *Il Progresso-Italo Americano,* September 17, 1970.

51. D'Ideville, II, 342.

52. *Il Progresso-Italo Americano,* September 17, 1970; Falconi, pp. 411–416; D'Ideville, II, 312.

53. D'Ideville, II, 367.

54. Falconi, pp. 415–416.

55. Blakiston, p. 292.

56. *The Roman Journals of Ferdinand Gregorovius,* p. 240.

57. Ibid., p. 253.

58. Sidney Sonnino, *Diario, 1866–1912,* ed. by Benjamin F. Brown (Bari: Laterza, 1972), I, 42, 49.

59. *The Roman Journals of Ferdinand Gregorovius,* p. 255; Blakiston, p. 329.

60. *Conversations with Napoleon III,* p. 284.

61. Lajos Lukacs, *The Vatican and Hungary 1846–1878; Reports and Correspondence of the Apostolic Nuncios in Vienna* (Budapest: Akademiai Kiado, 1981), p. 155.

62. Blakiston, p. 330.

63. *Conversations with Napoleon III,* pp. 317–318, 321.

64. Ibid., p. 321.

65. D'Ideville, II, 355.

66. Ibid., II, 247.

67. Martina, Pio IX (1851–1866), p. 144.

Chapter Twelve

1. Noel Blakiston (ed), *The Roman Question: Extracts from the Despatches of Odo Russell from Rome 1858–1870* (London: Chapman and

Hall, 1962), p. 338; Henry D'Ideville, *Journal d'un diplomate en Italie. Notes intimes pour servir a l'histoire du Second Empire: Rome, 1862–1866* (Paris: Hachette, 1873), II, 328, 345.

2. Lillian Parker Wallace, *The Papacy and European Diplomacy 1869–1878* (Chapel Hill: University of North Carolina Press, 1948), pp. 11–12.

3. Frederic Loliee, *The Life of an Empress (Eugenie de Montijo)*, trans. B. O'Donnell (London: E. Nash, 1908), p. 225.

4. Antonio Monti, *Pio IX nel Risorgimento Italiano con Documenti Inediti* (Bari: Laterza, 1928), p. 270.

5. Rufus King to William H. Seward, December 10, 1866, in Leo Francis Stock (ed.), *United States Ministers to the Papal States: Instructions and Despatches, 1848–1866.* (Washington, D.C.: Catholic University Press, 1933), p. 403.

6. R. De Cesare, *The Last Days of Papal Rome, 1859–1870*, trans. Helen Zimmern (London: A. Constable and Co., 1909), p. 410.

7. Giulio Andreotti, *La sciarada di Papa Mastai* (Milan: Rizzoli, 1967), p. 59.

8. Manifesto of Victor Emmanuel (October 27, 1867), *Archivio di Stato di Milano, Fondo Questura, carteggio* 75.

9. Carlo Falconi, *Il Cardinale Antonelli: Vita e carriera del Richelieu Italiano nella chiesa di Pio IX* (Milan: Mondadori, 1983), p. 428.

10. De Cesare, pp. 391–392.

11. *The Roman Journals of Ferdinand Gregorovius, 1851–1874,* ed. Friedrich Althaus, trans. Mrs. Gustavus W. Hamilton (London: George Bell and Sons, 1907), p. 297.

12. George Martin, *The Red Shirt and the Cross of Savoy* (New York: Dodd, Mead and Co., 1969), pp. 703–04.

13. *The Roman Journals of Ferdinand Gregorovius,* p. 301.

14. Vittorio Gorresio, *Risorgimento scomunicato* (Florence: Parenti Editore, 1958), p. 171.

15. Lajos Lukacs, *The Vatican and Hungary 1846–1878; Reports and Correspondence of the Apostolic Nuncios in Vienna* (Budapest: Akademiai Kiado, 1981), pp. 630–631.

16. Falconi, p. 428.

17. Pius to Monsignor Luciano Bonaparte, November 8, 1867, *Archivio Segreto del Vaticano, Archivio Particolare Pio IX, Stato Pontificio,* #163A.

234 NOTES

18. Blakiston, pp. 352–353.

19. Glorney Bolton, *Roman Century: A Portrait of Rome as the Capital of Italy, 1870–1970* (New York: Viking Press, 1970), p. 55.

20. Blakiston, p. 211.

21. De Cesare, 399.

22. Wallace, p. 26.

23. Falconi, pp. 431–38; D'Ideville, II, 349.

24. Blakiston, p. 362.

25. E. E. Y. Hales, *Pio Nono: A Study in European Politics and Religion in the Nineteenth Century* (Garden City, N.J.: Doubleday, 1954), p. 289.

26. Count Alessandro Adorni to Antonelli, March 14. 1869, *Archivio Segreto del Vaticano, Segreteria di Stato Esteri, rubrica 284, fascicolo 1*.

27. Wallace, p. 56.

28. Ibid., p. 62.

29. Baron John Acton, *The History of Freedom and Other Essays* (London: Macmillan and Co., 1922), p. 518.

30. Falconi, p. 438.

31. De Cesare, *The Last Days of Papal Rome*, p. 425.

32. *The Roman Journals of Ferdinand Gregorovius*, p. 343.

33. Falconi, pp. 441–42.

34. Blakiston, p. 403.

35. Ibid., p. 439; Roger Aubert, "Giacomo Antonelli," *Dizionario Biografico degli Italiani*, III, 490.

36. Falconi, 440; 444–45.

37. Acton, p. 519.

38. Blakiston, p. 369.

39. Andreotti, p. 50.

40. Ibid., p. 46.

41. J. B. Bury, *History of the Papacy in the 19th Century (1864–1878)*. ed. Rev. R. H. Murray (London: Macmillan and Co., 1930), p. 103.

42. Wallace, p. 73.

43. Giacomo to Gregorio Antonelli, March 1, 1870, *Archivio di Stato di Roma, Fondo Famiglia Antonelli, busta* 1.

44. Blakiston, p. 391.

45. Fernand Mourret, *A History of the Catholic Church: Period of the Early Nineteenth Century (1823–1878)*, trans. by Newton Thompson (New York: Herder Book Co., 1957), p. 658.

46. Aubert, *Dizionario Biografico degli Italiani*, III, 490.

47. *The Roman Journals of Ferdinand Gregorovius*, p. 351.

48. Blakiston, p. 417.

49. Wallace, p. 93.

50. Aubert, *Dizionario Biografico degli Italiani*, III, 490.

51. Wallace, p. 97; Shane Leslie, *Cardinal Manning: His Life and Labours* (New York: P. J. Kenedy and Sons, 1954), p. 100.

52. Blakiston, pp. 417, 426.

53. Ibid., pp. 428–429; Leslie, p. 100.

54. Falconi, pp. 450–453.

Chapter Thirteen

1. Giulio Andreotti, *La sciarada di Papa Mastai* (Milan: Rizzoli, 1967), p. 63; Lillian Parker Wallace, *The Papacy and European Diplomacy 1869–1878* (Chapel Hill: University of North Carolina Press, 1948), p. 118; Carlo Falconi, *Il Cardinale Antonelli. Vita e carriera del Richelieu Italiano nella chiesa di Pio IX* (Milan: Mondadori, 1983), p. 456.

2. J. B. Bury, *History of the Papacy in the 19th Century (1864–1878)*, ed. Rev. R. H. Murray (London: Macmillan and Co., 1930), p. 147.

3. Patrick Keyes O'Clery, *The Making of Italy* (London: Kegan Paul, French and Co., 1892), p. 469.

4. Emile Bourgeois and E. Clermont, *Rome et Napoleon III (1849–1870)* (Paris: Librairie Armond Colen, 1907), p. 310.

5. Andreotti, p. 68; Bury, p. 152; S. William Halperin, *Italy and the Vatican at War* (Chicago: University of Chicago Press, 1939), p. 337.

6. Andreotti, p. 69.

7. Bourgeois, p. 310; Italo De Feo, *Roma 1870. L'Italia dalla morte di Cavour a Porta Pia* (Turin: U. Mursia, 1970), p. 310.

8. Leo Francis Stock (ed.), *Consular Relations Between the United States and the Papal States: Instructions and Despatches* (Washington, D.C.: American Catholic Historical Association, 1945), p. 355.

9. Wallace, p. 120.

10. Falconi, pp. 457–458.

11. Andreotti, p. 78.

12. Paolo Dalla Torre, *Pio IX e Vittorio Emanuele II. Dal Loro Carteggio privato negli anni del dilaceramento (1865–1878)* (Rome: Istituto di Studi Romani Editori, 1972), p. 150.

13. Ibid., p. 151.

14. Falconi, p. 458.

15. Pius IX to Vittorio Emanuele II, September 11, 1870, *Archivio Segreto del Vaticano, Archivio Particolare Pio IX, Sardegna, Sovrani,* #83.

16. Dalla Torre, pp. 146–147.

17. Antonio Monti, *Pio IX nel Risorgimento Italiano con Documenti Inediti* (Bari: Laterza, 1928), p. 194.

18. Glorney Bolton, *Roman Century: A Portrait of Rome as Capital of Italy, 1870–1970* (New York: The Viking Press, 1970), p. 7; Stock (ed.), p. 354.

19. Falconi, p. 459; Raffaele De Cesare, *The Last Days of Papal Rome, 1859–1870* (London: A. Constable and Co., 1909), p. 451.

20. Dalla Torre, p. 33; Falconi, p. 464.

21. Falconi, p. 467.

22. Ibid., p. 468.

23. Stock (ed.), pp. 358–359.

24. John A. Thayer, *Italy and the Great War: Politics and Culture, 1870–1915* (Milwaukee: University of Wisconsin Press, 1964), p. 7.

25. Pietro Pirri, "Il Cardinale Antonelli tra il mito e la storia," *Rivista di Storia della Chiesa in Italia,* XII (1958), 99–100.

26. De Cesare, p. 459.

27. Monti, p. 167.

28. Wallace, p. 126.

29. Ibid., p. 132.

30. *The New York Times,* November 2, 1870.

31. Bolton, p. 66.

32. Francis B. Thornton, *Cross Upon Cross: Life of Pope Pius IX* (New York: Benziger Brothers, Inc., 1955), p. 232.

33. Andreotti, pp. 114, 119.

34. *The New York Times,* October 18, 1870.

35. Dalla Torre, p. 162.

36. *The Roman Journals of Ferdinand Gregorovius, 1852–1874,* ed. F. Althaus, trans. Mrs. G. W. Hamilton (London: George Bell and Sons, 1907), p. 396; Falconi, pp. 479–480.

37. Dalla Torre, p. 68.

38. *The Roman Journals of Ferdinand Gregorovius,* p. 390; Frank J. Coppa, *Pope Pius IX: Crusader in a Secular Age* (Boston: Twayne Publishers, 1979), p. 173; Great Britain, *British Foreign and State Papers,* LXV (1973–74), 638–642.

39. Stock (ed.), p. 429.

40. Fiorella Bartoccini, *Roma nell' ottocento* (Bologna: Cappelli Editore, 1985), p. 435; Falconi, p. 481.

41. Falconi, p. 488.

Chapter Fourteen

1. Carlo Falconi, *Il Cardinale Antonelli. Vita e carriera del Richelieu Italiano nella chiesa di Pio IX* (Milan: Mondadori, 1983), pp. 482–489.

2. Antonio Monti, *Pio IX nel Risorgimento Italiano con Documenti Inediti* (Bari: Laterza, 1928), p. 203; Lillian Parker Wallace. *The Papacy and European Diplomacy 1869–1878* (Chapel Hill: University of North Carolina Press, 1948), p. 268.

3. Pasquale De Franciscis (ed.), *Discorsi del Sommo Pontefice Pio IX Pronunziati in Vaticano ai Fedeli di Roma e dell' Orbe dal principio della sua prigionia fino al presente* (Rome: Tipografia di G. Aurelj, 1872–1878), I, 248.

4. Monti, p. 168.

5. S. William Halperin, *Italy and the Vatican at War* (Chicago: University of Chicago Press, 1939), p. 132.

6. Ibid., p. 68.

7. *The New York Times*, January 7, 1877.

8. Giacomo to Agostino Antonelli, his nephew, July 27, 1871, *Archivio di Stato di Roma, Fondo Famiglia Antonelli, busta 1, sottofascicolo* 313.

9. Giacomo Antonelli to Quintino Sella, November 13, 1872 in Luigi Luzzatti, *God in Freedom: Studies in the Relations between Church and State*, trans. Alfonso Arbib-Costa (New York: Macmillan Co., 1930), p. 567.

10. Antonio Monti, *La politica degli Stati italiani durante il Risorgimento* (Milan: Villardi, 1948), p. 230.

11. Falconi, pp. 491–492.

12. De Franciscis, I, 491–492, 498.

13. Ibid., II, 77; Monti, *Pio IX nel Risorgimento Italiano*, p. 171.

14. De Franciscis, I, 444.

15. *The New York Times*, November 5, 1872.

16. Wallace, p. 145.

17. De Franciscis, I, 371.

18. Giacomo to Agostino Antonelli, June 21, 1873, *Archivio di Stato di Roma, Fondo Famiglia Antonelli, busta* 1.

19. *The New York Times*, January 15, 1874; June 19, 1874.

20. De Franciscis, III, 334–335.

21. Ibid., III, 265.

22. Falconi, pp. 501–503.

23. *The New York Times*, March 23, 1873.

24. Luzzatti, p. 434.

25. Wallace, p. 192.

26. Frank J. Coppa, *Pope Pius IX: Crusader in a Secular Age* (Boston: Twayne Publishers, 1979), p. 184.

27. Falconi, p. 506.

28. Wallace, p. 194.

29. *American Catholic Quarterly Review*, XV (July 1890), 407; Erich Eyck, *Bismarck and the German Empire* (New York: Norton, 1964), p. 205; Edward Husgen, *Ludwig Windhorst* (Cologne: Verlog, 1907), p. 94.

30. Bismarck's speech in the Prussian Chamber of Peers in which he referred to his position during the *Kulturkampf,* April 12, 1886, in *Bismarck,* ed. by B. M. Holyday (Englewood Cliffs, N.J.: Prentice-Hall, 1970), p. 47; Falconi, p. 508.

31. Falconi, pp. 513, 518.

32. Giacomo to Agostino Antonelli, March 18, 1875, *Archivio di Stato di Roma, Fondo Famiglia Antonelli, busta* 1.

33. Giacomo to Gregorio Antonelli, January 30, 1876, *Archivio di Stato di Roma, Fondo Famiglia Antonelli, busta* 1.

34. Giacomo to Agostino Antonelli, Easter Sunday, 1876, *Archivio di Stato di Roma, Fondo Famiglia Antonelli, busta* 1.

35. *L'Union,* November 10, 1876.

36. *The New York Times,* January 24, 1876.

37. *The New York Times,* February 5, 1876.

38. *Le Monde,* November 7, 1876.

39. Falconi, p. 521.

40. *The Evening Post,* November 7, 1876.

41. Pietro Pirri, "Il Cardinale Antonelli tra il mito e la storia," *Rivista di Storia della Chiesa in Italia,* XII (1958), 119.

42. *The New York Tribune,* November 7, 1876; Falconi, p. 521.

43. *Rivista di Storia della Chiesa in Italia,* XII (1958), 119.

44. Falconi, p. 521.

45. *L'Unita' Cattolica,* November 7, 1876.

46. *Rivista di Storia della Chiesa in Italia,* XII (1958), 119.

47. Francis B. Thornton, *Cross upon Cross: Life of Pope Pius IX* (New York: Benziger Brothers, Inc., 1955), p. 245.

48. *The London Times,* November 7, 1876.

49. Giacomo Antonelli's Will, *Archivio di Stato di Roma, Fondo Famiglia Antonelli, busta* 6, *fascicolo* 4.

50. Ibid.; *The London Times,* December 7, 1876; *Dublin Review,* XVIII (January 1877), 83.

51. *Rivista di Storia della Chiesa in Italia,* XII (1958), pp. 105–118.

52. Ibid., pp. 114–115; *The New York Times,* July 22, 1877.

53. Wallace, p. 295.

54. *Rivista di Storia della Chiesa in Italia,* XII (1958), 106–107.

Chapter Fifteen

1. Noel Blakiston (ed.), *The Roman Question: Extracts from the Despatches of Odo Russell from Rome 1858–1870* (London: Chapman and Hall, 1962), p. 79.

2. *The New York Times,* November 7, 1876.

3. Giuliano Cataldi to Filippo Antonelli, November 15, 1859, *Archivio di Stato di Roma, Fondo Famiglia Antonelli, busta 7, fascicolo 3.*

4. Antonio Gramsci, *Il Risorgimento* (Turin: Einaudi, 1966), p. 166.

5. Ruggero Bonghi, *Pio IX e il Papa futuro* (3rd. ed.; Milan: Treves, 1877), p. 126.

6. *The New York Times,* November 25, 1876.

7. Paola Dalla Torre, "Il Cardinale Giacomo Antonelli fra carte di archivio ed atti processuali," *Pio Nono* VIII (1979), 160.

8. Will of Giacomo Antonelli's mother, *Archivio di Stato di Roma, Fondo Famiglia Antonelli, busta 6, sottofascicolo 2.*

9. Giuseppe Leti, *Roma e lo Stato Pontificio dal 1849 al 1870, Note di storia politica* (2nd ed.; Ascoli Piceno: Giuseppe Cesari Editore, 1911), I, 16.

10. Dalla Torre, *Pio Nono* VIII (1979), 155.

11. Gianfranco Radice, *Pio IX e Antonio Rosmini* (Citta' del Vaticano: Libreria Editrice del Vaticano, 1974), pp. 153–155.

12. Ibid., pp. 62–63.

13. Dalla Torre, *Pio Nono* VIII (1979), 185.

14. Raymond Corrigan, *The Church and the Nineteenth Century* (Milwaukee: Bruce Publishing Company, 1938), p. 57.

15. Dalla Torre, *Pio Nono* VIII (1979), 168, 171.

16. "Cardinal Antonelli," *Dublin Review* XXVIII (January 1877), 82.

17. R. De Cesare, *The Last Days of Papal Rome, 1859–1870,* trans. Helen Zimmern (London: A. Constable and Co., 1909), p. 124.

18. Carlo Gourand, *L'Italia: Sue ultime rivoluzione e suo stato presente* (Florence: Carletti, 1852), p. 55.

19. A. Rosmini, *Della Missione a Roma* (Turin: Paravia, 1881), pp. 143–144; Radice, p. 80.

20. Dalla Torre, *Pio Nono* VIII (1979), 172.

21. Ibid., p. 181.

22. *Dublin Review* XXVIII (January 1877), 81.

23. Ibid., pp. 81–82.

24. Fernand Mourrett, *A History of the Catholic Church: VIII—Period of the Early Nineteenth Century (1823–1878)*, trans. Rev. Newton Thomson (St. Louis: Herder Book Co., 1957), p. 404.

25. Ivan Scott, *The Roman Question and the Powers, 1845–1865* (The Hague: Martinus Nijhoff, 1969), p. 57.

26. Giovanni Maioli (ed.), *Pio IX da vescovo a pontifice. Lettere al Card. Luigi Amat. Agosto 1839-Luglio 1848* (Modena: Società Tipografica Modenese, 1943), p. 57.

27. De Cesare, p. 92.

28. Leti, I, 16.

29. *Archivio di Stato di Roma, Fondo Famiglia Antonelli, busta 2, fascicoli 13–14.*

30. Mourrett, VIII, 404.

31. Friedrich Engel-Janosi, "French and Austrian Political Advice to Pius IX, 1846–1848," *The Catholic Historical Review*, XXXVIII (April 1952), 9.

32. L. Thouvenel (ed.), *Le Secret de L'Empereur. Correspondance confidentielle ed inedite exchangee entre M. Thouvenel, Le Duc de Gramont et La General Compte de Flahaut 1860–1863* (2nd. ed.; Paris: Calmann Levy, 1889), I. pp. 169–170; II, 380.

33. Dalla Torre, *Pio Nono* VIII (1979), 183.

34. Pius to the Archbishop of Bourges, Dupont, June 10, 1849, *Archivio Segreto del Vaticano, Archivio Particolare Pio IX, Francia, Particolari*, #18.

35. Hippolyte Castile, *Le Cardinal Antonelli* (Paris: E. Dentu, 1859), pp. 9–11.

36. Dalla Torre, *Pio Nono* VIII (1979), 174.

37. De Cesare, pp. 163–164.

38. Guido Pasolini (ed.), *Carteggio tra Marco Minghetti e Giuseppe Pasolini, 1846–1854* (Turin: Bocca, 1924), I, 14.

39. Marco Minghetti, *Miei Ricordi* (3rd. ed.; Turin: L. Roux, 1888), III, 177.

40. Abbot Gasquet (ed.), *Lord Acton and his Circle* (New York: Longmans, Green and Co., 1906), p. 142; Scott, p. 70.

41. Antonelli's Circular Note of September 30, 1849 to the Powers, *Archivio Segreto del Vaticano, Segreteria di Stato Esteri, Corrispondenza da Gaeta e Portici, 1848–1850, Rubrica 68, fascicolo 1.*

42. Blakiston, p. 2.

43. Antonelli was one of the few people in the Curia willing and able to assume responsibility. On one occasion the Pope, showing the signs of fever, insisted upon saying Mass and collapsed at the altar. The other prelates, not knowing what steps to take, called Antonelli, who had the sense to call for a sedan chair and to have the Pope carried to his bedroom. Blakiston, p. 172.

44. For some indication of Antonelli's capacity to pay attention to detail and the plethora of responsibilities placed upon his shoulders see *Archivio Segreto del Vaticano, Segreteria di Stato Esteri, Corrispondenza da Gaeta e Portici, Rubrica 68, fascicolo 1, sottofascocoli 119–122* and *Rubrica 242, sottofascicolo 20.*

45. Pietro Pirri, "Il Cardinal Antonelli tra il mito e la storia," *Rivista di Storia della Chiesa in Italia,* XII (1958), 81.

46. Ibid.

47. Paolo Dalla Torre, *Pio IX e Vittorio Emanuele II. Dal Loro Carteggio privato negli anni del dilaceramento (1865–1878)* (Rome: Istituto di Studi Romani Editori, 1972), p. 29.

48. Cavour to Antonelli, March 29, 1853, *Archivio di Stato di Roma, Fondo Famiglia Antonelli, busta 1, fascicolo 2.*

49. Ettore Passerin D'Entreves, "Appunti nell' impostazione delle ultime trattative del governo colla S. Sede per una soluzione della questione romana (novembre 1860-marzo 1861) in R. Aubert, A. M. Ghisalberti and E. passerin D'Entreves (eds.), *Chiesa e stato nell' ottocento. Miscellanea in onore di Pietro Pirri* (Padua: Antinori, 1962), II, 584.

50. Federigo Sclopis di Salerano, *Diario Segreto (1859–1878),* ed Pietro Pirri (Turin: Deputazione subalpina di storia patria, 1959), p. 221.

51. "Le Cardinal Antonelli," *Gazette du Midi,* November 8, 1876.

52. Pius IX to Vittorio Emanuele II, April 2, 1860, in Pietro Pirri (ed.), *La qestione romana, 1856–1864. Parte II—I documenti* (Rome: Pontifica Università Gregoriana, 1951), p. 164.

53. Blakiston, p. 120.

54. Lajos Lukacs, *The Vatican and Hungary 1846–1878: Reports and Correspondence of the Apostolic Nuncios in Vienna* (Budapest: Akademiai Kiado, 1981), p. 196.

55. Frank J. Coppa, "Cardinal Giacomo Antonelli: An Accommodating Personality in the Politics of Confrontation," *Biography*, II (Fall 1979), 295.

56. Dalla Torre, *Pio Nono* VIII (1979), 186.

57. Carlo Falconi, *Il Cardinale Antonelli. Vita e carriera del Richelieu Italiano nella chiesa di Pio IX* (Milan: Mondadori, 1983), pp. 26–27.

58. Domenico Antonelli's administration of the affairs of Terracina, *Archivio di Stato di Roma, Fondo Famiglia Antonelli, buste* 4–5.

59. *Archivio Segreto del Vaticano, Fondo Particolare Pio IX, cassetta* 29, *fascicolo* 127.

60. *The New York Times*, November 5, 1872.

61. Dalla Torre, *Pio Nono* VIII (1979), 144.

62. *Unità Cattolica*, November 7, 1876.

63. Emile Ollivier, *L'Empire Liberal. Etudes, recits, souvenirs* (Paris: Garnier Freres, 1897), II, 338.

64. De Cesare, pp. 124–125.

65. Dalla Torre, De Cesare *Pio IX e Vittorio Emanuele II*, p. 29; Antonio Monti, *Pio IX nel Risorgimento Italiano con documenti inediti* (Bari: Laterza, 1928), p. 26.

66. Leo Francis Stock (ed.), *United States Ministers to the Papal States: Instructions and Despatches, 1848–1869* (Washington, D.C.: Catholic University Press, 1933), p. 274.

67. Mariano Gabriele (ed.), *Il Carteggio Antonelli-Sacconi (1850–1860)* (Rome: Istitutio per la Storia del Risorgimento Italiano, 1962), I, xl.

68. Pirri, *Rivista di Storia della Chiesa in Italia*, XII (1958), 81.

69. *The New York Times*, November 25, 1876.

70. Dalla Torre, *Pio IX e Vittorio Emanuele II*, p. 56.

71. *The New York Times*, January 16, 1874.

72. Ibid.

73. Pirri, *Rivista di Storia della chiesa in Italia*, XII (1958), 120.

Bibliography

I Archival Sources

1. *L'Archivio di Stato di Roma*

This is a rich source for the study of Cardinal Antonelli, the pontificate of Pius IX, and the Papal States during the turbulent years of the *Risorgimento*. This archive, and especially the *Fondo Famiglia Antonelli*, is the repository of the private and family papers of Cardinal Antonelli, and includes some of his public papers as well. *The Fondo Famiglia Antonelli* also includes the private correspondence and many of the business records of members of the Antonelli family, especially his father and brothers. Among the important private documents found herein are Giacomo Antonelli's last will, as well as the will of his mother, for which he served as executor.

The first 32 packets or *buste* of this *Fondo Famiglia Antonelli* contains the private correspondence and business affairs of Giacomo's ancestors and immediate family. The 33rd contains material on the financial arrangements for the reacquisition of the Beauharnais appanage, in which Giacomo and Filippo played a major role during the pontificate of Gregory XVI. In many respects the bulky *busta* 1, which contains the personal correspondence of the Cardinal, including some 328 letters, for the most part directed to his brothers and father, as well as important letters sent to Giacomo by various lay and clerical personages and heads of state, is most useful. However, much can also be gleaned from *busta* 3, which contains the correspondence with his father Domencio, and *busta* 5, which contains the papers of his mother, Loreta. Also useful are *busta* 6 and 12, which include the correspondence of his brothers Angelo and Filippo. *Busta* 13 focuses upon the relatively lucrative administrative affairs of Terracina and Sonnino.

The *Archivio di Stato di Roma* is also a rich source for an understanding of the governance and administration of the Papal States during the first half of the nineteenth century. Particularly useful are the *Carte Miscellanea Politiche O Riservate*, which are conveniently arranged chronologically, and contain a diverse selection of reports and political papers. The documents of the *Fondo Repubblica Romana* are invaluable for an understanding of the course of events in Rome in 1849, as are the papers of the *Consiglio di Stato* and the *Consulta di Stato*. The latter two archives place particular emphasis on the politics and policies of the Cardinal and chief minister of Pio Nono.

The correspondence between Antonelli and the Nuncio at Paris, Carlo Sacconi, found in the *Archivio di Stato di Roma*, was edited by Mariano Gabriele and published as *Il Carteggio Antonelli-Sacconi (1850–1860)* (Rome: Istituto per la Storia del Risorgimento Italiano, 1962).

2. *L'Archivio Segreto del Vaticano*

The papers of the pontificate of Pius IX in the Vatican Archives were opened to scholars in 1967. Within this vast repository a number of collections are particularly useful for a study of the political and diplomatic policies of Pio Nono and his chief minister, Cardinal Antonelli. Especially useful are *L'Archivio Particolare Pio IX*, which is subdivided into *Sovrani* and *Particolari* and catalogued by State, and the *Ogetti Vari*, grouped by number, and containing papers covering a wide series of events and issues of the pontificate.

The *Fondo Particulare Pio IX* contains many of the letters and sermons of Mastai-Ferretti as well as a number of his personal papers. Catalogs are available for the *Archivio Particolare* and the *Ogetti Vari*, although that for the former is far more detailed and useful than the catalog for the latter. The inventory for the *Fondo Particolare Pio IX* is sketchy at best, and one must request a *Cassetta* containing the papers of the archive, to determine the contents and importance of the papers therein.

Considerable can be learned about papal foreign and domestic policy from the *Archivio della Segreteria di Stato Esteri* and the *Archivii delle Nunziature*, especially the *Fondo Archivio della Nunziatura di Firenze*, the *Fondo Archivio della Nunziatura di Parigi*, and the *Fondo Archivio della Nunziatura di Vienna*. The rich mine of material found in the *Archivio della Segreteria di Stato* trace developments during the revolutionary period 1848–1849, for which the *Corrispondenza da Gaeta e Portici* is invaluable. Foreign affairs and Church matters were supervised by the Cardinal in the years following the restoration, and the record of his supervision can be traced in the papers of the *Segreteria di Stato* for the entire period. Additional light on the Secretary of State's modus operandi is shed by the papers of the *Stato Pontificio*, those of the *Miscellanea Corpo Diplomatico* and those collected in the *Nunziature e Delegazioni Apostoliche*, all found in the Secret Vatican Archives.

The *Archivio degli Affari Ecclesiastiche* contains the documentation regarding the elaboration and negotiation of the various concordats. The papers of the *Fondo del Concilio Vaticano* are still in the process of being reorganized.

Since the opening of the *Archivio Segreto del Vaticano* for the pontificate of Pio Nono some of the papers have been published including the correspondence between Antonelli and the Nuncio at Madrid, Monsignor Lorenzo Barili, which is drawn primarily from the *Archivio della Segreteria di Stato Esteri* and the *Archivio della Nunziatura di Madrid*. This correspondence has been edited by Carla Meneguzzi Rostangi under the title *Il Carteggio Antonelli-Barili, 1859–1861* (Rome: Istituto per la Storia del Risorgimento Italiano, 1973). Some of the papers drawn from the *Segreteria di Stato Esteri* and the *Nunziatura di Vienna* have been edited by Lajos Lukacs and published as *The Vatican and Hungary, 1846–1878: Reports and correspondence on Hungary of the Apostolic Nuncios in Vienna* (Budapest: Akademiai Kiado, 1981).

3. *Fondi Archivistici del Museo Centrale del Risorgimento*

These are rich in material for a study of the pontificate of Pio Nono and the activities of his Secretary of State. Included herein are the papers of Nicolà Roncalli and his *Cronaca di Roma*, some 51 bound volumes, providing a chronicle of events in the Papal States from 1844–1870. This newsletter, based on what the author saw, read, or heard about events in the capital and the provinces, provides a wide range of information about Papal Rome during these years. The archives of the *Museo Centrale del Risorgimento* also contains part of the correspondence of Michelangelo Caetani, Duke of Semoneta, Garibaldi, Callimaco Zambianchi, Luigi Carlo Farini, and others. The miscellaneous volumes on the *Stato Pontificio* numbered 114 contains a number of apostolic letters, encyclicals, and circulars regarding the Roman State from the Congress of Vienna to the collapse of the temporal power. *Busta* 11 of the *Archivio Amat* is useful as are the bound manuscript volumes and especially the *Notizie Politiche della Provincia Pontificia, 1833–1846* and the *Bollettini Politici di Roma*.

4. *L'Archivio Centrale dello Stato, E.U.R.*

This central archive of the Italian State contains the papers of the various ministries of unitary Italy and contains a number of archives that are useful for the earlier period, as well as the years from 1861–1878. Among the most useful papers for this particular study are some of the documents of the *Archivio Agostino Depretis*, those of the Famiglia Benso di Cavour, and those of the *Archivio Fanti*.

5. *L'Archivio Storico del Ministero degli Affari Esteri*

Contains diplomatic sources of the Italian State proclaimed in 1861 as well as considerable papers of the various states which were merged into the new Kingdom.

6. *L'Archivio della Congregagzione per la Cause dei Santi*

Contains a copy of the work by A. Cani and F. Vitozzi, *Processo Romano per la Causa di Beatificazione e Cannonizzazione del Servo di Dio Papa Pio IX. Articoli sopra la fama di Santita di vita, virtù e miracoli del Servo di Dio del processo ordinario da costruiri nella Curia Romana presentata da . . .* Torre del Greco: Palomba, 1908. Although many of the articles included herein are apologetic in tone, and focus on Pius IX, there are some that deal with his relationship to his government in general, and his relationship to Cardinal Antonelli in particular. Since there is a tendency to dwell on the virtues of the Pope, responsibility for failure and problems are often attributed to others, and the Cardinal bears much of the burden.

II Printed Works of the Pontificate of Pio Nono and the Ministry of Cardinal Giacomo Antonelli

1. *Acts, Allocutions, Encylicals and Statements*

Atti del Sommo Pontefice Pio Nono. Felicemente Regnante. Parte Seconda che Comprende i Motu-propri, Chirografi, Editi, Notifacazioni, ec. per lo Stato Pontificio. Rome: Tipografia delle Belle Arti, 1857.

This is particularly useful for a study of the first two years of the Pontificate and the role of the Cardinal during this initial period. It is indispensable for an understanding of the institutions provided by the Pope and his Secretary of State following the restoration of 1849. Included within these two volumes are a number of edicts of the early 1850s and the attempts at administrative reform.

Discorsi del Sommo Pontefice Pio IX Pronunziati in Vaticano ai Fedeli di Roma e dell' Orbe dal principio della sua prigionia fino al presente. 4 vols. Rome: Tipografia di G. Aurelj, 1872–1878.

Within these four volumes, edited by Pasquale de Franciscis, are the speeches and encylicals of Pius IX following the loss of Rome during his "imprisonment" in the Vatican. The tone and content of these messages reveal the intransigent mood of the Pontiff, and clearly establish his responsibility for the rigid stance assumed by the Papacy toward the Italian Kingdom following the loss of Rome. These discourses, at times a spontaneous outpouring on the Pope's part, also reveal Pio Nono's resistance to accomodation on the basis of his religious sentiments and scruples rather than the supposed *realpolitik* of Antonelli.

Pii IX Pontificis Maxima Acta . . . Rome: Artium, 1854–1875.

Contains the Pope's Allocutions and religious Encyclicals. Whereas the *Atti del Sommo Pontefice* is a compilation of Pius's secular acts—

decrees, notifications, edicts, *motu-proprii*, etc.—the *Acta* includes those documents of an ecclesiastical nature. They therefore reveal the religious basis for the Pope's actions minimizing the supposed political aims and ambitions of Antonelli. Pio Nono's encylicals can also be found in *Tutte le Encicliche dei Sommi Pontifici.* Milan: Dall' Oglio, 1959. A number of these are available in English in *Papal Teachings: The Church.* These encyclicals have been selected and arranged by the Benedictine Monks of Solesmes and translated by Mother E. O'Gorman. Boston: Daughters of St. Paul, 1962. Another important source in English is Roy J. Deferari's translation of Henry Denzinger's *Enchiridion Symboloroum,* 13th ed., which is published under the title *The Sources of Catholic Dogma.* St. Louis: B. Herder Book Co., 1957. Also see *Dogmatic Canons and Decrees* (of the Catholic Church). New York: The Devin-Adair Co., 1912, and *The Papal Encyclicals in their Historical Context.* Edited by Anne Fremantle with an Introduction by Gustave Weigel. New York: G. P. Putnam's Sons, 1956.

2. *Published Correspondence with Nuncios*

Gabriele, Mariano (ed.), *Il Carteggio Antonelli-Sacconi (1850–1860).* Rome: Istituto per la Storia del Risorgimento Italiano, 1962.

While the diplomacy of Cavour has been studied and restudied, the diplomacy of the counter-*Risorgimento* has not received the same scholarly attention. This discrepancy reflects the maxim that in history, as in life, it is success that counts, as well as the fact that until the mid-1960s the Vatican Archives remained closed for the Pontificate of Pio Nono. The unavailability of the papers of the Papal Secretariat of State during the years when the Italian State was born and the temporal power collapsed, assured that the record of these momentous events would be incomplete if not one-sided. In 1862 Mariano Gabriele edited the correspondence (found in the *Archivio di Stato di Rome*) between Cardinal Antonelli and Carlo Sacconi, the Nuncio at Paris. The documents included therein illustrate that Antonelli and Sacconi utilized the spiritual authority of the Pope in their attempts to persaude Napoleon III to defend the temporal power.

Meneguzzi Rostagni, Carla (ed.). *Il Carteggio Antonelli-Barili (1859–1861).* Rome: Istituto per la Storia del Risorgimento Italiano, 1973.

This correspondence is drawn mainly from the archives of the Secretariat of State and that of the Nunciature of Madrid. The dispatches included date from the beginning of 1859 to the summer of 1861. They reflect the initial Spanish reaction to the crisis facing the Papal States, the endeavors of Antonelli and the Nuncio to persuade Catholic Spain to assume the initiative in the defense of the temporal rights of the Holy See, and the documents reveal that the government did not have the will, if indeed it had the means to assume such a role, despite the great personal devotion of the Queen to the Holy Father. The diplomatic defense assumed by Antonelli in these pages follows the approach the Holy See had pursued since 1815, insisting that the temporal power owed its existence to the Catholic world on whose behalf it was exercised. Uncertain of Napoleon III's intentions, Antonelli hoped that Spain would galvinize the smaller Catholic states to champion the territorial rights of the Papacy. Despite the appeal to religious duty, the strategy did not succeed. Antonelli's instructions are typically laconic while the Nuncio is chatty if not loquacious, providing an almost day to day account of what is happening in Spain at almost all levels: the court, the government, and public opinion. Consequently, the correspondence sheds more light on Spanish developments than papal ones and will be of immense interest to students of Queen Isabella and General O'Donnell. The editor has written an Introduction which sets the stage for the material which follows, and has provided scholarly and informative footnotes which serve to clarify issues and identify individuals.

Cummings, Rayond L. "Come La Nunziatura di Napoli informava Roma nel 1859–1860." *Rassegna Storica del Risorgimento,* 67 (1980, n.2), 154–176.

   Based on the recently discovered papers of Gianelli and Antonelli in the Vatican Archives, it examines the relations between Naples and Rome during the final months of the Bourbon regime. Pietro Gianelli, the Nuncio, emerges as a patient observer of events, reluctant to embroil himself in the politics of the period.

Lukacs, Lajos. *The Vatican and Hungary 1846–1878: Reports and Correspondence on Hungary of the Apostolic Nuncions in Vienna.* Translated by Zsofia Karmos, Budapest: Akademiai Kiado, 1981.

   This correspondence between Antonelli and the various Nuncios in Vienna traces the relations of the Vatican with the Hapsburg Empire in general, and Hungary in particular, during the Pontificate of Pio Nono. It is ably edited by Lukacs but poorly translated by Kormos. Divided into two parts, the historical analysis is followed by a collection of documents, drawn principally from the Secretariat of State. Part I includes three sections: Reform and Revolution, 1846–1849, Counterrevolution and Absolutism, 1849–1867, and Liberalism and Ultramontism, 1867–1878. The five chapters and two hundred pages in the first section place the 368 documents which follow, in perspective. The narrative is scholarly, revealing the editor's extensive research, despite the awkwardness of the translation. Fortunately the documents selected for inclusion are presented in their original language (Italian) while the editor's precis of each has been translated. The documents reveal a considerable amount about Hungarian and Hapsburg developments, as well as the preoccupations of Rome during the turbulent years that witnessed first revolution, and then the collapse of the temporal power. The letters of Michele Viale Prelà (1845–1856), Antonio De

Luca (1856–1863) and Ludovico Jacobini (1874–1880) to Antonelli, and the Secretary of State's responses and instructions, contain a wealth of valuable information about Austria and the Papal perception of developments in Central Europe as well as the Italian peninsula. Since Lukacs includes some of the correspondence between Antonelli and De Luca, there is some overlap with Meneguzzi-Rostagni's volume.

Meneguzzi Rostagni, Carla. *Il Carteggio Antonelli-De Luca, 1859–1861*. Rome: Istituto per la storia del Risorgimento Italiano, 1983.

This volume of printed correspondence has an Introduction which places what follows in perspective as well as a series of scholarly and informative notes which serve to clarify issues and identify individuals. The survey of Austrian-Papal relations from Pio Nono's flight from Rome at the end of 1848, to the troubled triennial considered in this work, is particularly useful. The editor's analysis of the policies of a weak and anachronistic Papal States, and a Hapsburg Empire beset by internal divisions and diplomatic isolation, makes clear why they ultimately failed to preserve the temporal power.

Within the documents of this correspondence Antonelli emerges as an astute diplomat confronting a difficult situation. One of his problems was the fact that De Luca did not have much experience in defending the political affairs of the Holy See, preferring to dwell upon theological issues. Thus in a dispatch of March 10, 1859, Antonelli had to remind the Nuncio that in light of the Empire's importance for Papal diplomacy, the Secretary of State should be completely and promptly informed of all decisions made by its cabinet (p. 9). Again on March 25, 1859, Antonelli informed De Luca that while it was his responsibility to report on ecclesiastical matters, he had also to report on political developments, especially when these concerned affairs in Italy and impinged upon the Papal States (p. 19). In subsequent dispatches the Nuncio's skills improved, but the diplomatic situation deteriorated. In the face of Piedmontese hostility, French intrigue, Spanish immobility, and Austrian powerlessness, Antonelli had finally to concur with Pio Nono that only divine providence could provide relief.

3. *Diplomatic Dispatches and Correspondence with Heads of State*

Blakiston, Noel (ed.). *The Roman Question: Extracts from the Dispatches of Odo Russell from Rome, 1858–1870*. London: Chapman and Hall, L'td, 1962.

This volume contains the most important of Odo Russell's dispatches from Rome where he served as unofficial English representative, having frequent access to Antonelli. These dispatches gathered from the Public Record Office, the Clarendon Papers in Oxford, and the private Russell papers, provide an eyewitness account of the last decade of the Papal State and Antonelli's efforts to salvage the state and preserve the temporal power. Written by a Protestant, who believed that no satisfactory solution to Italian affairs could be attained without the end of the temporal power, Russell provides some interesting insights both into the activities and motivation of Pius IX and his Secretary of State, Antonelli.

Confederate States of America. *The Messages and Papers of Jefferson Davis and the Confederacy Including Diplomatic Correspondence 1861– 1865.* Introduction by Allan Nevins and compiled by James D. Richardson. New York: Chelsea House—Robert Hector, Publishers, 1966.
Includes information about the appointment and mission of Dudly Mann as envoy of the Confederate States of America to Papal Rome in 1863, and reports on the stance assumed by Antonelli.

Dalla Torre, Paolo. *Pio IX e Vittorio Emanuele II. Dal Loro Carteggio privato negli anni del dilaceramento (1865–1878).* Rome: Istituto di Studi Romani Editori, 1972.
The volume includes the last years of the correspondence between Pius IX and the first King of Italy, which is not found in Father Pirri's more extensive correspondence of the two. Although the title emphasizes their private correspondence, attention is provided to the Pope's correspondence with other sovereigns, particularly Napoleon III, and the Roman Question is almost always an underlying theme.

Elliot, Sir Henry. *Some revolutions and other diplomatic experience.* London: J. M. Murray, 1922.
Recollections of the English Minister at Naples and Turin; less than an objective observer, and not particularly favorable to the diplomacy of Naples and Rome.

Great Britain. *British and Foreign State Papers,* XXXVI (1847–48); XXXVII (1848–49); LXV (1873–74)
Are useful for the facts contained therein but the analysis is often biased, particularly in the post restoration years.

Il Carteggio Cavour-Nigra dal 1858 al 1861. Edited by the National Commission for the publication of the Papers of Count Cavour. Bologna: Zanichelli, 1961.
This correspondence provides some inkling of how Cavour and the Turin Cabinet viewed developments in Papal Rome and Cardinal Antonelli during the crucial years of the formation of the Italian Kingdom.

Il Regno di Sardegna nel 1848–49 nei carteggi di Domenico Bufa. Edited by Emilio Costa. Volume III: 20 febbraio 1848–29. Rome: Istituto per la Storia del Risorgimento Italiano, 1970.
This third volume of the correspondence of the political moderate Buffa, friend of Rattazzi, Castelli, and Cavour, and Minister of Agricul-

ture. These letters help to provide an understanding of Turin's position on domestic and diplomatic matters, including its policies towards Papal Rome.

Italia. Commissione per la pubblicazione dei Documenti diplomatici. *I Document Diplomatici Italiani. Prima serie (1861–1870)*. Rome: La Libreria dello Stato, 1952.
These documents help to reconstruct the policy of the new Kingdom of Italy in the decade from the formation of the Unitary State to the forcible acquisition of Rome.

La diplomazia del Regno di Sardegna durante la prima guerra d'indipendenza. II: Relazioni con lo Stato Pontificio (Marzo 1848–luglio 1849). Edited by Carlo Baudi di Vesme. Turin: Istituto per la Storia del Risorgimento Italiano, 1951.
Provides insights into why the Italian Confederation envisioned by Antonelli failed to materialize, and the impact, influence, and the responsibility for the Papal Allocution of April 1848.

Le relazioni diplomatiche fra il governo provvisorio siciliano e la Gran Bretagna. III serie: 1848–1860. Volume unico (14 aprile 1848–10 aprile 1849). Edited by Federico Curato. Rome: Istituto storico italiano per l'eta' modern e contemporanea, 1971.

Le relazioni diplomatiche fra L'Austria e il Granducato di Toscano. III serie: 1848–1860. Volume III: 10 maggio 1851–30 dicembre 1852. Edited by Angelo Filipuzzi. Rome: Istituto storico italiano per l'eta' moderna e contemporanea, 1968. Volume V: *19 maggio 1856—12 maggio 1859*. Rome, 1969.
These volumes on relations between Tuscany and Austria often cover issues and topics relating to the Papal States, particularly in the later 1850s.

Le relazioni diplomatice fra L'Austria e il Regno di Sardegna e la guerra del 1848–49. III serie: 1848–1860. Volume I: 24 marzo 1848—11 aprile 1849. Edited by Angelo Filipuzzi. Rome: Istituto storico italiano per l'eta' moderna e contemporanea, 1961.

Le relazioni dilomatiche fra L'Austria e lo Stato Pontificio. III serie: 1848–1860. I: 28 novembre 1848–28 dicembere 1849. Edited by Richard Blaas. Rome: Istituto storico italiano per l'eta' moderna e contemporanea, 1973.
Included herein are the Austrian documents on relations between Austria and the Pontifical State for the period between the flight of Pius to Gaeta and the restoration of papal power at the end of 1849. They reveal the differences between Vienna and Paris on matters concerning the Papal States, the nature and consequences of Papal diplomacy, the role played by Antonelli, and the impact of the events

of 1849 on Austrian policy. Although Austria had withdrawn its ambassador from the papal court, there is an excellent documentation in the instructions and dispatches of Prince Schwarzenberg, and in the letters of Count Esterhazy sent to Gaeta for the conference of the powers.

Le relazioni diplomatiche fra la Gran Bretagna e il Regno di Sardegna. III serie: 1848–1860. Volume IV: gennaio 1852–10 gennaio 1855. Edited by Federico Curato. Rome: Istituto per l'eta' moderna e contemporanea, 1968.

Examines the first phase of the diplomatic activity of the Cavourian and anti-papal James Hudson in Piedmont, and his approach both to Cavour and Antonelli.

Le relazioni diplomatiche fra lo Stato Pontificio e la Francia. III serie: 1848–1860. Volume I: 4 gennaio 1848–18 febbraio 1849. Edited by Michele Fatica. Rome: Istituto storico italiano per la eta' moderna e contemporanea, 1971.

The material included herein throws light upon the difficult situation confronted by the Papal States during the revolutionary period and the attempts of Antonelli to secure French support. The correspondence concludes with the eve of the Conference of Gaeta called by the Cardinal.

Le relazioni diplomatiche fra lo Stato Pontificio e la Francia. III serie: 1848–1860. Volume II: 19 febbraio 1849–15 aprile 1850. Rome: Istituto storico italiano per la eta' moderna e contemporanena, 1972.

Much of the correspondence in this volume concerns the French attempt to make their intervention against the Roman Republic conditional upon certain prescribed reforms to be given by the Pope to his subjects, and the means used by Antonelli to block this attempt.

L'Unificazione Italiana vista dei diplomatici statiunitinesi. Volume IV: 1861–1866. Edited by Howard Marraro. Istituto per la storia del Risorgimento Italiano, 1971.

This volume of diplomatic documents of the first minister of the United Kingdom of Italy George P. Marsh, includes correspondence from April 1861 to the end of 1866. The comments of Marsh are interesting, but not kind to Antonelli or the Papal States, and tinged with anticlericalism.

Marraro, Howard R. (ed.). *Diplomatic Relations between the United States and the Kingdom of the Two Sicilies.* 2 vols. New York: S. F. Vanni, 1952.

The first volume contains Instructions and Dispatches from 1816 to 1850, the second from 1850 to 1861.

Martina, Giacomo. *Pio IX e Leopold II*. Rome: Pontifica Università Gregoriana, 1967.
This 28th volume of the *Miscellanea Historiae Pontificiae* gathers the correspondence of the Grand Duke of Tuscany and Pio Nono, revealing the humanity of the Pope, his religious scruples and preoccupations, and his firm adherence to the confessional state. Antonelli, in turn, is shown as seconding and implementing the policies inspired by the Pope.

Olszamowska-Skowronska. *La correspondance des Papes et des Empereurs de Russie (1814–1878) selon le documents authentiques*. Rome: Pontifica Università Gregoriana, 1970.

Pirri, Pietro. *Pio IX e Vittorio Emanuele II dal loro carteggio privato. I. La laicizzazione dello Stato Sardo, 1848–1856*. Rome: Università Gregoriana, 1944. *Pio IX e Vittorio Emanuele II dal loro carteggio privato. II. La questione romana, 1856–1864. Parte I: Testo, Parte II: Documenti*. Rome: Università Gregoriana, 1951.
These volumes are invaluable for an understanding of the diplomacy and the war which led to the collapse of the Papal State, and the creation of the rump state which disappeared in 1870. Pirri was allowed access to the Vatican Archives prior to its opening to the broader scholarly community and published this important work, which is both scholarly and objective. Antonelli, in particular, is presented as an industrious diplomat attempting to fulfill the objectives of the Pope, which he shared.

Stock, Leo Francis (ed.). *Consular Relations between the United States and the Papal States: Instructions and Despatches*. Washington, D.C., American Catholic Historical Association, 1945; *United States Ministers to the Papal States: Instructions and Dispatches, 1848–1868*. Washington, D.C., American Catholic Historical Association, 1933.
As early as 1797 the United States commissioned a consul to represent them in the Papal States, and in 1848 opened formal diplomatic relations with the papal dominion, and supported a minister at the court of Pius until 1867. The reports of these ministers, though long neglected, provide invaluable and surprisingly objective accounts of developments in Rome and the Papal States. Removed from the bitter diplomatic struggle, the Americans provided some of the earliest objective accounts of Antonelli and his role in the counter-*Risorgimento*.

Zanichelli, Nicola (ed.). *Cavour e L'Inghilterra: Carteggio con V. E. D'Azeglio*. Bologna: Commissione Reale Editrice, 1933.

——— (ed.). *La questione romana negli anni 1860–61. Carteggio del Conte di Cavour con D. Pantaleoni, C. Passaglia, O. Vimercati*. Bologna: Commissione Reale Editrice, 1933.

III. Published Sources on Antonelli

1. *Memoirs, Diaries, Studies, and Correspondence of Those Having Access to Antonelli*

There is considerable consensus about events in Rome before and following the revolution of 1848 by those who had access to the Pope and his Secretary of State. Important light is shed on the period by such works as:

Balbo, Cesare. *Delle Speranze d'Italia.* 2nd. ed. Paris, 1944.

Bianchi, Nicomedè. *Le politica di Massimo D'Azeglio dal 1848 al 1859. I Documenti.* Turin: Roux e Favale, 1884.

Blakiston, Noel. "Con Odo Russell a Roma nel 1860," *Rassegna Storica del Risorgimento anno* XLVII (January-March 1960), 61–68.

Brazão, E. *L'Unificazione Italiana vista dai diplomatici portoghesi.* Rome: Istituto per la Storia del Risorgimento Italiano, 1962.

D'Azeglio, Massimo. *Degli ultimi casi di Romagna.* Florence, 1846;

———. *I miei ricordi.* Trans. into English by Count Maffei. *Recollections of Massimo D'Azeglio.* London: Chapman and Hall, 1868.

———. *L'Italie de 1847 a 1865. Correspondence Politique de M. D'Azeglio accompagnee d'une introduction per E. Rendù.* Paris: Didier et Cie, 1867.

A two volume recollection of events in the peninsula by a colleague of Antonelli and minister of the Pope, who eventually left the service of Rome to serve Piedmont, its political adversary.

Della missione a Roma di Antonio Serbati Rosmini negli anni 1848–1849. Turin: Paravia, 1881.

Published posthumously. In this work Rosmini accounts for both the failure of his mission to Rome as well as the increasingly conservative policy pursued by Pius after 1849. If the first could in part be explained by the bad faith of those Piedmontese ministers who had entrusted him with the assignment, the latter he tended to explain in terms of the increasing influence that Antonelli had upon Pius and the affairs of state. Thus in Rosmini's account, the Cardinal is presented as the villain and the enemy of the *Risorgimento.*

Diario di Nicola Roncalli dal anno 1849 al 1870. Edited by R. Ambosi de Magistris and I. Ghiron. Turin, 1884.

Included herein are selections from the *Cronaca di Roma* and sheds considerable light on Pio Nono, Antonelli, and the Counter-*Risorgimento.*

Farini, Luigi Carlo. *Lo Stato Romano dall' anno 1815 al 1850.* 3rd ed. 4 vols. Florence: Le Monnier, 1853.
 This is a well-documented work, even though this one-time colleague of Antonelli does not always indicate the sources he has employed. Farini reveals his constitutionalist and federalist bias in the work, giving it a marked political tone. Farini holds the democrats mainly responsible for the failure of the constitutional experiment in the Papal States and presents an interesting picture of Pius. Stressing the absolute moral integrity of the Pope, he nonetheless cites the religious basis of his political outlook. He also points to the political limitations of Pius including his emotionalism, his inability to resist the applause and condemnations of the crowd, and his indecision and uncertainty during difficult times. He sees far greater political ability in Antonelli, but questions his motivation.

Filipuzzi, Angelo. *Pio IX e la politica austriaca in Italia dal 1815 al 1848 [nella relazione di Riccardo Weiss di Starkenfels].* Florence: Felice Le Monnier, 1958.

Franco, Giovanni Giuseppe. *Appunti storici sopra il Concilio Vaticano.* Edited by Giacomo Martina. Rome: Università Gregoriana Editrice, 1972.
 Includes the quasi-daily observations of the director of the *Civiltà Cattolica* on the Vatican Council from the preliminaries, before its opening, to the declaration of infallability. The role of Antonelli is shown to be marginal and explanatory, while that of the Pope is shown to be central.

Gladstone, William. *Rome et le Pape.* Trans. Victor Oger. Paris: Edition Populaire, Sandoz et Fischbacker, 1876.

Hubner, Compte de. *Neuf ans de souvenirs d'un Ambassadeur d'Autriche à Paris sous le second Empire.* Alexandre de Hubner (ed.). Paris: Plon, 1904.
 Claims that Napoleon wanted to be arbiter of Italy, but found his moves checked by the convictions of Pio Nono and the politics of Antonelli.

Hudry, Marius. "Correspondance de Manfredo Bertone, Comte de Sambuy, Ministre plenipotentiare du gouvernment Sarde apres du Saint Seige (Nov. 1851–Nov. al 1852) à monsigneur André Charvaz, ancien precepteur du Roi Victor Emmanuel II," in *Chiesa e stato nell' ottocento. Miscellanea in onore di Pietro Pirri.* Edited by R. Aubert et al. Padua: Antenore, 1962, I, 327–54.

Kanzler, Hermann. *La Campagna romana dell' esercito pontifico nel 1867 descritta dal gen. Kanzler e documentata.* Bologna: Libreria della Immacolata, 1871.

The commander of the Papal forces describes the events of 1867 and the campaign.

Leccisotti, Tommaso. "La corrispondenza fra Don Luigi Tosti e l'ambasicatore d'Harcourt nel period della Repubblica Romana (1849)," *Pio IX, anno* V (September-December 1976), 312–39.

Lettere di Michelangelo Caetani duca di Sermoneta. Cultura e politica nella Roma di Pio IX. Edited by Fiorella Bartoccini. Rome: Istituto di Studi Romani, 1974.

This part of the liberal duke's correspondence deals with the collapse of the temporal power and the politics of the Pope, and his Secretary of State.

Maioli, Giovanni. *Pio IX da Vescovo al Pontefice. Lettere al Card. Luigi Amat. agosto 1839–luglio 1848.* Modena: Società Tipografico Modenese, 1943.

Includes the correspondence of Mastai-Ferreti while Bishop of Imola and during early period of his Pontificate. It provides one of the best printed accounts of the pastoral work of the future Pope as well as a good source for Pius's reaction to the main problems he had to confront upon becoming Pope.

Manno, Antonio (ed.). *L'Opinione religiosa e conservatirice in Italia dal 1830 al 1850 ricercata nelle corrispondenze di monsignor Giovanni Corboli Bussi.* Turin, 1910.

This is one of the most important sources for an understanding of the early years of the Pontificate of Pio Nono and the politics of Antonelli because Mons. Bussi was one of the closest and most-listened to collaborators of the Pope, in this period. With Antonelli he wrote the *statuto* of the Papal States in 1848. This young prelate, who shared the Pope's piety and desire to serve the Church, inspired many of the early reforms and often sustained an uncertain Pius. His correspondence is crucial not only for an understanding of the forces that impinged upon the Pope, but also important for an understanding of the mentality of Pius and Antonelli.

Manzotti, Fernando. "Il problema italiano nella corripondenza di Luigi Carlo Farini sulla *Presse,* sulla *Morning Post,* e sulla *Continental Review,*" *Rassegna Storica del Risorgimento, anno* II (1959) 43–60.

Memoires du Comte Horace De Viel Castel sur le Regne de Napoleon III, 2nd ed. Paris: Tous les Libraries, 1884.

Memorie biografiche di S. Giovanni Bosco. Turin: 1898 ff.

These memoires are not always historical and more often than not concentrate upon religious matters. However, they do reveal Pio Nono's religious beliefs and convictions which often underlay the political policies of Giacomo Antonelli.

Minghetti, Marco. *Miei Ricordi.* 3rd ed. Turin. L. Roux, 1888. Critical of Antonelli for continuing to serve Pius when he moved from a liberal to a conservative course.

Pasolini, Giuseppe. *Memorie, 1815–1876.* Ed. Pietro Desiderio Pasolini. 3rd. ed. Turin: Bocca, 1887.
Tends to place much of the responsibility for the conservative policies of Rome upon the shoulders of Antonelli rather than the Pope.

Pasolini, Guidi (ed.). *Carteggio tra Marco Minghetti e Giuseppe Pasolini.* Turin: Bocca, 1924.

Passaglia, Carlo F. *De l'obligation pour le Pape Eveque de Rome de rester dans cette ville quoique elle devienne la capitale du Royame Italien.* Trans. by Ernest Filalete. Paris: Molini, 1861.
Reveals that Antonelli opposed the Jesuits who wanted the Pope to abandon Rome at the time of the proclamation of the Italian Kingdom. In 1861 and again in 1870 Antonelli advised the Pope to remain in the Eternal City.

Rava. Luigi (ed.). *Epistolario di Luigi Carlo Farini.* Bologna: Zanichelli, 1911.

Roncalli, Nicola. *Cronaca di Roma. Volume I: (1844–1848).* Edited by Maria Luisa Trebiliani. Rome: Istituto per la Storia del Risorgimento Italiano, 1972.
The Institute for the History of the *Risorgimento* hopes eventually to publish the entire vast literature of the *Cronaca di Roma* of Roncalli. This first volume throws considerable light on the Rome of the last days of Gregory XVI, and the first two years of the Ponticate of Pius IX.

Rosmini, Antonio. *Epistolario Completo.* 13 vols. Casale: Pane, 1887–92.
Within these volumes one finds the basic Rosminian position sympathetic to the piety of Pius but somewhat critical of his political approach and especially critical of the person and policies of Antonelli.

Stafanutti, J. A. *La Lega Italiana promossa da Pio IX, Il 1849 romano negli scritti editi e inediti di mons. Corboli Bussi.* Tarcento: Grafiche D. Stefanutti, 1951.

The Roman Journals of Ferdinand Gregorovius, 1852–1875. Edited by Friedrich Althaus. Translated by Mrs. Gustavus W. Hamilton. London: George Bell and Sons, 1907.
Although the author is hostile to the Papacy, he reports a number of amusing incidents that occurred in Rome which he enjoyed, despite his antipathy to the Papacy. He presents Pius as alternately weak and vacillating one moment, and dictatorial and intransigent the next. A

dichotomy is likewise found in his view of Antonelli, though he is fairer to the Cardinal than most of his other critics.

Thouvenel, L. (ed.). *Le Secret de L'Empereur. Correspondance confidentielle et inédite éxchangée entre M. Thouvenel, Le Duc de Gramont et Le Général Comte de Flahault 1860–1863.* 2 vols. 2nd. ed. Paris: Calmann Levy, 1889.

Provides insights into the position of France and Napoleon III towards Papal Rome during these years. In many of the reports of Gramont Pius is depicted as the source of the hard line assumed by Rome, and Antonelli is seen as the moderating figure, who sought to moderate the intransigent stance of his sovereign.

2. Memoirs, Diaries, Correspondence and Studies of Contemporaries of Giacomo Antonelli

Acton, Lord. *Historical Essays and Studies.* Edited by John N. Figgis and R. V. Laurence. London: Macmillan and Co., 1908.

Adamoli. G. *Da San Martino a Mentana. Ricordi di un voluntario.* Milan: Treves, 1892.

An account by one of Garibaldi's volunteers who was with him at Mentana.

Antologia degli scritti politici di Carlo Cattaneo. Edited by Giuseppe Galazzo. Bologna: Societa editrice Il Mulino, 1962.

The references of this federalist to Pius and Antonelli tend to be somewhat more balanced than most other moderate liberals, but they are nonetheless critical of Papal policy.

Barrili, A. G. *Con Garibaldi alle porte di Roma (1867). Ricordi e note di A. G. Barili.* Milan: Treves, 1895.

Mentana seen from a Garibaldian perspective.

Beust, Comte De. *Trois-quarts de siècle. Mémoires du Comte de Beust.* Paris: L. Westhausser, 1888.

Provides insights into Franco-Papal relations among other things.

Bianchi, Nicomede (ed.). *Il Conte Camillo di Cavour. Documenti editi e inediti.* Turin: Unione Tipografico Editrice, 1863.

Within these pages as well as Cavour's diary, correspondence, and the columns of his newspaper *Il Risorgimento*, one finds a generally hostile attitude towards Antonelli and Papal policy after 1848. This reflects, in part, Cavour's own sentiments, the needs of his domestic policies in Piedmont, particularly his alliance with the Center-Left of Urbano Rattazzi, the secularization of the state, as well as his anti-Austrian orientation and his ambitions for expansion in the Italian peninsula.

Bismarck, Otto von. *Reflections and Reminiscences.* Edited by Theodore
S. Hamerow. New York: Harper and Row Publishers, 1968.

Carteggio di Bettino Ricasoli. Edited by Sergio Camerani. Volume
XXVI: *12 aprile 1867–27—dicembre 1869.* Rome: Istituto storico italiano per l'eta contemporanea, 1972.
The documents published in this volume are important for clarifying
a number of ministerial activities and positions of the Iron Baron as
well as the political crisis of 1867–69 during the ministries of Rattazzi
and Menabrea.

*Carteggio di Camillo Cavour. La Liberazione del Mezzogiorno e la for-
mazione del Regno D'Italia.* 5 vols. Edited by the commission for the
publication of the correspondence of Cavour. Bologna, Nicolà Zanichelli,
1949–54.

Costa, Emilio (ed.). "Le carte di Francesco Balbi Senarga," *Rassegna
Storica del Risorgimento, anno* LXV (April-June, 1978), pp. 207–217.

*Count Cavour and Madame de Circourt. Some Unpublished Correspon-
dence.* Edited by Costantino Nigra. Translated by Arthur John Butler.
London: Cassell and Co., 1894.
Contains a series of critical references to Rome and Papal policy.

Craven, A. *Lord Palmerston, sa correspondance intime pour servir a'
histoire diplomatique de l'Europe de 1830 a' 1865.* Paris: Didier, 1879.

Crispi, Francesco. *L'Italia e il Papa ed altri scritti.* Milan: Istituto Edi-
toriale Italiano, 1917.

Crispolti, Filippo. *Pio IX, Leone XIII, Pio X, Benedetto XV. Ricordi Per-
sonali.* Milan: Treves, 1932.
Presents a short, but interesting, picture of Pius IX.

Deiss, Joseph Jay. *The Roman Years of Margaret Fuller.* New York:
Thomas W. Crowell, 1969.
Although sympathetic to the person of Pio Nono, Fuller's writings
from Rome during the troubled days preceding the revolution and during the Republican period reflect the Mazzinian beliefs on the matter
of the temporal power.

Feo, Fancesco De (ed.). *Carteggi di Cesare Guasti. Il Carteggio con Enrich Bindi.* Florence: Leo Oschki Editore, 1972.

Gajani, Gugliemo. *The Roman Exile.* Boston: John B. Jewett and Co.,
1856.
An account of events in the Papal States, the Roman Republic, and
the fall of the Republic of 1849, told by a member of the Roman Constituent Assembly.

Garibaldi, Giuseppe. *Autobiography of Giuseppe Garibaldi.* 3 vols. Trans. by A. Werner with a supplement by Jessie White Mario. London: Walter Smith and Innes, 1889.

Gioberti, Vincenzo. *Del primato morale e civile degli Italiani.* Brussels, 1843.
The 1932 edition was published in Turin by Unione Tipografico Editrice Torinese.

————. *Del Rinnovamento civile d'Italia.* Turin: Bocca, 1851.
Within these pages Gioberti places the responsibility for the failure of the program he had envisioned in his *Primato* upon the shoulders of the statesmen of Piedmont, the democrats, Antonelli, and the Pope. He holds the Piedmontese accountable for not being able to transcend their own immediate, narrow goals, and for placing obstacles in the way of the political league of Italian states. He accuses the democrats of obstinancy in pursuing utopian goals that could not be realized, and thus impeding that which was possible at the time. As regards Pio Nono, Gioberti recognizes that his actions provided the *Risorgimento* with momentum, but accuses him of later destroying the very work he had initiated. He attributes the Pope's actions not only to political inexperience and uncertainty but also to his fear of weakening the Church by provoking a schism in the German-speaking countries. He attributes his failure, in part, to his unfortunate choice of advisors, and above all, his movement away from Rosmini and his increasing reliance on Antonelli.

Gregorovius, Ferdinand. *The Ghetto and the Jews of Rome.* Trans. Moses Hadas. New York: Schocken Books, 1948.
An analysis of the Jewish community of Rome by this medieval historian who lived in Rome from 1852–1874.

Hubner, Count Joseph. *Neuf ans de souvenirs d'un ambassador d'Autriche a' Paris sous le Second Empire, 1851–59.* Paris: Plon, 1904.
An understanding if not sympathetic, view of the problems faced by Antonelli and the Roman government.

Leicht, Pier Silverio. "Memorie di Michele Leicht," *Rassegna Storica del Risorgimento, anno* XXII (July 1935), 56–109.

Lettere edite ed inedite di Camillo di Cavour. Edited by Luigi Chiala. Turin: Roux e Favale, 1882–87.

Lezzani, Mario. "Noterelle epistolari di un Romano dei Mille," *Rassegna Storica del Risorgimento, anno* XXII (December 1935), 928–31.

Martini, Ferdinando (ed.). *Due dell' estrema. Il Guerrazzi e il Brofferio. Carteggi inediti (1859–1866).* Florence: F. Le Monnier, 1920.

Within this correspondence one finds expression of their anticlerical sentiments, and their opposition to the policies of Papal Rome.

Massari, Giuseppe. *Diario dalle cento voce.* Bologna: Cappelli, 1959.

Mazzini, Giuseppe. *Italy, Austria and the Pope: A Letter to Sir James Bart.* London: Albanesi, 1845.

————. *Scritti editi ed inediti.* Milan: G. Daelli, 1861–91.
Within these volumes one finds Mazzini's radical attitude towards Rome and the Papacy, which stresses the incompatability between the papacy and Italian liberty.

Memoirs of Prince Chlogwig of Hohenlohe-Schillingsfuerst. Edited by Friedrich Vurtius. New York: Macmillan, 1906.
Provides some insights into events that led to the *kulturkampf.*

Menabrea, Luigi Federico. *Memorie.* Edited by Letterio Briguglio and L. Bulferetti. Florence: Giunta-Berbera, 1971.
This books says a number of things about the events of 1848.

Metternich, Klemens von. *Mémoires, documents et écrits divers laissés par le prince de Metternich.* Edited by Prince Richard Metternich with the papers being arranged and classified by M. A. de Klinkowstroem. 8 vols. Paris: 1880–84.
The seventh volume is particularly important for assessing the doubts that the Austrian Chancellor had about the new Pope.

Ollivier, Émile. *Journal, 1861–1869.* Edited by Theodore Zedlin and Anne Troisier de Diaz. Paris: Juliard, 1961. 2 vols.
In this, as in his other works, Ollivier assumes a balanced position on events in Rome.

————. *L'Eglise et l'état au Concile du Vatican.* Paris, 1879. 2 vols.
This work does not restrict itself to the Council but focuses on the personality of Pius IX, providing a picture drawn from the memoirs of Princess Caroline de Wittgenstein who lived in Rome.

Ozanam in his Correspondence. Edited by Monsignor Baunard. New York: Benzinger Brothers, 1925.
By and large sympathetic to the work of Pius IX both as Pope and prince.

Pallavicino, Giorgio. *Memorie di Giorgio Pallavicino. Publicate per cura dei figli.* Turin: Roux, Frassati, et. Co., 1895.

Perfetti, Filippo. *Ricordi di Roma.* Florence: G. Barbera, 1861.

Perraud, Cardinal. *Mes relations personelles avec les deux derniers Papes Pie IX et Leon XIII. Souvenirs, notes lettres (1856–1903).* Edited by François Léon Gauthey. Paris: Pierre Tequi, 1917.

Pio Nono ed i suoi Popoli nel MDCCCLVII ossia Memorie intorno al viaggio della Santità di N.S. per L'Italia Centrale. Rome: Tipografia degli SS Palazzi Apostolici, 1860.
A detailed account of Pio Nono's visit to the northern parts of his state in 1857. Although its objectivity is questionable, it is useful for an itinerary of the voyage.

Posthumus Papers of Jesse White Mario: The Birth of Modern Italy. Edited with an Introduction by Visconti-Arese. New York: Scribner's sons, 1909.
Devoted to Mazzini and Garibaldi, her papers reflect their attitude towards Rome and Papacy.

Proceedings of the Public Demonstration of Sympathy with Pope Pius IX and with Italy, in the City of New York, on Monday, November 29 A.D. 1847. New York: William Van Norden, 1847.
Among the documents of interest are letters from Martin van Buren, George M. Dallas, former vice president of the United States, James Buchanan, Secretary of State, William H. Seward, and Albert Gallatin. Also included is an address to Pius IX.

Ricordi di Micelangelo Castelli, 1847–1875. Edited by Luigi Chiala. Turin: L. Roux, 1888.
The views of this political moderate approximate those of Cavour as regards Rome.

Sclopis di Salerano, Federigo. *Diario Segreto (1859–1878).* Edited by Pietro Pirri. Turin: Deputazione subalpina di storia patria, 1859.
Although profoundly Catholic, Sclopis tends to be objective and balanced in his assessment of events in Rome, relations between Church and State first in Piedmont, and later in Italy, and in his evaluation of Pio Nono and Cardinal Antonelli.

Secrets of the Second Empire: Private Letters from the Paris Embassy, Selections from the Papers of Henry Richard Charles Wellesly, 1st Earl Cowley, Ambassador at Paris 1852–1867. Edited by F. A. Wellesley. New York: Harper and Brothers Publishers, 1929.

Senior, Nassau William. *Journals Kept in France and Italy from 1848 to 1852.* London, 1871.
Volume one provides an eyewitness account for the governance of Rome under French occupation following the fall of the Republic.

Settembrini, Luigi. *Ricordanze della mia vita.* Milan: Feltrinelli, 1961.

Sonnino, Sidney. *Diario, 1866–1912.* Edited by Benjamin F. Brown. Bari: Laterza, 1972.

Spaur, Countess de. *Relations du voyage de Pie IX a Gaete.* Paris: Didier, 1852.

An eyewitness account of the flight by one who rode in the carriage which brought Pio Nono to Gaeta.

The Memoirs of Francesco Crispi. Edited by Thomas Palamenghi-Crispi. Translated by Mary Prichard-Agnetti. New York: Hodder and Stoughton, 1912.

Visconti-Venosta, Giovanni. *Ricordi di gioventù. Cose vedute e sapute, 1847–1860.* Milan: Rizzoli Editore, 1959. Trans. by William Prall from the third edition as *Memoirs of Youth: Things Seen and Known, 1847–1860.* Boston: Houghton Mifflin Co., 1914.

Extremely hostile to the Papal government following the restoration, but there is no attack on the person of Pio Nono.

3. *Contemporary Accounts of Giacomo Antonelli and the Policies of Papal Rome*

About, Edmund. *The Roman Question.* Trans. by H. C. Coape. New York: Appleton and Co., 1859.

Originally published in French as *La question romaine* this work is critical of Pius IX, the papal monarchy, and even more so of Cardinal Antonelli, who is presented as a minister grafted on a savage and held responsible for most of the problems and abuses in Rome.

Bianchi-Giovini, A. *Quadro dei costumi della corte di Roma.* 3rd. ed. Florence: Libreria speciale della novità, 1861.

This short work is political and polemical and ultra-critical of the Papal Regime following the second restoration. While there are few kind words for the Pope, the Antonelli family is specially criticized, with the Cardinal depicted as the real power in Rome and the root cause of many of its problems.

Boero, Giuseppe. *La rivoluzione romana al giudizio degli imparziali.* Florence, 1850.

Despite its claim for impartiality, the sentiment of the author is decidely Catholic and conservative. Nonetheless, this is not just an apologetic work, and is based upon a number of sound sources.

Brennan, Richard. *A Popular Life of our Holy Father Pope Pius IX Drawn from the Most Reliable Authorities.* New York: Benzinger Brothers, 1877.

An apologetic, popular, clerical biography which makes no attempt to be critical or to assess objectively the life of the Pope, or the policies pursued by his Secretary of State.

"Cardinal Antonelli," *Dublin Review,* XXVIII (January, 1877), 74–84.

Published after the death of the Cardinal, the account is apologetic but provides useful information about the life and policies of Pio Nono's Secretary of State.

"Cardinal Antonelli," *Littells's Living Age,* Volume 67 (1860) 57–58.
An unfavorable presentation of the Cardinal who is depicted as a machiavellian schemer who absorbed the Pope's political power almost completely.

"Cardinal Antonelli," *The New York Times,* January 16, 1874; November 7, 1876.

Castille, Hippolyte. *Le Cardinal Antonelli.* Paris: E. Dentu, 1859.
A short, ultra-critical, and polemical study of Antonelli, which stresses the unfortunate influence he allegedly had upon Pius and the governance of the states of the Church.

D'Arlincourt, Viscount. *L'Italia Rossa o Storia della rivoluzioni dall' elezione di Pio IX al di lui ritorno in sua capitale.* Trans. by Francesco Giuntini. Florence: Published by the author, 1851.
This volume is inspired by conservative, clerical sentiments and considers the revolution inspired by the diffusion of incredulity whose ultimate aim is to undermine the temporal power and destroy religion.

"Death of Cardinal Antonelli," *Annual Register* (1876), 210–211.

De Boni, Filippo. *La congiura di Roma e Pio IX.* Lausanne, 1847.
Reflects the author's early enthusiasm for the first policies of Pio Nono. The author was to change his attitude following the Pope's Allocution and flight to Gaeta. In his subsequent work *Il Papa Pio IX* (1849), both Pio Nono and Antonelli are seen as enemies of the national cause.

De Goddes Le Liancourt, Count C. A. and James A. Manning. *Pius the Ninth: The First Year of His Pontificate.* 2 vols. London: Thomas Cautley Newby Publishers, 1847.
Within these pages Pius can do no wrong.

De Grandeffe, Arturo. *Pio IX e L'Italia.* Turin: Reviglio, D'Ideville, H. Pio IX, sa vie, sa mort. Souvenirs personnels.* Paris: Palme-Albanel, 1878.

Gennarelli, Achille. "Giacomo Antonelli," in *Il Risorgimento Italiano. Biografie storico-politico d'illustri Italiani contemporanei.* Edited by Leone Carpi. Milan: Antica Casa Editrice, 1886.
Provides some interesting information and insights.

"Giacomo Antonelli," *Unità Cattolica,* November 7, 1876.

Gourard, Carlo. *L'Italia: Sue ultime rivoluzione e suo stato presente.* Edited by Mario Carletti. Florence, 1852.

Hassard, John R. G. *Life of Pope Pius IX.* New York: Catholic Publication Society, 1878.

Yet another apologetic biography which provides little insight into the actual role played by Antonelli during the Pontificate.

Jourdan, Louis and Taxile DeLord. *Les Célebrités du jour, 1860–61.* Paris: Aux bureau du journal *Le Siècle,* n.d.
Presents an unflattering picture of the person and policies of this "celebrity."

Liverani, Francesco. *Il Papato, L'Impero, e il Regno d'Italia.* Florence: Barbera, 1861.

Maguire, John Francis. *Pontificate of Pius the Ninth.* London: Longmans, Green and Co., 1870.
This is the third edition of *Rome: Its Rulers and Its Institutions* originally published in 1857, and carries the history of the pontificate through the Vatican Council. Like the earlier volume it is clerical in its orientation, but factually accurate in most instances. Within its appendix is the important "Report from the Count de Rayneval the French Envoy at Rome to the French Minister for Foreign Affairs" of May 14, 1856, on conditions in the Papal States.

O'Reilly, Bernard. *A Life of Pius IX Down to the Episcopal Jubilee of 1877.* 8th ed. New York: P. F. Collier, Publishers, 1878.
An apologetic, clerical biography which has few notes and lacks a bibliography.

Quinet, Edgar. *La question romaine devant l'histoire, 1848–1867.* Paris: Armand Le Chevalier, 1868.
This study tends to be harsh on the Jesuits and critical of Papal policy.

Ransford, E. "Cardinal Antonelli," *The Canadian Monthly.* December 1876, 534–538.
Presents a few personal recollections of the Secretary of State of Pio Nono.

Roux, E. "Le Cardinal Antonelli," *Gazette du Midi, November 8, 1876.*
An account of the life and career of Cardinal appears in this obituary article.

Silvagni, David. "Il Cardinale Antonelli," in *La corte e la società romana nei secoli XVIII e XIX.* Naples: Arturo Berisio Editore, 1967. III, 490–532.
Published originally in 1882, the last chapter of this three volume work is devoted entirely to Giacomo Angonelli, and provides useful information about his early years. It is one of the less biased of the contemporary accounts. Nonetheless it is not always objective and lacks notes.

Shea, John Gilmary. *The Life of Pope Pius IX and the Great Events in the History of the Church during his Pontificate.* New York: Thomas Kelly, 1878.

This is among the better of the apologetic biographies of Pius IX written in English.

Spada, Giuseppe. *Storia della Rivoluzione della restaurazione del governo pontificio dal 1 guigno al 15 luglio 1849.* 3 vols. Florence: 1868–69.

This antirevolutionary history is well documented and the author's ideological preconceptions and his attachment to the Papacy do not mar his objective account of events.

Veillot, Louis. *Vita di Pio IX.* Trans. by L. Gibelli. Paris, 1863.

An apologetic study by one of the leading ultramontanes.

Vetere, Veturio. *I ventidue anni di governo del Cardinale Antonelli.* Rome: Stabilimento Giuseppe Civelli, 1871.

A critical assessment of the government over which Antonelli presided.

4. *Later Studies of Giacomo Antonelli*

Aubert, Roger. "Antonelli, Giacomo," *Dizionario Biografico degli Italiani,* Volume III, 484–93.

One of the best accounts of the Cardinal Secretary's background and career in article form. Objective and scholarly.

Coppa, Frank J. "Cardinal Giacomo Antonelli: An Accomodating Personality in the Politics of Confrontation." *Biography,* II (Fall, 1979), 283–302.

Delves into the personality and policies of Cardinal Antonelli. Commencing with the polemical picture that has persisted to the present, an attempt is made to assess his character and career as well as his relationship to Pio Nono.

———. "Cardinal Antonelli, the Papal States and the Counter-Risorgimento," *Journal of Church and State,* XVI (Autumn, 1974), 453–71.

Examines the political responsibility of Pio Nono and Cardinal Antonelli in initiating and executing the policies of the Counter-Risorgimento.

———. "Giacomo Antonelli." *Clio* (of Rome), IX (April-June 1973), 183–210.

A study of the myths and realities of the person and policies of the controversial Secretary of State of Pio Nono.

Dalla Torre, Paolo. "Il Cardinale Giacomo Antonelli fra carte di archivio ed atti processuali." *Pio IX,* VIII (1979), 144–95.

This long and scholarly article examines the historiography on the Cardinal on both his personal and political life placing his contribution in historical perspective.

Falconi, Carlo. *Il Cardinale Antonelli. Vita e carriera del Richelieu italiano nella chiesa di Pio IX.* Milan: Mondadori, 1983.
This is the first full-length quasi scholarly study of Antonelli in Italian or any other language. Falconi has utilized the papers of the family archive in the *Archivio di stato di Roma,* the archives of Frosinone, Sonnino, Macerata, Naples, Stresa and Paris. He has also had recourse to the Antonelli documents of the *Archivio Secreto del Vaticano* although he might have gleaned more from the papers of the Secrertariat of State also found in the Vatican archive. Falconi's bibliography, which encompasses some forty pages, includes Antonelli's printed correspondence with a number of nuncios, the diaries of contemporaries, the principal encyclicals of the Pontificate as well as the major works on Pius IX, the Roman Question, and the Papal States. This exhaustive research has produced a treasure trove of information on the Cardinal's life and career. The first fourteen chapters, which dwell upon the family background and economic activities, as well as Giacomo's youth and early career, are particularly useful, providing information not readily available elsewhere. The remaining twenty-two chapters, which trace the Cardinal's career from 1848–1876, recount more widely-known developments, but are useful for the depth of their coverage and their insights. There are some limitations. First, while the work is historical rather than apologetic or polemical, the author's friendliness to his subject is sometimes excessive. The publisher has not included the author's notes—a serious omission for any scholarly work and especially so in the study of a figure as controversial as Antonelli. Despite these shortcomings, this is the only serious full-length study of the Cardinal we have to date, and will have to be consulted by all those working on the Secretary of State and the Pontificate of Pio Nono.

Ghisalberti, Alberto. "Appunti sull' attento al Cardinale Antonelli." in *Chiesa e Stato nell' Ottocento. Miscellanea in onore di Pietro Pirri.* R. Aubert et al. editors, Padova, 1962.
This was republished by Ghisalberti as chapter XII in his *Momenti e Figure del Risorgimento Romano* (Milan: Giuffrè Editore, 1965), pp. 233–248. It provides one of the best accounts of the June 12, 1855 attempt to take the life of Cardinal Antonelli.

Lai, Benny. *Finanze e finanzieri Vaticani fra L'Ottocento e il Novecento, da Pio IX a Benedetto XV.* Milan: Mondadori Editore.
Provides a good picture of how Antonelli managed to set the Vatican finances in order following the loss of the Papal State, with particular emphasis on the Cardinal's role in the reorganization and restructuring of Peter's Pence.

Lodolini, Armando. "Un archivio segreto del Cardinale Antonelli. I *Studi Romani, anno* I (July-August, 1953), 410–24; Part II, *Studi Romani, anno* I (September-October 1953), 510–20.

Relying on the papers found in the *Archivio di Stato di Roma*, Lodolini focuses on the family, early life, and career of Giacomo Antonelli in these two interesting articles.

Marlow, B. "Cardinal Antonelli." *Truth* (July 1932), 19–20.

A short and apologetic study of the man and his policies.

"Mezza città sotto accusa." *Il Progresso Italo-Americano*, September 21, 1970.

Provides information on De Merode's struggle with Antonelli and the series of acusations made against Antonelli's servant and thus against the Cardinal himself.

Omodeo, A. "Fonti e memorie. Antonelli, Giacomo, Cardinale," *Rassegna Storica del Risorgimento, anno* XLVII (July-September, 1960), 319–324.

This short article presents useful data for an understanding of the life and career of the Cardinal.

Pirri, Pietro. "Il Cardinale Antonelli tra il mito e la storia." *Rivista di Storia della Chiesa in Italia,* XII (1958), 81–120.

Although apologetic in part—perhaps as a reaction to much of the earlier literature on the Cardinal, which is polemical—this is one of the best studies on Antonelli, dispelling many of the generalizations about his life and policies.

Randall, A. "The Pope's Alter-Ego: Consalvi and Antonelli." *Tablet* (April 20, 1963), 419–20.

Although apologetic in tone, attempts to assess the interaction between Pius IX and his Secretary of State.

IV Contemporaries of Giacomo Antonelli

1. *Studies of Pio Nono*

Andreotti, Giulio. *La sciarda di Papa Mastai.* Milan: Rizzoli, 1967.

Provides some interesting anecdotes about the Pope and his Pontificate.

Aubert, Roger. *Le Pontificate de Pie IX.* Paris: Bloud and Gay, 1952.

This remains one of the best general studies of the Pontificate of Pio Nono. It includes an excellent, though now dated, bibliography of the history of the Church during his reign. It is neither kind nor always objective towards the person and policies of Antonelli. The Cardinal's "dictatorship" is criticized by Aubert who in this work attributes the inspiration as well as the execution of Papal diplomacy to him.

Browne-Olf, Lillian. *Their Name is Pius.* Milwaukee: Bruce Publishing, 1941.
A short survey of the Pontificate of the Modern popes called Pius.

Case, Lynn M. "Anticipating the Death of Pius IX in 1861." *Catholic Historical Review,* XLIII (January, 1958), 309–23.

Clerici, E. *Pio IX. Vita e Pontificato.* Milan: Federazione Giovanile diocesana milanese, 1928.
A moderate study inspired by conciliatory sentiments.

Coppa, Frank J. *Pope Pius IX: Crusader in a Secular Age.* Boston: Twayne Publishers, 1979.
A critical account of the life and times of Pius IX. It focuses on the political events of the Pontificate, avoiding the polemical tone of many of the earlier works on the counter-*Risorgimento*. It utilizes the papers of the Secret Vatican Archives, as well as a broad range of primary and secondary works, catalogued in its annotated bibliography.

————. "Pessimism and Traditionalism in the Personality and Policies of Pio Nono." *Journal of Italian History,* II (Autumn 1979), 209–217.
Traces the religious conservatism of the "liberal" Pope, noting that his alleged liberalism never extended to religious and theological matters. Reveals that from the first Pius' had the interests of religion uppermost in his mind and showed himself conservative in the defense of the rights of religion and the errors of the day. Thus there was not an early Pius and a later one—he was remarkably consistent. The liberal image of the Pope was created by others but dismantled by Pius himself.

De Grandeffe, *Pio IX e L'Italia Libera.* Turin: Reviglio, 1959.

De Saint-Albin, Alexandre. *Pie IX.* Paris: Dentu, 1860.

Fernessole, Pierre. *Pie IX Pape.* Vol. I, 1792–1855; II, 1855–1878. Paris: Lethielleux, 1960–63.
Despite the fact that the author was allowed access to the Vatican Archives prior to their opening to the scholarly community, this study suffers from a number of shortcomings. It is one-sided in its attitude towards the pontificate and fails to place the events in Pius' reign within the broader context of nineteenth century Church history.

Gordini, Gian Domenico. "Giudizi ed opinioni di Pio IX prima del pontificato." *Pio IX, anno* I (1972), 130–156.
Provides insights into personality and policies of Pius prior to his assuming the Papacy. It appears in the quarterly review *Pio IX. Studi*

e ricerche sulla vita della Chiesa dal Settecento ad oggi which since 1972 has been published under editorship of Antonio Piolanti and has provided a constant stream of articles on Pius and his Pontificate.

Hales, E. E. Y. *Pio Nono: A study in European Politics and Religion in the Nineteenth Century.* Garden City, N.J.: Doubleday and Co., 1954.
　　This short study, written before the opening of the Vatican Archives, is so sympathetic to the Papacy and the Pope so as to call its objectivity into question. It is important because it is the first biography of Pius IX in the twentieth a century written in English, and also because it is generally fair towards Antonelli.

Hayward, Fernand. *Pie IX et son temps.* Paris: Plon, 1948.
　　Provides an anecdotal format and does not include notes. Maintains that Antonelli rather than Pius prevented the success of the Siccardi mission to Portici and that the Cardinal was therefore at the source of the conflict between the Holy See and Piedmont. Also charges Antonelli with corruption and having replaced the nepotism of the popes by his own.

Martina, Giacomo. *Pio IX (1846–1850).* Rome: Università Gregoriana Editrice, 1974.
　　This is the first of a projected three volume biography of Pius IX which begins where the study of Serafini ends and includes important documents in the text and appendices. In his first chapter Martina provides a comprehensive survey of much of the printed material dealing with the life and pontificate of this Pope. It is an objective and scholarly study, but this is less a study of Pius than it is one of the Papal States and the Pontificate.

———. *Pio IX (1851–1866).*
　　This second volume of the "biography" examines the Pontificate following the Pope's restoration to Rome to the mid-1860's. As in the earlier volume, Pius is often lost in the maze of developments in the Papal States, Italy, Europe, and the world. Having had recourse to the recent historiography on Antonelli, Martina has somewhat moderated his earlier and more critical assessment of the Cardinal. The author's reevaluation of the Cardinal has played a part in his overall evaluation of the regime, which is far more balanced than that of the liberal and national historiography and that of the clerical school. Among other things, Martina reveals that Giacomo and his brothers were distressed by brigandage which frightened the family at Terracina, and was discouraged by the Minister and his government, contrary to the long-held assumption that Rome encouraged brigandage to overturn the newly formed Kingdom of Italy.

———. *Pio IX Chiesa e mondo moderno.* Rome: Edizioni Studium, 1976.

While completing research for his larger work, Martina produced this brief synthesis of the history of the Church during the Pontificate of Pio Nono. It has a good annotated bibliography.

———. *Pio IX e Leopold II.* Rome: Pontifica Università Gregoriana, 1967.
As much a study of the relations between the Papal States and Tuscany as it is between the two rulers.

Menucci, Angelo. "La riapetura del museo 'Pio IX' in vista delle celebrazione di Senigallia," *Pio IX,* VI (January-April 1977), 117–123.

Monti, Antonio. *Pio IX nel Risorgimento Italiano con Documenti Inediti.* Bari: Laterza, 1928.
Included in this volume is part of the correspondence between Pius IX and his brother the Count Gabriele Mastai in the years from 1830 to 1867, as well as other letters of interest. They appear in the appendix of the volume.

Palazzini, Cardinal Pietro. "Spiritualita' di Pio IX, il Papa della Croce," *Pio IX,* VI (January-April 1977), 3–21.

Radice, Gianfranco. *Pio IX e Antonio Rosmini.* Città del Vaticano: Libreria Editrice del Vaticano, 1974.
This revisionist study examines the relationship between Pope Pius IX and the priest and philosopher, Antonio Rosmini. Radice attempts to disprove the commonly held notions that the relationship between the two churchmen was determined essentially by the political events of 1848–49, and that Pius was inconsistent in his treatment of Rosmini.

Sencourt, R. "Rosmini and Pius IX." *Contemporary Review,* CXIIC (1955), 387–89.

Serafini, Alberto. *Pio IX. Giovanni Maria Mastai Feretti dalla giovinezza alla morte nei suoi scritti e discorsi editi e inediti. I: Le vie della Divinia Provvidenza (1792–1846).* Citta' del Vaticano: Tipografia Poliglotta Vaticana, 1958.
The author was only able to complete the first volume of his projected multi-volume work. The one volume he has produced is based on primary source material, and reveals all sorts of important information about the youth of Mastai-Ferretti. Indeed it is the most important printed source for these early years. The biography is being completed by Martina who has produced two volumes which commence where Serafini finished his first volume.

Thornton, Francis Beauchesne. *Cross Upon Cross: The Life of Pope Pius IX.* New York: Benziger Brothers, Inc., 1955.
An apologetic, clerical biography without footnotes, which includes a number of stories and anecdotes which cannot be substantiated.

Pelczar, Giuseppe Sebastiano. *Pio IX ed il suo Pontificio.* 3 volumes. Turin, 1911.
The best of the older apologetic biographies.

Quazza, Romolo. *Pio IX e Massimo D'Azeglio nelle vicende romane del 1847.* Modena: Societa' Tipografica Editrice, 1954.

Vercesi, Ernesto. *Pio IX.* Milan: Edizioni Corbaccio, 1930.
Provides some insights into the personal life and thoughts of Pio Nono and his policies.

2. *Studies of Other Contemporaries of Antonelli*

Adams-Daniels, Elizabeth. *Jesse White Mario, Risorgimento Revolutionary.* Athens: Ohio University Press, 1972.

Anzilotti, Antonio. *Gioberti.* Florence: Valecchi, 1922.

Aubry, Octave. *Eugenie: Empress of the French.* trans. F. M. Atkinson. Philadelphia: Lippincott, 1931.

Barker, Nicholas. *Distaff Diplomacy: The Empress Eugenie and the Foreign Policy of the Second Empire.* Austin: University of Texas, 1967.

Biaggini, Carlo Alberto. *Il Pensiero politico di Pellegrino Rossi di fronte ai problemi del Risorgimento Italiano.* Rome: Vittoriano, 1937.

Bianchi, Nicomede. *La politica di Massimo D'Azeglio dal 1848 al 1859. Documenti.* Turin: Roux e Favale, 1884.

Bismarck. Edited by F. M. Hollyday. Englewood Cliffs: Prentice-Hall, 1970.

Brodsky, Alyn. *Imperial Charade* New York: Bobbs-Merrill, 1978.

Cappelletti, Licurgo. *Storia di Vittorio Emanuele II.* 3 vols. Rome: Voghere, 1892–93.

Cognasso, Francesco. *Vittorio Emanuele II.* Turin: Unione tip. Editrice Torinese, 1942.

Collodi, C. *Biografie del Risorgimento.* Florence: Casa Editrice Marzocco, 1941.

Coppa, Frank J. *Camillo di Cavour.* New York: Twayne Publishers, 1973.

Fleury, Comte. *Memoirs of the Empress Eugenie.* New York: Appleton and Co., 1920.

Gasquet, Abbot (ed.) *Lord Acton and his Circle.* London: Longmans, Green and Co., 1906.

Ghisalberti, A. M. *Massimo D'Azeglio, un moderate realizzatore*. Rome: Edizioni Ateneo, 1953.

Griffith, G. O. *Mazzini: Prophet of Modern Europe*. London: Hodder and Stoughton, 1932.

Hales, Edward E. Y. *Mazzini and the Secret Societies: The Making of a Myth*. New York: Kenedy, 1956.

Halperin, S. William. *Diplomat under Stress: Visconti Venosta and the Crisis of July 1870*. Chicago: University of Chicago Press, 1939.

Higginson, Thomas Wentworth. *Margaret Fuller Ossoli*. 10th ed. Boston: Houghton, Mifflin and Co., 1895.
    She was in Rome during the reformist period and during Mazzini's Republic as well.

Himmelfarb, Gertrude. *Lord Acton: A Study in Conscience and Politics*. Chicago: University of Chicago Press, 1952.

Howe, Julia Ward. *Margaret Fuller (Marchesa Ossoli)*. London: W. H. Allen and Co., 1883.

Kurtz, Harold. *The Empress Eugenie 1826–1920*. Boston: Houghton Mifflin Co., 1964.

Leetham, Claude. *Rosmini: Priest, Philosopher and Patriot*. Baltimore: Helicon Press, 1957.

Lodolini, Armando. *Mazzini: Maestro Italiano*. Milan: Dall'oglio, 1963.

Mack Smith, Denis. *Cavour.* New York: Knopf, 1985.

Matthew, David. *Lord Acton and His Times*. Tuscaloosa: University of Alabama Press, 1968.

Morley, John. *The Life of William E. Gladstone*. New York: Macmillan and Co., 1904.

Omodeo, Adolfo. *L'Opera politica del Conte di Cavour.* 2 vols. Florence: La Nuova Italia, 1945.

Orsi, Pietro. *Cavour and the Making of Modern Italy, 1810–1861*. New York: Putnam's Sons, 1914.

Redlich, Joseph. *Emperor Francis Joseph of Austria*. New York: Macmillan, 1929.

Rodolico, Niccolo'. *Carlo Alberto*. 3 vols. Florence: Le Monnier, 1936–48.

Romeo, Rosario. *Cavour e il suo tempo*. 4 vols. Bari: Laterza, 1969–84.
    This is the most important and exhaustive work on Cavour and his times.

Sauvigny, G. De Berbier De. *Metternich and His Times.* Trans. Peter Ryde. London: Darton, Longman and Todd, 1962.

Thayer, William Roscoe. *The Life and Times of Cavour.* 2 vols. Boston: Houghton Mifflin Co., 1911.

Thompson, J. M. *Louis Napoleon and the Second Empire.* New York: W. W. Norton and Co., 1955.

Trevelyan, George MaCaulay. *Garibaldi and the making of Italy (June-November 1860).* New York: Longmans, Green, and Co., 1948.

Ward, Wilfrid. *The Life of John Henry Cardinal Newman Based on his Private Journals and Correspondence.* London: Longmans, Green, and Co., 1912.

V Rome and Risorgimento

1. *Papal Rome in the Age of Antonelli*

Amminstrazione Provinciale di Roma. *Studi in occasione del Centenario. I-Scritti sull' amministrazione del territorio romana prima del Unita'* Milan: Giuffre, 1970.

Andrieux, Maurice. *Rome.* Translated by Charles Lam Markmann. New York: Funk and Wagnalls, 1968.
  Chapter XXXI entitled "The Stormy Years" is pertinent for the Pontificate of Pius and Ministry of Antonelli.

Bartoccini, Fiorella. *La "Roma dei Romani."* Rome: Istituto per la Storia del Risorgimento Italiano, 1971.
  This work concentrates on the Italian attempts to acquire Rome 1859–1870, and the failure of the Romans to take the initiative for their inclusion in the unitary state. The author's description of the capital's population is perceptive and she suggests that the Roman's obvious satisfaction with their own institutions and way of life was instrumental in the failures of the revolutionary groups to overturn the government of Antonelli.

———. *Roma nell' Ottocento. Il Tramoneto della "Citta Santa" nascità di una capitale.* Bologna: Cappelli, 1985.
  This 16th volume published by the National Institute for Roman Studies concentrates on Rome in the nineteenth century. Divided into two parts, the first concentrates on developments in Rome from the French intrusion to the Italian arrival in 1870. The second half treats developments during the first three decades of Rome's existence as capital of Italy. The book examines political, cultural, social and economic

Bibliography 277

developments, albeit in a confused manner. The economic and demographic data are particularly useful and will be welcomed by the specialist.

Berkeley, G. F. H. and J. Berkeley. *The Irish Battalion in the Papal Army of 1860.* Dublin: Talbot Press, 1929.
Contains much valuable information about the makeup of the Papal forces and examines events leading to the defeat of the Papal army at Castelfidardo.

Biagini, Antonello and F. Maurizio. "La riorganizzazione dell' esercito pontificio e gli arruolamenti in Umbria tra il 1815 and il 1848–49." *Rassegna Storica del Risorgimento, anno* LXI (April-June 1974), 214–25.

Bolton, Glorney. *Roman Century: A Portrait of Rome as Capital of Italy, 1870–1970.* New York: Viking Press, 1970.
Some of the early chapters deal with the Rome of Antonelli.

De Cesare, Raffaele. *Roma e lo stato del Papa dal Ritorno di Pio IX al XX Settembre, 1850–1870.* Milan: Longanesi and Co., 1970. Abridged and translated into English under the title *The Last Days of Papal Rome.* Trans. by Helen Zimmern. London: Archibald Constable and Co., 1909.
This study of the Papal States concentrates on the period that commences with the return of Pius to his capital and concludes with the fall of Rome. Long considered a classic, its reputation rests not only on its own merit but on the scarcity of earlier studies of Papal Rome and Cardinal Antonelli. In the work the author uses a series of anecdotes, memorabilia, and a host of oral reports to create a study which is more social than political. Those pages which describe the customs, institutions, religious life, and social climate are the best in the book providing an almost photographic view of a world long since lost.

Ghisalberti, Alberto M. *Momenti e figure del Risorgimento Romano.* Milan: Giuffrè, 1965.

———. *Roma da Mazzini a Pio IX. Ricerche sulla restaurazione papale del 1849–50.* Milan: Giuffrè, 1958.

Ghisalberti, Carlo. "Il Consiglio di Stato di Pio IX," *Studi Romani, anno* II (1954), 165–75.

———. "Lo Stato Pontificio dal 1849 al 1870." in *Studi in occasione del Centenario,* pp. 3–11.

Isastia, Anna Maria. *Roma nel 1858.* Rome: Istituto per la Storia del Risorgimemto, 1978.

Leti, Giuseppe. *Roma e lo Stato Pontificio dal 1849 al 1870. Note di Storia politica.* 2 vols. Ascoli Piceno: Giuseppe Cesari Editore, 1911.

Despite the use of some important documents, this presents a caricature of Papal Rome and from time to time degenerates into a bitter verbal attack on Pio Nono and Cardinal Antonelli.

Monsagrati, Giuseppe. "Un episidio della Seconda Restaurazione pontificia: il caso Calendrelli." *Rassegna Storica del Risorgimento, anno* LIX (October-December 1972), 531–62.

Mori, Renato. *Il tramonto del potere temporale. 1866–1870.* Rome: Edizione di storia e letteratura, 1967.

Roma capitale d'Italia nel primo centenario. Milan: Mondadori, 1971. This volume put out by the Ministry of Public Instruction in Italy for the centennial of Rome as Italy's capital is superficial in its history of the capital in general, but provides a good treatment for the decade 1860–70.

Silvagni, David. *La corte e la società romana nei secoli XVIII e XIX.* Naples: Arturo Berisio Editore, 1967.

Travaglini, Carlo M. *Il dibattito sull' agricoltura romana nel secolo XIX, 1815–1870. Le accademie e le societa' agrarie.* Rome: Università degli Studi, 1981.
This monograph focuses on the agrarian accademies that materialized in Rome before the Italian annexation.

2. General Studies of the Risorgimento

Bersezio, V. *Il Regno di Vittorio Emanuele II. Trent anni di vita Italiana,* 8 vols. Turin: Roux e Favale, 1878.

Di Nolfo, Ennio. *Storia del Risorgimento e dell' Unita' d'Italia.* Milan: Rizzoli Editore, 1965.

Garrone, Alessandro Galante. "Risorgimento e antirisorgimento negli scritti di Luigi Salvatorelli," *Rivista Storica Italiano, anno* LXXXVIII (September 1966), 513–43.

Gay, H. Nelson. *Scritti sul Risorgimento.* Rome: La Rassegna Italiana, 1937.

Gramsci, Antonio. *Sul Risorgimento.* Edited by Elsa Fubini with an Introduction by Giorgio Candeloro. Rome: Editori Riuniti, 1967.

Grew, Raymond. *A Sterner Plan for Italian Unity: The International Society in the Risorgimento.* Princeton: Princeton University Press, 1963.

Hearder, Harry. *Italy in the Age of the Risorgimento, 1790–1870.* London: Longman, 1983.

This volume deals both with the Italian states in the nineteenth century as well as the *Risorgimento*. While it provides no new revelations, it is a good overview.

Holt, Edgar. *The Making of Italy. 1815–1870*. New York: Atheneum, 1971

King, Bolton. *A History of Italian Unity*. 2 vols. 4th ed. London: Nisbet and Co., 1934.
This remains the most complete survey of the *Risorgimento* in English and therefore useful, despite its strong anticlerical bias and particular attack on Antonelli.

Lovett, Clara M. *The Democratic Movement in Italy, 1830–1876*. Cambridge: Harvard University Press, 1982.
Explores the impact of democratic movements upon the *Risorgimento* and the unitary state. Utilizing a prosopographical approach, focuses upon the lives of 146 Italian radical leaders of the nineteenth century, probing the role of social origins, religious attitudes, early education and political socialization in their formation.

Mack Smith, Denis. (ed.) *The Making of Italy, 1796–1870*. New York: Harper, 1968.

———. *Victor Emmanuel, Cavour, and the Risorgimento*. New York: Oxford University Press, 1971.
Includes fifteen articles which provide an overview of developments from 1840 to 1870 while concentrating on the roles of Cavour and Vittorio Emanuele in the creation of Italy.

Marchetti, Leopoldo. "Ottaviano Vimercati," *Risorgimento*, 14 (1962), 22–37.

Martin, George. *The Red Shirt and the Cross of Savoy*. New York: Dodd, Mead and Co., 1969.

Mazzini. Tra Insegnamento e ricerca. Rome: Edizione Dell' Ateneo, 1982.
The proceedings of a 1981 conference on Mazzini, it underscores the current state of research and studies on this Italian patriot.

Nada, Narciso. *Guliemo Moffa di Lisio*. Bra: Società Amici del Museo, 1982.
This slim volume is interesting in that it clearly shows the personal toll revolutionary activity had upon the lives of those involved in the national movement.

O'Clery, Patrick Keyes. *The Making of Italy*. London: Kegan, Paul, French and Co., 1892.

Omodeo, A. *Difesa del Risorgimento*. Turin: Einaudi, 1951.

Ramm, Agata. *The Risorgimento*. London: Routledge and Kegan Paul, 1962.

Salvatorelli, Luigi. *Pensiero e azione del Risorgimento*. 2nd ed. Turin: Einaudi, 1963.

Stillman, W. J. *The Union of Italy, 1815–1895*. Cambridge: University Press, 1909.

Thayer, William Roscoe. *The Dawn of Italian Independence and Rebirth of Italy*. 2 vols. Boston: Houghton-Mifflin, 1892.

Walker, Mack (ed.). *Plomières: Secret Diplomacy and the Rebirth of Italy*. New York: Oxford University Press, 1968.

Woolf, S. J. *The Italian Risorgimento*. New York: Barnes and Noble, 1969.

3. Role of Other States During Risorgimento

Acton, Harold. *The Last Bourbons of Naples (1825–1861)*. New York: St. Martin's Press, 1961.

Barrie, Ottavio. *L'Inghilterra e il problema italiano nel 1848–49*. Milan: Giuffre', 1965.

Bianchi, Nicomede. *Storia documentata della diplomazia in Italia dall' anno 1814 all' anno 1861*. 8 vols. Turin: Unione Tipografico, 1872.

Blumberg, Arnold. "George Bancroft, France, and the Vatican: Some Aspects of American, French, and Vatican Diplomacy: 1866–1870," *Catholic Historical Review*, L (January 1965), 475–93.

Bourgeois, Émile and E. Clermont. *Rome et Napoleon III (1849–1870)*. Paris: Librarie Armand Colen, 1907.

Bourne, Kenneth. "The British Government and the Proposed Roman Conference of 1867," *Rassegna Storica del Risorgimento, anno* XLIII (October-December 1956), 759–35.

Case, Lynn M. *Franco-Italian Relations, 1860–65: The Roman Question and the Convention of September*. Philadelphia: University of Pennsylvania Press, 1932.

Coppa, Frank J. "Italy, the Papal States, and the American Civil War," *La Parola del Popolo* (November-December 1976), 364–67.

Di Nolfo, Ennio. "Austria e Roma nel 1870," *Rassegna Storica del Risorgimento, anno* LVIII (July-September 1971), 409–36.

Engel-Janosi, Friedrich. "French and Austrian Political Advice to Pius IX, 1846–1848," *Catholic Historical Review.*, XXXVIII (April 1952), 1–20.

Hearder, Harry. "La politica di Lord Malmesbury verso L'Italia nella primavera del 1859," *Rassegna Storica del Risorgimento, anno* XLIII (January-March 1956), 35–58.

Leonardis, Massimo de. *L'Inghilterra e la Questione Romana, 1859–1870.* Milan: Università Cattolica del Sacro Cuore, 1980.
A clear analysis of England's policy towards the Roman Question during a crucial decade. Reveals the Protestant influence on English policy towards Italy and the English Catholic critique of that policy.

Monti, Antonio. *La politica degli Stati Italiani durante il Risorgimento.* Milan: Casa Editrice Francesco Vallardi, 1948.

Saint-Armand, Imbert De. *France and Italy.* Translated by Elizabeth Gilbert Martin. New York: Charles Scribner's Sons, 1899.

Scott, Ivan. *The Roman Question and the Powers, 1848–1865.* The Hague: Martinus Nijoff, 1969.

Simon, Alois. "Palmerston et les États Pontificaux en 1849," *Rassegna Storica del Risorgimento,* anno XLIII (July-September 1956), 539–46.

Taylor, A. J. P. *The Italian Problem in European Diplomacy, 1847–1849.* Manchester: Manchester University Press, 1934.

Tarle, Eugenii. *Le blocus continental et le Royaume d'Italie.* Paris: Alcan.
Maintains that the Risorgimento was the work of the bourgeosie rising to a consciousness of its class interests.

Ugolini, Romano. *Cavour e Napoleone III nell' Italia Centrale.* Rome: Istituto per la Storia del Risorgimento Italiano, 1973.
Perhaps the definitive account of the revolt in Perugia and its suppression by the Pope's Swiss forces in 1859.

Urban, Miriam. *British Opinion and Policy on the Unification of Italy 1856–1861.* Scottsdale, Pa.: Mennonite Press, 1938.

Wallace, Lillian Parker. "Pius IX and Lord Palmerston, 1846–1849." in Wallace and William C. Askew, *Power, Public Opinion and Diplomacy.* Durham, N.C.: Duke University Press, 1959.

———. *The Papacy and European Diplomacy, 1869–1878.* Chapel Hill, N.C.: University of North Carolina Press, 1948.

4. *Role of Religion in the Risorgimento*

Amabile, G. *La Legge delle Guarantigie.* Catania: Gianotta, 1897.

Aubert, R. and A. M. Ghisalberti, E. Paserin D'Entreves (eds). 2 vols. *Chiesa e stato nell' Ottocento.* Padua: Editrice Antenore, 1962.

Aubert, R. *Essais sur la liberte' religieuse.* Paris: Fayard, 1965.

Barry, Colman J. (ed.). *Readings in Church History: The Modern Era.* Westminister, Md.: The Newman Press, 1965.

Bastgen, Hubert. *Die Romische Frage: Dokumente und Stimmen.* 3 vols. Freiburg: Herder, 1917–19.

Belardinelli, Mario. *Il conflitto per gli exequatur (1871–1878).* Rome: Edizioni dell' Atteneo, 1971.

———. "L'Exequatur' ai vescovi italiani dalla legge delle guarentigie al 1878," in *Chiesa e religiosità in Italia dopo L'Unità, Communicazioni* I, 5–42.

Bernhart, Joseph. *The Vatican as a World Power.* New York: Longman's Green and Co., 1939.
In treating the role of Cardinal Deacons in the Church, the author stresses the impact of Consalvi and Antonelli.

Berselli, Aldo. "Il problema della liberta' religiosa nel pensiero di Marco Minghetti," *Rassegna Storica del Risorgimento, anno* XLIII (1956), 234–43.

Boggio, P. C. *La questione romana studiata in Roma. Impressioni, reminicenze, proposte.* Turin, 1865.

Bonfanti, Giuseppe. *Roma capitale e la questione romana. Documenti e testamonianze di storia contemporanea.* Brescia: La Scuola, 1977.
A good survey of the Roman question with text and documents.

Bonghi, Ruggero. *Pio IX e il Papa futuro.* 3rd ed., Milan: Treves, 1877.

Bury, J. B. *History of the Papacy in the 19th Century (1864–1878).* Edited by F. H. Murray. London: Macmillan, 1930.

Cadorna, C. *Illustrazione giuridica della formula del Conte di Cavour, "libera Chiesa in Libero Stato."* Rome: Tipografia Badoniana, 1882.

Camiani, Pier Giorgio. "Motivie riflessi religiosi della questione romana," in *Chiesa e religiosità in Italia dopo L'Unità. Relazioni* II, 65–128.

Caracciolo, Alberto. *Roma capitale. Dal Risorgimento alla crisi dello stato liberale.* Rome: Edizioni Rinascita, 1956.

Chiesa e religosità in Italia dopo L'Unita'. Atti del quarto Convegno di Storia della Chiesa, La Mendola 31 Agosto-5 Septembre 1971. 4 vols. Milan: Università Cattolica del Sacre Cuore, 1973.

The papers concentrate upon the Church and religion in the peninsula from the creation of the Kingdom in 1861 to the death of Pius in 1878. They are indispensable for those interested in the post unification Church, neglected by much of the historiography which dwelt upon the Roman Question.

Coppa, Frank J. "Realpolitik and Conviction in the Conflict between Piedmont and the Papacy during the Risorgimento," *Catholic Historical Review*, LIV (January 1969), 579–612.

――――. "The Religious Basis of Giuseppe Mazzini's Political Thought," *Journal of Church and State*, XII (Spring 1970), 237–253.

Corbet, James A. *The Papacy: A Brief History*. New York: Van Nostrand Co., 1956.
Shows Antonelli's policy to be determined by needs of the Church and Papacy.

Corrigan, Raymond. *The Church and the Nineteenth Century*. Milwaukee: Bruce Publishing Co., 1938.

Dalla Torre, Paolo. *L'Anno di Mentana*. Milan: Martello Editore, 1967.

Daniel-Rops, Henri. *The Church in an Age of Revolution*. 2 vols. Garden City, N.Y.: Image Books, 1967.

De Feo, Italo. *Roma 1870. L'Italia dalla morte di Cavour a Porta Pia*. Turin: U. Mursia, 1970.

Del Cerro, E. *Cospirazioni romane (1817–1868). Rivelazioni storiche*. Rome: E. Voghera, 1899.

Del Potere temporale dei Papa: Opuscoli e documenti. 3 vols. Turin: Tipografia De Agostini, 1859.

Eckhart, Carl Conrad. *The Papacy and World Affairs As Reflected in the Secularization of Politics*. Chicago: University of Chicago Press, 1937.

Engel-Janosi, F. "The Roman Question in the Diplomatic Negotiations of 1869–70," *Review of Politics*, 101 (1941).

Falconi, Carlo. *The Popes in the Twentieth Century: From Pius X to John XXII*. Boston: Little, Brown and Co., 1967.

"F. Curci and the Roman Question," *Dublin Review*, XXX (January 1878), 1–32.

Gorresio, Vittorio. *Risorgimento scomunicato*. Florence: Parenti Editori, 1958.

Graham, Robert A. *Vatican Diplomacy: A Study of Church and State on the International Plane.* Princeton: Princeton University Press, 1959.

Hales, E. E. Y. *Revolution and Papacy.* Notre Dame: University of Notre Dame, 1966.

——. *The Catholic Church in the Modern World.* Garden City, N.Y.: Image Books, 1964.
Reveals that Pius was not dominated by anyone and shows that Antonelli knew the limits of his position and authority.

Halperin, William S. "Catholic Journalism in Italy and the Italo-Papal Conflict of the 1870's," *Catholic Historical Review,* LIX (January 1974), 587–601.

——. *Italy and the Vatican at War.* Chicago: University of Chicago Press, 1939.

——. *The Separation of Church and State in Italian Thought from Cavour to Mussolini.* Chicago: University of Chicago Press, 1937.

Hayward, Fernand. *A History of the Popes.* New York: Dutton, 1931.

Jacini, Stefano. *La crisi religiosa del Risorgimento. La politica ecclesiastica italiana da Villafranca a Porta Pia.* Bari: Laterza, 1938.

Jemolo, Arturo Carlo. *Chiesa e Stato in Italia negli ultimi cento anni.* Turin: Einaudi, 1952. David Moore has translated this into English as *Church and State in Italy, 1850–1950.* Oxford: Blackwell, 1960.

——. "I Cattolici e la formazione dello stato nazionale unitario," in *Partecipazione dei Cattolici alla vita dello stato Italiano.* Edited by E. Clerici. Rome: Editrice Studium, 1958.

——. *La questione romana.* Milan: Istituto per gli studi di publica internazionale, 1938.

——. "Libera Chiesa in Libero Stato," in *Cavour 1861–1966.* Turin: Bottega D'Erasmo, 1962.

MacCafrey, James. *History of the Catholic Church in the Nineteenth Century.* 2 vols. Dublin: M. H. Gill and Son, 1909.

Manning, Henry Edward. *Miscellanies and Independence of the Holy See.* New York: Catholic Publication Society, n.d.

——. *The Temporal Power of the Vicar of Jesus Christ.* 3rd ed., London: Burns and Oates, 1880.

Martin, Michael. *The Roman Curia as it Now Exists.* New York: Benzinger Brothers, 1913.

Masse, Domenico. *Cattolici e Risorgimento*. Rome: Edizione Paoline, 1961.

Mellano, Maria Franca. *Il caso Fransoni e la politica ecclesiastica piemontese (1848–1850)*. Rome: Pontifica Università Gregoriana, 1964.

Minghetti, Marco. *Stato e Chiesa*. Milan: Hoepli, 1878.

Misner, Paul. *Papacy and Development: Newman and the Primacy of the Pope*. Leiden, N.Y.: Brill, 1976.

Mollat, G. *La Question Romaine de Pe VI a Pie XI*. Paris: Librairie Lecoffre, 1932.

Montale, Bianca. "Gustavo di Cavour e *L'Armonia*," *Rassegna Storica del Risorgimento*, XVI (1956), 456–66.

Mori, Renato. *Il Tramonto del Potere Temporale 1866–1870*. Rome: Edizioni di Storia e Letteratura, 1967.

———. *La questione romana, 1861–1865*. Florence: Felice Le Monnier, 1963.

Mourret, Fernand. *A History of the Catholic Church*. Volume VIII: *Period of the Early Nineteenth Century (1823–1878)*. New York: Herder Book Co., 1957.

Nielson, Fredrik. *The History of the Papacy in the XIXth Century*. London: John Murray, 1906.

Nippold, Friedrich. *The Papacy in the 19th Century*. New York: Putnam's Sons, 1900.

Odegard, Peter H. (ed.). *Religion and Politics*. Rutgers: Oceana Publications, 1960.

Parsons, Wilfrid. *The Pope and Italy*. New York: America Press, 1929.

Passerin D'Entreves, Ettore. "Appunti sull' impostazone delle ultime trattative del governo cavouriano colla S. Sede per una soluzione della questione romana (novembre, 1860-marzo, 1861)," in Aubert et. al., *Chiesa e Stato nell' Ottocento*, II, 563–95.

Pellegrino, Bruno. "Nicolà Caputa (1714–1802) tra religione e politica," *Rassegna Storica del Risorgimento, anno LXIII (January-March 1976)*, 8–35.

Pitocco, Francesco. *Utopia e riforma religiosa nel Risorgimento*. Bari: Laterza, 1972.

Quintavalle, Ferruccio. *La questione romana negli opuscoli liberali fra il 1850 e il 1870*. Bologna: Forni Editore, 1972.

Salvatorelli, Luigi. "Il problema religiosa nel Risorgimento," *Rassagna Storica del Risorgimento,* XLIII (1956), 193–216.

Santini, Luigi. *Alessandro Gavazzi: Aspetti del problema religiosa del Risorgimento.* Modena: Societa' Tipografica Editrice, 1955.

Scoppola, Pietro. *Dal neoguelfismo alla democrazia cristiana.* Rome: Editrice Studium, 1957.

Sini, Aurelia. "Il movimento cattolico librale nelle province pontificie (in particolare sui profili giuridici del pensiero religioso di Terenzio Mamiani)," in *Studi in Occasione del Centenario,* pp. 13–36.

Suardo, Dino Secco. "Liberali e cattolici nel Risorgimento," *Civitas.* anno XXVI (1975), 45–59.

Traniello, Francesco. *Cattolicesimo conciliatorista.* Milan: Marzorati, 1970.

Vidler, Alec R. *The Church in an Age of Revolution.* Baltimore: Penguin Books, 1961.

VI Critical Events of the Pontificate of Pio Nono and Ministry of Antonelli

1. *Revolution and Restoration*

Andrisani, Gaetano. "Il viaggio di Pio IX a Gaeta," *Gazzetta di Gaeta,* anno V (1977), 1–6.

Ara, Angelo. *Lo statuto fondamentale dello Stato della Chiesa (14 marzo, 1848).* Milan: Giuffrè, 1966.

Berkeley, George F. and J. Berkeley. *Italy in the Making: January 1st, 1848 to November 16, 1848.* Cambridge: University Press, 1940.
  This work is important because it is the first to have used the Florentine archives for an understanding of the genesis of the Allocution of April 1848. It also provides a balanced picture of the general political situation in the Papal States prior to the revolutionary outburst.

Berra, Luigi Francesco. "La fuga di Pio IX a Gaeta e il racconto del suo scalco segreto," *Studi Romani, anno V* (1957), 672–86.

Bonomi, Ivanoe. "Ricordi della Repubblica Romana del 1849," in *Strenna dei Romanisti,* 3–9.

Boyer, Ferdinand. "Pie IX a Gaete e amiral Baudin," *Rassegna Storica del Risorgimento, anno* XLIII (April-June 1956), 244–51.

Colonna, Gustavo Brigante, "Mazzini al Quirinale," in *Strenna dei Romanisti*, 146–49.

Coppa, Frank J. "Papal Rome in 1848: From Reform to Revolution," *Proceedings of the Consortium on Revolutionary Europe, 1979*, pp. 92–103.

————. "Rome and Revolution: From Pius VI to Pius IX," *Proceedings of the Consortium on Revolutionary Europe, 1984*, pp. 268–276.

Demarco, Domenico. *Pio IX e la rivoluzione romana del 1848. Saggio di Storia economico-sociale*. Modena, 1947.
Stresses the Social aspects of the revolution.

————. *Una rivoluzione sociale. La repubblica romana del 1849*. Naples: M. Fiorentino, 1944.

Ghisalberti, A. M. *Roma da Mazzini a Pio IX. Richerache sulla Restaurazione Papale del 1849–1850*. Milan, 1958.

Giovangini, Luigi Armando. *Dalla Elezine di Pio IX alla caduta della Repubblica Romana*. Genoa: Lanterna, n.d.

Gouraud, Carlo. *L'Italia: Sue ultime rivoluzione e suo stato presente*. Florence: Carletti, 1852.

Johnston, R. M. *The Roman Theocracy and the Republic 1846–1849*. London: Macmillan and Co., 1901.

Laureano, Edoardo. "Il plauso del clero alla Repubblica romana del 1849," *Rassegna Storica del Risorgimento, anno* LVII (April-June 1970), 226–32.

"Le Pape Pie IX a Gaete," *Correspondant*, new series, tome 279, 172–195.

Leroy-Beaulieu, Anatale. *Un Empereur, Un Roi, Un Pape, Une Restauration*. Paris: Charpentier, 1879.

Malvezzi, Nino, "Pellegrino Rossi, Marco Minghetti, e Carlo de Mazade," *Nuova Antologia, anno* LXI (October 1926), 437–53.

Migliori, F. (ed.). *Roma nel 1848–49*. Florence: La Nuova Italia, 1968.

Minocci, Carlo. *Pietro Sterbini e la rivoluzione romana (1846–1849)*. Naples: Edizioni "La Diana," 1967.
Provides a clear and fairly comprehensive account of the events that led to the proclamation of the Roman Republic and Sterbini's part in bringing it about.

Mollat, G. "La Fuite de Pie IX a Gaeta," *Revue Histoire Ecclesiastique, annee* 40, 266–282.

Morinelli, Ugo. *Pie IX e Ciceruacchio.* Rome: Tipografia "La Precisa," 1937.

Pennacchini, Luigi Enrico. "Dopo la caduta della repubblica romana," *Rassegna Storica del Risorgimento, anno* XXII (July 1935), II, 161–73.

Perini-Bembo, A. "Breve considerazioni demodossa-logiche sul'allocuzione pontificia del 20 aprile 1848," *Rassegna Storica del Risorgimento, anno* XLIII (July-September 1956), 525–32.

Pivano, Livio. "Mazzini Dittatore (1849)," *Nuova Antologia, anno* LXI (February 1926), 265–69.

Quarra, Alberto. *"Nonno Toto" e le vicende risorgimentali romane.* Rome: S. T. Pinto, 1973.

Robertson, Priscilla. *Revolutions of 1848: A Social History.* New York: Harper and Row, 1960.

Rodelli, Luigi. *La Repubblica Romana del 1849.* Pisa: Domus Mazziniana, 1955.

Rota, Ettore (ed.). *Il 1848 nella storia italiana ed europea.* 2 vols. Milan: Villardi, 1948.

Salvaggi, Carlo. "La costituzione della Repubblica Romana," in *Studi in occasione del Centenario.* Milan: Giuffrè, 1970.

Strenna dei Romanisti. Edited by Giuseppe Romani. Rome: Staderini Editore, 1947.

Thayer, William Roscoe. *The Dawn of Italian Independence.* Boston: Houghton Mifflin Co., 1893.

Trevelyan, George Macaulay. *Garibaldi's Defense of the Roman Republic 1848–49.* London: Longmans, Green and Co., 1914.

Tupputi, Carla Lodolini. *La commissione governative di Stato nella Restaurazione pontificia (17 luglio, 1849-12 aprile, 1850).* Milan: Giuffrè, 1970.

———. "Ricerche sul Consiglio di Stato pontificio (1848–1849)," *Archivio della Società Romana di storia patria, anno* XCV (1972), 237–315.

Wollomborg, Leo. "Lo Statuto Pontificio nel quadro constituzionale del 1848." *Rassegna Storica del Risorgimento, anno* XXII (October 1935), 527–94.

2. *The Syllabus of Errors*

"A Text of the Syllabus," Translated by George McHugh and Clement McNaspy. Found in Raymond Corrigan's *The Church and the Nineteenth Century.* Milwaukee: Bruce Publishing Co., 1938.

Aubert, Roger, "Mgr. Dupanloup et les Syllabus," *Revue d'Histoie Eclesiastique, LI (1956), 79–142.*

Guzzetti, Giovanni Battista. "Il Sillabo di Pio IX nel suo contesto storico-dottrinale," *Pio IX, anno* V (September-December 1976), 366–81.

Hull, R. R. *The Syllabus of Errors of Pope Pius IX: The Scourge of Liberalism.* Huntington, Indiana: Sunday Visitor Press, 1926.

I documenti citati nel Syllabus edito per ordine del Sommo Pontefice Pio IX preceduti da analoghe avvertenze. Florence: Tipografia S. Antonino, 1865.

Manning, Henry Edward. *"The Syllabus," Characteristics: Political, Philosophical and Religious from the Writings of Henry Edward.* Edited by William S. Lilly. London: Burns and Oates, 1885.

Martina, Giacomo. "Nuovi documenti sulla genesi del Sillabo," *Archivio Historiae Pontificiae,* VI (1968), 319–69.

––––––. "Osservazioni sulle varie redazioni del 'Sillabo,'" in *Chiesa e Stato nell Ottocento.* Padua: Antenore, 1962., pp. 419–523.

McElrath, Damian. *The Syllabus of Pius IX. Some Reactions in England.* Louvain: Editions Nauwelarts, 1964.

Papa, Egidio. *Il Sillabo di Pio IX e la stampa francese, iglese e italiana.* Rome: Cinque Lune, 1968.

Pepe, Gabriele. *Il Sillabo e la politica dei Cattolici,* Rome, 1945.

Petroncelli, M. *Il Sillabo, encicliche ed altri documenti di Pio IX.* Florence, 1927.

Quacquarelli, Antonio. *La crisi della religiosita' contemporanea. Dal Sillabo al Concilio Vaticano.* Bari: Laterza, 1946.

Rinaldi, G. *Il Valore del Sillabo.* Rome, 1888.

Rossi, Ernesto. *Il Sillabo.* Florence: Parenti Editore, 1957.

The Syllabus of Pius IX: A Review of the Propositions Condemned by His Holiness Pope Pius IX with a text of the Condemned List. Ramsgate, N.Y.: Catholic Publication Society, 1875.

"The Syllabus of the Principal Errors of our times, which are stigmatized in the Consistorial Allocutions, Encyclicals and other Apostolic Letters of our Most Holy Father, Pope Pius IX," in *Documents in the Political History of the European Continent.* Edited by C. A. Kertesz. Oxford: Oxford University Press, 1968, pp. 233–44.

3. The Vatican Council

Adrianyi, Gabriel. *Ungarn und das I. Vaticanum.* Cologne: Bohlau Verlag, 1975.
Concentrates on the role of the Hungarian and Rumanian bishops at the Council and their opposition to Papal infallibility.

Altholz, Josef L. "The Vatican Decrees Controversy, 1874–1875," *Catholic Historical Review,* LVII (January 1972), 593–605.

Aubert, Roger. "Il primo Concilio Vaticano," *Studi Romani, anno* XVIII (1970), 318–39.

──── . "L'Eglise en Italie avant et apres Vatican I," in *Chiesa e religiosita' in Italia dopo L'Unita', Relazioni,* I, 3–31.

Biagione, Gazzoli Francesco. *Memoire di Monsignor Tizzani con biografia e note.* Rome, 1945.

Butler, Cuthbert. *The Vatican Council: The Story Told from Inside in Bishop Ullathorne's Letters.* 2 vols. New York: Longmans, Green, and Co., 1930.
Provides a clear analysis of the work of the Council based upon the diary kept by Bishop Ullathorne of Birmingham as well as a number of other sources. It was written to refute the attacks of Döllinger and other hostile critics of the Council, and is one of the most important works available in English on the subject.

Catta, Etienne. "Mgr. Edouard Pie, Pie IX, le Syllabus et le premier Concile du Vatican d'apres les oeuvres de L'Eveque de Poitiers. IV—Le Concile," *Pio IX, anno* VI (January-April 1977), 60–93.

Cecconi, Eugenio. *Storia del Concilio Ecumencio Vaticano scritta sui documenti originali.* 4 vols. Rome: Tipografia Vaticano, 1878.
These volumes published shortly after the death of Pius IX are primarily concerned with the preliminaries of the Council and in many ways represent an official collection of documents more than a history of the Council proper.

Ceccuti, Cosimo. *Il Concilio Vaticana I nella stampa italiana (1868–1870).* Rome: Edizioni Cinque Lune, 1970.

Cwiekowski, Frederick J. *The English Bishops and the First Vatican Council.* Louvain: Publications Universitaries de Louvain, 1971.
This is a well documented study of the English participation in the First Vatican Council. It is not restricted to the role of the Bishops and also considers the activities of men such as Acton and probes the concerns of the liberal Gladstone government.

Döllinger, von Johann Joseph Ignaz. *Letters from Rome on the Council by Quirinus.* 2 vols. New York: Da Capo Press, 1973.

In addition to the 69 letters in these volume there is a preliminary history of the Council, and a series of speeches and other documents in the appendices. All of the material in this work has a strong bias against infallibility, is critical of the Council and its majority, and presents an unflattering picture of Pius IX.

Fessler, Monsignor Joseph. *Le Concile du Vatican. Son Caractere et ses Actes.* Paris: Plon, 1877.
An apologetic and pro-Papal work.

Franco, Giovanni Giuseppe. *Appunti storici sopra il Concilio Vaticano.* Edited by Giacomo Martina. Rome: Università Gregoriana, 1972.
Reveals that Pius was not a passive instrument of the majority but shows him to be independent and decisive on a number of issues, and above all, that of infallibility. The diary also makes clear that while Pius made his position known on a number of issues, he by and large respected the liberty of the assembly.

Gadille, Jacques. "Albert du Boys. Ses Souvenirs du Concile du Vatican, 1869–1870." in *L'Intervention du gouvernment Imperial a Vatican I.* Preface by Roger Aubert. Louvain: Publications Univesiaries de Louvain, 1968.

Gladstone, W. E. *The Vatican Decrees in their Bearing on Civil Allegiance: A Political Expostulation.* New York: Harper and Brothers, 1875.

Granderath, Theodor. *Geschicte des Vatikanischen Konzils.* 3 vols. Freiburg. Translated into French as *Histoire du Concile du Vatican.* 5 vols. Brussels, 1907–13.
This work is solidly based upon sources available in the Vatican Archives which were opened to Father Granderath of the Society of Jesus. It presents a good account of the various problems and controversies and offers considerable insight into the role of the Pope. However, it is at times apologetic and sometimes fails to appreciate the role and view of the minority in the Council.

Hennesey, James. *The First Council of the Vatican: The American Experience.* New York: Herder and Herder, 1963.

Hergenrother, Dr. *Anti-Janus: An Historico-Theological Criticism of the work entitled "The Pope and the Council by Janus,"* Trans. J. B. Robertson. Dublin: W. B. Kelley, 1870.

Lord Acton and the First Vatican Council: A Journal. Edited by Edmund Campion. Sydney: Catholic Theological Faculty, 1975.
The volume contains journal notes of Acton from 1870 to 1871 and provides insights into his contacts with the political figures in Rome as well as the attempt to thwart the majority of the council on the issue of infallability.

Maccarrone, Michele. *Il Concilio Vaticano I e il "giornale" di Mons. Arrigoni*. 2 vols. Padua: Antenore, 1966.
    This is a solid piece of work which covers more than the title might indicate. It concentrates primarily upon the relations between the Council and the Italian government, on the attitude of the Italian bishops, and on the conduct of Pius during the Council. On the last issue it has made an important contribution in correcting the impression left by Dollinger and others that the Jesuits directed the Council. Maccarrone notes the important role played by the Pope, especially on the question of infallibility.

Manning, Henry Edward. *The Vatican Council and its Definitions*. New York: P. J. Kenedy, 1905.
    An ultra-apologetic work by one of the chiefs of the infallibilist party in the Council.

Mansi, Johannes. *Amplissimo Conciliorum Collectio*. Paris, 1923–27.
    Five volumes (49–53) contain official documentation of Vatican I.

Mourret, Fernand. *Le Concile du Vatican d'apres des Documents inédits*. Paris: Bloud and Gay, 1919.
    One of the earliest of the objective and more scholarly works on the Council. It is based upon the Journal of Monsignor Icard, Director of the Seminary of St. Sulpice, Paris, who was in Rome throughout the sessions of the council.

Mozley, Thomas. *Letters from Rome on the Occasion of the ecumenical Council, 1869–1870*. London: Longmans, Green and Co., 1891.
    Provides an eyewitness account of Rome by Newman's brother-in-law, at the opening and early days of the Council. Rather critical of developments.

Tamborra, Angelo. "Il Concilio Vaticano I e gli orientali ortodossi. Illusioni e disinganni (1868–1870)," *Rassegna Storica Italiano, anno* LVII (October-December 1970), 507–19.

The Letters and Diaries of John Henry Newman. Edited by Charles Stephen Dessain and Thomas Gornall. Volume XXV: *The Vatican Council, January 1870 to December 1871*. New York: Oxford University Press, 1973.

Veuillot, Louis. *Rome pendant le concile*. Paris, 1872.

Vitelleschi-Nobili, Francesco. *Il Papa infallibile. Cronaca del Concilio ecumenico vaticano primo*. Milan: Giordano editore, 1963.

4. *The Kulturkampf*

Alexander, Edgar. "Church and Society in Germany: Social and Political Movements and Ideas in German and Austrian Catholicism, 1789–

1950," in *Church and Society: Catholic Social and Political Thought and Movements, 1789–1950.* Edited by Joseph N. Moody. New York: Arts, Inc., 1953.

Bismarck and Europe. Edited by W. N. Medlicott and D. K. Convey. New York: St. Martin's Press, 1971.
  The chapter "France and the Catholic Question, 1871–1875" provides insights into Bismarck's fears of a Catholic conspiracy and the internal and international factors that prompted the *Kulturkampf.*

Bismarck: Some Secret Pages of his History.—Being a Diary kept by Dr. Moritz Busch. New York: AMS Press, 1970.
  Volume II is the more useful for an understanding of Bismarck's attitude toward the Center Party and Rome.

Gherardini, Brunnero. "Pio IX, episcopato e 'Kulturkampf,'" *Pio IX* (January-April 1977), 22–59.

Goyau, G. *Bismarck et l'Eglise. Le Kulturkampf, 1870–1887.* 4 vols. Paris, 1911–13.
  Though dated, in part, this is still a very useful work for an understanding of the *Kulturkampf.*

Helmreich, Ernst. *A Free Church in a Free State?* Boston: D.C. Heath, 1964.

Husgen, Edward. *Ludwig Windhorst.* Cologne: Bachem Verlog, 1907.

Kent, George O. *Arnim and Bismarck.* Oxford: Oxford University Press, 1968.
  In addition to delving into Prussia's policies during the course of the Vatican Council this work provides insights into the impact of the "diplomatic revelations" of Arnim on the *Kulturkampf.*

Ross, Ronald J. *Beleaguered Tower: The Dilemma of Political Catholicism in Wilhelmine Germany.* Notre Dame: University of Notre Dame Press, 1976.
  Although it concentrates on the post Bismarckian period, the first chapter provides insights into the *Kulturkampf.*

"The Impregnable Fortress: Prince Bismarck and the Centre Party," *American Catholic Quarterly Review,* XV (July 1890), 390–421.

Schmidt, Erich. *Bismarcks kampf mit dem Katolizimus. Teil I: Pius der IX und die Zeit der Rustung, 1848–1879.* 2nd ed. Hamburg: Hanseaticsche Verlagsanstalt, 1942.

———. *Der Kulturkampf in Deutschland, 1871–1890.* Gottingen: Musterschmidt, 1962.

Based on an impressive documentation, this work disagrees with those of historians such as Heinrich Bornkamm and Erich Eyck which stress that Bismarck made a sudden decision to enter the *Kulturkampf*. While it sees the conflict emerging as a consequence of the Catholic minority's reluctance to reconcile itself to Prussian leadership in Germany, it stresses that Bismarck decided to cross swords with the Church when Rome refused to support his government against the Center Party which opposed some of Bismarck's policies.

Stehlain, Stewart A. *Bismarck and the Guelph Problem, 1866–1890: A Study in Particularist Opposition to National Unity*. The Hague: Martinus Nijhoff, 1973.

Places Bismarck's fear of the Center Party and the *Kulturkampf* within the context of the Chancellor's broader fear of particularism after unification.

Windell, George G. *The Catholics and German Unity, 1866–1871*. Mineapolis: University of Minnesota Press, 1954.

Provides a good account of the Catholic reaction to emerging Prussian leadership in Germany. It is an excellent source for the background of the *Kulturkampf*.

Index